ADMIRALS OF AMERICAN EMPIRE

ADMIRALS
of
AMERICAN EMPIRE

The Combined Story of

GEORGE DEWEY
ALFRED THAYER MAHAN
WINFIELD SCOTT SCHLEY
and
WILLIAM THOMAS SAMPSON

By

RICHARD S. WEST, JR.

GREENWOOD PRESS, PUBLISHERS
WESTPORT, CONNECTICUT

359.0092
W519

To

EDITH MAE WEST
and
KAREN MARIE WEST

"An hour or two at Manila, an hour or two at Santiago, and the maps of the world were changed . . ."

—ADMIRAL A. S. BARKER

CONTENTS

Part One
YOUNG OFFICERS IN BATTLE

Part Two
NAVAL DECLINE AND RESURGENCE
1865—1890

Part Three
THE NEW NAVY
1890—1898

CONTENTS—*Continued*

Part Four

THE BRIEF WAR OF EMPIRE
April 22—August 12, 1898

Part Five

FULFILLMENT

ACKNOWLEDGMENTS, NOTES AND INDEX

LIST OF ILLUSTRATIONS

Part One

YOUNG OFFICERS IN BATTLE

1. FOUR NAVAL CADETS

SOME forty years before America plunged into her fateful naval war with Spain the four young men who were to become her chief naval leaders in that war took their oaths of office as naval cadets in Annapolis. Dewey entered the Naval Academy in 1854, Mahan and Schley in the fall of 1856, and Sampson became a "plebe" in September 1857, just as Dewey was commencing his final or "First Class" year.

It would have been impossible to pick at random from the muster roll of the Naval Academy four youths more widely different in temperament and social background than George Dewey, Alfred Thayer Mahan, Winfield Scott Schley and William Thomas Sampson.

George Dewey was the son of Dr. Julius Yemans Dewey, a genial and prosperous physician of Montpelier, Vermont, whose ancestors—after the son's victory in Manila Bay in 1898—were immediately traced back through early Pilgrim settlers in Massachusetts to the French Huguenot family of Douai, who had reached Kent in England about the time of Drake and the Spanish Armada.[1]

Dewey owed his appointment to the Naval Academy—as he owed his assignment to the Asiatic Station in 1897—largely to chance. Another Montpelier youth, who had received the naval appointment from Dewey's district, decided at the eleventh hour to become a clergyman instead. Dewey's father spoke to Senator Foote. Young Dewey got the vacated appointment. The boy who had changed his mind lived to become the Reverend George Spaulding and to preach a sermon in Syracuse in honor of Admiral George Dewey's victory at Manila Bay.

For short and athletic Cadet George Dewey with his quick black eyes and boundless energy the Naval Academy of the middle fifties was disappointing. It smacked of the Latin school. Too much reading, writing and arithmetic and not nearly enough athletic sports. At home in Montpelier, where he was often called "the black-eyed cuss," he would attract attention by racing blindfolded down the steps of the statehouse on the day the state legislature opened. Once in a spirit of bravado he had driven his father's horse and wagon across the Winooski when the river was at flood stage. The current swept the wagon under and smashed it, but the boy crawled onto the horse's back and floundered to safety. Another time he almost drowned himself to establish a record in swimming. When George at sixteen asked his father to let him go to sea, the latter compromised by sending him to a staid and semimilitary institution at Norwich, Vermont, where the boy found relief from the boredom of studies by playing pranks. George and four other students once broke up a religious meeting by singing Negro songs outside the window, for which irreverence he and his companions were bound over to the county court at Woodstock.

His father extricated him from the toils of the law and brought him down to Annapolis in September of 1854. Here, if anywhere, he would surely get a touch of needed discipline.

Commander Louis M. Goldsborough, the Naval Academy's "green sea" superintendent, had a gruff manner and a confirmed sea dog's ideas about discipline. At assemblies, in a booming voice long practiced in shouting orders above a gale, Commander Goldsborough would lecture the cadets on discipline. But to obtain discipline in the Naval Academy of the middle fifties was next to impossible. The student body lacked homogeneity and even minor infractions of the regulations had to be handled through the Navy Department in Washington. Goldsborough was energetically laboring to get this situation changed when Dewey reached Annapolis.[2]

Dewey, an impressionable boy of seventeen, had never been outside of Vermont before. In Annapolis he was thrown into intimate association with bearded Oldsters, cadets up to twenty-seven years of age who already had served several years in the fleet, and who, on returning to Annapolis to complete their schooling and pass their final examinations, had brought all their seamen's vices with them. These older cadets were given to "Frenching out" and carousing in Hemsley's Tavern at the foot of Annapolis' Slippery Hill. The upperclassmen resented Professor Henry Lockwood's efforts to inflict artillery drill upon them, considering it too military and landlubberly; but Lockwood, who was a graduate of West Point, was constitutionally unable to see it their way and the drills continued. In retaliation, the cadets one day took advantage of Professor Lockwood's impediment of speech and marched over the sea wall and into the Severn River, before "the Honorable Henry" could stutter out the command to halt. For this sort of boyish practical joke George Dewey developed a special fondness.

"Shang" Dewey, as the midshipmen nicknamed him, at once acquired the popular habit of chewing tobacco and smoking, for which he repeatedly acquired demerits. The records show that ten demerits came his way for "ungentlemanly and unofficerlike conduct—hissing at mess," six for being "absent from recitation," four for being "very inattentive at recitation" and six for "disrespectful conduct at and after roll-call."[3] Tardiness in getting to formation, cutting classes and entertaining visitors in his room during study hours were his chief recorded faults. Formal studies he considered a grind and examinations relentless; yet his relative standing in his class improved each year. He finally stood Number Five in a class of 15.

Like most normal midshipmen he was quick to resent an affront to his dignity. At mess a Southern cadet called him a "doughface Yankee." Shang went for his plaguer and beat him until he fell under the table, thereby garnering an additional ten demerits. He was once teased by several faculty children because of his youthful appearance. "Don't he look pretty! Don't he look pretty!" Cadet Dewey caught one of the offenders, the young son of Professor Chauvenet, and gave him a spanking which he was later to recall with pride after Dewey's brilliant victory in 1898; although at the time it occurred the boy's mother was so incensed that she carried her complaint against Dewey to the superintendent.[4]

Years later, in his *Autobiography*, Dewey reminisced with undisguised zest of how a class of Oldsters once took it upon themselves to discipline Professor William R. ("Bull Pup") Hopkins for assigning them low marks in Natural and Experimental Philosophy, and of how Bull Pup was "captured and imprisoned in a glass wall-case in the chemical laboratory."[5]

Alfred Thayer Mahan, tallest and most sophisticated of the quartet of naval cadets, was better grounded than any of the others in military discipline. Namesake of a general, he had been born at West Point in 1840, where his strict, puritanical father, Dennis Hart Mahan, was Professor of Mathematics.[6]

Owing to his father's excellent connections, young Mahan ought to have experienced little difficulty in obtaining an appointment to the Naval Academy. The father, however, was convinced that Alfred was better fitted for some civilian pursuit and declined to assist him in his desire.

Alfred's mother, by sending him to an Episcopal boys' school at Hagerstown, Maryland, did what she could to divert the boy into the ministry; and a year later his father sent him to board at the home of a minister uncle in New York City while he attended Columbia College. Thus between fifteen and seventeen Alfred came under the influence of the Reverend Milo Mahan, author of an extensive work on ecclesiastical history. Although the exposure to a religious environment was to bear fruit many years later in essays and a book on the Christian life, Alfred persisted, over his father's objection, in his original choice of a career. At sixteen he took a train to Washington and talked Secretary of War Jefferson Davis into obtaining for him a Naval Academy appointment. Whether he was cut out for naval life only time would tell.

The Naval Academy was but ten years old in 1856 when Mahan was sworn in as a naval cadet. As its traditions had not yet jelled, no official objection was offered when Mahan proposed, since he had had two years at Columbia College, to take the examination for entering the Third Class at Annapolis. To the dismay, no doubt, of the other members of the Third Class, Mahan entered their group directly without first having had to pass through the ordeal of Plebe Year. Subsequently, after Mahan's experience, the Naval Academy traditions congealed on this point. For his own good no other midshipman has ever been permitted to skip Plebe Year.

At the Naval Academy sober, serious, religious Cadet Mahan had difficulty keeping a straight face in chapel. Chaplain George Jones's sermons seemed to him "rant and cant," fit only for "milk sops." "Old Slick," as Mahan and the other cadets dubbed the chaplain, he caricatured as an "intolerable old poker," "old mummy," "most delightfully and successfully stupid," who "gave me a most unlovely idea of religion generally." Nor, because of its undue emphasis on hell fire and damnation, was the sermon of a visiting Presbyterian preacher judged much better: "I can't stand what looks like an effort to bully you into religion. . . . A man who is religious because he fears to go to hell is as despicable as one who remains irreligious because he fears the world's opinions." Sincerely devout, Cadet Mahan resisted the efforts of Holy Joe—Professor Joseph E. Nourse—who taught ethics and rated Mahan as his best student, to have him participate in the Bible class. In private the boy read and selected from the Bible the passages he especially admired as literature. "But really, Sam," he wrote to his friend Ashe, "It is a great pity that they would not send a decent parson here, there is a large field perfectly innocent of cultivation."[7]

From the beginning, partly because of his entry into an upper class, Mahan lived a life apart from his classmates who could not forgive him for having escaped the rigors of Plebe Year. Had it happened that Shang Dewey or the garrulous and affable Schley had vaulted over Plebe Year, it is safe to say that within a week or two they would somehow have made their peace with their irate classmates, but not Mahan. There was, too, Mahan's effeminately beautiful face. He had sat for the artist as model for the face of Rose Standish in the painting "Landing of the Puritans" which is one of the murals in the rotunda of the National Capitol. This fact in itself was enough to prejudice his classmates against him. Six feet two inches tall, as ramrod straight as an honor student at West Point, with steel-gray eyes that looked through or beyond rather than at you and a manner shy, self-conscious, diffident, waiting for the other fellow to make the advances— little wonder that half his classmates at once sized him up as a pillar of conceit.

Young Mahan proved to be a model student academically. Aside from his ability to count his friends on the fingers of one hand, his first two years at the Naval Academy were not unusual. With only one of these friends was he really intimate, his roommate Samuel A'Court Ashe, a thin six-foot spindle of a boy from North Carolina, and like Mahan in temperament and outlook. To Sam Ashe, Mahan poured out his innermost thoughts and with Ashe he planned a two-man crusade to brighten the discipline of the Naval Academy when the two of them should become First Classmen. One of the main faults, they believed, was the unwritten law that First Classmen never report First Classmen for violating Academy regulations. Mahan and Ashe agreed that together they would break away from this discipline-dissipating tradition *by reporting classmates and lower classmen alike.*

Heretofore the First Classmen had been bearded veterans of the fleet, but this situation was now in process of change. After Captain George S. Blake relieved Commander Goldsborough as superintendent in 1857, the practice of sending back to the Academy the Oldsters from the fleet was abandoned. Mahan, however, a sort of other-worldly perfectionist, went ahead with his unusual plans in complete disregard of the new situation and of the self-immolation that their carrying out entailed. Even after Ashe resigned because of excessive seasickness on the cruise, Mahan, convinced of the rightness of his decision, did not hesitate to undertake the crusade alone.

In October of 1858, at the beginning of his First Class year, Mahan reported a classmate for talking in ranks. . . .

His shocked classmates put Mahan in Coventry. Almost to a man they stopped speaking to him except when official duty required.

From West Point came the strictest paternal counsel to stiffen the lonely youth's moral fiber. "As to what your crew may think or do," wrote Professor Dennis Mahan, "so long as you pursue a consistent line of conduct, and a courteous gentlemanly bearing, do not let it trouble you for a moment. Call no man friend who expects your friendship to be shown in violating your duty with respect to him."[8]

The undisguised warmth of his father's moral indignation proceeded in part from the circumstance that the father was at this moment prosecuting a former pupil for slander. Alfred, sensitive, self-centered and as yet unaware of his parent's personal difficulty, accepted the admonition literally.

There was no one in Annapolis to whom he could confide his troubles. Even his new roommate, Tom Spencer, declined to take sides in the feud and soon Alfred was despising him along with all the rest. His sense of military fitness prevented him from seeking a confidant among underclassmen, and the barriers of age and rank prevented any simple outpouring of the heart to officers and professors. The commandant, Commander T. T. Craven, apparently sensed Mahan's difficulties but hesitated to embarrass him since Alfred often called at the commandant's quarters to pay his respects to Miss Nannie Craven. Occasionally the lonely cadet would visit for a few moments in the rooms of lower classmen where he witnessed some of the uproarious antics of Ye Pelicans Club led by Winfield Scott Schley.

Cut off from the world about him, Mahan vented his innermost feelings in letters to his ex-roommate Sam Ashe. Sam alone knew the character of the offending classmates as Alfred knew them and Sam alone appreciated all the complications of the situation.

To occupy his leisure Mahan devoured one or two novels a week, delved into Froissart's *Chronicles,* and found inspiration in the history of Britain's "glorious" navy. As his final bleak year at the Naval Academy dragged itself out, Mahan absented himself more and more from his dormitory, the unloved "Apollo Row," and visited in the homes of townspeople and naval officers. He called often to see Miss Nannie Craven—whose delightful impartiality in entertaining both Alfred and his unfriendly classmates rather nettled and disturbed him. Commander Craven on occasion would misread the clock in order to permit the boy to remain after study hour in the evenings. "Damme, if I know which I like best, father or daughter,"[9] Alfred wrote Ashe, his most understanding friend, who was in North Carolina, out of the Navy, studying law. The letters to Ashe, waxing fatter and fatter, sometimes ran to 19½ pages, and down to graduation day itself the rift with his classmates continued.

Not without reason Alfred feared his own "jealous and exacting" temperament and wondered whether he had been "destined to be a persecuted individual through life." "In fact, to acknowledge my true estimate of myself, I think I am very good-looking, very talented, and a favorite in society, and with more moral *character* than nine-tenths of the midshipmen in the school, and I also feel that I would give anything if to this were added in its highest degree the Christian virtue of humility. I do not, however, think . . . that my self-conceit . . . is disagreeably conspicuous." With himself he could be ruthless and with others too. "As to my making up with the fellows in the class that have fallen out with me," he wrote, in answer perhaps to a suggestion from Ashe, "of course the offer must come from them and come as a request coupled with an apology." No offer of this sort ever came to break the deadlock between the lonely and introspective Mahan and the "damned grinning asses," as he termed his classmates.

Winfield Scott Schley, the only Southerner in the group and the only one accustomed even to moderate luxury, was born in his father's gracious manor house Richfields in Frederick County, Maryland. Young Schley could boast a family tree that had Scotch, Irish, Bavarian and Huguenot branches. His ancestors on both sides had come to America before the Revolution, because—as the picturesquely imaginative Schley wrote in later years—they "preferred the dangers lurking in the Wilderness of America . . . to the militarism, the discriminations and distinction of caste and class, and the intolerant religious bigotry of their day in the older countries of Europe."[10]

Schley's appointment came as a reward for the political services of his relatives in the election of Representative H. W. Hoffman to Congress. Almost any Congressman might have been delighted to sponsor him, however. He was a pleasant, happy-go-lucky youth, fond of hunting and fishing, gregarious and a lively spinner of yarns. He always regretted the fact that the general whose name he bore was temporarily at outs with the powers in Washington when he needed his appointment, and when he wrote his memoirs years later Schley practically apologized for General Winfield Scott's omission to obtain it, "although he [the general] showed an active interest [in Schley] by means of letters and good advice ever afterward while he lived."[11]

Midshipman Winfield Scott Schley entered the Naval Academy in 1856 at the same time as Mahan, but entered as a plebe and took the regular four-year course with its two practice cruises. The breezy and carefree Fourth Classman from the rolling hills near the contented little town of Frederick, Maryland, differed in every way from the introvert son of the West Point professor. He was a robust boy who, in his own words, "held pleasure and holidays in higher esteem than plodding study, which was more interesting in some such ratio as the square of the distance separating us from books."[12]

Whereas Mahan, with little effort stood next to the top of his class in his studies, Schley, with equal ease, stood next to the bottom of his class. Shang Dewey by firm determination pulled himself up from anchor man to star as Number Five, but Schley—a leading spirit in the high-jinx order of Ye Pelicans Club—was content to leave scholarship to "savvys" and plodders. That he was capable of better is indicated by his once standing sixth in drawing and tenth in Spanish. By graduation time his class had shrunk to 25 members, with Schley standing Number 18.

In conduct his demerits ranged between 38 and 84 per year, which was only average. This unimpressive statistical record, however, was compiled by the officials. The whimsical youth had a genius for avoiding the usual traps laid by the duty officer.

One Sunday, while the midshipmen were in chapel, religious tracts were distributed in their rooms. Mahan resented this business as an intrusion. Schley, on the other hand, amused his friends by holding a mock-serious prayer meeting over the tracts.

One night Schley's antics broke down even Mahan's reserve. "A crowd of fellows," wrote Mahan to Ashe, "had assembled in Paddock's room to hear music and some of them prevailed on Jim [O'Kane] to give them a tune on the violin. . . . He struck up a dance, not much time in it I must say, and 'Ye Pelicans,' . . . each a cigar in mouth, gyrated around in the mazes of the dance. But alas! a change came o'er the spirit of the scene. One of 'Ye Pelicans,' Yclept Schley, unwarily trod on Jim's pedestal where a very sore corn had made its appearance. Away went violin in one corner of the room, bow in another, while Jim, exclaiming with shocking profanity. . . . The room was convulsed with laughter . . . while Schley, taking possession of the discarded violin, commenced a series of performances that only Schley could give."[13]

Naval Cadet Schley made his first cruise in the sailing sloop *Preble* in the summer of 1857. On the return voyage the practice ship sailed over heavy seas littered with the wreckage of the passenger steamer *Central America*, that had foundered a few days earlier. Two summers later he enjoyed the responsibility of an upperclassman in the practice cruise in the sloop of war *Plymouth* under Commander T. T. Craven, the commandant of midshipmen. Reefing and furling the sails aloft on a wet night with a stiff salt breeze blowing was more to young

Schley's taste than covering a blackboard with a calculus problem. Taking a turn at the wheel or in the chains heaving the lead, pulling an oar in small boat drills, sleeping in hammocks in crowded and poorly ventilated quarters, "living upon rations . . . of hard tack, salt junk, pork and beans, weevily rice, wormy cheese, rancid butter" were hardships that Schley could recall with pleasure in after years, since they developed a "*camaraderie* of the older officers and men . . . which bound them together in loyal attachment to country and to each other."[14]

In his last year at the Naval Academy Schley and his companions of Ye Pelicans found time to argue over John Brown's raid at Harper's Ferry and the growing rift between North and South. A native of the border state of Maryland, he debated for the fun of argument and felt no strong leanings toward either side. "Nobody imagined that war between the States was possible."[15] Of greater moment to Schley was the ceremonial of Burying Math! On January 21, 1859, with naval Cadets Schley and "Dunker" Ames at their head, the Second Class, solemnly and with all the honors of war, buried copies of their Calculus and Analytical Geometry textbooks. "The turn out was elegant," reported onlooker Mahan. "The whole class with inverted broomsticks (sign of mourning you know) marched in a decent and reverential manner behind the Battery and there and then consigned them to their last repose. According to military rule they marched back to an enlivening tune nearly resembling 'One-Eyed Riley.' "[16]

Naval Cadet William Thomas Sampson was the son of Presbyterian Scotch-Irish immigrants who settled in Palmyra, New York, about four years before William's birth. As the oldest son in a large family, William helped his father at whatever labor could be found in the village, wood sawing, gardening, road building, bricklaying, and he earned a reputation for making a clean job of anything he undertook. "Will used to hoe corn and potatoes for me when he was a little shaver for two shillings a day," C. D. Johnson, a Palmyra farmer reminisced in 1898, "and he went at it with a grim earnestness, and never let up till he finished it thoroughly."[17] Studying under his mother's oil lamp at night, he made a brilliant record in school. His teachers backed him for an appointment to the Naval Academy, and Congressman E. D. Morgan obtained one for him in 1857. The story is told that young William was helping his father at work on a road when the postman handed him the all-important letter containing his appointment, and that William kept it, seal unbroken, until he reached home that night in order that his mother might share the joy of opening it.

Cadet Sampson, entering the Naval Academy in September of 1857 at nearly eighteen years of age, was about seven months older than Second Classman Mahan to whose gun crew Sampson was assigned. The impression made by the slender, slightly awkward country boy who appeared in Annapolis clad in "a loose mixed suit, ready-made and ill-fitting," lasted in Mahan's memory for nearly fifty years.[18] Everything connected with ordnance fascinated young Sampson, who would ask all sorts of questions, with a steady, fixed expression in his great luminous brown eyes.

The old fort or battery on the southeast corner of the Academy grounds was the point which especially attracted Sampson. Academy authorities had roofed it over. Inside its parapet on the seaward side was built a platform for four great guns, and around this was a wooden wall pierced with windows simulating the gunports of a ship. Exercising at the great ordnance was sheer pleasure for Sampson. Mahan, who had a thorough grasp of theoretical knowledge, even if his clumsy hands could manage only the simpler forms of seaman's knots, was mildly puzzled by the older underclassman's hunger for technical knowledge: "at our first meeting, Sampson began as he afterwards continued, putting me through a searching series of questions concerning the matters around him. He clearly, if unconsciously, intended not to wait till knowledge came to him of itself, if he could compel it to hasten."[19]

Throughout his last three years Cadet Sampson stood at the head of his class and during his First Class year he was cadet adjutant, or commander of the battalion. "There was in him an inherent modesty and simplicity through which there transpired no evidence of consciousness that he had made himself more than others."[20] His bearing now was erect and military, quite different from his appearance as a plebe. His attention centered almost altogether upon his studies, and he did not permit his grades to suffer because of his extra duties as midshipman commander.

Midshipman Sampson could never have understood Midshipman Dewey's unadulterated lack of interest in book learning.

Like Mahan, he may occasionally have witnessed a ceremony of Ye Pelicans, but a talent for riotous funmaking was totally lacking in him. As fond of ideas as Mahan, Cadet Sampson was also serious-minded and aloof. Yet his aloofness apparently proceeded from his underprivileged upbringing or from preoccupation with scientific subjects, rather than from any such social maladjustment as that from which Mahan suffered during his last year at the Academy. That Sampson in a dignified way evoked the awe of lower classmen is the testimony of Charles E. Clark, later captain of the *Oregon* and a plebe when Sampson was a first classman. Clark tells how Sampson once overheard and quashed a midshipman argument on secession. A disloyal remark brought Sampson "to an abrupt halt. . . . He was the ranking cadet officer, as adjutant wore the most gold lace and, being strikingly handsome moreover, was probably a greater man in the eyes of the junior classmen than any of their officers or instructors.

" 'You say,' he slowly and deliberately repeated the words of the last speaker, 'if the capitol of the nation is attacked, Northern troops will not be permitted to march through Baltimore to protect it? Well, then,' his voice, usually so quiet, rang out like a call to arms, 'the North will march *over* Baltimore—or the place where it stood!' He said nothing further and went his way, leaving a silent group behind him and with the Northern boys an indescribable sense of comfort."[21]

Another time, arm in arm with a resigning Southern classmate, Cadet Adjutant Sampson led a song-singing farewell procession to the Main Gate. The commandant, Lieutenant C. R. P. Rodgers, rushed out of his house to demand "the meaning of this rioting."

"No riot, sir," replied Cadet Sampson, "we are only bidding our classmate goodby."[22]

The commandant motioned them to go on with their farewell party.

The quick-tempered, impetuous Dewey graduated from the Naval Academy in 1858; introspective Mahan, still kept in Coventry by his classmates, in 1859; the fun-loving "Pelican" Winfield Scott Schley in 1860. Sampson, the scholarly ordnance enthusiast, completed his course of studies in the fateful spring of 1861.

Spain, Cuba, the Philippines lay far ahead in the undreamed future, as the admirals for 1898 completed their course of instruction at the Naval Academy and plunged almost immediately into the grueling postgraduate experience of warfare in the Civil War.

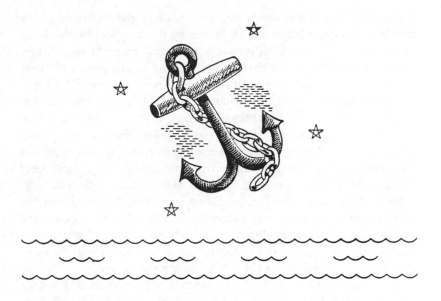

2. DEWEY IN ACTION

Sampson stepped from the classrooms of Annapolis into the wardroom of a warship on active wartime service, but the other future admirals of 1898, having graduated earlier, spent a more normal one to three years in the steerage mess as midshipmen in the peacetime Navy at sea.

Between 1858 and 1861 Dewey served on the *Wabash*, the *Powhatan* and the *Pawnee*. These excellent ships were equipped with steam engines and boilers below decks and a full outfit of sails aloft.

The *Wabash*, a 4,000-ton screw frigate of the *Merrimack* class, was flagship of the Mediterranean Squadron, and Dewey was proud to be a member of her company. Discovering in Gibraltar and Malta that British officers and society held the chewing of tobacco to be a mark of ill breeding, Shang Dewey promptly gave up this frowned-on habit. Perhaps because of his neatness in dress he was often taken ashore in Mediterranean ports by Flag Officer E. A. F. LaVallette. Places and people interested him.

"Harbor of Genoa, January 20th, 1859," reads an entry in young Dewey's neatly written diary. "Light variable airs and rains. At

8 A M, at Merid., and at sunset fir'd a salute of 21 guns in honor of the marriage of Prince Napoleon of France to the daughter of the King of Sardinia . . ."[1] Youthful, romantic, uncritical, he made no mention of the widely known fact that the bridegroom in this case, a kinsman of Napoleon III, was a seasoned libertine of forty-three and his bride a princess aged fifteen and obviously sacrificed to the minotaur for reasons of state. In Constantinople the sight of the Sultan's harem trailing their lord to the Mosque was indelibly fixed in the young man's memory. And the American consul's daughter, to whom he was introduced at this time, he distinctly remembered forty years later when at the height of his fame he called again at Constantinople.

From the deck of the *Pawnee* Dewey saw the Caribbean and the gulf. Captain Hartstene was an intemperate Southerner who, on the eve of the Civil War, might have debated within himself whether to deliver over the *Pawnee* to the Confederates. On the voyage home in 1861 Dewey was officer of the day when the ship was coming abreast of Charleston, South Carolina. At this moment the eccentric Hartstene bustled up to the quarter-deck in his crazy-quilt blouse "made of remnants of his wife's silk dresses" and commanded Dewey, "Take in the top-gallant sails!" Dewey had them taken in. "Now set them again!" Dewey did as ordered. "Now call all hands and take them in properly!"[2] A third time Dewey obeyed, as it was his duty to obey. But the captain's petulance stuck in his crop, for he considered that the maneuver had been executed properly the first time. Hartstene's later resignation and enlistment on the side of the Confederates lent color to Dewey's theory that off Charleston he had come within an ace of turning over his ship to the Confederates.

At the Boston Navy Yard in 1861 the obsolete side-wheeler *Mississippi* was being outfitted as temporary flagship of the Gulf Squadron to put Lincoln's blockade into effect. Her captain, T. O. Selfridge, who in forty years of naval service had never before commanded a steam man-of-war, watched the yard workmen with an anxious eye because saboteurs had just put the regular flagship *Colorado* out of action for four weeks. Mechanics, going over the *Mississippi's* antiquated engines, cleaning, adjusting, added here and there a patch of new metal to strengthen a weak section of boiler plate. In spite of the wariness of the ship's officers, however, a pro-Secessionist saboteur sawed half through two port delivery pipes, filled the breaks with gutta-percha and painted them over. This knavery, detected immediately after the ship got under way, delayed her departure for four days.

Lieutenant George Dewey reported for duty aboard the *Mississippi* on May 10, 1861, when the outfitting was at its height, and he served aboard her until she went down under him two years later at Port Hudson. The last chapters in the story of the *Mississippi* are the first chapters in the story of George Dewey as a fighting man of action. The veteran wooden side-wheeler was to carry him so frequently under fire and her extreme vulnerability would require all hands to be so constantly on the alert that, as Dewey wrote later, "war appeared to be almost a normal state of affairs to us."[3]

On his way south, Dewey was anxious for his ship to get into the fighting, but for several months the *Mississippi* was anchored at Key West. From blockaders farther west she received reports about Confederate raiders sneaking out of Southern harbors. From Washington came instructions on neutral prize cargoes, requests by Unionists to be evacuated from Southern coast towns and rumors of Confederate preparations. At Key West she never sighted a hostile ship or fired anything larger than a signal gun, and once she spent four days fishing for a lost anchor without finding it. The *Mississippi* was in effect a mere office for her superannuated flag officer. In July when the flagship *Colorado* arrived, Flag Officer Mervine shifted his flag back to her, and the *Mississippi*—to Lieutenant Dewey's vast relief—took a blockade station off Mobile Bay.

In September Dewey's vessel was stationed off the Mississippi River deltas. Anchored athwart Pass a l'Outre or Southwest Pass, the *Mississippi* fired an occasional shot at Confederate craft trying to sneak through the blockade. The Southerners were often successful, for there were several secondary passes navigable to shallow vessels and the one or two heavy blockaders like the *Mississippi* were neither numerous nor agile enough to intercept them.

In the spring of 1862 Farragut came down to attack New Orleans, and George Dewey got his first real break. . . .

A shift of officers brought Captain Melancton Smith to command the *Mississippi* and Smith, influenced by Dewey's four years of service in steam vessels, picked Dewey, in spite of his youth, to be his execu-tive officer and second in command. Lieutenant Dewey was twenty-four and busy sprouting a mustache to make himself look older, for there were officers in Farragut's fleet twice his age who held billets that were less desirable. One day Farragut, half joking, mentioned this circumstance to Smith.

"Dewey is doing all right," contended Smith. "I don't want a stranger here."

"Then we will let him stay," said Farragut.[4]

Spurred by pride in an assignment beyond his years and by boundless gratitude toward Captain Smith and Flag Officer Farragut, Lieutenant Dewey worked as he had never worked before. And there was plenty to do, for the awkward and heavy *Mississippi* normally required sea room to maneuver in and was never intended to fight in a river as Farragut had now ordered her to do. Her high sides and mammoth paddle boxes, moreover, would present a large silhouette to Confederate gunners in the forts below New Orleans, making her more vulnerable than any other ship in Farragut's fleet; but Farragut needed her gunpower.

At Ship Island, Farragut's advance base near the deltas, her coal bunkers were swept clean. At Southwest Pass her cannon and ammunition were transferred to lighters. When everything movable had been taken out, a team of small steamers was hitched up to cables run out through her bow hawse holes and these dragged her, inches at a time, across the bar. It required two weeks to get her inside the bar to deep water.

At Pilot Town—a few ramshackle houses standing on poles in the swamp which had been converted into a temporary storage depot—Dewey supervised the remounting of her guns and essential gear, and reloaded her coal from lighters.

The third week in April she moved up the river and anchored below the hostile forts. Inside the river, even in broad daylight, the unwieldy vessel was in constant danger of running aground. Day and night now while Commander David D. Porter's mortar boats were bombarding the forts, Dewey was kept busy stowing cables around exposed machinery and sending out boats' crews to fend off fire rafts which had been drifted downstream by the Confederates. "We, with the fleet," Dewey wrote, "were too busy to sleep much, but we were soon so accustomed to the noise, and so dog-tired when we had a chance to rest, that we could have slept in an inferno."[5]

Captain Smith's plea of poor eyesight having failed to budge Farragut from his plan to rush past the forts at night, Smith turned over to Dewey the job of navigating the ship and himself took Dewey's appointed place on the gun deck.[6]

Short, thick-set Lieutenant Dewey trod the *Mississippi's* hurricane deck with quick decisive steps, thoroughly relishing his new responsibility. Shortly after midnight of April 23-24 he lifted his muddy chains and anchors. At 3:00 A.M. he caught Farragut's signal of two red lights perpendicular at the peak of the *Hartford* and gave orders to get under way. This was to be Dewey's baptism of fire.

The *Mississippi* was the third ship from the head of the line, and throughout the dangerous run past the forts Dewey kept her in her appointed position in spite of his vessel's crankiness in the river currents and in spite of the fact that the *Pensacola*, the ship next ahead, twice stopped dead in the water to let her gunners take aim.

Apparently Dewey paid little attention either to the fire of the enemy or the weird lighting effects of the battle scene itself, but devoted himself entirely to keeping his ship in its station astern of the *Pensacola*. At the height of the fireworks a Mr. Waud, an artist for an illustrated weekly who had Captain Smith's permission to witness the spectacle from the *Mississippi's* foretop, yelled down to Dewey that there was "a queer-looking customer on our port bow." Dewey looked and ordered, "Starboard the helm!" A moment's delay and the much-feared Confederate ironclad ram *Manassas* would have sheared off the *Mississippi's* port paddle wheel. As it was the ram butted against the ship abaft the wheel and merely skinned off a few planks. Dewey automatically shouted, "Sound the pumps!" Leaning far out over the side, he saw in the flame light about fifty gleaming ends of copper bolts "cut as clean as if they were hair under a razor's edge."[7] The damage, however, caused no leak, for the *Mississippi's* inner planking had held.

Above the forts about daybreak Captain Smith, now on the hurricane deck, received a megaphone order from Farragut to run down the *Manassas*. "Can you turn the ship?" Smith asked Dewey. "Yes, sir." Dewey did not know whether he could turn her or not. She had not yet turned under her own power in the narrow river "but I knew that either I was going to do so or else run her aground."[8] Dewey's attempt succeeded. As the giant *Mississippi* charged down

like a steam roller upon a turtle, the *Manassas'* commander ran ashore
and abandoned the vessel.

The *Mississippi's* losses were only two killed and six wounded, appreciably lower than in the other ships. "I have much pleasure,"
beamed Captain Melancton Smith in his official report, "in mentioning
the efficient service rendered by Executive Officer George Dewey,
who kept the vessel in her station during the engagement, a task exceedingly difficult from the darkness and thick smoke that enveloped
us from the fire of our vessel and the burning [Confederate] gunboats. . . ."⁹

For ten months after the battle of New Orleans the side-finned
Mississippi was like a stranded whale, too heavy, Farragut decreed, to
move upstream with the other vessels against Vicksburg, and too heavy
to flounder back out of the river to a blockade station without a tow
from small steamers which could not be spared for this purpose. It fell
to her lot to be tied up to a New Orleans wharf where her guns could
overlook the city and support the unpopular army of occupation under
General Butler.

After his thrilling ordeal below New Orleans Lieutenant Dewey
accepted with an effort the sudden letdown from battle action to sentry
duty. The injuries to the ship were repaired. He exercised the gun
crews. He shut his eyes to the monotonous view of an idle water front.
Many were the errands ashore that he performed for Captain Smith.
He enjoyed, as would any zestful, impatient and mildly annoyed young
man, the petty disputes over rank and official prerogatives that arose
between the shellback Commodore Morris of the *Pensacola* and the
rough-and-tumble politician, General Butler. In French restaurants
Dewey consumed quantities of good food, but the hostility of his con-
quered fellow countrymen perplexed and worried him. Social life
ashore, Dewey wrote, "was limited mostly to the scowls of the people
we passed . . . the true Southern woman would as soon have invited
Satan as a Union officer to her house."¹⁰ In the spring of 1863 when
Farragut ordered the *Mississippi* to accompany him farther upstream
in the thrust past Port Hudson, Dewey was happy.

It was a hazardous mission. At Port Hudson, where the Mississippi
River makes a horseshoe turn under high bluffs, the Confederates had
fortified a "little Gibraltar" which defied the Federal forces ascending
the river. The *Mississippi's* station in the run past Port Hudson was

W. T. Sampson as a Naval Cadet.

A. T. Mahan at Seventeen.

Dr. Julius Y. Dewey, Father
of the Admiral.

George Dewey in 1867.

Dewey as Lieutenant.

Lieutenant Dewey about the
Time He was Executive Officer
on the *Mississippi*.

that of "whipper-in" at the rear of the line. Again, as at New Orleans, the operation was undertaken at night.

After sundown on March 14, 1863, not a breath stirred the sultry air on the river below Port Hudson. Opaque and soot-laden clouds, cascading from the funnels, poured over the decks of the warships and hovered in dense layers on the water, obscuring the outlines of the shores. At ten o'clock, when Executive Officer Dewey ordered the engineer to open the throttles, he could scarcely make out the three pairs of stern lights disposed *en echelon* upstream ahead of the *Mississippi*. A rowboat lashed under the port bow of the *Mississippi* held the crouched figure of the river pilot, upon whose vision and skill the fortunes of all hands depended.

At eleven the flagship *Hartford* sent up a rocket as signal for the mortars stationed below Port Hudson to open fire. On the low west bank the Confederates set fire to a pile of pitch pine and the hilltop batteries to the east blossomed with flame as Confederate guns fired down on the ships. Dewey, dividing his time between the gun deck and the hurricane deck, now lost sight of the ships ahead. He directed his gunners to fire at the flashes on shore. He passed the *Monongahela* without seeing her through the choking smoke. Farther ahead the *Richmond*, disabled by a shot and carried around by the current, fired a broadside at the flashes of the *Mississippi's* guns before her gunners discovered their error. As the *Mississippi's* gun crews were decimated by friendly as well as enemy fire, men from the unengaged port batteries fell into their places, and young Dewey felt a rush of almost paternal pride in the efficiency of the men he had drilled at New Orleans.

The *Mississippi* had now reached the curve of the horseshoe directly under the loftiest of the enemy's cannon and abreast of the treacherous underwater tongues of mud reaching out from the left bank.

Suddenly the pilot called, "Starboard the helm! Full speed ahead!" The helmsman reeled the *Mississippi's* steering wheel rapidly to the right. The ship caught in the current, swung around a hairsbreadth too far. At full speed she ran on a mud bar, heeled over "three streaks to port"—and there she stuck.[11]

"With our own guns barking, and the engines pounding, and the paddle-wheels making more noise than usual, because we were aground, it was difficult to make commands heard," wrote Dewey. "In half an hour the engines never budged us, while steadfastly and even unconcernedly the engine-room force stuck to their duties. We were being more frequently hit. . . . I remember hunting about the deck for Captain Smith and finding him lighting another cigar with a flint as coolly as if he were doing it when he lay anchored off New Orleans."

"Well, it doesn't look as if we could get her off," he said.

"No," agreed Dewey, "it does not!"[12]

A plunging shot tore through the deck and set fire to a paint storage room which was below the water line forward and under normal circumstances well protected. The fire raging beyond control and threatening the magazines, Captain Smith ordered, "Abandon ship."

Dewey sent the wounded men downstream in the first boat. The second and third boats he directed to land the remainder of the men where they could wade ashore to the west bank. These latter boats were so slow in returning from the shore to the ship that on the next trip Dewey impulsively swung himself down into one of the boats to speed their return.

Free of the ship, with shells splashing all around his small boats, he suddenly realized that whatever might be his motive he had left his ship in distress and had violated the old and honorable rule of the sea: "the last man to leave her should be the captain, and I as executive officer should be next to the last."[13]

He whipped out his pistols and compelled the boats' crews to pull faster. He made it back to the doomed ship.

Captain Smith sent him below decks to search once more for other wounded who might still be alive. In the darkness Dewey pulled a fainting youngster from under a pile of mangled bodies. Then, with Ensign O. A. Batcheller, he descended to the wardroom to set fire to the ship. "I had a lantern with me. . . . I ran into my stateroom, and pulling the mattress off the berth hurried back with it to the wardroom"; he ripped it open and crammed it with several chairs under the dining table, poured oil over it from the lantern and set it ablaze.[14]

As the flames leaped through the hatches, the officers abandoned ship, the ensigns, then Dewey, then the captain.

Several hours later on board the *Richmond*, Dewey and Captain Smith watched the burning shell of the *Mississippi* float past them down the river.

"She goes out magnificently, anyway!" remarked Dewey.

"I don't think so!" retorted the solemn captain.[15]

Later in the day Melancton Smith, who according to Dewey "would have made a most dignified bishop," wrote to the Secretary of the Navy, "I consider that I should be neglecting a most important duty should I omit to mention the coolness of my executive officer, Mr. Dewey, and the steady, fearless, and gallant manner in which the officers and men of the *Mississippi* defended her, and the orderly and quiet manner in which she was abandoned."[16]

As an officer without a ship, Dewey was given temporary duty as prize agent to dispose of vessels and cargoes captured by blockaders in the Western Gulf. The breather ashore enabled him to procure a new outfit of uniforms and further to indulge himself as a connoisseur of New Orleans' famed pompano fish and upland plover. In June a berth was found for him as executive officer on the *Monongahela*.

Farragut himself was now spending much of his time on the *Monongahela* patrolling in the lower river while the flagship *Hartford* was marooned above Port Hudson. Occasionally the genial Farragut interfered with the holystoning of Dewey's deck to swap yarns with the seamen. Often the flag officer would clap Dewey on the shoulder with a "Come along, youngster!" and go over the side into his little steam cutter for a reconnaissance under the batteries of Port Hudson.[17] In these journeys Farragut never turned back until he had drawn fire from enemy batteries. Though frequently under fire Dewey himself was never struck. His luck in this respect was cut from the same cloth as Farragut's.

The closest call of Dewey's career came at 9:00 A.M. on July 7, 1863. A new Confederate guerrilla battery which ambushed his ship near Donaldsonville sent a shell through the bulwarks on the *Monongahela's* port quarter. It burst on the quarter-deck, mortally wounded Captain Abner Read, killed one seaman, seriously wounded four others and knocked down Captain Thornton A. Jenkins, Farragut's chief of staff. Dewey, who had been standing near enough to chat with the two captains, was untouched. Temporary command of the ship now fell to Dewey as executive officer; Captain Jenkins the same day wrote Farragut an official report praising Dewey's "unrivaled coolness and courage."[18]

Three days later the U. S. S. *New London* grounded at White Hall Point where Confederate musketry on shore kept her men below decks. Dewey for the first time exercising full command of a battleship in action, went to her rescue. Sharpshooters' bullets kicked up splinters all over the *Monongahela*. Dewey, completely without a sense of danger and possessing the rare ability to devote his entire attention to the business in hand, tugged the *New London* off the shoal and shepherded her down the river to safety. "Lieutenant Commanding Dewey displayed coolness, skill and judgment," reported the rescued commander.[19]   The word "coolness" had become monotonous in official commendations of George Dewey.

In midsummer, the Mississippi River having been opened from Cairo to the Gulf, Lieutenant Dewey was detached from Farragut's squadron and ordered north.

He returned to his home in Montpelier, Vermont, for his first leave of absence in two years. Dr. Julius Yemans Dewey was doubtless startled to discover on his son's face a near imitation of his own sideburns. For all the hirsute decorations, however, the strenuous life had only slightly altered George's youthful appearance. There was, perhaps, a more purposeful look in his bright black eyes. At twenty-six his skin was as smooth, his forehead as free of lines as that of a girl of sixteen.

At Portsmouth, New Hampshire, where he spent several weeks putting into commission the double-ender *Agawam*, Dewey met Susan Boardman Goodwin, the beautiful daughter of Ichabod Goodwin, Governor of New Hampshire. "Old Ichabod," a fighting governor who personally raised and financed a regiment in the first weeks of the war, was the sort of man who would not neglect entertainments for fighting young officers of the fleet who were assigned to duty in his state. Dewey's autobiography merely mentions, without giving particulars, that he met his future bride in Portsmouth.

On the East Coast, where the Navy was closer to Washington and political surveillance, Dewey found the rules of seniority to be more strictly followed than they had been in the West. Life on the stuffy harbor gunboat *Agawam*, a midget side-wheeler compared with either the *Mississippi* or the *Monongahela*, was strenuous enough, but her role as a gunboat supporting General Butler, as Dewey put it "vegetating" in the James River, gave her no real chance for distinction.

On the eve of the Fort Fisher campaign Admiral Porter sent for Dewey to become executive officer of the big steam frigate *Minnesota*. "But I was on the *Minnesota* less than one day. Her captain voiced the old complaint about my youth, and Porter not being of the mind to assign him an executive whom he did not want, I returned to the *Agawam*."[20] The unconventional Admiral Porter—himself a lieutenant at the outbreak of the war and able to sympathize with the young fighter's desire to get ahead in his profession—at length found a welcome for Dewey on Commodore H. K. Thatcher's huge and obsolete *Colorado*.

Thatcher, unfortunately for Dewey, was Porter's second in command, and when the time came for the assaulting force of seamen from the fleet to go ashore for the attempt to storm Fort Fisher, Thatcher declined to allow Dewey to lead the *Colorado's* contingent, as did the executive officers on other ships. If anything should happen to Porter, Thatcher would have to command the squadron, and Dewey must be available to take over from Thatcher the command of the *Colorado*. The new executive's job on the *Colorado*, however, enabled him to cut his teeth as a commander of men.

Ever since the beginning of the war the *Colorado's* crew had suffered from low morale. The ship was not adapted to any sort of fighting thus far experienced in the war. Her deep draft had deprived her of a part in the New Orleans campaign. She was too slow to catch blockade runners. Moreover, during the past year many of the *Colorado's* trained seamen had been transferred to more active ships and their places had been filled with draftees and "bounty jumpers."

Dewey learned that his predecessor on the *Colorado* "had had a pretty wearing and unhappy time of it," that he had had as many as a hundred disciplinary cases at a time chained between the guns and that these ruffians had called out insulting remarks as officers passed by.[21]

His first morning on board Lieutenant Dewey summoned all hands to muster, and many failed to turn out. Obviously the junior officers were afraid of some of their men. Dewey went below and wherever he found a hammock occupied the quick-tempered, muscular, square-shouldered executive officer tumbled the man out on the deck. Thereafter he had no trouble with late sleepers. Gradually he singled out the troublemakers, and, instead of chaining them on the relatively pleasant gun deck, he locked them in the brig. The worst character, a red-haired giant named Webster, he shackled in the hold.

The enraged giant worked himself free of his irons and terrified the master-at-arms by breaking up stone bottles of soda and ale and hurling threats up the ladder. Dewey cocked his revolver and went below.

"Webster, this is the executive officer, Mr. Dewey," he called down to him. "I am coming down, Webster. You may be sure of this, if you raise a finger against me I shall kill you."[22]

Dewey descended quickly. Webster dropped the upraised bottle and submitted to arrest.

The *Colorado* found a deep-water anchorage within a mile of Fort Fisher, and in the bombardments of December and January, as the war drew toward its close, Dewey's gun crews at last saw clean hard fighting. Several of their guns were knocked out and a number of men killed. In one emergency Dewey ran along the gun deck calling: "Fire! Fire as fast as you can! That is the way to stop their fire!"[23]

Commander Thatcher officially praised the crew for their "cool" and "deliberate" firing. Dewey he commended for "invaluable assistance . . . in having all departments of the ship in perfect order for battle, as well as for the valuable aid in the management of the ship during the action."[24]

The war closed with Dewey wearing, as a reward for his coolness and his ability to inspire coolness in others, the four narrow gold stripes of a lieutenant commander. Lieutenant Commander George Dewey, in the photograph on a *carte de visite* which he had made at this time, looked more youthful than ever. He had shaved off the late lieutenant's sideburns.

3. THE INFLUENCE OF WAR ON MAHAN

FOR Mahan a leisurely cruise on the Brazil Station filled the two-year interval between Annapolis and the Civil War. His ship, the flagship *Congress*, one of the last of the Navy's exclusively sail-driven frigates, had been built 19 years before, in 1840, in the year Mahan himself was born and this experience of life on an outmoded canvas-powered-man-of-war would lend authority to Mahan's later writings on the age of sail. The vessel's captain, Louis M. Goldsborough, had been superintendent during Mahan's first year at the Naval Academy, and the broad pennant which she flew was that of Flag Officer Joshua Sands. As it turned out, this was fated to be the *Congress'* last cruise, for soon after her return home she won death and fame in Hampton Roads in an unequal clash with the Confederate converted-ironclad *Merrimack*.

The crowded decks of the *Congress* brought to life for Mahan the characters he had known in Marryat's novels. Her bosun, carpenter, sailmaker and 200-odd able-bodied seamen might only yesterday have been transferred from Nelson's *Victory* or Collingwood's *Royal Sovereign*.

Flag Officer Sands chose Mahan to be his aide. Sands was a veteran of 1812 with eccentricities which Mahan quickly learned to associate with officers of the old school. Sands had been married three times. He had fought three duels and in his last duel had killed his man.

Mahan accompanied him ashore on a visit to the scene of his last duel, on an island in the harbor of Rio de Janeiro. Solemnly reminiscent, the flag officer paced off the field, meditated a few moments in silence and then marched back to his barge. For hours on end Mahan watched him measure the quarter-deck with mincing steps, a queer little slouching figure beside the towering bulk of Captain Goldsborough. At night Mahan trailed the flag officer down the gun deck, carefully picking his way, like Sands, among the men sprawled in sleep between the guns, to the smoking compartment forward. Mahan was often irked by this enforced tagging along. "The life of an aide," he wrote later, "is literally that of a dog . . . following around, or else sitting in a boat at a landing, just as a dog waits outside for his master, to all hours of the night, till your superior comes down from his dinner or out from the theatre. A coachman . . . has only his own behavior to look to, while the aide has to see that the dozen bargemen also behave, don't skip up the wharf for a drink, and then forget the way back to the boat."[1] Quite likely Flag Officer Sands sensed young Mahan's scrupulously repressed rebellion. One day as he was about to go ashore he noticed that Mahan was wearing a handsome necktie his mother had given him. "Humph!" he growled. "Don't wear a thing like that with me. You look like a privateersman!" As aide to Sands, Mahan enjoyed many a "whiff of the naval atmosphere of the past."[2]

Mahan at nineteen, of meditative turn and fond of daydreaming, did not enjoy being "utilized for every kind of miscellaneous and non-descript duty." He found, however, considerable private amusement in characterizing people. The first lieutenant, for example, was "great with the paintbrush and tar-pot" and "mighty in that lavish swashing of sea-water which is called washing decks."[3]

From his own lyrical apostrophes to naval life as it was on the *Congress*, written 50 years later, one gathers that he was fondest of the midwatch, from midnight to four, when human activity was considerably less than in either of the other night watches. He loved the sight of the ship's sails in good weather and was thrilled by the musical vibrations of her taut rigging. But he never enjoyed a storm. He accepted the responsibilities assigned to him at such a time and felt lucky if no mishap occurred while he was in charge. He derived little if any thrill out of being an integral part of the ship. His mind was not always where his body was. He was undoubtedly even more isolated and lonely aboard ship than he had been in his last year at Annapolis. Four of his classmates who had put him in Coventry in Annapolis served with him on this cruise of the *Congress*. They argued for and against secession, but Mahan remembered none of the other topics of their conversation.

The world was large in 1861. The *Congress* at distant Montevideo did not learn of Fort Sumter until two and a half months later. Not cables, but a lumbering windjammer brought the alarming news. The *Congress* was immediately headed back for Boston on a return voyage that required 62 days. What excited Mahan was the chance that the war might bring him quickly into a command of his own. The Navy would have to be rapidly expanded and at the same time the number of its officers would be reduced through the resignations of Southerners. He was not particular as to the kind of ship he wished to command, nor could he be. He was still only a midshipman.

The prospects in Boston looked bright, and in Washington, whither he was at once transferred to the *James Adger*, brighter still. Boston shipowners and insurance men were in a panic and clamoring for the Navy to scour the seven seas and run down the Confederate raider *Sumter*. Confederate Commander Raphael Semmes, lately of the United States Navy, had eluded the slow blockaders off New Orleans about the time Mahan's ship had departed from Montevideo, and, at the very time that the *Congress* was tacking north through the West Indies, the Rebel raider was seizing and burning American shipping in those waters. Captured dispatches of Semmes to the Confederate Navy Department were published in Washington under lurid headlines the first week in September when Mahan joined his new ship, the merchant steamer *Adger*, newly acquired by the Navy, and being outfitted for service as a blockader.

Twenty-one-year-old Midshipman Mahan set on paper his dream of a separate command. "The ravages of the pirate *Sumter* have reached a pitch that, if long continued, will cast an undeserved stigma on the Navy." The raider, being a fast steamer, would always be able to take advantage of neutrality rules and elude pursuers. Why not try a decoy? An innocent-looking merchant vessel "with a heavy pivot gun and a light house built over it such as are often seen in merchant ships, and which could not excite suspicions," might lie in wait for the raider in the West Indies. Would there not be a probability of the raider's "approaching confidently . . . so as to be disabled or sunk with your heavy guns?" The youthful naval strategist was aware that his idea might appear harebrained. "But suppose it fail, what is lost? A useless ship, a midshipman, and a hundred men." If successful, "look at the prestige such an affair would give the service." Finally, if the idea were accepted and the Department "should not wish to risk a better man, I beg to offer myself to lead the enterprise."[4]

He mailed his idea to Gustavus Fox, Assistant Secretary of the Navy, and while he was waiting for an answer his ship proceeded to Hampton Roads, where he shortly received his commission as lieutenant and was transferred to the U.S.S. *Pocahontas* as executive officer. That Midshipman Mahan's idea of a decoy ship was entirely feasible was proved by its successful use in World War I. In the confusion of 1861, however, the novel suggestion was filed away, and it failed to win for its author the coveted quick promotion to an independent command.

As executive officer of the *Pocahontas,* Mahan enjoyed an unusual measure of both pleasure and pain. Percival Drayton, his captain, was a well-read South Carolinian and one of the pleasantest commanders in the Navy for a junior officer of literary taste to serve under. Drayton, moreover, remembered the son of Professor Dennis Mahan of West Point as one of the cadets he had examined at the naval school only two years before, and when Lieutenant Mahan joined his ship Drayton made a diary note that he was "young enough not to have too fixed ways and is quite clever."[5] This meant, in effect, that Drayton intended to leave most of the deck duty to Mahan.

In late October 1861 the *Pocahontas* steamed south with 99 other naval craft and army transports under Flag Officer S. F. Du Pont. The forthcoming naval attack against the Confederate forts at the entrance to Port Royal Sound was to be Mahan's first chance to fight a ship in battle. As events proved, it was also to be his *only* chance.

Off Hatteras, the *Pocahontas* was separated from the rest of the fleet by a gale that sank or blew on shore several of the river ferries that had been converted into transports. The *Pocahontas* also had difficulty replenishing her coal supply at sea. Owing to the fantastic optimism of her designers, her coal bunkers had a capacity of only 67 tons. Thus handicapped, she failed to make the rendezvous on November 7 with the fleet off Port Royal before Du Pont sailed in to battle. When in the distance they heard Du Pont's guns opening up against the Confederate forts, Drayton and Mahan were still two hours away, taking on the last load of coal. Casting off the coal ship, they hurried into the sound. It was imperative for them to get into this battle. Percival Drayton's brother, the Confederate General Thomas Drayton, commanded the Port Royal forts, and a failure to get his ship into battle would automatically impeach Percival's loyalty.

Chuffing in two hours late, the *Pocahontas* let fly several broadsides into the already beaten forts. In return she received a token damage in her rigging.

Mahan experienced no great thrill in his first and only battle. "After the action, there followed the usual scene of jollification." The transports steamed into the sound, "bands playing, troops hurrahing, and with the general expenditure of wind from vocal organs which seems the necessary concomitant of such occasions," Mahan wrote later.[6]

As the Federal ships milled about in the harbor celebrating the first Union naval victory of the war, Commander Drayton peered through his glasses at his Confederate brother's forts and beyond Fort Walker to the Drayton family's cotton fields, now furrowed by cannon balls. Executive Officer Mahan, whose eye should have been on the drift of his ship in the crowded harbor, was fascinated by the mixture of emotions on his commander's face. Meanwhile the tide carried the *Pocahontas* afoul of the rigging of the anchored sloop *Seminole*. "Down came one of the big blocks from our masthead, narrowly missing the captain's head," while the *Seminole* lost her bowsprit rigging.[7] Henceforth Mahan, having learned the hard way, would become a more careful deck officer. Never again would he be able to relax on a quarter-deck. Unlike Dewey, whose mind ran smoothly in the single groove essential to the business in hand, it always required an effort for Mahan to fix his attention on any simple, monotonously repetitious task and steadily hold it there.

Mahan, after ten months of desultory blockade duty off South Carolina and Florida, was sent north to teach seamanship to the midshipmen at Newport.

Here at last, in the temporary wartime quarters at Newport, Mahan found an environment congenial to his tastes. The head of his department, Lieutenant Stephen B. Luce, well-read and affable, was like Mahan of a scholarly temperament. Despite a difference of thirteen years in age the two men became fast friends. Later Luce was to become founder of the Naval War College, and his chief service to American history was to be his success in persuading Mahan to go there, to nurse the college through its first troubled years, and to make his studies of "the influence of sea power upon history."

At Newport also, Mahan suffered an affair of the heart which was to have a lasting effect upon him. He fell thoroughly, hopelessly in love with a young married woman of the Newport social set. Torn by the age-old conflict of love and honor, and aided no doubt by the coolness of the lady herself, whom he called "Nonpareille,"—the unequaled— the young Naval Academy instructor in seamanship chose the honorable course, and forbore to urge the lady to obtain a divorce. The decision, however, left Mahan emotionally unsettled for the next ten years.[8]

Mahan in the final year of the war was whisked off from congenial Newport to the "desperately tedious" blockade. He spent three months on the small steam corvette *Seminole*—the same that had been stripped of her bow rigging at Port Royal.

The *Seminole's* station off Sabine Pass in the Western Gulf was regarded by Mahan as the ultimate in dullness. In port there were "the resources of the shore to fill up the chinks." On a voyage, "the vicissitudes of successive days provide the desultory succession of incidents, which vary and fill out the tenor of occupations." But on the blockade dead monotony . . . "The crew, once drilled, needed but a few moments each day to keep at the level of proficiency; and there was practically nothing to do, because nothing happened that required either a doing or an undoing." Mahan solemnly took to chewing onions. He even wished for a gale of wind to offset the monotony. "Day after day, day after day, we lay inactive—roll, roll." "The largest reservoir of anecdotes was sure to run dry. . . . I have never seen a body of intelligent men reduced so nearly to imbecility as my shipmates then were."[9]

After three months of self-torture in this solitary outpost Lieutenant Mahan was transferred to Admiral Dahlgren's squadron off Charleston and Savannah. The blockaders here, as Mahan found, were better off than in the Gulf. They got their newspapers earlier. They fed on the first tier of beef from the supply boats. Mahan's friend Commander Luce was now in a ship on this station. In this altogether more congenial environment, Mahan chewed fewer onions.

As exigencies required, Mahan was shifted around from one small ship to another, his main duty in the final months of the war being to maintain communications with, and to run reconnaissance patrols for, various units of Sherman's army which were operating back of Charleston and Savannah. Admiral Dahlgren, who found Mahan most useful as a staff officer, several times entrusted him with temporary command of a vessel and for a while had him serving as ordnance officer for the squadron as a whole.

As the war ended, Mahan, as Dahlgren's aide, tall, handsome and much better pleased with himself than at any time during the war, wore his gold braid with dignity at the official rehoisting of the flag over Fort Sumter and at Admiral Dahlgren's reception for General Sherman at Savannah.

"What?" Tecumseh Sherman's unbarbered face grinned in reminiscence when Mahan was introduced. "What, the son of old Dennis?"[10]

4. SCHLEY TRIES "THIS NELSON BUSINESS"

WHEN Midshipman Winfield Scott Schley reported aboard the steam frigate *Niagara* in New York in June of 1860, he found carpenters erecting cabins for distinguished guests on the poop of the ship just above Captain W. W. McKean's quarters. Schley deposited his duffel bag in the steerage forward and discovered there a strange character dressed in formal attire who identified himself as Mr. Hollenback, a reporter for the *New York Herald*. Hollenback, impressed by his assignment to report the homeward voyage of the three princes who comprised the first Japanese mission to the United States, had come aboard the *Niagara* apparently expecting to mess with the captain, and when he discovered that he was to be quartered with midshipmen in the steerage, it was too late for him to go ashore for another rig.

Schley and his companions jumped him at once. "What are you doing in that hat?" "Get out of that nail keg!" When the reporter affected surprise, the midshipmen launched an attack with swords and slit the silk stovepipe into ribbons. Hollenback took it in good part. Someone found him a cap, and throughout the voyage to Japan he swapped yarns with the midshipmen, ate the same fare and slept on their hard board bunks without squeamishness.[1]

At the Cape Verde Islands the *Niagara* took on coal. At São Paulo de Loanda on the equatorial coast of Africa they delivered mail to the U. S. S. *Constellation,* flagship of the Navy's West African Squadron. Rounding Africa and crossing the Indian Ocean, the *Niagara* sped under full canvas. To Schley, whose watch station was on the forecastle, every sail they sighted offered a challenge to a race. Usually the *Niagara* outsped her unwitting rivals. She was extraordinarily narrow in beam to assure speed as a commerce raider, and her gun deck, mounting the latest 11-inch shell guns, stood so high out of the water that many an old seaman believed she would upset in a gale, an element of danger which Schley relished.

In September the *Niagara* reached Anger Point on the Straits of Sunda, and the Japanese princes, several of whom spoke Dutch, spent a few days on shore. On returning to the ship they brought a pet monkey aboard. Their pet was cared for by the Japanese cooks in the temporary galley erected in Schley's territory on the forecastle. Though monkeys are normally a welcome diversion to sailors, this individual made a game of upsetting Japanese saucepans on the holystoned deck and seemed aware of the diplomatic immunity he enjoyed. When the sailors tried to discipline him, he would leap into the rigging beyond reach, swing by the tail and jabber at them. This demoralizing situation lasted until someone thought of greasing his tail. The next pan he upset was his last. In the rigging his customary tail hitch slipped and he was lost overboard.

To Midshipman Schley, who had been officer of the watch when the incident occurred, fell the duty of explaining it to the first lieutenant, and then to the captain and the Japanese. "In the confusion of interpreting from Japanese to Dutch and from Dutch to Japanese and then from Japanese to English, the impression was left on the captain's mind that the writer [Schley] had really caused the death of the monkey . . . but as the monkey had been careless in holding on, the suggestion was made that he had committed suicide, and for this the writer ought not to be held responsible. The explanation was accepted as sufficient and closed that international incident in diplomacy."[2]

In Tokyo the Japanese princes repaid the hospitality of the Americans with ceremonials and entertainments for officers and crew. The

Niagara then retraced her course via Capetown and reached Boston in May of 1861. Anxiety over secession was uppermost in all minds, since the latest news anyone had had—in a letter received by the chaplain— told of Lincoln's election. Captain McKean himself was at the gang- way to greet the Boston pilot.

"Pilot, what is the news?"

"Captain, where have you come from?"

"From Hong Kong."

"And you ain't heard anything at all?"

"No, not a word."

"Why, Captain, the country is all busted to hell!"[3]

A few days later Midshipman Schley watched the waves curl under the *Niagara's* bowsprit pointed south.

Merchantmen returning from abroad were boarded by a lieutenant from the *Niagara,* notified of the blockade and threatened with seizure should they try to go into Southern ports. Before the midship- men in the *Niagara's* steerage mess arose visions of captures—and of *prize money.* What percentage of the prize money would fall to the midshipmen? How much prize money would enable a man drawing a midshipman's pay to get married?

More immediate seemed the prospect of action. Arriving off Charleston on May 11, young Schley could see near the South Channel lighthouse 28 armed launches filled with men. Would these Confederate launches row out after dark and try to take the *Niagara* by boarding? They did not come out the first night. And by noon next day Midshipman Schley was on his way back north in command of the first prize.

The prize, a two-masted, square-rigger named *General Parkhill,* had made a signal to men on shore in open violation of the *Niagara's* block- ade warning. Captain McKean at once sent Schley with ten seamen on board of her with orders to deliver her to the admiralty court in Philadelphia. In the opinion of Captain McKean, Schley's competence in seamanship considerably outweighed his recent prank of greasing the tail of the Japanese monkey, for the captain wrote to the Secretary of the Navy that he would like to have "Mr. Schley . . . returned im- mediately" to the *Niagara.*[4]

In Philadelphia, however, Schley was assigned to one of the many merchant ships undergoing conversion to naval service. Having obtained a leave of absence he visited his home in Frederick, Maryland. Also, he visited Annapolis; and in Annapolis the former member of the Pelican Club fell passionately in love with Annie Rebecca Franklin, whom he had known since Naval Academy days.

Annie Franklin possessed, according to Cadet Alfred Mahan, a pretty face that "takes the shine off" the "foreign articles" which the midshipmen imported from Baltimore and Washington for dances. "She has a beautiful complexion, and whenever she smiles the dimples all over her face seem to light up and smile at the same time."[5] She had also, it appears, a rare ability to listen. Midshipman Winfield Scott Schley, mantled in the glamour of a trip to the Orient and of his recent command of a prize vessel and in love with Miss Franklin, pleasantly overflowed with good humor and good stories. The two became engaged.

In August 1861 Schley was promoted to "master" and transferred from a ship being outfitted in Philadelphia to another ship being outfitted in New York. Schley's new ship, the *Potomac*, was a 40-year-old sailing frigate. Master Schley was her sixth officer—with Captain L. M. Powell and four lieutenants above him and nine masters and midshipmen below him. Immediately below Master Schley on the list of the *Potomac's* officers was Master W. T. Sampson, honor student of the Naval Academy class just graduated. For about twelve months the two future principals in the Battle of Santiago lived in closest proximity as junior officers on the *Potomac*. Poles apart in temperament, the one athletic, loquacious and not at all scholarly, the other reticent and bookish, they got along without friction.

Schley's billet on the blockade was fully as dull as Mahan's, but he accepted his lot with a better grace. Moreover, the prospect for prize money had all but vanished. The blockade in the Eastern Gulf was now well established and Schley's sailing frigate, too slow to overhaul a prize, was useful to plug an otherwise empty space off Mobile Bay only because the Confederates did not know that her glowering guns were obsolete smoothbores.

Schley frequently volunteered for hazardous duty in small boats. Once, with the captain's permission, he led a party in two small boats in an effort to seize a blockade-runner that had stranded under the Confederate Fort Morgan. Though the odds were against him, he advanced up the channel "directly against the wind's eye and against a heavy sea."[6] Cannon balls from the fort sent up mounds of frothy water around the little cutters. It was the first time Schley had come under fire. Keeping his boats headed end-on toward the fort to present the smallest possible target, he came within a mile of the coveted goal before he gave up the attempt as too great a strain on his men. "The men under my command behaved well under fire," he reported.[7] A month later he led a brilliant rescue mission.

Twelve miles east of Fort Morgan three cutters from the *R. R. Cuyler* had ventured ashore to capture a stranded blockade-runner. As they touched sand a volley of musketry rang out from behind the dunes. One boat was capsized and several men in the other two were wounded. The *Cuyler*, though able to shell the sharpshooters on shore, to protect her men, had no other small boats to send in to bring out her wounded. Schley with two cutters from the *Potomac* went to their rescue. "The concealed enemy," reported Schley, "choosing his time, waited until he had my boats fairly under his fire, welcomed us with a volley, followed by another and still another."[8] Schley's crews returned the fire, rowed on into the surf, hitched a line to the *Cuyler's* boats and towed them out through a succession of fusillades from the marksmen on shore. Enemy fire took a nick out of the brass oarlock on Schley's cutter, but did no further injury.

The *Potomac's* journey to Vera Cruz to investigate Napoleon III's invasion of Mexico carried Schley away from the blockade area during Farragut's campaign against New Orleans. Schley was promoted to lieutenant and transferred to the steam gunboat *Winona* as executive officer in July of 1862.

The bedraggled *Winona* looked, and was, unlucky. Jerry-built out of green timber and less than a year old, she was already cracking open in her seams. She had suffered humiliation as one of the rear ships in Farragut's line which had failed to get past the gantlet of the New Orleans forts. A few weeks after Schley joined the ship, she was subjected to a first-rate insult off Mobile Bay. The Confederate raider *Florida*, flaunting English colors and ignoring the blockaders' challenge, shouldered her way past the *Winona* and the *Oneida* into Mobile Bay. The *Oneida's* captain was promptly cashiered by the Navy Department for not sinking her in spite of her neutral flag. The *Winona's* captain, a man of whom Schley was personally very fond, brooded and drank himself into delirium tremens.

To the dismay of Executive Officer Schley, the captain [James S. Thornton] now insisted on steering the *Winona* up the main channel within the screen of cannon shot from Fort Morgan. Here he milled around aimlessly, dodging shell splashes from the fort, but unable because of the range to use his own guns effectively. Schley directed the ship's surgeon to examine the captain, and with the surgeon's written diagnosis in hand Lieutenant Schley placed the captain under confinement.[9] Senior Officer, Captain James Alden, approved Schley's action, detached Thornton and placed Schley in temporary command of the ship. Rocked by December storms, the *Winona's* seams started leaking so badly that Farragut ordered her to patrol duty inside the Mississippi River where, as her officers had predicted, the mud in the river water partially stopped her leaks.[10]

Schley's service with Farragut in the lower river, he was to write many years later, "was a trial to the young man which was to fit him into the heroic mold."[11] There was plenty of strain, and Schley experienced much the same sort of rough work as Dewey, who was here at this same time. Schley's ship was so often ambushed by Confederate guerrillas that he never lay down at night without first arranging his clothes so that he could literally jump into them when the alarm sounded. Talkative and effervescent, he unloaded much excellent though unsought advice upon his commanding officer, and on at least one occasion when his suggestions were disregarded the *Winona* was caught at anchor under a guerrilla battery and rather thoroughly shot up. Schley had Dewey's luck in never receiving a scratch himself, though others near him were shot down. Like Dewey, he was assigned for a short period as acting commander of the *Monongahela*.

During the final stages of the campaign against Port Hudson, Lieutenant Schley served as third officer on the large steam sloop *Richmond* under Captain James Alden. Since the second officer, Terry, was detailed to command a naval battery on shore with the Army, Schley now became acting executive officer on a large ship. He reveled in the responsibility. Fleet bombardment of Port Hudson became an almost daily routine. At times when Captain Alden was absent from the ship Schley enjoyed the part of acting captain.

Schley was thus commanding the *Richmond* on the sultry Sunday afternoon of May 24, 1863, when Farragut—using Dewey's *Monongahela* as a temporary flagship—signaled the fleet to bombard Port Hudson. Schley's ship, moving up the left bank with the flagship on her starboard quarter, led the line. Schley, whose individual target was a high battery known as the "citadel," was anxious to make a good showing before the admiral.[12] So intent was he after firing commenced that he ignored Farragut's signal "retire from action." There being scarcely a breath of air on the river, Farragut's signal bunting hung limp from the flagship's masthead, and a haze of smoke from the funnels and guns served further to obscure it. For the moment Schley hoped that the signal applied to some other ship, and kept on battering his target until the other ships had all retired and Farragut's intention became too obvious for Schley to ignore.

A bit sheepish, Schley went aboard to report his action. Farragut returned his salute.

"Captain," the admiral lectured, "you begin early in your life to disobey orders. Did you not see the signal flying . . . to withdraw from action?"

Schley's stammering explanation about the difficulty in reading the signal was cut short by Farragut's admonition that he "wanted none of this Nelson business in his squadron about not seeing signals."[13]

Following this scene on the quarter-deck, Farragut invited the young lieutenant into his cabin and poured him a glass of wine. "Had to blow you up, Scott, but, by God! that's the way to fight. Have a drink."[14]

Port Hudson's fall in July 1863, which finished the task of opening the Mississippi River, also finished Schley's battle experience in the war. He returned north in August. On September 10, 1863, at the age of twenty-four, he was married to petite, dark-haired and vivacious Annie Rebecca Franklin. On a honeymoon and business trip to Washington he ran into Captain H. A. Wise, ordnance expert who had been his shipmate on the trip to Japan. Wise obligingly found for the newlywed a temporary shore billet in the Bureau of Ordnance. In December 1863 he was detailed to the double-ender *Wateree* and sent to the Pacific in a needle-in-the-haystack search for the Confederate raider *Shenandoah*. In the vast reaches of the Pacific the search was without success. The end of the war found Lieutenant Schley chuffing up and down the Pacific coast of Nicaragua, protecting American lives and property from the hazards incident to a Nicaraguan election.

5. SAMPSON AFLOAT AND ASHORE

In the spring of 1861 a crowd of irate Annapolis citizens, disturbed by the sight of Union troopships in the bay, milled in Maryland Avenue, alternately cheering Jeff Davis and denouncing Old Abe. They threatened immediate violence to Yankee midshipmen within the locked gate and emphasized their threats by hurling stones and brickbats over the Naval Academy wall.

Receiving these missiles and imprecations and vigorously tossing them back from the other side was a company of midshipmen cadets armed with rifles and itching for a chance to use them. Cadet Commander William Thomas Sampson commanded the midshipmen and held the Main Gate, while the New York Seventh Regiment and the Massachusetts Eighth disembarked from their transport steamer and occupied the Academy grounds. When the troops had been put ashore, the bewildered underclass cadets were hustled aboard the school ship *Constitution* and sent to Newport; while the more fortunate First Classmen were ordered at once into active service—a fortunate emergency which did away with final examinations.

Sampson was assigned to the Washington Navy Yard. He apparently made the trip to the threatened capital in company with the Seventh New York Regiment.

Sampson reported to Commander John A. Dahlgren at the navy yard on April 29 when the first war panic in the capital was at its height, and for a week he served on shore.[1] That the threat to the capital was real cannot be doubted. The city's communications via Baltimore had been severed by the cutting of telegraph wires and the dismantling of rail bridges, and its Potomac steamer line was menaced by Confederate artillery hurriedly mounted on the Virginia cliffs of the river. Indeed, for some weeks the State of Maryland hung precariously in the balance.

Around the navy yard there was much work that a bright midshipman could do. A mosquito fleet of commandeered river steamers was being fitted with light guns to patrol the Potomac River near Alexandria and keep it open to essential traffic. The bridge across the East Branch to the navy yard had to be guarded against Maryland insurgents. There were a hundred details relating to equipping and messing the Seventh New York Regiment now garrisoning the Washington Navy Yard. During his one week here Sampson made himself so useful that Commander Dahlgren, the noted gun inventor, remembered him later and placed him in a responsible post with the Monitor fleet off Charleston.

For three weeks, in May of 1861, Midshipman Sampson served aboard the U. S. S. *Pocahontas* in the patrol of the Potomac River and the lower Chesapeake Bay. Even under ideal conditions it would have been difficult for this dull-sailing, seagoing sloop to navigate the Potomac. And now, with lights and channel buoys continually being destroyed or shifted by the Confederates, she frequently ran aground. Her powerful guns, however, enabled her to give safe convoy to troop and ammunition ships during this critical period. On June 1 Sampson was detached from the *Pocahontas* and ordered to the U.S.S. *Potomac* at New York.[2]

Since the *Potomac's* repairs in the crowded Brooklyn Navy Yard required three months, Midshipman Sampson spent part of the summer at his home in Palmyra, New York. His mother, Hannah Sampson, proud of her tall and handsome officer son, William, her one boy, as she expressed it, "who won't have to carry a sawbuck all his life," now felt rewarded for the sacrifices she had made to put him through the Palmyra District School. As loyal to his family as ever, William helped his father at common labor, and in the evenings he and his mother laid plans for the education of several of his younger sisters. He planned to, and did, save money from his Navy pay to make this possible. Probably also in these few weeks at home Midshipman Sampson paid court to Margaret Sexton Aldrich of Palmyra, who two years later became his wife.[3]

On August 20, after six weeks in lodgings on shore in New York, he went aboard the *Potomac* as an acting master. As a member of the junior officers' mess, Master Sampson stood next in rank below the convivial, fun-loving Master Schley. For nine months he served in the Gulf and observed the European naval intervention at Vera Cruz. In the late spring of 1862 Sampson was ordered to the Naval Academy at Newport as an instructor.

For a young man of Sampson's scientific interests in modern armor, ordnance and steam engines, the wooden, sail-driven *Potomac* with its antiquated smoothbores had offered little. The Naval Academy, too, especially in its makeshift quarters, was considerably off the track of his dominant interests. A more self-assertive man in Sampson's position might have requested some other duty. But Sampson's hard-working parents had taught him to accept without question whatever task was assigned to him.

The somnolent wartime Naval Academy in Newport was a billet shunned alike by the fighter and by the officer interested in the scientific aspects of naval development. With too few officers to fill the needs of an expanding Navy, and with many officers pulling political strings to avoid assignment to the Academy, it was throughout the war difficult for the Navy Department to find suitable officers to instruct midshipmen. Too often the assignment fell upon men who were misfits afloat or too old for sea service. William T. Sampson, a happy combination of sea officer and student, was kept at the Naval Academy for two full years, through the entire second and third quarters of the Civil War.

Wartime promotions made him a lieutenant by the time he joined the Naval Academy faculty at Newport in the summer of 1862. He was now twenty-two years old, sober, erect, somewhat shy but well poised, and like other junior officers of his day he had grown a mustache and beard.

As an executive officer he had living quarters on board one of the school ships which was being used as a dormitory for midshipmen. After routine inspections of the berth deck, Sampson's chief responsibility was drilling the midshipmen on the parade field ashore and exercising them aboard the practice ships in handling sails and spars and in lashing, unlashing and training guns. French E. Chadwick, Charles E. Clark and Park Benjamin, who came under Sampson's charge at this time, have left written testimonials to the respect and awe which they as midshipmen had felt toward their instructor.

Sampson became a shipmate of Mahan on the practice cruise of the *Macedonian* in 1863. In spite of the danger from the Confederate raider *Alabama*, this cruise was routed over the normal course to Plymouth, Southampton and Cherbourg. At Spithead near Southampton Sampson first saw the inside of a British Navy Yard, and his enthusiasm over machinery, which was never shared by Mahan, overflowed in table talk which Sampson's austere messmate did not relish. "The ingenuity of the machinery," wrote Mahan, "the variety and beauty of the blocks, the many excellencies, had the changes rung upon them meal after meal, till I could hear the whir of the wheels in my head and see the chips fly."[4]

At Cherbourg, Sampson watched crowds of Frenchmen celebrate the landing of France's conquering army in Mexico. He had himself witnessed France's naval maneuvers at Vera Cruz the year before—a clear violation of the Monroe Doctrine which the United States, tied up in Civil War, had been unable to oppose. These French celebrations impressed Sampson with the importance to America of a fleet capable of supporting her overseas interests.

As the practice ship headed homeward across the Bay of Biscay, where an encounter with the *Alabama* was considered to be possible, the *Macedonian's* skipper, Stephen B. Luce, lowered the vessel's topmasts, painted her superstructure yellow and her hull black and hoisted the flag of Spain, a ruse which everyone hoped might enable them to get near enough to the *Alabama* to pour a broadside into her. Lieutenant Sampson conscientiously drilled his midshipmen at the great guns, but his efforts bore no immediate fruit because the Confederate raider was not sighted.[5]

Eventually, however, the midshipmen whom Sampson drilled on a ship masquerading as Spanish became the fighting commanders in America's war with Spain in 1898. The list of midshipmen whom

Sampson instructed during his wartime duty at Newport includes the following officers of 1898: Captain Arent S. Crowninshield of the Naval War Board in Washington, Captain Henry Clay Taylor of the battleship *Indiana* at Santiago, Captain Charles E. Clark of the *Oregon*, Captain Francis A. Cook of Commodore Schley's flagship *Brooklyn*, Captain Robley D. ("Fighting Bob") Evans of the battleship *Iowa*, Captain Charles V. Gridley of Commodore Dewey's flagship *Olympia*, Captain Charles D. Sigsbee of the ill-fated battleship *Maine*, Captain French E. Chadwick of Rear Admiral Sampson's flagship *New York*, and Captain Caspar F. Goodrich of the *St. Louis*, whose boats put General Shafter's men ashore near Santiago.[6]

Lieutenant Sampson enjoyed teaching the restless midshipmen in Newport. Living with them aboard an anchored school ship, he shared their thoughts about the first-rate war being waged down the blockade coast.

In 1863, after his marriage to Margaret Sexton Aldrich, he divided his time between his home ashore and classrooms afloat. His leisure he devoted to the technical problems of the war as well as these could be followed in published dispatches. This study completely absorbed him. Unlike Lieutenant Mahan, he felt no urgent inner need for social contacts, but was quiet, studious, so modest that he often appeared to outsiders as diffident.

In August of 1864 Sampson was ordered to the South Atlantic Blockading Squadron under Rear Admiral John A. Dahlgren, under whom he had already served at Washington, and was assigned to be the Executive Officer of the Monitor *Patapsco*.

Sampson was at last able to study at firsthand the famed, but grossly misrepresented, new type of iron warship. The *Patapsco's* designer had taken advantage of the original *Monitor's* battle experience and placed her pilot house on top of her gun turret beyond danger from her own 11 and 15-inch guns; and the smokestack (which in the first *Monitor* had been quickly riddled and knocked overboard by the *Merrimack*) was protected by heavy armor. Internally her construction was about the same. The *Patapsco*, however, in service for a year and a half without a dockyard overhaul, looked little better than a floating wreck.

At her lonely station in the entrance to Wassaw Sound—where she acted as an iron cork to plug one of the lesser gaps in the blockade—

her new executive officer examined the ironclad from stem to stern. The scars from her early battles against Forts Sumter and Moultrie had not yet been repaired. During Du Pont's attack on Sumter the year before she had come under a rain of projectiles which bounded off the wrought-iron laminated armor of her turret but snapped some 40 of the cast-iron bolts that had riveted this armor together. Bolt-heads had caught in the base of the turret and scotched it. Her engineers—men of the old wooden navy—in trying to force the turret despite these obstructions had broken off a tooth or cog from the ten-foot pinion wheel that supported and turned the turret. Into the gap in the pinion wheel these shade-tree blacksmiths had inserted a new tooth of wrought iron, which in turn had broken out, along with several more of the original cogs. The result of these mishaps was that, instead of being able to turn through an intended arc of 360 degrees, the turret-turning mechanism could now operate through only 90 degrees. The ship itself had to be turned in order to point her guns.

Only one of her two cannon was now serviceable. Her 11-inch rifle, damaged by a premature powder explosion which had killed two men, had been idle for more than a year. It had been impossible to replace the gun outside of a navy yard, for the turret armor itself would have to be dismantled and the ship would scarcely have been worth sending back to New York for repairs even had it been possible to spare her from the blockade.

On the *Patapsco's* smokestack armor Lieutenant Sampson studied the effect of a 15-inch shell fired by accident from the *Patapsco's* own 15-inch smoothbore. In October when the *Patapsco* was laid up at Port Royal for emergency repairs Sampson superintended the removal of this battered smokestack and Admiral Dahlgren whimsically sent it north as a souvenir for the Naval Academy.

The emergency repairing at Port Royal also revealed to Sampson why the *Patapsco* could make no headway at all in breasting a flood tide. Her barnacle-encrusted bottom trailed a beard of seaweed. Salt deposit encrusting her boiler tubes had reduced their mean diameter from 1.75 to 0.916 inches.

Throughout the entire ship Sampson could detect new problems that were to require research and experimentation in order to perfect the Machine Age Navy of the future. The science of steel metallurgy was yet in a primitive stage. Obviously tougher alloys were necessary.

The stresses of all the intricate parts of a battleship made of iron were unequal. There must be better metal for guns and armor, better designs for guns and gun carriages, better marine engines. Some efficient means must be found to compensate for variations of the compass aboard an iron ship. Also the Confederates at near-by Charleston in the last phase of the war were pointing the way toward future naval development with their experimental semisubmersible torpedo boats and harbor torpedoes or mines. For Sampson these technological problems marked the course he was to follow in his later career. Like Dahlgren he was to devote his best years to study and experiment, unspectacular, secluded, hidden from the public.

While his main interest was scientific, Sampson coolly accepted the dangers of war and the hazards inherent in warlike machinery. In the last days before Charleston, when the *Patapsco* was sunk by a Confederate mine, Sampson had a chance to display his remarkable calmness while under stress.

General Sherman had taken Savannah, and Admiral Dahlgren, anxious for the Navy to make what contribution it could toward winning Charleston, sent the *Patapsco* after nightfall on January 15, 1864, to lift a string of mines between Forts Sumter and Moultrie.

In this hazardous operation the *Patapsco's* task was to shepherd a flock of picket launches while they did the actual dragging and to protect them with her howitzers. The night was without a moon and Sampson, piloting the ship from his station on top of the turret, kept track of the launches largely by means of sound. The monitor, encumbered by what proved an utterly useless torpedo guard of logs and rope netting, shuttled to and fro outside the supposed location of the mines, alternately drifting in on the tide and moving back out under steam.

On her third run outward, and about 800 yards north of Fort Sumter, she ran on a torpedo. "The torpedo struck the vessel on the port side, just abreast the bitts," reads the report Sampson wrote the next day, "and appeared to raise the deck, through which the smoke issued. My first impression on hearing the report was that a shot had struck the overhang just below the water; but the column of smoke and water which immediately shot upward convinced me of the real nature of the explosion."[7]

The captain shouted to man the boats and at the same instant, before

Sampson could relay the order, the stern lifted clear of the water and the whole ship slid under. In an estimated 15 seconds from the moment of concussion everything but the tip of the *Patapsco's* smokestack had disappeared. As the turret went down one of Sampson's feet became entangled in some rope netting and he was dragged under. Beneath the swirling, steam-flecked water, he disengaged his foot and bobbed to the surface, where he was hauled on board one of the picket launches.

At 11:00 P.M. Lieutenant Sampson and Commander Quackenbush reported the sinking in person to Admiral Dahlgren. "I would state," reads Quackenbush's final report, "that the cool intrepidity displayed by Lieutenant Sampson, my executive officer . . . deserves the highest praise."[8] Lieutenant Mahan, who the next morning heard Sampson's calm description of his experience, testified that "when I saw him he was as unaffectedly and without effort unperturbed as though nothing remarkable had occurred."[9]

For the future admirals of America's war with Spain the Civil War had served as a postgraduate school in the art of war. Thrown by circumstances into assignments not of their own choosing, they had nevertheless reacted in ways that would be characteristic of their future careers.

George Dewey had discovered for himself an ideal of a fighting commander in Admiral Farragut whom he was to remember in the lean years that were now to descend upon the Navy. "What would Farragut do?" became the question he would eventually ask himself while steaming into Manila Bay.

Mahan, the most self-conscious intellect, was as yet uncertain in his aims. His niche in the Navy had yet to be created. Later he would himself formulate his aim, and he possessed the necessary stubbornness to buck half the Navy in achieving that aim.

Schley, like Dewey, was to remember fighting under Farragut. But he was unable to accept the too modest Farragut as a complete ideal. There was a flamboyant streak in Schley's character that had already manifested itself during his Annapolis days in his tendency to play to a gallery. In later years Schley was to think of himself more and more as belonging to the naval tradition of Lord Nelson. He was an individualist. He courted fame and conceived of himself as bred up in the heroic mold. His career like that of the great prototype he admired was destined to have its spectacular moments, and inevitably to evoke popular controversy.

Sampson, as indicated already, took the scientist Dahlgren for his model. Let the public breath blow hot or blow cold, Sampson, the scholar and scientist, would never be deflected from his purpose.

Meanwhile there was room in the Navy for all four of these divergent types. Each in his own way had fought and proved himself. In July 1866, when the Navy was being slashed right and left in the interests of economy, all four were promoted to the grade of lieutenant commander on the dwindling Navy's list of active officers.

Part Two

NAVAL DECLINE AND RESURGENCE
1865-1890

INTERNATIONAL CARTOON COMMENTS ON OUR WAR WITH SPAIN.

From the *Minneapolis Journal*

From the *Minneapolis Tribune*

(*Left*) Very Kind of Him

President Dole: "Accept a little gift from me. You might need it in your business."

(*Right*) Cluck! Cluck! Cluck!

Both cartoons reprinted in *The American Monthly Review of Reviews*, July, 1898.

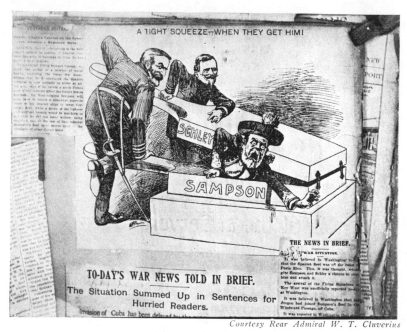

A Tight Squeeze—When They Get Him!

A Washington Donkey Party.

6. GENTLEMAN GEORGE DEWEY

THE war over, George Dewey's thoughts turned to Portsmouth, New Hampshire, to Susie Boardman Goodwin. But his immediate assignment to the *Kearsarge* and the European Station perforce postponed marriage. He made a quick trip to Portsmouth. Susie and her sister, Mrs. Stone, returned with him to Boston to be near him that last week before his ship sailed.[1] Usually the European cruise lasted two years. These would be long years.

His courtship in April of 1864 had been a worried, wartime courtship on time snatched from his many duties in outfitting the *Agawam* at the Portsmouth Navy Yard. Susie, Governor Ichabod Goodwin's youngest daughter, upon whom Dewey had called almost every other day, had a twinkle in her eye. The lines of her pretty mouth were firm without being domineering. Her wide shapely forehead was topped with neatly kept curls.

There had been entirely too little time, and, to complicate the situation, Dewey's skipper, Commander A. C. Rhind, a bachelor of forty-three, also called frequently at the Goodwin house. The commander's calls, in fact, since the two men had to take turn about leaving the ship, alternated with the lieutenant's.[2] Town gossips insisted that young Dewey and his commanding officer, who was old enough to be the girl's father, were rivals. This situation, very nettling to a young man seriously in love, lay back of a skirmish with the law that Dewey had at this time.

With his speaking trumpet in hand, Dewey at the navy-yard dock was directing work on his ship on April 6, 1864, when he fell into an argument with one George Garland, a yard worker. Quick as lightning Dewey landed a blow on the fellow's head. Next day Garland had Dewey arrested and hailed before Squire Alexander Dennett, a navy-yard inspector of timber who held a magistrate's commission. The trial, held in the barroom of Union House, a stone's throw from the navy yard, resulted in Dewey's being fined $5.00 and assessed $8.50 costs, the magistrate adjudging it to be "proved beyond a doubt that Lieut. Dewey struck Geo. W. Garland one blow on the head with the speaking trumpet so hard as to bruise the trumpet."[3]

The commandant of the navy yard, deciding not to try Dewey a second time, under military law, felt rather pleased that the case had been so quickly and cheaply disposed of in magistrate's court.

Not so Dewey. Dewey scanned Squire Dennett's list of costs and decided that $2.00 for a half hour's rental of Union House barroom was exorbitant. Commander Rhind concurred in Dewey's opinion. Dewey hired an attorney and threatened to bring a lawsuit against Dennett for extortion. Magistrate Dennett, coming under the jurisdiction of the commandant of the navy yard, was required to justify his entire procedure in writing. The papers which Dennett prepared show Dewey to be clearly wrong but the action of the commandant indicates that Dewey enjoyed the moral support of his brother officers on the station.

The *Kearsarge* was famous in Europe as the victor over the *Alabama* off Cherbourg, and it was fitting that she should be one of the first ships to return the American flag in peacetime to the European Station. As her executive officer Lieutenant Commander George Dewey enjoyed a privileged position.

Mrs. G. W. Van Horne, wife of the United States consul and Dewey's hostess at Marseilles, wrote that "the *Kearsarge's* officers were mostly young fellows of 22 and 24, full of life, and delighted at being on shore. Lieut. [Comdr.] Dewey was like an elder brother to them in everything, and they looked up to him accordingly." The famed singer Patti had been booked for one night only in Marseilles, and all the seats of the opera house had been sold. Dewey and his seamen were "wild to hear Patti," wrote Mrs. Van Horne, "for we claimed her as an American." Mrs. Van Horne called on the singer at her hotel, and Patti herself interceded for the Americans, threatening, "No seats, no opera!" Finally the mayor of Marseilles tendered one of his box seats for Dewey and arranged chairs on the stage behind the scenes for the rest of the party from the ship. At the concert, continues Mrs. Van Horne's story, "It fell to me to do the most of the talking as Dewey (modest then as ever) did not seem inclined to air his French. We looked from the box, which was in the second tier above the stage, and waved our hands to the boys below us, and heard Patti at her best."[4]

Dewey also had his troubles—troubles that afflicted the entire Navy at this time. Immediately after the Civil War there was a marked increase in desertions among the crews. Some men who had volunteered late in the war were restless to return to civil life, some were foreigners interested only in prize money, others were professional bounty jumpers. In various ports Dewey was compelled to publish advertisements offering ten-dollar rewards for the return of deserters. A typical entry in the *Kearsarge's* log shows disciplinary actions at Brest on July 21, 1865: "Samuel Augustus (boy) for insolence to an officer; Charles Villalla (coxswain) drunkenness & insolence; John Slatterly—disorderly, stealing, lying." Two weeks later at Flushing, Villalla had to be court-martialed for threatening an officer. In January of 1866, shortly before Dewey was transferred to the flagship, mass desertions occurred in the squadron, with eight men deserting from the *Kearsarge*, six from the flagship *Colorado*, and 11 from the other ships of the squadron.[5]

From Dewey's ten months of service on the *Kearsarge* there has been handed down an apocryphal mutiny story which is indicative of Dewey's reputation as a disciplinarian. The *Chattanooga News* published this yarn as a true story at the time of Admiral Dewey's death and the *Literary Digest* quoted it on February 3, 1917. Although it had appeared several times during the admiral's lifetime, Dewey never troubled to refute it.

"Dewey was a stern disciplinarian. Arming himself with twelve revolvers, it is recorded that he ordered the ship's writer in front of him and entered the hatch where the [mutinous *Kearsarge*] crew were assembled.

" 'Call the roll,' Dewey ordered the writer, a pistol in each hand and the rest in the breast of his coat. The writer called 'John Jones.' 'Here,' was the mechanical reply.

"Dewey picked out Jones and said, 'John Jones, I see you. I am going to have your name called once more, and if you do not answer and immediately go up on deck you are a dead man. Call the roll.'

" 'John Jones,' called the writer.

"No answer.

"Dewey fired, and Jones dropt.

" 'Now, men,' continued Dewey, cocking his pistols, 'the roll will be continued. As each man's name is called he will answer and go up on deck. Call the roll.'

"The mutiny was ended."

At twenty-nine George Dewey was hardly the martinet that the shellback yarnspinners depicted in the mutiny story. He could be stern. All five feet, seven inches of his stocky, square, wrestler-type body were as hard as nails. His bushy mustache, so heavy it drooped, belied perhaps the firm set of the square chin. The black eyes, which generally wore a look of genial repose, were quick to snap in anger, as when he spanked a professor's youngster at the Naval Academy or bruised his speaking trumpet over a man's head at Portsmouth.

John L. Veimard, ensign, and a shipmate with Dewey in 1866 after the latter's transfer to the *Colorado*, wrote that Dewey "was smarter than chain lightning, quick, passionate, and always demanded perfect discipline of his men. He never would have a drunkard near him, and any man found in the least bit intoxicated aboard ship was dealt with in the severest manner."[6] This testimony, too, must be accepted with qualifications in view of other testimony that Lieutenant Commander Dewey presented a bottle of wine to each of the *Colorado's* bluejackets at Christmas in 1866.[7]

Charles E. Rand describes one of Dewey's impulsive actions on the *Colorado*. A gale was blowing in the Bay of Biscay. The vessel could make only eight knots under steam and was being rapidly drifted on a lee shore. In the crisis the admiral took the bridge and sent Dewey to get the sails set to supplement the power of the creaky engines.

Dewey ordered the men aloft, and "just to encourage us Dewey himself mounted the ladder, and in less time than I can tell it, was on the yard unfurling sail."[8] Recklessness of this kind, an occasional gift of wine and a penchant for releasing miscreants from the brig a day or two before their time was out were devices well calculated to win the loyalty of his crews.

After 26 months in Europe, the *Colorado's* return to the States gave Dewey a long-looked-for leave of absence. On October 27, 1867, in the Episcopal church of Portsmouth, New Hampshire, Lieutenant Commander George Dewey, U. S. Navy, aged 30, was married to curly-haired Susan Boardman Goodwin. George's father, Dr. Julius Yemans Dewey, and his younger sister Mary, by then the wife of Dr. George Preston Greeley, were among the members of his family who attended the wedding. At the elm-shaded Goodwin homestead a gala reception was held. "Fighting" Governor Ichabod Goodwin, chortling with pride and perhaps recollecting the episode of the speaking trumpet, commented: "George is sort of reckless sometimes, but hang me, if I can help liking him. He's honest and full of grit, and he'll be heard from one of these days."[9]

In foreseeing a future for his son-in-law, ex-Governor Goodwin was shutting his eyes to the already apparent decline of the Navy.

During the five brief years of ideally happy married life with his "Dear Susie," George Dewey seems not to have been greatly concerned over the drastic curtailment of the United States Navy. For three years, while he was on duty in Annapolis, he was out of touch with the general picture of the Navy as a whole; and the Naval Academy, at this time under the jovial but feverishly energetic Admiral David Dixon Porter, was not only escaping the economizer's hatchet but alone of all naval establishments was experiencing a boom. The early Naval Academy, whose Latin-school routine Cadet Dewey had cordially disliked, was being literally uprooted and rebuilt as an up-to-date naval school. New buildings were mushrooming all over the yard for laboratories, dormitories and gymnasiums.[10] For the first time in its 22 years of existence the Naval Academy furnished homes on the reservation for young married officers. Dewey's assignments to administrative work and later as aide to the superintendent were pleasant duties. When the Deweys moved into the yard, there was under way an elaborate program of dances and dramatic entertainments designed to bring midshipmen into social contact with officers and their families. George and Susie Dewey—for all their sly winks at "Porter's dancing Academy!"—slipped congenially into the new Annapolis scene.[11]

For a brief time, indeed, there was a chance that the Navy as a whole might find a new justification for its existence and so escape the historic pattern of postwar decline. That ardent imperialist William H. Seward, continuing as Secretary of State under Andrew Johnson, was using all his wiles to promote an overseas empire for the nation. Alaska ("Seward's ice-box!") he managed to get into the bag, but Providence interposed to thwart him of the Virgin Islands purchase. On November 18, 1867, the *Monongahela*, a ship Dewey had briefly commanded on the Mississippi River and one upon whose deck he had narrowly escaped death, was by a tidal wave lifted bodily from her anchorage off Fredericksted, Island of St. Croix, floated over the tops of docks and warehouses and set down in the streets of the town.[12] Unhappily for the Navy this spectacular freak convinced Congress that the Virgin Islands would be a poor investment for naval bases. Anti-Johnson politics subsequently killed Seward's further dreams of expansion, and with these died all other hopes for peacetime naval expansion.

Detached from the Naval Academy in October 1870 and ordered to command the *Narragansett*, Dewey received at last his first regular command; and at the navy yards in Portsmouth, Boston and New York he was able to see for himself the inroads that five years of peace had made upon United States naval power. Nowhere was there any new construction under way. Skeleton forces in the navy yards were by law restricted to repair operations whose cost often ran as high as the original price of a vessel. Peace was the passion of the average American. Economy was in the ascendant. Wooden ships were rotting at their moorings; ironclads, not one of which was now in commission, were rusting in ordinary. The Navy, first-rate in 1865, had fallen to third place in 1870, inspiring the witticism of a foreign observer that "the scream of the American eagle ceases to be more alarming than that of a parrot or a popinjay."[13] "What signs of activity!" exploded the commandant of the Brooklyn yard; "I'd give a champagne dinner to the man who'd show me such a thing. The navy yard is rotting away, the buildings are going to wrack and ruin, and we are drifting into a thin apology for a station."[14] A backwoods Tennessean's idea "that our Navy ought to consist of two logs tied together and surmounted by the American flag" seemed to have taken root in Congress.[15] The *Army and Navy Journal* estimated that, whereas 25 percent of the government's income had been allotted to the Navy in 1800, only seven percent was allotted in 1870.

Dewey was fortunate to get command of the third-rate steam sloop *Narragansett*. There were 200 officers senior to Dewey in 1870 and only 49 serviceable ships in commission. Dewey felt unlucky, however, in the *Narragansett's* assignment to the South Pacific. He sailed her from Portsmouth to New York, where she went into the navy yard for major repairs. Dewey, impetuous, tired of waiting, managed to get shifted in the spring of 1871 to the antiquated store ship *Supply*. The Germans were besieging Paris and a generous American public was sending shiploads of food to Frenchmen reported as starving. At Cherbourg, where Dewey found earlier cargoes of American relief stores rotting on the dock, he was ordered instead to dispose of his cargo in London. Upon returning to New York he was sent to the Torpedo Station at Newport.

Dewey found a house and brought his wife down from Portsmouth. Susie was expecting a child.

The Torpedo Station on Coaster's Harbor Island near Newport represented America's sole effort to keep abreast of the rest of the world in any branch of naval development. During the Civil War the United States had done expensive pioneering in armor-clad ships, and European navies were now building on the foundations America had laid. A tremendous technological race had developed between armor and ordnance, with the latter in the lead. Armor was being made thicker, but always it could be pierced by the newer and more efficient weapons built by the ordnance men. Why not, many Americans reasoned, wait until one could see the outcome of this wasteful race between guns and armor; and then rebuild the Navy accordingly? There were other arguments to justify delay. Had not the United States improvised a Navy in 1861? In a future war emergency might not American inventive genius again be relied on? Such arguments carried the day in Congress.

On Coaster's Harbor Island, however, the Navy established a small factory for building torpedoes. Confederate success in mining harbors and Union success in sinking the ironclad *Albemarle* with an inexpensive steam launch and a torpedo on the end of a pole, had given some warrant for the belief that with better torpedoes and better torpedo boats the United States might protect her harbors against a marine invader.

George Dewey remained at Newport less than a year. He was not there long enough to become genuinely interested in the novel mechanisms which he saw being built and demonstrated in adjacent waters. On December 23, 1872, Susie gave birth to a son whom they named George Goodwin. But Susie, his bright-faced, curly-haired young wife, failed to recover. Five days after the birth of her child she died.

Henceforth he would avoid Newport. Until late in life he would but rarely visit the son whom he left in the care of relatives. Susan Dewey's picture he would carry inside his watchcase for many a year. As quickly as official channels would permit, he obtained once more the command of the *Narragansett* and left for the most uninteresting duty afloat for a man of Dewey's normally convivial temperament— survey duty in the South Pacific.

Dewey, in mourning, made the trip from New York to Panama as a passenger on a mail steamer. Entering the Caribbean for the first time since the Civil War, he doubtless recalled his old fighting days on the Mississippi River before he had met Susie. His campaigning with Farragut was now ten years in the past. Nothing could remind him less of war than the peacetime, government-subsidized mail packet whose length he paced, and no work was more peaceful than his assignment to survey duty off the western coast of Mexico. The contrast may have struck him with considerable force, for, as his steam packet rounded Cuba, there were centered in this island all the symptoms of a first-class war in the making. Cuba for five years had been in insurrection against Spain. Cuba lay athwart United States trade routes out of New Orleans, and toward an uncontrollable insurrection in Cuba America could not remain forever indifferent. There were already rumors of war because of the numerous filibustering expeditions organized by professional Cuban insurrectionists on neutral American shores and sent out from American harbors in defiance of our naval patrol to operate against the Spanish authorities in Cuba.

Dewey boarded the diminutive Isthmian train at Colón. As the smoke-belching symbol of modern civilization chugged and puffed its winding course over jungle-clad mountains, he was aware that in recent years American marines, some of whom he knew personally, had landed several times to protect this immensely important American concession, the right-of-way across the Panamanian Isthmus.

At the Bay of Panama on April 6, 1873, following the usual ceremony, Dewey relieved Commander R. W. Meade as commanding officer of the U.S.S. *Narragansett*. Commander Meade, a seadog of the imperialist variety, had just returned from a cruise over the Pacific. At the Samoan Islands, where swarms of natives clad "in the ancient costume of Mark Twain's ancestors" had clambered over the ship, Meade had plied them with food and drink and—to the horror of his isolationist fellow countrymen back home—had raised the American flag and negotiated a treaty, which gained for Americans the exclusive use of the harbor of Pago Pago, on the Island of Tutuila.[16] There would be no such gala opportunity for Dewey.

After loading on his surveying instruments at Panama, Dewey pointed the nose of the *Narragansett* northward to the Gulf of Lower California. Here, hemmed in between the narrow, mountain-studded peninsula of Lower California and the mainland of Mexico, he spent two years surveying and charting these little-known coastal waters. Surveying in this torrid and enervating region was a job to stifle a man's domestic grief.

La Paz, inside a fishhook bay at the southern end of the peninsula, offered sufficient shelter against storms to enable Dewey to use this anchorage as headquarters for collating data and drawing the charts. On May 10, when Dewey dropped anchor at La Paz and paid his first call on the Mexican governor, the latter's aloofness struck Dewey as distinctly unpleasant. Next day Dewey was compelled to order double irons for Seaman Michael Hurley, whose frank Irish reaction to the dullness of La Paz had been to go on a binge.

Forty miles inland from La Paz lived an American named Brook, whose friendship Dewey prized while he was on this out-of-the-way station. Brook was manager of a silver mine jointly owned by British and American investors and he supervised the labor of some 500 or 600 peons. "I was made to feel very much at home at his residence at the mines and enjoyed many delightful rides from that point as a base, in company with him and his ten-year-old son," wrote Dewey.[17] Twice a year the *Narragansett* steamed north to San Diego for supplies and repairs.

News of the *Virginius* Affair reached distant La Paz after the *Narra-*

gansett's second respite at San Diego. Spain's high-handed butchery of
Captain Fry and 53 of his American and Cuban filibusters angered
Americans and particularly naval officers whose duty it might be to
fight our run-down Navy. Feverish revamping of decommissioned
Civil War tubs was under way on the East Coast.

Dewey entered the *Narragansett's* wardroom to find Midshipman
Charlie Badger and other officers depressed at the prospect of war with
Spain when they were marooned on the West Coast, thousands of
miles from a possible scene of action around Cuba. "On the contrary,
we shall be very much in it," Dewey promised his officers. "If war
with Spain is declared, the *Narragansett* will take Manila!"[18]

In May of 1875 a courier brought Commander Dewey an urgent
note from his friend Brook at the silver mines. Brook in resenting an
insult had shot two Mexicans. He was now, with his family and a few
English and American foremen, barricaded in his home and menaced
by a mob of peons. Could Commander Dewey send a file of marines
to rescue him?

The *Narragansett* as a survey ship lacked a full complement of men,
and Dewey weighing the hazard of sending a small force 40 miles into
the interior decided against it. The governor of La Paz, a colonel in
the Mexican army and unfriendly toward Americans, might conceivably turn his garrison of 600 troops against Dewey's handful of seamen.

Instead Dewey sent his executive officer, Lieutenant George C.
Reiter, ashore to ask the governor himself to send a party to rescue
Mr. Brook.[19]

"Oh, he got into trouble. Let him get out," said the governor.

Dewey did not like this reply, and the more he thought about it the
angrier he became. The next morning he sent a note to the Mexican
official telling him that an American citizen's life was at stake and that
Dewey would insist that he be rescued and given a fair trial. Dewey
warned that if troops were not sent within 24 hours the *Narragansett*
would bombard the town.

"Does he mean it?" Master Frank Winslow asked Midshipman
Badger. Dewey overheard and answered the question. "Get those
howitzers ready for tomorrow morning," he ordered Winslow, "and
inspect all the small arms and ammunition." Dewey mustered his crew
of 120 men and drilled them all afternoon and into the night. He

lifted anchor and moved the ship into a position to command the Mexican governor's house on the main street of La Paz. As the sun rose the next morning a Mexican corporal brought off a note from the governor, announcing compliance with Dewey's demand; and the lookout in the maintop reported seeing a party of about 300 Mexican soldiers heading out of town toward the mining camp.

Having achieved his object, Dewey considered the incident closed. Months later, however, the Secretary of the Navy, having read about it in a New York editorial headed "The Right Man in the Right Place," prompted Dewey to submit a report of the happening. This Dewey did. His action was fully approved by the Secretary.

In July of 1875 Dewey was detached from his "practical isolation" on the *Narragansett* and ordered home. He paid a brief visit to Montpelier to see his two-and-a-half-year-old son and the following month was assigned to duty in Boston as inspector for the Second Lighthouse District. The assignment had the advantage of being close to his home. Dewey's job entailed semiannual visits of inspection to the lighthouses and lightships extending from Hampton Harbor, New Hampshire, to Sakonnet Point, Rhode Island.

Lighthouse keepers, though poorly paid ($600 per year), were permitted to engage in any supplementary business which did not interfere with their tending of the lights.[20] At their isolated stations Dewey often found them working as tailors, cobblers, schoolteachers, justices of the peace or even filling a neighboring pulpit. Dewey looked after their creature comforts and apparently enjoyed swapping stories with them. For John Ferraro at the Fort Schuyler Lighthouse, whose fiancée insisted upon having a honeymoon, Commander Dewey obtained the necessary furlough, and a year later an infant Ferraro—the first of a small army of babies to be named after the future admiral—was christened George Dewey Ferraro.[21]

In September of 1877 Dewey became a member of the Lighthouse Board and the following April was appointed naval secretary to the board, with an office and residence in Washington. His duties here brought him into association with scientists like Professor Henry of the Smithsonian Institution, with whom Dewey debated the relative merits of lard oil and mineral oil as fuel for lights. Gas-lighted buoys and electric lamps for large lighthouses were installed during Dewey's four-year tour of duty in Washington. Inspection trips were made along the Atlantic Coast and in the upper reaches of the Mississippi River.

Aside from his social contacts with naval officers, Dewey might as well have been outside of the Navy at this time. The Navy was on the rocks politically, Secretary Robeson and Congress having reached an impasse over appropriations. For a time the Navy Department had hard scrabbling to pay even family allotments of men on foreign stations. During these trying years for the Navy, Dewey seems to have drifted with the tide. There is no evidence, for instance, of his ever petitioning Congress for naval reform as dozens of his brother officers of all ranks were doing.

When not on duty, Dewey passed his time pleasantly enough. At the Metropolitan Club he often chatted with Admiral Porter and General Sherman, both of whom he admired. To the detriment of his health he indulged his appetite for good food. "Washington social life, with its round of dinners and receptions," he later recalled, "were a new and enjoyable experience to me, if exhausting physically."[22] He acquired a reputation as a genial companion, "rather a club-man of the Pendennis type than a rough and ready sailor."[23] He was gracious and suave and—some thought—"unfathomable." He was interested in, and willing to talk on, almost any subject under the sun.

After seven years in the Lighthouse service, Dewey obtained an assignment to the Asiatic as skipper of the *Juniata*. The Far East was the most important area in which he had never served and, since the *Virginius* war scare in 1874, when he had contemplated striking westward to the Philippines with the *Narragansett*, Dewey had looked forward to Asiatic duty.

Dewey put to sea from New York the last of November 1882 and, after a few days out, his years of good living caught up with him. He began running a temperature. The ship's doctor ordered the course shaped for the Azores, as this would give the easiest passage and minimize the commander's discomfort.

In Gibraltar Dewey, stubbornly determined not to co-operate with the doctors in locating the cause of his trouble, bore without wincing the thumping given him by British physicians.[24] In Malta he had to be eased ashore to the naval hospital, more dead than alive, to be operated on for abscess of the liver. While he was recovering with a tube in his side, he was attacked by typhoid fever. "At one time I fully expected to die," he wrote his sister, Mary Greeley, on April 11, 1883, "and nothing but an excellent constitution and God's mercy brought me through. . . . The climate of Malta is much like that of Florida, and we are enjoying oranges, roses, etc.,—and now and then a mosquito. Your affectionate brother, George Dewey."[25] The *Juniata* continued on to the Far East under another skipper and Dewey spent the next two years convalescing.

In October of 1884, at forty-seven, Dewey was promoted to captain. If his health held out he might make the next grade of commodore before reaching the statutory retirement age of sixty-two. The chances for achieving distinction in the Navy were practically nil, Dewey had come to believe.

On October 7 Captain Dewey was assigned to command the *Dolphin*. The *Dolphin*—the newest ship in the Navy—was the first of a group of steel cruisers. Although she was only a small experimental craft, her appearance in 1884 marked the upturn after 20 years of steady naval decline. The *Dolphin* represented a promise for the future. She was of all-steel construction, of American-made steel and of American design. But her quarters were stuffy, her shaft had broken in two during her trial run and she had a hundred mechanical "bugs" that had to be eradicated. Had Dewey been a well man he might gladly have accepted the interesting mechanical challenges which this craft afforded her skipper. Instead, Dewey rather resented the prospect of becoming a center of technical controversies. A few months later when the chance opened to transfer to the command of the *Pensacola*, Captain Dewey, the convalescent, "gladly" stepped down off the newest deck in the Navy and on board the superannuated *Pensacola* found sanctuary from so much novelty and clamor.

The circumstance that ex-Secretary of the Navy Chandler was at the moment indulging in an altercation with Admiral Earl English of the European Squadron saved Dewey from a relatively uninteresting cruise off Montevideo and sent him instead to the European Station, as captain of the flagship and chief of staff to Rear Admiral S. R. Franklin.

The *Pensacola* was a Civil War relic well remembered by Dewey and one of the ships whose repairs in the postwar years had amounted to more than her original cost. She had been given horizontal-action engines, a steam-driven capstan for hoisting anchor and an electrical battery for firing her guns. Aside from these modest changes she was her old self. Her hull was of wood and her broadside guns were Civil War muzzle-loading smoothbores. Above Captain Dewey's catwalk on her quarter-deck were billowing mounds of canvas—30,000 square feet of it—ship-rigged to the royals.

On the eve of Dewey's departure from Norfolk a fire broke out in the navy yard and only the skill of her junior officers saved the *Pensacola* from injury. After an inspection in Hampton Roads, in which the *Pensacola's* crew hoisted powder, bent on sails and manned the yards in the best ancient tradition, Captain Dewey got his ship under way for her impressive four-year cruise in European waters.

At Funchal, Madeira, while sailors manned the yards and fired salutes, the somewhat pompous Admiral Franklin officially relieved Admiral English as commander of the Mediterranean Squadron and announced that Captain George Dewey would be his chief of staff. Tied to a dock in Funchal was a once famous American clipper *The Red Jacket;* to all Americans who saw her she symbolized America's lost prestige on the seas, for she was stripped of tophamper and her beautifully molded hull was relegated to the menial role of coal hulk.

Admiral Franklin and Captain Dewey exchanged entertainments with the governor of Gibraltar. The *Pensacola's* gun deck was draped in bunting for the "at home" and an "excellent collation" was served to officers' guests in the wardroom. As always whenever Dewey had a hand in it the table creaked "with elaborate menus."

At Lisbon in the fall Admiral Franklin, Captain Dewey and a party of officers "went fifteen miles into the country to the estate of a Colonel Campbell and breakfasted there."[26] Campbell was a grandson of William IV, and his wife a daughter of Admiral of the Fleet Sir George Sartorius. The American consul at Tangiers arranged a boar hunt to entertain the *Pensacola's* officers.

Mrs. Franklin joined the admiral at Villefranche and throughout the winter Admiral Franklin spent much of his time ashore at the Hotel Cosmopolitan. There were theater parties, whist parties, church parties and sight-seeing tours to the casino at Monte Carlo. New Year's Day, 1886, was "a quiet one," but a week later there was a "dancing reception on board the *Pensacola* given by the Admiral, Captain, and officers."[27]

James Gordon Bennett entertained Captain Dewey and a large naval party with an excursion out of Nice on the millionaire publisher's yacht *Namouna*, and the following day Dewey had Bennett to a return dinner on the ship. Around these bits of fact Dewey's yarn-spinning seamen wove a fiction about their commander "and the nabob." According to the story, Dewey had given orders that no visitor be allowed on board until noon of the next day, as the ship needed cleaning. "A New York nabob in port on his steam yacht sought to go aboard. He was told of the order. 'But you must let me on now,' the nabob urged. 'I am Mr. So-and-So, you know,' mentioning his charmed name. 'I pay more taxes in America than any other two men, and, in fact, I own half the United States Navy.' 'Let him come up,' came an order from the commander. The man of millions clambered aboard and was met by Dewey. 'I heard your remark that you owned half of the United States Navy,' said the commander; and then, stooping, he cut a sliver of wood from the deck and handed it to the boastful visitor. 'Take this souvenir of the Pensacola and keep it,' remarked the commander. 'It is yours; it is all you have ever owned or ever will own of the Navy of the United States. Shall be glad to see you with other visitors any time after noon tomorrow.' So saying, Dewey turned and walked aft, and a crestfallen Croesus crept back to his launch."[28]

Captain Dewey was never one to scorn money and the guinea stamp of social position. Yet it is very likely that on occasion he may have waxed caustic on professional topics. Life on the *Pensacola*, with its endless round of diplomatic ritual and social entertainment—however varied that life might be by comical boat races between clowning cooks, or by black-faced minstrel shows on the quarter-deck, or even by extended excursions ashore to Florence or Athens or Damascus— was not a satisfactory life for any American naval officer in the 1880's. Looking back on it years later Dewey deplored "the wounds to my sense of professional pride as captain of the *Pensacola*." The *Pensacola* might be picturesque as a survival of happier days in the Navy, but, measured in a European port alongside such modern English ships as the *Agamemnon*, or even such newcomers as the Japanese Navy's *Namiva-kau*, she was—in Dewey's bitter words—"an old tub." "As we had no commerce or interests to protect in Europe, and were unable to protect them if we had, the presence of our squadron in European waters was perfunctory. It used to be a saying among the officers that we went from port to port to meet our wives who were travelling

ashore, and to get letters from sweethearts."[29] To the widower, whose
only sweetheart was the picture in his watchcase, life undoubtedly
must have seemed futile at times. After four years of parade as skipper
of an impotent flagship on a station where displaying the flag was designed to impress foreigners with one's naval might, Dewey was recalled in 1889.

In midsummer, at age 52, he obtained his first important billet in
the Navy Department—that of chief of the Bureau of Equipment and
Recruiting. This was a post which Winfield Scott Schley, two years
junior to Dewey, had obtained four years earlier. Dewey obtained it
solely by virtue of the seniority rule. The honor carried with it for
"Gentleman George Dewey," as some of his fellow club members were
now wont to call him, the courtesy title of "commodore."

7. MAHAN TURNS NAVAL PHILOSOPHER

THE war clarified for Mahan the fact that *he did not like the Navy*.
The breach with his classmates who had put him in Coventry never
healed.[1] He was as unresilient as ever, was still unreconciled to such
dull duty as the blockade, and in the peacetime years ahead he might
expect a share of monotonous assignments.

Upon the cessation of activity at Charleston, Mahan was detailed to
convoy duty in the Gulf where, along with three-fourths of his crew,
he contracted a virulent type of malaria, known as Chagres fever. His
side-wheeler *Muscoota* had to be sailed back to Norfolk by a crew of
volunteers from other ships.[2]

He was months ridding himself of fever germs. He had saved some
money and might at this time have changed his profession. But jobs
were scarce and he was too conscious of the fact that his entire training had been for a naval career. In an uncertain world, moreover, his
commission of lieutenant commander was not to be lightly tossed overboard. At twenty-six he held a rank which few men under fifty had
held before the war. Then there was his father, Professor Mahan of

West Point, against whose wishes Alfred had entered the Navy in the first place. He could not now brook his stern and aging parent's displeasure by resigning from the service. His friend Samuel Ashe in Wilmington, North Carolina, with whom Mahan resumed the correspondence interrupted by the war, was struggling against Negro rule in his state and trying desperately to make ends meet in his newly established law business. Mahan solved Ashe's dilemma, and incidentally his own, by lending Ashe $500, the first of several loans.

Still in love with the Nonpareille of Newport, unwilling to break up another man's home to satisfy his desire, he accepted duty on the Asiatic Station as a means of getting clear of his difficulties. That he was distraught is indicated by a reproach he sent Ashe on the eve of his departure: "You say, 'Some time has imperceptibly lapsed since I last wrote,' when you know damned well, that your god damned laziness allowed ten weeks to go by without uttering or writing a syllable. You're a hell of a man, aren't you? Yes, you'll be a lawyer, never fear!"[3]

In February of 1867 the ice broke up in New York Harbor and Executive Officer Mahan in the U.S.S. *Iroquois* set out via Cape Town for Japan. From this roundabout route the future historian of British sea power derived an elementary education in the geography of the British Empire. At Cape Town a file of Tommies marching smartly down the street startled him by saluting him with an "eyes right."[4] The strategic town of Aden, controlling the mouth of the Red Sea, at once fascinated and repelled him with its incongruous population of English, Arabs, Parsis, Somalis, Sepoys and Jews. The Jews, with long curls falling to their shoulders and features "brutalized by ages of oppression and servility," enabled him to imagine vividly the kind of mob that had crucified Christ.[5]

In Japan Mahan had a part in the ceremonial opening of the new treaty ports Osaka and Hiogo, and two weeks later, following the tragic drowning of Admiral H. H. Bell, it became Mahan's duty to fire the *Iroquois'* minute guns during the admiral's funeral on shore.[6] News of the revolt in Spain took him to Manila to look out for American interests by showing the flag in that harbor.

In Asia he found himself no fonder of the details of shipkeeping than ever, but here he was able to get ashore often for sight-seeing. From Hakodate he journeyed inland for several days on a scraggy pony to climb a famous volcano. The countryside around Osaka he considered the most beautiful in the world. Medieval Japan was as yet free from Western innovations; her two-sworded samurai still rode through the city streets. The isolationist, antiforeign spirit of the Japanese people compelled Americans to carry pistols and to restrict their travels inland. A group of elderly Japanese women whom Mahan saw at a theater were stripped to their waists, "making a display which we might call immodest, but hardly alluring. We were objects of curiosity to these venerable dames—who smiled at us displaying in addition to their other witcheries, irregular sets of black teeth." To Ashe he confided that he preferred men in general to women, "perhaps a little on the sour grapes ground." He could not forget his first love, "whom I am devoted to, and think charming."[7]

Thoroughly tired of Asia after a year and anxious to get back home, Mahan obtained six months' leave and permission to return by way of Europe. "I am a victim of indecision and shyness. The hope that thus throwing myself into a different and more lively sphere may tend to correct these faults is not the smallest inducement I have to this present course."[8] While waiting for his passage he went to see a Japanese execution—"a not very commendable curiosity—but I did want to see a man's head taken off by one blow of a sword. There were three victims—I only watched the first—and paid little attention to the accessories. The execution was perfect—the head dropping instanter—once was enough, and as I said, I left—unpleasantly affected, but not to the extent I had feared."[9]

He left Hong Kong on the steamer *Glenartney* in October 1869. From Calcutta he traveled overland across the tip of India to Bombay, thence by steamer to arrive in Marseilles December 17, 1869. Here he heard that the U.S.S. *Sabine* was in Nice. His brother Dennis Mahan was a midshipman on the *Sabine*. He went to Nice.

But in Nice he encountered not only his brother but the Nonpareille! She was older now and more fascinating than ever. Her husband had died. She was free. His old passion flamed, and he remained in Nice for a month only to have his offer declined. "Absence," as he put it to his bosom friend Ashe, "seems to have done its work on her, and it is too evident to me."[10]

For distraction he flung himself into a sight-seeing trip to Rome. In his discouraged frame of mind he found the city "filthy, disgustingly so," and he was bored by the " 'expurgated' heathen columns and obelisks every few squares." The Vatican bewildered him. Only the Colosseum, St. Peter's and a few art treasures he found interesting. While he stood in awe before the Dying Gladiator, a sudden memory of Byron's lines brought tears to his eyes. "The marble face seemed to gain life and you could grieve for the dying man thinking of his wife and children far away." Mahan was in a mood to grieve. "I have been a good deal harassed in my mind," he wrote Ashe. "I presume things of this sort are continually occurring in the histories of human life, yet to be the one concerned they each seem peculiar in themselves; and I so find myself incapable of imagining any one equal to her in loveableness and fascination. The effect upon me personally however is bad—for I have no occupation requiring my mind to leave what is perhaps a very morbid condition. If ever a man needed praying for I do just now; for I am in sore straits to do right—even to know what is right. The best hope for me humanly speaking, would be to form some stronger and more natural attachment; but is it possible? This is the only one of her sex I ever desired to possess, to call my very own."[11]

Having returned to West Point with his fresh resolve to seek out a wife, he found the atmosphere of his boyhood home not conducive to romance. Professor Mahan, crotchety after forty-six years of teaching cadets, was fighting a movement on the campus to have him retired for age. The presence of a Negro cadet at the Point was a startling sight, evidence enough of topsy-turvyness in the political world. Mahan read a little, rode horseback a little. The mere thought of returning to active duty was enough to induce "apathetic indolence." "I am perfectly satisfied to remain ashore as long as the Navy Department may see fit to permit me."[12]

An attack of malaria and "perpetual headache" took him to the sulphur baths at Sharon in the Adirondacks. And here, in a convalescent state, he met Ellen Lyle Evans.

The courtship developed on a very lofty plane. Miss Evans was considerably younger than Mahan, and for some time their relations were very tentative, owing to a prejudice of the young woman's father against naval officers.

His courtship was interrupted by the death of his uncle, the Reverend Milo Mahan, in whose house he had lived as a student at Columbia, and whose advice in theological matters Mahan now felt he needed. After several months he was on the verge of inviting Miss Evans down to the Point to meet his parents when he received orders from the Navy Department assigning him to duty on the receiving ship at the New York Navy Yard.

Mahan accepted the assignment and explained to the Department's detailing officer that he had "strong personal reasons for desiring to remain in or near New York during the succeeding winter." To Ashe he revealed his resolution "at least [to] have the opportunity of getting in love . . . that certain vague unquietness that from time to time disturbs me is due to the unnatural state that celibacy undoubtedly is."[13]

The winter, however, brought the siege of Paris, and an assignment like Dewey's to command a ship carrying relief foodstuffs to France. Like Dewey's Mahan's trip proved to be unnecessary, and after a "boisterous and tedious" passage his cargo had to be sold in England. While Dewey, similarly situated, was enjoying the hospitality of the London clubs, Mahan took the opportunity to visit St. Paul's. He was deeply stirred. "The service was full choral . . . and the effect was very moving . . . the more so when joined to the remembrance of the vast numbers of the faithful who during five centuries have worshipped under the same arches. . . . I shall go to Canterbury from London. Next Sunday St. Albans; the great ritual church is my objective point."[14]

Mahan's first real interest in history seems to have awakened during his visits to these ancient cathedrals. There was a solemn impressiveness about them, the "vague awful mystery of great age which peoples the building with the ghosts of those many generations now gone to their rest."[15] As with every great historian these ghosts were like living people to Mahan.

He returned home in July to resume his visits to Sharon. "I am not entrainé by that mad wild instinct, dignified by the name of love, which I have known of old," he wrote.[16] During the nine months that intervened before their marriage, Ellen Evans had to overcome her father's opposition to having a naval officer for a son-in-law, and Alfred suffered one of the greatest shocks of his life in the tragic death of his father.

On September 16, 1871, Professor Dennis Hart Mahan committed suicide. In June the Board of Visitors had recommended his retirement after forty-seven years of service, with the rank of brigadier general. The old man resented this act as a personal affront and refused to accept the generalship. During the summer he was several times seized with violent nervous paroxysms. His moodiness grew worse and on the day he died he was being taken by steamboat down to New York to consult a doctor. Mrs. Mahan and two colleagues, Professors Michie and Church, were attending him. Suddenly, when no one was looking, he strode quickly aft and threw himself under the churning paddle wheel. . . .

The *Army and Navy Journal* noted that the bearing of Professor Mahan was "a peculiar blending of military with the scholastic." Fastidious in dress and manner, austere in the classroom, he had had frequent clashes with his students because of his sensitiveness, "but he never remembered it and the students' affection and esteem for him was very strong."[17]

In his father's fate the introspective Alfred beheld a premonition of his own. Five years after his father's death and four years after his own marriage, Alfred wrote Sam Ashe: "The knowledge that one's family has any hereditary tendency to disease is one of the very sore burdens that some have to bear. I used to believe that we were free from such but since my father's death, and recognizing in most of us a disposition to nervous and mental excitement and worry, I have myself gone through seasons of great apprehension."[18]

On June 11, 1872, the bride having won her father's consent, Lieutenant Commander Alfred Thayer Mahan, thirty-two, and Ellen Lyle Evans, twenty-one, were married. The philosophical bridegroom had been self-sufficient for so long that he feared the process of adjustment to "the little constant rubbings of family life."[19] Yet from the outset his domestic life seemed in many respects ideal. Aware that he was hard to live with, he imposed a rigid discipline upon himself. His interest in theology, though it continued after marriage, became overshadowed by his interest in religion as an attitude toward life. "Religious faith," he later confessed, "I, at least, did not for a long time apprehend."[20] He now learned that the "poor are not only they who have little money. There are also the poor in native good dispositions, whose hearts know their own bitterness; who fain would in temper, in love, joy, peace, long-suffering, gentleness, meekness, self-control, give to Christ abundantly, if only they could; who from the poverty of a

weak or an arid, or a perverse nature, can give only the rare cup of
cold water, wring the few mites of kindly impulse, realize here and
there something of love, not in bare act, which is cheap, but in that
steady burning purpose which is life and light."[21]

A generous leave of absence made easier the transition from bache-
lorhood. In November he received his promotion to commander. His
next active service, as captain of the *Wasp* on the South Atlantic Station with headquarters in Montevideo, enabled him to take Mrs. Mahan with him. Their first child, Helen Evans, was born in Montevideo
August 6, 1873. Mahan rejoiced that she was a daughter. She was an
intelligent child who quickly learned that she could have more fun
with her daddy if she refrained from clutching his whiskers.[22]

His relief arriving in January of 1875, Mahan relinquished command
of the *Wasp* and with his family returned home via Europe. In France
they paid a visit to Mrs. Mahan's mother and invalid father who were
living in the quiet mountain village of Pau in southwest France. Mahan gave little Helen Evans, still under two, a high rating as a seafarer
and proudly noted that "she was the wonder of all our fellow passengers as she trundled unaided along the deck during heavy weather."[23]

A tour of duty at the Boston Navy Yard brought Mahan into immediate touch with the malpractices of naval administration under Grant,
and revived those latent instincts of the reformer which Mahan had
displayed as a cadet at the Naval Academy. The employment of navy-
yard workmen to do work for private contractors during working
hours for which the government paid, Mahan branded as "an indirect
fraud upon government." Just before elections many new workers
were foisted upon the yard by politicians, "a most barefaced bribery."
"The Commodore of this yard was brought up before a Court and
compelled to deliver up a letter written by the Chief Constructor of
the Navy directing him to take in as many as necessary, to throw open
the gates, 'that the Administration attached great importance to the
election of so and so.' "[24] One officer known to Mahan, who had been
dismissed from the service for drunkenness and incompetence, was
subsequently, and contrary to law, restored to his position in the line
by Secretary Robeson.

It was not in Mahan's nature to sit idly by or leave agitation to
others. Through his friend Ashe, he got in touch with the lawyer's friend Senator Merriman, of North Carolina, who, though not a

member of the Naval Committee, might yet be expected to get the ear of the committee. "I honestly believe the Naval Service to be undergoing very serious demoralization and injury from the neglect of the present Secretary, and from his corrupt use of his office to promote political, personal and pecuniary gain."[25] The great "flurry" of naval demonstrations off Key West that followed the *Virginius* affair Mahan interpreted as the Department's effort to circumvent a Congressional investigation. In a letter Mahan put his ideas forcefully before Senator Merriman, and wrote also to many others. Entering into the notorious line-and-staff controversy, he excoriated Chief Naval Constructor Hanscom for his part in the decline of the Navy. "What a stench there is in the mere thought that party intrigues should be mixed up with the question of building sound ships and doing good work in a Navy Yard."[26]

Through the good offices of Merriman, Mahan was called upon by the Congressional committee to state his case. He spent considerable time over his indictment of the Navy's administrators, endlessly revising his composition "to combine conciseness and clearness."[27] The excitement incident to his reform activities induced one of those "seasons of great apprehension" from which he had occasionally suffered since his father's death; and to overcome this strain he turned to religion and sought to emulate the calm Christian faith and discipline of his mother.

From a trustworthy source he learned that Secretary Robeson planned to economize by placing a number of officers on furlough and that he was among the number. What he would do he did not know. The maneuver would slice even waiting orders pay in half, allowing in his case a pittance of $1,150 on which to support his family. In anticipation of the financial stringency, he moved Ellen and the little daughter into his mother's home at 232 South Broad Street, Elizabeth, New Jersey. In August the anticipated blow came.

The passage of a Naval Deficiency Bill, which followed almost immediately, however, restored him to the active list in October, with temporary duty at the Naval Academy. The brief financial depression set him to puzzling over the uncertainties of his lot as a naval officer. Expected by the Department to hold himself in constant readiness for duty afloat, facing unusual expense in moving at any and all times, he felt that he was by circumstances denied the right to accept a supplementary job. What, in this case, should one do?

Given a year's leave of absence in December, he spent it abroad with his wife's family in Pau, France. Though poverty restricted further travel and Mrs. Mahan was expecting a second child, he did manage to take short trips to the medieval walled town of Carcassonne and to Toulouse. "I became very much interested in the history of that part of the country and after my return to Pau, I availed myself of the city Library to read up, then formed the idea of writing a couple of magazine articles, afterwards a small book, for which I collected a number of photographs as illustrations."[28] Might not writing become the solution to his problem?

On July 10, 1877, a baby sister of four-year old Helen Evans arrived. The infant was named Ellen after her mother. And the very next day Mahan received orders to report for duty at the Naval Academy on September 1. There was barely sufficient time for the mother to recover before the Mahans embarked for home. Mahan reached Annapolis on September 4, and Mrs. Mahan with the children, after a month's recuperation at the home of relatives in Philadelphia, followed in October.

Nominally Commander Mahan was head of the Department of Gunnery. Actually he managed only the instruction. Gunnery drills, somewhat to his dismay, were taken over and "run by the Sup't. and Commandant of Midn., so much so that I have nearly washed my hands of any concern with them, finding that I could do nothing. Our present superintendent is an able man, of very polished and elegant manners etc, but very fond of running everything himself—so after some ineffectual efforts to get a certain allowance of time and management for myself within it I have given over and let him run the ranch."[29]

The superintendent and the commandant, whatever their motives for such gratuitous assistance, ultimately proved to be instruments of fate. Their interference contributed to Mahan's sense of insecurity— "we always expect the knife"—*and it gave him time for writing.*

Harper's Magazine rejected his manuscript on provincial French history. Lippincott offered to publish it as a book—at Mahan's expense! Mrs. Mahan, a most competent mother and encourager, kept him from losing heart. Mahan turned to the study of naval policy. For years he had subscribed to the *Manchester Guardian*. In 1878 when the U. S. Naval Institute offered a prize for the best essay on "Naval Education for Officers and Men," Commander Mahan's essay placed third and became his first signed publication for which he was paid.[30] He had passed his first milestone. But not even the general direction of the road where the next milestone lay was as yet clear.

In private, to his friend Sam Ashe, he began to expound ideas to which he was not yet ready to sign his name in print. He felt much deep-seated bitterness toward Secretary Robeson and also, without the same justification, toward Robeson's successor, Secretary Thompson, whose chief faults seem to have been his seventy years of age and his utter lack of training to take on an office "loaded with a bad name and traditions of dishonesty." As Mahan saw things in 1880, the country's prime strategic need, since we had no overseas colonies, was "a strong defensive force for our coast line; offensive operations to be directed mainly against an enemy's coast." Though not inclined to go to sea himself, he yet deplored the deterioration of the Navy's vessels because it deprived officers of the kind of sea service necessary to gain experience. "Now the [projected de Lesseps] Canal at the Isthmus *may* bring our interests and those of foreign nations in collision—and in that case—which it is for statesmen to forecast—we must without any delay begin to build a navy which will at least equal that of England when the Canal shall have become a fact. We have for such a purpose *no* navy. . . . We must begin to build as soon as the first spadeful of earth is turned at Panama." He had scant hope that this would be done; "but unless it is we may as well shut up about the Monroe doctrine at once."[31]

He was transferred to the Navigation Office at the New York Navy Yard, and while he was stationed here his son, Lyle Evans, was born on February 12, 1881.

From this metropolitan vantage point he viewed an alarming contradiction in the nation's mind. The jingo outbursts of Blaine in the State Department he considered grotesque and criminally reckless in view of our naval decrepitude. "Immersed as the people are in peaceful and material pursuits, the military establishment is necessarily one of our lesser interests. . . . Practically we have nothing. Never before has the navy sunk so low . . . we have not six ships that would be kept at sea in war by any maritime power." Our Navy was no match even for Chile's. "Spain a near and troublesome neighbor is our superior."[32]

Mahan's second milestone loomed ahead in December of 1882, when *Scribner's* asked him to write the third book in their series on the Civil War. They wanted the manuscript by April 10 following.

Elated with the opportunity, he obtained a month's extension of the deadline and set to work on *The Gulf and Inland Waters*. He wanted the money, his wife's family having recently returned from abroad to live with the Mahans. Though Mahan had misgivings as to whether he could do justice to the book, he felt that he could "do as well as another who would accept the same time."[33] Spurred by the thrill of authorship he sent in the first six chapters on April 12 and got a further extension of time for the remainder. He hurried his last chapter and later made copious changes on the galley proofs.

Mahan was in the middle of this writing project when Dewey in the Mediterranean was taken desperately ill with abscess of the liver. Mahan, offered the chance to relieve Dewey as commander of the *Juniata*, requested to be, and was excused. A year later, apparently on the strength of his book, which had been well received, Mahan hoped to obtain command of the *Pensacola*, flagship of the European Squadron—a prize which fell, however, to the convalescent and lucky Dewey. To Ashe Mahan exposed his chagrin that Dewey had had "sufficient favor with the powers that be to cut me out."[34] Literary work, Mahan discovered, did not measurably increase his professional stature in the eyes of the Navy Department. On the contrary, as if to discourage him from pursuing his new avocation, the Navy proceeded to "banish" him to the Pacific Station as commander of the U. S. S. *Wachusett*.

The exile traveled by mail steamer to Aspinwall and crossed the Isthmus by rail, "on the line nearly of de Lesseps' ditch"; then took another steamer to Callao, Peru, where he found the *Wachusett*. The small ship, just in from a four-year cruise in the southwest Pacific, was now, owing to the "nitrate" war between Chile and Peru, literally tied down to shuttle-cruising along the monotonous coast between Callao and Valparaiso. Along the entire stretch the shore is "so bold that you can run a ship almost against the barren cliffs, which rise abruptly to heights varying from 1500 to 7000 feet." Along the whole stretch "not a shred of green is to be seen, except in rare cases when a mountain torrent breaking through to the sea has a narrow fringe of green fields and small trees"—a stretch interesting enough to the traveler, the naturalist, the antiquarian or the explorer, but not to Mahan the writer who was interested in naval history.[35]

The philosophy of naval imperialism had not yet taken root in

Mahan's mind. Why America, with no overseas colonies, should keep *three* ships of her negligible Navy in this vicinity was more than Mahan could fathom. Three wooden hulls mounting outmoded Civil War muzzle loaders! *"Où sont les neiges d'antan?"* A French officer from a modern ironclad, returning Mahan's official visit, let fall his hand condolingly on the breech of one of these old guns. "Where are the snows of yesteryear? Ah yes, the old system. We used to have it!"[36]

The remark stung Mahan's sense of national pride. Though he approved of Secretary Chandler's airing of abuses in our naval system, Mahan did not believe that the United States would ever support so aggressive a naval program as expansion overseas would entail. He was, at this time, opposed to such expansion: "to me the very suspicion of an imperialist policy is hateful." "Though identified, unluckily, with a military profession," he confessed to Ashe, "I dread outlying colonies, or interests, to maintain which large military establishments are necessary."[37]

The Pacific Station was not at all congenial to Mahan. Endlessly doling out petty punishments to seamen for "skylarking on the quarter-deck," for "calling boatswain's mate a son of a bitch" or "over-staying leave"; forever trying to save money for a parsimonious government by using sails instead of steam; even conducting divine services on Sundays when there was no chaplain aboard—these routine chores sapped his energy.[38] Next to the Gulf blockade, which had so nearly "reduced him to imbecility," this assignment on the Pacific Station was, he felt, the worst assignment he had ever had.

Admiral Hugh Rodman, in his jocular *Yarns of a Kentucky Admiral*, relates an occurrence which must have irked Mahan at the time and which made him famous from then on for his unusually elaborate collision drills. Rodman was at this time a shipmate with Mahan on the *Wachusett*, with the curious rank of "ensign j.g." "The greatest naval strategist the world has ever known," writes Admiral Rodman, was "no good afloat. . . . Our ship collided with a bark under sail, which without question had the right of way. It was our duty to keep clear. We were under sail before the wind, steering north; she was on the port tack heading about W.S.W. and was sighted broad off our starboard bow, distant several miles. Yet we collided with her and were badly damaged, and all hands [were] called to abandon ship, though this was later found to be unnecessary. There was never a court-martial of any kind, but when one of our officers, who was something of a wag, was asked the reason of the collision, he answered, 'Why, the Pacific Ocean wasn't big enough for us to keep out of the other fellow's way.' "[39]

To Ashe Mahan deplored the wretched condition of the Navy's ships. "If we are made to go from port to port in ships which are a laughing stock, knowing that we are, must be, laughed at behind our backs . . . you cannot expect that our pride and self respect will escape uninjured."[40] His third and greatest milestone, however, a truly congenial occupation, was at this moment taking shape for him back home.

Mahan's old friend Commodore Stephen B. Luce had initiated a move to establish a Naval War College for officers at Newport. A board had reported favorably and Luce himself had been made president of the new institution. He now wrote Mahan inviting him to become a member of his staff as a lecturer on Naval Tactics and Naval History.

Mahan at Callao, "drifting on the lines of simple respectability as aimlessly as one very well could," eagerly accepted Luce's offer.[41] At the English Club, a pleasant oasis in Callao, he began devouring history books in preparation for his new assignment. Now more than ever he found the petty details of shipkeeping irksome. As the Navy Department, less anxious than he, declined to order a relief for him, he remained aboard the *Wachusett* until she was decommissioned in San Francisco, at 12:53 P. M., on September 9, 1885. Thus he missed the opening term of the college.

Commodore Luce, lean, wiry, of medium height, with sharp gray eyes, hawk nose and thin lips hedged in between a voluminous spread of iron-gray side whiskers, officially opened the Naval War College on September 20, 1885. After landing from his barge, and being accompanied up the slope of Coaster's Harbor Island by a smart group of naval aides, the little commodore briskly ascended the steps of the old poorhouse building which had been deeded over to the United States. His hand touched the doorknob. "Know all men by these presents—" a whimsical twinkle lighted his gray eyes—"and in the name of the Father, Son and Holy Ghost, I christen this building the War College of the American Navy!"[42] Captain Yates and Lieutenants Symonds, Very, Tilley and Mulligan, after rendering him a well-wishing salute, returned down the hill to their barge, leaving him on the almshouse porch alone, except for his Negro orderly. Eight students, officers attached to the near-by Torpedo Station, attended the historic first term of the college in the fall of 1885.

Mahan, now a captain, arrived in Newport at the close of this term to find the new Naval War College beset by difficulties. Luce had quarreled with the outgoing Secretary and had been detached. An old guard faction in the Navy's high command, unalterably opposed to the college, had already prejudiced both the new Secretary, Whitney, and Chairman Herbert of the House Naval Affairs Committee against the college. Mahan was named to replace Luce as president of an institution which was already threatened by extinction.

Accepting Luce's mantle and ignoring the sniping of objectors, Captain Mahan buried himself for a year in the New York Public Library studying and writing his first lectures.[43] Sir William Napier's *History of the War in the Peninsula* and Theodor Mommsen's *History of Rome* he had digested already. His main idea of sea power, as he now conceived it, included not merely the chronology and factual details of naval battles, but also all the elements that combine to make a nation powerful on the sea: commerce, geographical position, natural resources, character of the people, character of the government, diplomatic and naval policy. His plan was to study history from a naval point of view and to analyze naval warfare in the light of the established principles of military war in so far as the latter were applicable. Possibly—he thought—he might formulate or discover the principles that govern the art of naval war.

To this task he addressed himself with a consuming zeal. Realizing that his work was too broad to admit of ordinary research in original documents, he took secondary histories, but studied them from a new point of view—the naval one in its widest aspects—and worked toward a new science or philosophy: that of sea power. The subject, thus approached, unfolded of itself.

His attitude toward his work was almost one of religious devotion. Regarding his new work as distinctly providential, he spoke of it as "my call." "I think any scheme of education is defective," he had written in his prize essay for the Naval Institute *Proceedings*, "that makes no effort to teach the learner to believe in and depend upon God; to bear constantly about him the consciousness of one perfect friend who knows how painful it often is to *him*, just how faithfully he had worked when to men he had seemed to fail."[44]

In part his deep-seated belief in the value of a War College had sprung out of his own unpleasant experience of life afloat. Shipboard life permitted desultory reading only; it was scarcely conducive to study. "The temptations to pleasure, the novelty of many scenes, the constant distractions, the close and heavy air of the sleeping compartments, all tend to compel men to social outdoor life, and to deter from strong mental effort."[45] Moreover, as modern technology was developing in the Navy, officers were tending more and more to become mere servants of science who trusted blindly in formulas and closed their eyes "to the magnificence of the war seaman's career."[46]

If his ship would make a certain speed, she might, for all Mahan cared, be driven by a tallow candle; if his gun would do the requisite amount of work, it might be made of pasteboard. The War College should train officers to go beyond the mechanical gadgets of science; it should seek through historical studies to develop the rarer qualities of "the artist in war . . . intuition, sagacity, judgment, daring, inspiration—which place great captains among creators, and war itself among the fine arts."[47]

Mahan read his prepared lectures to an audience of 20 officers in the fall of 1886. Other lecturers on his regular teaching staff included Army and Navy officers who were specialists in various fields. Lieutenant John F. Meigs, U.S.N., gunnery expert from the staff of the Atlantic Fleet; Captain Tasker H. Bliss, U.S.A., later a general in World War I; and Lieutenant McCarty Little, U.S.N., retired because of an eye injury and living in Newport, were Mahan's right-hand supports. Among the occasional speakers whom he drew in from the outside were Professor J. R. Soley, a specialist in international law, and Theodore Roosevelt, a young B.A. just out of Harvard, who had written a creditable book called *The Naval War of 1812*.

Yet all was not merry as a marriage bell. The "old guard," whom Mahan had been ignoring, moved into action at the end of Mahan's first year. Captain F. M. Ramsey, superintendent of the Naval Academy, challenged the right of the War College to exist as a competitor of the Academy. As an economy measure Chairman Herbert of the House Naval Committee argued that the college ought to be nipped in the bud, since like other new Federal offices if allowed to continue it might become a perennial drain on the public purse. On the floor of Congress it was noted with innuendo that the new institution was conveniently located "not far from the Newport casino!"[48] Did we want our naval officers to become socialites or fighters?

Economy, clew up and furl, away with all this stuff! The place to learn naval tactics was at sea! During the controversy a cocky reporter for a New York paper came up to see what Mahan was doing in the old ex-almshouse. "To my bad luck," recorded Mahan, "a plan of Trafalgar hung in evidence, as he stalked from room to room. 'Ah,' he said, with superb up-to-date pity, 'you are still talking about Trafalgar,' and I could see that Trafalgar and I were thenceforth on the top shelf of fossils."[49] Unhappily for Mahan the old guard had its day before the Naval Committee. No appropriation was made to support the college in 1887.

Mahan was dismayed but not stumped. Student officers who had come to his lectures prepared to scoff had enjoyed this new and invigorating intellectual discipline and had emerged from the ex-almshouse as converts to the idea of the Naval War College. And Mahan had Commodore Luce's blessing. At the close of Mahan's last lecture the little gray commodore had come to the front of the room and dramatically hailed Mahan as a naval philosopher comparable to the great military philosopher Jomini![50]

Thus encouraged Mahan took his case to Washington. Secretary Whitney refused to alter his unfavorable views but gave Mahan permission to interview Congressmen and muster what support he could. Ashe had sent Mahan a letter of recommendation to Congressman Cowles. Mahan searched for it among his papers in vain and wrote hurriedly requesting Ashe to forward him another letter. Several members of the House Committee were won over, but Chairman Herbert, though perfectly good-natured, had set his teeth and compressed his lips. "In vain did I try to divert his thoughts to the magnificent endings that would come from the paltry ten thousand the college asked."[51]

Although Congress failed to appropriate funds to support the War College, the Navy Department made no change in Mahan's orders.

Back in Newport, Mahan determined to pull the college through on a shoestring. Shrewdly he put through the customary channels a requisition for coal. Navy Department clerks passed it as routine and his winter's supply of coal had already been delivered in the basement before the authorities discovered that there were no funds to pay the bill! Then they charged it to the adjacent Torpedo Station and let it go at that. A pile of scrap lumber left by the carpenters the year before, Mahan sold on the ancient naval principle of the "slush" fund

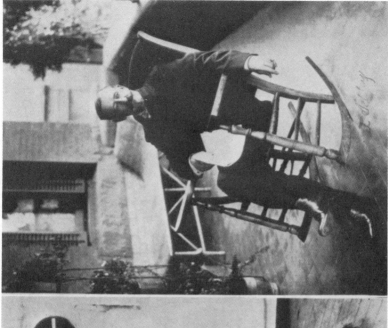

Rear Admiral W. S. Schley.

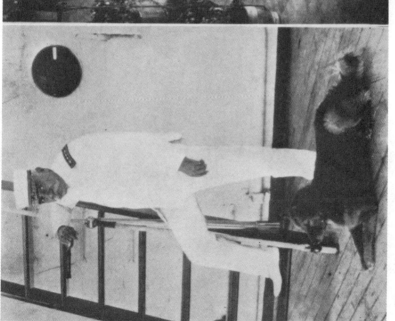

Admiral Dewey and His Faithful Companion "Bob."

Rear Admiral Alfred Thayer Mahan.

Rear Admiral W. T. Sampson on Board the
New York.

and the $100 thus obtained he hoarded to defray minor incidentals. He got back to his studies, and trusted to God—and to the enormously capable Mrs. Mahan—to look out for the practical side of his existence.

He got through the second year most successfully as far as the teaching program was concerned. That he had to put up with oil lamps when an electric line to the Torpedo Station ran within a few yards of the ex-almshouse did not matter, any more than the board fence mattered, which the Bureau of Ordnance put up to protect its Torpedo Station property from being trespassed upon by officer students from the War College, which came under the Bureau of Navigation!

The next year Tasker Bliss was suddenly detached without the courtesy of an advance notice to the president of the college. Then Mahan learned that a bill was up in Congress to eliminate the War College as a separate entity by amalgamating it with the Torpedo Station. Mahan rushed to Washington. For the time being at least the action would have to stand. Secretary Whitney himself, so a Naval Committee member informed Mahan, had appeared on Capitol Hill "and by his personal influence, accompanied by a threat of what he would do if his wishes were not complied with," had put through the amalgamation. In view of Whitney's assurance a year ago that he would not oppose Mahan, the latter now felt that he had been tricked. To Ashe he denounced the Secretary's "overruling me unheard in a matter immediately under my charge, and then posing in the press as a man who is overruling the folly of men whom he has not even consulted and of whose reasons for their course he has heard nothing."[52]

As if to forestall any further lobbying on the part of the president of the unwanted Naval War College, which was now legally disbanded and temporarily, for the sake of appearances, amalgamated with the Torpedo Station, Captain Mahan was himself detached and ordered to duty on a board to select a site for a navy yard on Puget Sound. Only a lifetime of discipline enabled Alfred Mahan to control himself.

The work which he had so well started, however, had enlisted genuine support from such rapidly rising younger officers as William T. Sampson, Caspar F. Goodrich, French E. Chadwick and Bradley A. Fiske. And there was still a lot of fight left in Commodore Luce. The leaven was working and the philosopher Mahan was to triumph in the fullness of time.

8. SCHLEY'S TOWERING FAME

IN THE two decades of rapid naval decline which followed the Civil War Winfield Scott Schley matured into a companionable, easygoing individual who never quibbled over an assignment and always managed to discover a great deal that was interesting and exciting, no matter where the Department happened to send him. As he cared little what foreign duty he drew, his assignments to Asia, the South Atlantic and the Arctic were not "blue ribbon"; but at home, when he could be with his family, he was rewarded with choice berths in Annapolis, Boston and Washington. "Scott is very fond of his family," Schley's stepmother affirmed, "a man of very pleasant and amiable character, always in a good humor and never out of temper."[1] Of medium height, his leanness made him appear taller than he was. He parted his hair in the middle and pin-pointed his mustaches. Some time after the Civil War he grew tired of his chin whiskers and shaved them clean and later compromised with an imperial, which he dutifully waxed and pointed.

Inevitably his always getting agreeable locations on shore evoked the envy of some who had had blue ribbon assignments abroad; and, while he did not actually belong in the category popularly known among naval men as the "gilded social aristocracy," he was frequently credited with membership therein, and, perhaps because he felt somewhat flattered by the charge, he never denied it. Of fashionable cut and fancy, he carried on as in cadet days at the Naval Academy. He wore a boutonniere in his lapel, led the german and was a center of merriment in every party.

He possessed an unusual gift as a raconteur and made a specialty of a type of endless chain story. The story of the mischievous monkey, whose tail Master Schley once greased with such calamitous effect, grew with the telling. A bumboatman brought an orangutan on board at the Straits of Sunda. Schley bought it for a dollar and the animal became a member of the crew. Schley turned him over to an old chief bosun's mate to whom the animal took a fancy. The sailors named him Porkchops, and from the sailors he learned much. He slept in a regular hammock within two days and could pick out his hammock by number. Porkchops was very smart and much quicker than the other bluejackets. Worth five sailors on the yards in a storm, he many a time saved the lives of the whole ship's company by getting in the big spread of canvas in the nick of time. The bosun's mate handed him a lighted pipe one day and ran. But Porkchops pulled away at it like a royal marine. He began to use the spit kits for expectorating. Schley had to include an extra two pounds of tobacco for Porkchops' allotment. Schley thought it was a touching and amiable sight to see the bosun's mate and Porkchops strolling on the spar deck, linked arm in arm after mess, both chewing on black clay pipes and thinking over the day's happenings. Schley gave the animal a drink of old nutty sherry. Porkchops smelled it first, and took a swallow. Then he rubbed his stomach and gulped the rest. He was the drunkest orangutan that ever put a marine's cap on one side of his head and looked rakish. He had to be put in his hammock that night but in the morning he was penitent and would never touch alcoholic beverages again. . . . There was never an end to Schley's saga on Porkchops. Schley told the first episode to a news reporter in the smoking compartment of a sleeping car en route to New York and followed it with later installments at chance meetings over a period of ten years. The reporter, who seems to have been truly affected, wrote solemnly that he had "seen the dampness come into Schley's eyes when he would be talking about the orang-outang."[2]

Beyond doubt Schley told episodes in the life of Porkchops to the midshipmen during his tours of duty at the Naval Academy. Schley was first assigned to Annapolis in 1867 as acting assistant professor of Spanish. Dewey and Sampson arrived later in the same year for duty in other departments. Schley and Dewey, aged thirty and thirty-two, respectively, both enjoyed the social entertainments of Admiral Porter's regime, and their lifelong friendship appears to have been cemented at this time. Always fond of dramatics, the highly imaginative Schley devised ideas for theatrical skits which he helped to direct and acted in. Mrs. Schley's father having made her a wedding present of a fine brick house in Annapolis, the Schleys lived off the Naval Academy reservation. As communicants of colonial St. Anne's Episcopal Church, they enjoyed a wider circle of friends than most naval families.

In November of 1869, Lieutenant Commander Schley set out as executive officer of the *Benicia* for thirty-four months of duty on the Asiatic Station. Mahan's wearisome service in Asia was just ending when Schley's tour of duty there began, and it was typical of the disparity in luck of the two men that Schley should appear on the scene after the trying period of diplomatic uncertainty, and in good season to play an active role when there was acclaim to be won.

The merchantman *General Sherman* with its American crew and cargo of Yankee notions had recently disappeared off the coast of Korea. Inquiries were being made in Pekin and in the treaty ports of China and Japan. Everywhere the finger of suspicion pointed to the pirates of Korea. Korea itself could not be approached through diplomatic channels, for there were none. The Hermit Kingdom by ancient custom permitted no contacts with the outside world. Now that China, the Maritime Provinces of Siberia and Japan had all been opened to commerce, it exasperated Western merchants that Korea, a huge uncharted peninsula jutting out into and menacing navigation between the Japan and China seas, should continue to bar her doors to trade. Moreover, all along Korea's dangerous coasts, as the *New York Commercial Advertiser* fulminated, lived "pirates of the worst sort. No one escapes them. They capture a ship, pillage it, burn it, and kill all the crew."[3]

When Schley early in 1870 was weathering hurricanes on the voyage east around Africa and enjoying the feel of his well-found and seaworthy *Benicia*, Count Otto von Bismarck in Berlin was suggesting to the American Secretary of State Hamilton Fish that America enter a British, French and German naval combination to stamp out piracy in Asia. Although Bismarck's project evaporated at the outbreak of the Franco-Prussian War, the United States now strengthening its Asiatic squadron with better units like the new 2,400-ton *Benicia*, and influenced by growing commercial interests, moved ahead alone in the direction of "bombshell" diplomacy.

A new and aggressive skipper for the *Benicia*, Captain L. A. Kimberly, arrived in the East by steamer from San Francisco. And as a passenger on the same steamer came the Honorable William H. Seward, the ex-Secretary of State to whose ardent imperialism the purchase of Alaska had been due.[4] Seward became the first foreigner to whom the mikado in Japan accorded a face-to-face interview. Schley, traveling in Seward's wake, enjoyed a similar reception a short while later. In Pekin, Seward, together with the American minister, Mr. Low, prepared the Chinese emperor for the forthcoming American effort to open Korea. The Americans hoped to carry it off as Perry had in Japan, peaceably, with only a parade of naval force. To this end the American Admiral "Jack" Rodgers had been furnished a copy of Perry's treaty. Rodgers was to negotiate a similar treaty with Korea, if possible, or at least to get an agreement which would protect the lives of Americans shipwrecked on the Korean coast. Rodgers, with Minister Low on board the flagship, planned to take five of his gleaming black-hulled warships up the Kang-Hoa River and conduct his negotiations a few miles below the Korean capital city, Seoul.

The Korean expedition left Nagasaki in May of 1871 and steamed slowly through dense fog up the southern coast of Korea. Their only map, one that had been roughly drafted by the French a few years before, was found to be inaccurate when they repeatedly ran on hidden or uncharted rocks. Off the mouth of the Kang-Hoa River communication was established with the natives through Chinese interpreters. Several local officials who came aboard the flagship were assured that the mission was peaceful and that the American admiral sought to inquire into the circumstances surrounding the loss of the *General Sherman*. While this message was being transmitted to Seoul,

Admiral Rodgers sent his two lightest vessels, *Palos* and *Monocacy*, together with a flotilla of steam launches from the *Benicia* and the *Alaska*, to survey the lower river where there were treacherous shoals and a tide of eight feet. As the survey party ascended the river many fishermen, who took fright, abandoned their junks and swam ashore; yet natives in white kimonos who lined the bluffs seemed friendly enough. Upstream at a bend in the river, the "Gates of the Kingdom" were defended by five forts. An estimated 2,000 white-clad Korean soldiers lining the parapets fingered their large-mouthed blunderbusses and brandished their spears. The largest red stone fortress on the left bank at the curve had an advantageous elevation of 150 feet.[5]

When the survey party reached this curve, a stream of fire poured suddenly down upon them from the forts. The flotilla of launches at once fired their 12-pounders, while the *Palos* and *Monocacy*, rushing up on a five-knot tide, rattled away over the heads of the flotilla with their eight-inch rifles. The *Monocacy* grounded on a rock and was held fast till the tide came in full.[6]

During the firing a note signed by a chief counsellor of the king was brought to the admiral. This contained no satisfactory explanation of the *General Sherman* incident but stated that the Koreans "refused to hold any intercourse whatever with foreign nations."[7]

Rodgers in return demanded an explanation and apology for their firing upon his survey party. For want of a better means of transmission this message was affixed to a pole at the water's edge. Next morning it was found to have been removed. To allow ample time for transmission to Seoul a second note also tied to the pole announced that the squadron would wait ten days for a satisfactory answer.

Landing parties from each ship were detailed and drilled during the interval of waiting for a reply. Rations for several days were cooked and packed and ammunition was got up on deck. Apparently hoping to propitiate the foreigner and make him go away, the natives drifted down the river a barge of cattle as a present. This was towed ashore and returned. Admiral Rodgers received no reply to his notes.

Accordingly, on June 10, the landing party under Captain Kimberly was put ashore. Schley, enjoying as Kimberly's adjutant a sort of roving commission, had a hand in all phases of the operation. He saw the boats towed ashore, the howitzers tugged through the marshes to high ground, the men assembled at their appointed places. Several boats were lost in the swamps, and many trouser legs were torn off of men who had mired to their hips. Covered by fire from the *Monocacy* and *Palos*, the sailors on this first day overran the lesser batteries and obtained a favorable position for assaulting the main fort at the bend of the river three miles upstream from the point of landing.

For the final assault on June 11, Schley obtained Kimberly's permission to "represent him in the advance."[8] Schley took a station with the *Benicia's* seamen under Lieutenant Hugh McKee. Between his position and the fort lay a ravine with a steep incline up its farther side to the escarpment of the fort. During the forenoon the ships knocked out a section of this escarpment. At 12:40 P. M. the officers ordered a charge at the double quick.[9] The assaulting sailors rushed down into the ravine and up the incline to the shattered escarpment. Hugh McKee, a likable youth from Kentucky whose father had fallen at Buena Vista, was the first man inside the enemy's citadel. Schley was directly in back of him. A discharge from a blunderbuss caught McKee and threw him back against Schley. A spear point caught Schley's left sleeve and momentarily pinned it to his coat. Schley shot McKee's assailant and charged with his men. The Korean soldiery, dismayed to find that their helmets and shields of forty thicknesses of cotton cloth offered almost no protection against the Americans' bullets, scattered in disorder.

Schley now discovered that his companion McKee had been mortally wounded by a shot through the spine. Schley admired the desperate courage of the Koreans who with antiquated brass cannon and small arms had sought to defend their country against naval guns and breech-loading Remingtons. To many of the enemy wounded he gave surgical aid, and he took some of them to the ships for further care. Lieutenant McKee and two others had been the only Americans killed.

The first American effort to open relations with Korea, though without success, undoubtedly influenced Korea in 1876 to establish relations with Japan and, in 1882, to sign the treaty of friendship and commerce with the United States negotiated by Commodore R. W. Shufeldt.

Not without envy, some Englishmen, by whom the doctrine of empire had been long cherished, saw America in the Korean incident of 1871 reaching out for a protectorate in Asia. "It has been a dream of certain buccaneering spirits for a long time past 'to have a go in at the Corea,'" commented the *Army and Navy Gazette* of London; "There are magnificent bays and matchless harbors on the coasts. Gold, silver, lead, and iron mines exist in large tracts, and the country is exceedingly fertile. . . ."[10] Such premonitions, however, were premature. There were few Sewards in America in 1871: commercial interest in the Far East was yet in its infancy, and a rejuvenated United States Navy to back it lay a quarter of a century in the future. Schley himself, like the majority of his fellow countrymen, saw the event merely as a simple vindication of the nation's honor. And Alfred Mahan, who was capable of divining the Korean expedition's imperial implications, was at this early date opposed to overseas possessions.

After his adventures in the Orient, Schley served four years at Annapolis, three in the South Atlantic, one in Washington and four in the Lighthouse Service. They were lean years, perhaps, but with no languishing, as in Mahan's case, on furlough pay.

At the Naval Academy, upon reaching the grade of commander, Schley became head of the Modern Languages Department. Recalling his own experience as a midshipman, he required less nicety of accent on the part of the midshipmen and emphasized conversation in Spanish and French, with the instructors doing most of the talking. One of Commander Schley's duties as head of department was to visit classes to see how the subject was going over with the students. On these inspections—usually very austere occasions in other departments—he would seat himself in the front of the room and slightly behind the chair of the professor, who was a native Frenchman or Spaniard. While midshipmen were reciting, Schley could not resist the impulse to signal them by hand warning them if wrong, encouraging them if they were on the right track.

From 1876 to 1879, Commander Schley enjoyed his first regular naval command as skipper of the U.S.S. *Essex* in the South Atlantic. The State Department, expecting disorder in Mexico, kept him three months in Vera Cruz. Schley, vigorously practicing his Spanish, got on well with the Mexicans.[11]

He accommodated himself easily to unusual situations. When official etiquette required him to yield his cabin to the United States minister to Monrovia, who was a Negro, Commander Schley did so entertain the Honorable J. Milton Turner. Away from home and his Southern upbringing, he was able to ignore the African descent of his official guest and even to pass "many delightful hours . . . in his society."[12] As a reward for his settling a quarrel in Liberia, a native king wished to bestow one of his wives on him. The dusky young woman was recommended as a good companion, never sick a day in her life and "able to manage a kraal perfectly."[13] Owing to the "contrary" laws of his country, Schley tactfully explained, he felt obliged to decline.

On board the *Essex* the greater part of the crew was made up of apprentice boys, and with Schley in the dual role of captain and schoolmaster life was never dull. Running low on coal at the mouth of the Congo and hearing that years ago an American collier had cached her cargo up the river, Schley organized a treasure hunt. His apprentice boys, entering into the spirit of the game, combed both sides of the river and located the coal under a heavy growth of jungle vegetation. After they packed it on board the *Essex* Commander Schley complimented them and pronounced the coal as good a grade of anthracite as anyone could wish.

In the Atlantic ports of Africa and South America Schley entertained port officials on board the *Essex* and in turn was invited to the usual balls and dinner parties ashore. Sir Bartle Frere, governor of Cape Colony, and Emperor Dom Pedro of Brazil headed the list of dignitaries whose hospitality Schley and his officers enjoyed. On several crossings of the South Atlantic, Schley took deep-sea soundings and charted the ocean floor. Occasionally the commodore of the South Atlantic Station would dispatch the *Essex* to rescue Americans shipwrecked in out-of-the-way places. Such a mission to the remote island of Tristan da Cunha brought Schley an unusual role, which his never failing sense of the dramatic enabled him to fill.

The merchantman *Mabel Clark* had been wrecked on Tristan da Cunha, and Schley was sent to pick up her survivors. Schley found that one Marcus Johnson, a member of the shipwrecked crew, had fallen in love with the granddaughter of the local governor and did not wish to leave. There being no minister of the gospel on the island and no prospect of one any time soon, Schley was asked to officiate. The couple came on board and Commander Schley read the Episcopal marriage service on the *Essex's* hospitable but gently rolling quarter-deck. The service was interrupted several times by the young woman's spells of seasickness. Schley's apprentice boys aided the bride as best they could and merrily showered her with rice as she left the ship. At the moment, as Schley reported to his admiral, he was not sure "in what degree it would be legal if brought to the test," but as time went on and he reflected over the incident he decided that the Archbishop of Canterbury himself could scarcely have done better.[14] "Love conquers all things," Schley reminisced with clerical pride; "when it fills the soul there is no wall too high, no sea too deep, no island too desolate, and no land too remote to defeat its purposes."[15]

Upon his return to the States, Schley ran into difficulty with the health inspectors at Norfolk. A few days earlier he had obtained a clean bill of health from quarantine authorities at Port Royal, South Carolina, and with this he proceeded to ignore the Norfolk inspectors who were not ready to inspect the ship the moment he arrived. Schley was arrested when he reached the city and bound by a $1,000 bond to answer a charge of violating the quarantine. In court he might have put up a creditable defense for himself had he been so minded. But the genial and easygoing Schley elected to pay the fine of $20 and costs rather than "to be declared innocent after a lengthy contest of several days, costing him two or three hundred."[16] In a similar situation Mahan might have fulminated but would have waited a month if necessary for the inspector; while Dewey would neither have waited for the inspector nor surrendered his case in court.

Schley returned to Philadelphia after three years at sea with his ship in such good condition that Secretary Thompson tendered him the "congratulations and thanks" of the Department. "The Essex, after a cruise of unusual activity and often exposed to the severest weather both in the tropic and temperate zones, returns in an almost perfect condition save ordinary wear and tear, and could again be dispatched on distant service. All this is most gratifying evidence of the excellent qualities of the ship, the faithful manner in which she was fitted and her able and careful management. The fact that she has sailed and steamed over 40,000 miles, without losing a spar or sail, is a high compliment to her officers and crew, especially to the apprentice boys who composed the greater part of the latter."[17]

Eight months of duty in Washington, where he was a member of a board to rewrite the Navy's allowance book, and four years as Lighthouse Inspector in Boston until 1883, intervened before Schley's great merit as a commander became known to the world at large. In 1883 he was back in Washington in a minor bureau post when his chance of a lifetime arrived.

In that red letter year the Navy won its first political victory since the Civil War. And Schley's being stationed in Washington enabled him to help out in the political jousting, for he was on intimate terms socially with a number of Congressmen. Toward the end of the year, moreover, he was able to benefit personally by simply being on the ground when a new and important naval mission was conceived and to obtain the assignment as its commander.

The Secretary of the Navy at this time—the man chiefly responsible for ending the long naval decline and starting the Navy on its road to recovery—was William E. Chandler. To turn the tide Chandler had to be a determined political scrapper. Nominated for the cabinet by Chester A. Arthur, he was accorded a routine confirmation by a Senate which probably knew him vaguely as a native of New Hampshire and a friend of James G. Blaine, but which probably was unaware that in his youth Chandler had been hired by Secretary of the Navy Gideon Welles to smoke out a nest of fraudulent naval contractors in Philadelphia and had thereby acquired a permanent taste for sleuthing. As Secretary of the Navy, in his own turn, Chandler's first move in 1882 was to lift the lid off the Department in an investigation which shocked the country with its revelation of our naval weakness. The small-town politician from Navy-conscious New Hampshire achieved an overnight reputation for stamping on the toes of admirals and Congressmen. An astonished press roared applause, and before the furor subsided Chandler had wrung from Congress the first important authorization of naval construction in a generation.

This milestone in naval legislation, signed March 3, 1883, about the time Schley was assigned to duty in Washington, called for the construction of four new steel cruisers and for the completion of four monitors whose engineless hulks had been occupying costly space in their builders' shipyards for the past eight years.

The affable Schley at once became a useful handyman to Secretary Chandler, who in the course of his political battle had become *persona non grata* to certain Senators. A ticklish problem which Schley helped to solve was the determination of how much money the government now owed the shipbuilders as rent for the shipways that for eight years had cradled the unfinished monitors. As a member of the board appointed to study this matter, Schley personally visited the shipyards of William Cramp & Sons in Philadelphia, of John Roach in Chester, and of Harlan & Hollingsworth in Wilmington. He had a knack for pouring oil on troubled waters. The companies allowed him to examine their books to ascertain how much money the shipways adjoining those of the uncompleted monitors had earned over a period of years, and with these standards a satisfactory settlement was agreed upon.

Chandler was deeply interested in the apprentice system. Schley's skill with apprentices, as demonstrated on the *Essex*, brought him the assignment as chief of the apprentice system under the Bureau of Equipment and Recruiting. Schley's natural enthusiasm for a project so close to Chandler's heart paved the way for a free discussion between Chandler and Schley in December 1883, when the project of rescuing the Arctic explorer Greely was placed in the hands of the Navy Department.

The Greely case was already notorious. In the summer of 1881— the year the *Jeannette* explorers came to grief off Arctic Siberia, but before word of the *Jeannette* misfortune could reach home—Lieutenant A. W. Greely of the Army Signal Corps established a base for Arctic exploration on Lady Franklin Bay, Grinnell Land, north of Greenland. The S. S. *Proteus*, which carried Greely and his 25 colleagues north, left them with enough food and supplies to last three years, and according to plan the *Proteus* was to return at the end of two years to bring the party home. Should the relief ship fail to reach Greely by the end of the second summer, Greely was to break camp and head south by whaleboat or sledges, subsisting upon stores of food which were to be deposited for him at convenient locations along the route. During the summer of 1882 the supply ship sent north to deposit these provisions along Greely's possible route reached only as far as Cape Sabine, 200 miles south of Greely's base, before being turned back by the ice pack. Unfortunately for Greely, as it turned out, the inept commander of the supply ship cached only a mere 250 rations at Cape Sabine and brought the remainder home! In the summer of 1883 the relief ship *Proteus*, on reaching Cape Sabine also neglected to land food here and a few miles north of this point was crushed in the ice and with her precious cargo of foodstuffs sank.

Through bungling and bad luck some 50,000 rations intended to supply Greely had been either brought back home or destroyed. The *Proteus'* crew returned home on their small tender, but arrived too late for another expedition to be sent north in this year. Greely, according to the original plan, would now start south, to find no stores cached along his route until he reached Cape Sabine, and only a handful there.

The harrowing details of the *Jeannette* tragedy, which had been drifting back in piecemeal installments throughout 1883, now alternated in the nation's press with equally grim conjectures over Greely's present plight. While a protracted and futile investigation of the *Proteus* disaster was under way, minority party politicians blamed Greely's plight on the War Department. In December a joint Army and Navy board, appointed by President Arthur to decide what could be done, handed over to the Navy the mission to rescue Greely. Secretary of the Navy Chandler broached the matter tentatively to Schley who fairly jumped at the chance to lead a rescue mission. The assignment was his![18]

Chandler honored Schley's request that his assignment be kept secret as long as possible to shorten the period of anxiety for Mrs. Schley and the children and also gave him a free hand in selecting the officers who were to accompany him.

In Congress the appropriation for the expedition was passed by the House and then for more than three weeks was held up in the Senate to allow individual Senators to settle old scores with Chandler. By mid-February when the bill finally became law Secretary Chandler on his own initiative had already purchased two stout whaling ships, the *Thetis* and the *Bear*, and the work of strengthening and outfitting them was already under way. That Greely was not left "to die in a parliamentary manner" was due equally to Chandler's political courage and to Schley's energy and professional skill.[19]

The British public, too, evinced great interest in the rescue and tendered to the United States Government the steamer *Alert*, an offer which Minister James Russell Lowell was glad to accept.

Several officers whom Schley selected to accompany him belonged to the social set; hence Congressmen who felt that the Secretary had taken advantage of them talked loudly about "naval dudes" and "gilded favorites" who prowled around Washington in search of soft jobs. How any mission to the Arctic could be considered "soft" was not explained. Both Chandler and Schley were too busy to parry these thrusts. In Washington the Secretary, cutting through the red tape of the bureaus, required all administrative snarls relating to this expedition to be brought to his attention immediately. In New York Commander Schley personally supervised the preparations. At 11:00 each forenoon his officers reported on their work and suggested further purchases. Money was spent freely. Congress had authorized $500,000. Schley, with a blank check from Chandler, spent $763,000. For the first time in several decades a naval expedition equipped itself adequately. And it sailed on schedule! The *Bear* sailed on April 24, the *Thetis* on May 1, the *Alert* on May 10.[20]

To Schley's dismay a few days before he sailed Congress voted a reward of $25,000 for any private search party which should either rescue the explorers or bring back satisfactory evidence of their fate. The offer was designed to enlist the aid of the Dundee whaling fleet, which went north each year at this time. The imaginative Schley foresaw whalers pushing into all sorts of dangerous ice floes and posing new rescue problems every few miles along his route. The first result of the offer was a flurry of contradictory reports telegraphed from St. John's, Newfoundland, which asserted that Greely's party had been seen on ice floes in several widely separated areas.[21]

On May 1, 1884, Schley served a luncheon on board the *Thetis* for the Secretaries of War and of the Navy. Photographs were made of the visitors and of the rescue party, including even Commander Schley's French chef and his mess boy Yong Sing.

With the navy-yard band playing "Home Sweet Home," the *Thetis* at 2:20 P. M. cast off. Crowds on shore shouted good luck. Whistles tooted all over the harbor. Schley's sailors ran up the ratlines and waved their hats or tossed them as souvenirs to their well-wishers on the sea wall. The *Tallapoosa* with the two Secretaries aboard accompanied the *Thetis* down the bay. Salutes of 21 guns were fired at Governor's Island, Fort Wadsworth and Fort Hamilton. The *Thetis*, not carrying a salute gun, responded by dipping her colors. Outside of Sandy Hook, Schley directed Lieutenant Uriel Sebree to lay a course for Nantucket lightship and went below, exhausted, to sleep with almost no interruption for 24 hours.[22]

From St. John's, Newfoundland, where he picked up Elsinore caps, sealskin boots and Labrador dogs, Schley raced north to take advantage of the first spring openings in the ice pack. On the way to Godhaven on Greenland he dodged icebergs in dense fog and battled headwinds. From Godhaven to Disko and Upernivik Schley himself spent 12 to 15 hours a day in the crow's-nest. Often what appeared on his map as a headland turned out to be an island, between which and the shore Schley found broken ice that he could push through. He kept a bright lookout for "water-blinks," reflections on the mists above possible channels of clear water. At first it seemed to Schley in the crow's-nest that the *Thetis'* ice-coated masts would snap at the shock of ramming. But soon he grew accustomed to these shocks and also to the continuous grinding of ice against the hull.

Following the hard-learned lessons of Arctic procedure, Schley deposited in cairns on the chief headlands notes of his progress and future intentions to guide the *Bear* and the *Alert*. When Dundee whalers were in his vicinity, Schley would invite their captains aboard the *Thetis* for smokers, or "mollies," as they were called in whaling vernacular. On these occasions, contrary to his usual habit, Schley spoke little and listened to the amusing and harrowing adventures of the whalers. He thus picked up many tricks of Arctic navigation not found in textbooks.

The presence of the Dundee whalers on the trip to Upernivik lent excitement, since there was always the chance that one of them might be the first to sight Greely and claim the $25,000 reward. Above Upernivik, however, the whalers fell behind. The *Thetis* and the *Bear* pushed on alone to the northwest across Baffin Bay through rifts in the ice pack which in mid-June had just begun to open. Sometimes they ran on submerged rocks. The rocks, however, had been ground so smooth by the ice that Schley soon lost his fear of them. A seasoned Arctic explorer upon whom Schley depended was George W. Melville, chief engineer and a survivor of the *Jeannette* expedition. Melville and the Eskimos hired at Upernivik gave Schley a confidence which he might not have gained so quickly without them, and in the rescue of Greely not days, but hours, counted.

At 8:00 P. M. on June 22 Ensign Harlow, who had been sent to examine a cairn on Brevoort Island, signaled, "Have found Greely records."[23] Schley, directed by this find, hurried on the same night to Cape Sabine, where at 10:00 P. M. he found Greely with seven of his men, exhausted but still alive.

Greely's tent, which had blown down upon him, was quickly raised and a fire was made to heat some milk. Greely himself had not eaten for two days, during which time the others had had nothing to eat either but a few squares of soaked sealskin. At the joyful shrill of Schley's whistle they had trickled their last spoonful of whisky down the throat of the feeblest survivor.[24]

As the emaciated survivors were carried off to the ships, some in delirium begged the sailors not to shoot them. In the last terrible weeks Greely, unable to rise from his sleeping bag, had been compelled to order the military execution of a man whose thieving of rations had imperiled the lives of the others.[25] Schley's men discovered what was left of this unfortunate individual on the beach below the camp. His face was intact and recognizable but the rest of his bones had been gnawed clean.

Schley, intent on returning to their relatives for decent burial the remains of those who had starved to death, had his sailors open the 12 graves on the hill back of the camp and move the corpses on board. Finding that these, too, had been mutilated by the removal of muscular tissue, he had the bodies carefully padded with batting and sewed into winding sheets. By so doing he hoped to hide from their relatives and from the world at large the ghoulish details of hunger-mad cannibalism to which some members of the party, possibly without Greely's knowledge, had been driven.

One survivor died during the trip south. When others regained sufficient strength to answer the sailors' questions, Schley found it necessary to prohibit all conversation on the cannibalism at Cape Sabine. His anxiety to spare the relatives of the deceased, at least until they had buried their dead, moved him to stop at St. John's, Newfoundland, to have the dead sealed up in metal caskets. Schley's telegram to the Secretary of the Navy, revealing in general terms the success of the Relief Expedition, declared that "forty-eight hours' delay in reaching them would have been fatal to all now living." After answering the general questions the world had been waiting to ask, he tucked away in his 900-word message the suggestion "that bodies now on board be placed in metallic cases here for safe and better transport in a seaway. This appears to me imperative." Chandler's telegram matched Schley's in subtlety: "Preserve tenderly the heroic dead; prepare them according to your judgment and bring them home."[26]

Secretary Chandler and Greely's superior, General Hazen of the Signal Corps, together with the entire Atlantic Fleet under Admiral Luce, were on hand in Portsmouth, New Hampshire, preparing an ovation for the Greely Relief Expedition. With some trepidation Schley raced into Portsmouth a day ahead of schedule and maneuvered the Secretary with General Hazen into his cabin for a secret session. Greely and the six other survivors were whisked ashore to permit them "to recuperate" unmolested by press and public. The next day the fanfare of Chandler's proposed naval parade—a long planned publicity affair in view of both the oncoming Presidential election and of Chandler's program of naval construction—came off according to plan.

In New York, where the well-bolted caskets were landed, the Greely Relief Expedition was accorded a second naval demonstration and popular ovations. President Arthur welcomed Commander Schley with a reception at the Fifth Avenue Hotel. After Schley had introduced his officers to the President, Chandler informed him that the President as a reward for his fine work had decided to appoint him chief of the Bureau of Equipment and Recruiting.

Commander Schley now rode the crest of popular favor. "Not a whisper of hostile criticism has been heard on Commander Schley's management of the expedition, but he receives credit for good judgment and energy from all quarters," noted the *Army and Navy Journal*.[27] The *New York Tribune* reported in detail the banquet at Delmonico's for Schley and his officers. "When coffee had been served and the curling smoke of cigars had produced a pleasant haze . . . three cheers were given for Commander Schley." In a few generous remarks Schley insisted that the honor for the rescue be shared by Secretary Chandler and by the men who accompanied him.[28] As one survivor put it, "Death had us by the heel, boys, when you pulled us out by the neck!"[29]

"It was a notable feat, this dash through howling tempest and ice straight to the goal, and the American heart was thrilled as it had not been since Richmond fell," summarized a writer in the *United Service Magazine*.[30]

As chief of the Bureau of Equipment and Recruiting Commander Schley, still a comparatively young man of forty-two, enjoyed the courtesy title of commodore and a position of special privilege in

Washington. Efficient and agreeable, he suffered no decline in fortune under the Democratic administration of Chandler's successor, Mr. Whitney, and at the end of his four-year term President Cleveland reappointed him for another four years.

As indicated by his elaborate preparations for the Greely Relief Expedition, Schley was no penny pincher. A great talker and mixer, he was generally well informed on the new technical equipment which the Navy was building up in the latter 1880's, but his personal specialty was not so much "equipment" as "recruiting." All matters affecting both the enlistment and the well being of the Navy's personnel were his special interests. Schley believed that the Navy should offer a career for the seaman as well as for the officer, and he did much to improve the seaman's lot. Heretofore on entering the service a sailor had to purchase $50 worth of shoddy clothing and was allowed no shore liberty until this initial debt had been cleared. Frequently this meant six months' confinement aboard ship. Schley was the chief instigator of the change to government-issued clothing of standard quality. Although he was no connoisseur of fine food like Dewey, he yet had the good sense to establish at the Washington Navy Yard the first school to train Navy cooks, for which a grateful Navy sang his praise. He also advocated a system of pensions for the common seaman, similar to that of the Army.

Promoted to captain in 1887, he applied at once—and before her keel was laid—for command of the new cruiser *Baltimore*. Assignments afloat for captains were still scarce, and Schley, influenced not a little by sentimental considerations, felt that it was only fitting that the new cruiser *Baltimore* should be commanded by a Marylander.

Never satisfied to sit long at his Washington desk, he was always traveling about the country on inspections. In 1889 when the *Baltimore* was commissioned he was delighted to resign from the Bureau of Equipment and Recruiting in favor of his old friend George Dewey and to be off once more on the green seas of the South Pacific. He probably would have been delighted could he have known in advance that he would soon have a share in a serious international incident.

9. SAMPSON WHETS NEW WEAPONS

As a watch officer on the *Colorado* for two years after the Civil War, Lieutenant Commander W. T. Sampson divided his time between the old "brine bruiser's" weather deck and her engine room. In the drydock at Cádiz to replace the ship's stern bushing no detail of the overhaul escaped the machine-minded Sampson. The lignum vitae boxing for the propeller shaft had been so worn away as to score the metal shaft. Better materials must be found for this and every other special purpose in the complex machinery of modern ships. Sampson's intelligent wardroom discussions of this fundamental machine-age fact led his junior shipmate Ensign Caspar F. Goodrich to consider him the most brilliant officer of his time. The youthful Goodrich also thought him exceedingly handsome, with his "dark hair and beard, brown eyes, bright complexion, and engaging personality," and on the topside whenever Sampson's rich, full basso sang out "Ready about! Stations for wearing!" it always gave the young ensign a thrill.[1]

With Dewey and Schley, Sampson came ashore in 1867 to teach in

Annapolis, where for three years he was head of the new Department of Physics and Chemistry. He was allowed a free hand in building up laboratory equipment and was given a large percentage of the midshipmen's carefully rationed study time.

"Every branch of a naval officer's profession," wrote Sampson in a statement of the purpose of his department, "furnishes many illustrations of the application of science. . . . It may not be absolutely necessary that an officer should understand the chemical and physical difference between cast-iron, wrought-iron, or steel gun; yet, I think there can be no question that such knowledge will be serviceable many times. . . . The objects of the course in this department are to develop the cadet's powers of observation, and make him prompt and correct in interpreting the impression of his senses."[2] From 1869 to 1871 a brilliant and impressionable cadet named Albert Abraham Michelson sat in Sampson's classes and absorbed his passion for scientific experiments.

Sea duty as executive officer of the *Congress* in 1871-1874 took Sampson away from his Naval Academy laboratory for an unsatisfactory interlude. This apparently was the only time that Sampson took his family with him to a foreign station. In the Sampson family there were now three daughters: Margaret Aldrich, Catherine and an infant, Susan. Little Susan died at the age of two in Naples on January 1, 1873, and her remains were brought home to Palmyra for interment in the Aldrich family burial plot.

Professionally, Sampson's patience was sorely tried on this cruise. In various European ports the *Congress* berthed alongside modern armor-belted ships flying the flags of fifth-rate powers whose modern, breech-loading cannon could outrange the *Congress'* cast-iron smoothbores and in a matter of minutes reduce her white oak walls to rubble. The sorry plight of the United States Navy became a breeder of ill will between staff officers (engineers, surgeons and paymasters) and officers of the line. On the *Congress* Commander Sampson as executive officer was technically outranked by the ship's paymaster. Sampson, who was responsible for the military discipline on board, overruled Paymaster George Cochran in a trivial matter relating to the writing of a receipt for stores taken on board at Liverpool. Cochran's biased version of the tilt that occurred inside the executive officer's office on the *Congress'* half deck depicts Sampson as follows:

"He was sitting at the desk at the time, and turning to me in a very rude and excited manner, at the same time shaking his head and pointing at me, said, 'I order you at once, Sir, to go and sign that receipt for those stores.' I replied, 'I won't do it,' and walked off."[3] The difficulty was referred to Captain A. C. Rhind and the paymaster was shortly transferred to another ship. Sampson's cruise on the *Congress* was climaxed in February of 1874 by the fleet maneuvers off Key West that followed the *Virginius* affair. During these widely publicized maneuvers, for which a number of Civil War monitors were hastily put into commission, the inadequacy of our naval force even for fighting the fifth-rate navy of Spain was clearly revealed to Sampson. The United States at this time had neither a modern fleet nor the industrial machinery for manufacturing one. At the end of the maneuvers, when the *Congress* was sent back to Europe, Sampson was ordered to Washington, whence, after reporting on the fleet maneuvers, he was returned to Annapolis.

Back in his old Department of Physics and Chemistry, Commander Sampson found a situation ideal for advancing the cause of science in the Navy. Under the authorization of a new law a class of cadet-engineers was assigned to the Naval Academy to be given four years of scientific training along with the cadet-midshipmen. With few, if any, good engineering schools in the country at this time, the competition for these appointments was so keen and the group selected so well grounded in elementary physics that Sampson was able to introduce advanced studies in the general principles of wave motion, the theory and application of electricity, the sources of compass error in iron ships, the pressure of gases and the chemistry of steel, gunpowder, guncotton, nitroglycerin, dynamite and the various fulminates. "The means of attack and defense in naval warfare are constantly becoming more complicated, and naval officers have, in the same proportion, more and more to learn to master their profession," wrote Sampson in a report to the superintendent.[4]

To prepare them for war in the future, Sampson sought to arm Naval Academy graduates with the indispensable weapon of scientific training. "Great and rapid changes are liable at any moment to arise in his profession. If a naval engagement were to take place today between two modern fleets, the result might entirely revolutionize our ideas of naval warfare. He who would be most prompt to appreciate the new condition of things, and adapt himself thereto, will be the best officer. Now, I think this readiness for the future is only to be secured by arming the graduates of this institution at all points by such scientific training as will best prepare them for any contingency."[5]

To further this program Sampson in the fall of 1874 made a tour of Northern universities and industrial plants in search of new ideas in education.[6] As a result of the trip he was able to transform the summer practice cruises for cadet-engineers into conducted tours of the chief manufacturing establishments along the Atlantic seaboard. To Sampson's delight several companies, like the Morse Twist-Drill Company of New Bedford, explained even their secret processes to the students. Important shipyards (Roach & Sons, Harlan & Hollingsworth, William Cramp & Sons), the navy yards in Philadelphia and New York, locomotive works and steel companies were visited. At Newport Sampson and his cadets watched the Navy's new Torpedo Station manufacture nitroglycerin and fuses for torpedoes. Sampson was greatly pleased that the new studies at the Naval Academy had prepared his students to understand what they saw and his report to the superintendent glows with quiet excitement in the quest for scientific knowledge that might have practical applications in naval ships.[7]

Cadet-Engineer Ira N. Hollis, whose course at the Academy coincided with Sampson's present tour of duty (1874 to 1878) and who like Sampson graduated at the head of his class, has left a description of Sampson as a science lecturer. "The lecturer never failed to impress his students as he stood quietly behind a long wooden desk covered with apparatus set up for experimental demonstration. His speech came slowly. . . . His sentences were models of clearness and accuracy, but what I have come to regard as marvelous was the uniform success of his experiments. I do not recall a single failure. He never had to apologize for the behavior of the electric current or to lay blame on the atmosphere. Everything did precisely what he said it was going to do."[8]

Sampson's brilliant former student, A. A. Michelson, now an ensign, was assigned in 1875 as assistant in Sampson's Department of Physics and Chemistry. In December of 1875 Margaret McLean Hemingway came to Annapolis to visit her aunt, Mrs. W. T. Sampson, and here in the Sampson home she met Michelson. The young woman recalled having seen Michelson once before in London at the tomb of Charles Dickens, and the friendship thus begun led to their marriage in 1877.[9]

In 1876 Ensign Michelson began work on his famous experiment to determine the velocity of light, with Sampson's help and encouragement, using equipment from the physics laboratory. After his marriage Michelson obtained $2,000 from his father-in-law, and at the western end of the north sea wall of the Naval Academy he built a frame building in which he housed a steam engine and precision equipment to revolve the tiny mirror which was to reflect the light in his experiment. The revolutions of this mirror were so accurately controlled that a variance in speed of one or two hundredths of a turn could be easily detected. Two thousand feet away from this revolving mirror, at the eastern end of the sea wall, a theodolite and other instruments were mounted to measure the beam of light.[10]

In view of the basic significance of Michelson's experiment for astronomy and practical navigation, Sampson relieved Michelson of many routine duties to allow him time for setting up his apparatus, taking observations and performing calculations.

In the midst of this exciting renaissance of science at the Naval Academy, domestic tragedy struck in Sampson's home. His wife died of typhoid fever on January 10, 1878. The bereaved husband and four motherless daughters, ranging in age from one to 14, accompanied the remains to Palmyra. The funeral was held from the home of Sampson's father-in-law, David S. Aldrich, at 2:00 P. M. on the nineteenth, and Mrs. Sampson, who according to all accounts had been gentle and socially gracious, was buried beside little Susan in the Aldrich plot.

Sampson left the children with relatives in Palmyra and returned to Annapolis to witness the successful completion of Michelson's experimental determination of the velocity of light. The feeling of Sampson, the teacher, for precision machinery is undoubtedly reflected in the words of his student. "One comes to regard the machine," wrote Michelson, "as having a personality—I had almost said a feminine personality—requiring humoring, coaxing, cajoling, even threatening. But finally one realizes that the personality is that of an alert and skillful player in an intricate but fascinating game, who will take immediate advantage of the mistakes of his opponent, who 'springs' the most disconcerting surprises, who never leaves any result to chance, but who nevertheless plays fair, in strict accordance with the rules he knows, and makes no allowance if you do not. When *you* learn them, and play accordingly, the game progresses as it should."[11]

A contribution to science was made by Commander Sampson on July 29, 1878, when he observed the total eclipse of the sun at Creston, Wyoming. His data would enable corrections to be made in the Navy Department's Nautical Almanac.[12]

During the next year Sampson, a widower of thirty-nine, spent the greater part of his free time in Palmyra, caring for his four daughters, visiting with his parents and making the acquaintance of a growing host of nieces and nephews. During this period he met Elizabeth Susan Burling who probably taught his two eldest daughters in the Palmyra school. Elizabeth Burling was from Rochester. A woman of great dignity and charm, she had previously taught in Wells College at Aurora, New York. She was widely read and her specialty, like Sampson's, was mathematics.

A story of Sampson's courtship of Elizabeth Burling is told by a Palmyra woman who as a girl used to remain after school to sweep the room.[13] One afternoon, the slender, neatly groomed naval officer came to the school to walk home with Miss Burling. When the teacher went behind the door to get her wraps, her escort followed and gave the teacher a kiss. Whether the incident occurred before or after Sampson's uneventful cruise to the Orient as commander of the U. S. S. *Swatara*, it is impossible to say. In 1882, shortly after his return from the Asiatic Station, Commander Sampson and Elizabeth Burling were married. The ceremony was held in the home of the bride's brother, George W. Burling, in Rochester.

Sampson, now attached to the Naval Observatory in Washington, was able once more to have his family with him. The second Mrs. Sampson, largehearted and motherly, won the confidence and love of Sampson's daughters, whose child sayings she recorded in a diary. A minister sent Sampson a request to look at the sun through the observatory's large telescope. In her diary Mrs. Sampson records that Robin, as Mrs. Sampson called her husband, "said to us at table that even a clergyman could not be allowed that privilege; the precious instrument is never to be subjected to the sun's rays; that the power of the heat at the point of the telescope would be great enough to melt diamonds." "Then," said Nannie, a philosophical child of eight, "very probably, people had better take care how they try to take their diamonds with them when they die."[14]

The location of the observatory where Sampson lived, on the foggy flats north of Constitution Avenue, was not a healthful one. Sampson put up a board fence to keep out the cows and pigs that roamed the commons in this section of the city; and as a further precaution to guard the health of his family, as well as that of observatory employees, he caused a thorough sanitary survey to be made.

Sampson held the position of assistant to the superintendent for two years, and during this time there were no less than four senior officers holding the office of superintendent. This meant, in effect, that in practically all transactions except the signing of the annual report, Sampson was the actual head of the institution. His two years here fell during a period of transition. A new quarter-million-dollar plant to be built on Georgetown Heights had been appropriated for, and its architectural plans were now being drawn.

The Naval Observatory's new "Ephemeris," an astronomical table predicting future positions of celestial bodies and thus enabling navigators accurately to determine longitude, had been tentatively completed. Calculations for it, based on data from the first Transit of Venus expeditions, had been made and there remained now to be undertaken a series of new expeditions organized and sent out with equipment and instructions supplied by Sampson to take additional observations wherewith to make further checks on the accuracy of the Ephemeris. These expeditions were dispatched to Florida, Texas, Chile, Patagonia and South Africa.[15]

Sampson and his staff made endless observations of the "clock stars" and performed mathematical calculations. Often, after other workers had finished their work for the day, Sampson would enter the observatory and spend an entire night at the large telescope checking the stars and taking off by the aid of oil lamps the almost microscopically fine readings from his instruments. Sampson requested funds to install electric lights, but this innovation did not materialize until after his time. He did, however, obtain funds to install a small steam engine to turn the dome of the 26-inch telescope which had sagged so that it could no longer be revolved by hand.

On February 27, 1883, the Sampsons' first son was born. The infant, whom the affectionate father declared to be "ugly as a mud fence," was christened William Burling Sampson and was the joy of his parents and of a house full of older sisters ranging in age from six to nineteen. The "diary," which Mrs. Sampson kept for the baby, gives an intimate picture of the household while the Sampsons were at the observatory. The new baby had been expected to arrive on Washington's birthday; but even though he was five days late "Papa calls me 'February Washington' or 'Bill' which my little sisters don't seem to like. . . ." Sampson was often preoccupied or absent-minded around the house, and he utilized this trait in developing a sort of game to get the two younger girls all excited over the baby's welfare. "This morning," the diary reads, "he came in and sat down exactly where I was lying. My sister Olive & dear good nurse Marfa screamed out & thought there wasn't any baby left, and papa jumped up & looked awfully scared, but he didn't hurt me a bit, and some way I think he knew I was there all the time. Papa weighed me today, and I weigh $10\frac{1}{2}$ lbs. not counting my clothes."[16]

During Sampson's tour of duty there, Western Union was granted permission to run a private wire to the observatory for the purpose of transmitting Naval Observatory time signals throughout the country. This innovation led immediately to the unifying of railroad time systems which hitherto throughout the nation had been operating within a chaos of 53 different systems. The country was now divided into five longitudinal time belts; new railroad schedules were printed, and at noon on November 18, 1883, when the time ball on the roof of the Naval Observatory was dropped to indicate the hour, all the principal railroads of the country reset their clocks and watches and their trains began moving on the Naval Observatory's "Standard Time." The Standard Time, next extended to government offices, was not adopted by private business until later, owing to difficulty in making over the habits of workers.[17]

In the fall of 1884 Commander Sampson was chosen as a delegate to represent the United States at the International Conference on the prime meridian. Much confusion in the maritime world had grown out of the coexistence of two different systems of reckoning longitude, the Greenwich and the Parisian. British and American maps of the globe assumed Greenwich as the prime meridian; whereas France and certain Latin-American nations used Paris. America's increasing trade with Latin-American states led President Arthur to call the international conference to iron out this world-wide confusion.

In the conference, which was held in Washington, the French delegates, loyal to Paris, resisted the general view that Greenwich was the most logical and feasible choice, and advocated establishing a prime meridian which did not run through the territory of any great power. Bering Strait or the Azores, they proposed. British delegates held out for Greenwich.

Commander Sampson, in the role of compromiser, urged "that a prime meridian, to be accurately determined and fixed, should run through some established national observatory, and should be in telegraphic communications with the rest of the world."[18] Furthermore since more than 70 percent of the world's shipmasters already used the meridian of Greenwich, and since a change to any other meridian would entail an expense in excess of $10,000,000 to make the necessary changes in the charts, he urged that Greenwich be selected. Twenty-one nations voted for Sampson's proposal. Little Santo Domingo alone opposed. France and Brazil abstained from voting. President Arthur held a reception for the delegates at the White House, and an important problem of the Machine Age, into which the world was rapidly rushing, had been adjusted.

Upon the completion of his work with the Prime Meridian Conference, Sampson was transferred to Newport, Rhode Island, as inspector of Ordnance and head of the Torpedo Station. The first appropriation bill for naval construction since the Civil War had been passed, and Newport, the location both of the Torpedo Station and the base for the apprentice training system, was soon to acquire its third naval establishment, the Naval War College. During the two years from 1884 to 1886, when Sampson quartered his family in the superintendent's one-and-a-half-story bungalow, the foundations and basement of which had been the casement of a colonial fort, Newport was a center of the Navy's intellectual and scientific revival. Here at Newport ancient and modern ideals in naval equipment were ludicrously juxtaposed. On board the several obsolete sailing ships apprentice seamen achieved proficiency in the now useless technique known as "gilguy." Yankee smartness of an earlier era was here pushed to ridiculous extremes as seamen learned to "strip a ship to a girtline" in a matter of minutes. Eight-inch cast-iron cannon were fired, transferred to the opposite side of the ship and fired again—in 28 seconds flat! No gunnery in it, but trickery, with no little danger to the scurrying artists of "serve-vent-and-sponge."[19] Gilguy represented the ultimate and quixotic perfection in the use of guns and gear that would never be used again in battle.

The Torpedo Station, within a stone's throw of these sailing ships, had also its quixotic side. Since 1867 the station had been gingerly playing with mines, offering 19-explosion salutes to visiting Secretaries of the Navy and toying ineffectually with spar torpedoes like the Civil War improvisation with which Cushing had sunk the *Albemarle*. General William Tecumseh Sherman at a New England Society dinner had poked fun at this weapon by calling it a "devil-fist, a great proboscis, with some kind of explosive at the end."[20]

For a while Sampson experimented with the spar torpedo, working out improvements in rigging the spar so that it would not snap when the torpedo boat attained a speed of 18 knots. But he soon became more interested in the explosives inside the torpedo's warhead. Inside the service torpedo Sampson found the guncotton to be too loosely packed around the primer. He experimented. First he wedged pieces of oak into the spaces between the cylindrical bars of guncotton, then he had guncotton molded into flat disks which could be packed still more tightly. To ascertain the relative effectiveness of his experimental torpedo and of the regular service torpedo he exploded one of each kind in a pond beneath six inches of ice. His experimental torpedo blew a larger crater in the ice. More complicated experiments followed. In the manufacture of guncotton, Sampson's variations of the formula led to a more stable and effective product.

Sampson installed in Newport Harbor special buoys to be used in compensating the compasses of the four new steel cruisers whose engines were now being mounted. He trained naval personnel as instructors in deep-water diving and widened the range of laboratory study in electricity. A system of electric lighting was installed in Torpedo Station buildings. In classroom methods Sampson at once scrapped the practice of requiring officer students laboriously to transcribe verbatim and hand in to instructors fair copies of all lectures. Instead, having learned much in his years of teaching at the Naval Academy, he had all lectures printed and issued to the students in advance so that they might predigest them and ask intelligent questions of a speaker during the lecture period. Cramming, if not eliminated, was no longer encouraged.[21]

In addition to his duties at the Torpedo Station Sampson served on several naval boards. With Commodore Luce and Lieutenant C. F. Goodrich he canvassed the question of the Navy's need for advanced theoretical study in a War College, and Sampson along with Luce and Goodrich shared the responsibility for getting the Naval War College started in 1885 as a next-door neighbor to the Torpedo Station on Coaster's Harbor Island.

When the shipbuilder John Roach ran into bankruptcy trying to overcome technical difficulties in the construction of the four new steel cruisers, the A.B.C.D.'s (*Atlanta, Boston, Chicago* and *Dolphin*), Sampson was appointed to membership on a board of naval officers to recommend changes in the designs of these cruisers. Since the original plans for these first steel ships of the new Navy had been ineptly drawn—Congress having been unwilling to incur the added expense of purchasing suitable plans aboard—these ships would never be made entirely satisfactory. The *Dolphin*, the command of which Dewey had turned down, was relegated to nominal assignments as a dispatch boat, though the other three were made moderately serviceable as warcraft.

The international situation having induced President Cleveland to call for a general examination of our coast defense system, Sampson was appointed as one of a commission of eight Army and Navy officers headed by the Secretary of War to consider the whole defense problem and to make recommendations. As an advocate of armor, guns, self-moving torpedoes, electrical equipment, etc., Sampson was able to give impetus to all these developments. That the government would eventually have to subsidize the steel industry in order to obtain American-made metal for guns and armor, Sampson clearly foresaw. Without his early and clear-headed proposals the Navy's "coast defense" battleships of 1898 could scarcely have materialized in time to strike the blows for American empire when the moment for the first time became psychologically right.

In September 1886, Commander Sampson, now forty-six years of age, with his brown hair graying at the temples, was ordered to Annapolis as superintendent of the United States Naval Academy.

Sampson was one of the youngest officers ever assigned to this post. While his selection by Secretary Whitney was hailed by the *Army and Navy Journal* as "a conspicuous instance of the office seeking the man," the "well deserved honor" had probably been bestowed to afford him a rest from his strenuous labors and at the same time to keep him within commuting distance of Washington, where his assistance on technical problems was needed.[22]

Quite naturally the Naval Academy's science departments flourished during Sampson's tenure as superintendent. Professor Ira Remsen of Johns Hopkins University and other eminent scientists were brought to Annapolis to lecture to the midshipmen. Large orders of machine tools and of equipment for the blacksmith shop, the boiler shop and the pattern shop were procured. Never losing sight of the needs of the New Navy, Sampson took an interest in the Ordnance proving ground at Fort Severn, across the river from Annapolis, and in the Ordnance factory in Washington. Sampson presided at meetings of the U. S. Naval Institute when foremost scientists from all over the country discussed technical problems of the Machine Age.

Although summer practice cruises continued to be made by the midshipmen in ancient white-oak ships with superannuated engines and smoothbore cannon, Superintendent Sampson went repeatedly to Washington to ask Congress to appropriate funds for a modern cruiser with the latest model engines and the best rifled guns. Congress at length authorized the new training vessel.

Partly out of sheer frustration the midshipmen of the early 1880's had fallen into cheating and hazing. The "economy" law of 1882, which sought to reduce the number of officers by lengthening the Naval Academy course from four to six years and then by granting commissions to only a fraction of each graduating class, had undermined the morale of the midshipmen. A First Classman posted the answers to an examination and denied having committed the act. When it was announced that he had been given 22 demerits and deprived of his cadet rank, he was cheered by his classmates. Officers who disciplined those who had cheered the culprit were themselves hissed and booed. Hazing of plebes included pulling their noses, shaving one side of their heads, forcing them to drink bottles of ink and swinging them out of a third-story window in a blanket. One religiously inclined youth was stripped naked and made to preach a sermon. Various superintendents had tried to check these breaches of discipline with harsh punishment.[23]

Sampson's punishments were thorough, but he also sought to remove the chief cause of delinquency by urging Congress to abandon the six-year course in favor of the four-year one and by persuading the Navy Department to find for Academy graduates, not commissioned in the Navy, places in the revenue service, Coast Survey and related government activities. Sampson abolished the offensive demerit and conduct grade system, and substituted in its place a system of privileges based on conduct during the preceding month. Hazing in its worst forms disappeared into the limbo of tradition and was commemorated in the midshipmen's jocular ballad, "Hazing Plebes So Green."

During 25 years of inadequate naval appropriations, the dormitory buildings had fallen into decay. The so-called "New Quarters," jerry-built in 1866, represented the newest construction of living quarters in 30 years. The brick walls of the New Quarters, resting on "made" ground, had cracked from the third story to the basement and wide seams had opened in its flooring. It was impossible to heat the structure, and impossible to prevent odors of the kitchen and the laundry in the basement from permeating classrooms on the first deck and midshipmen's rooms on the two upper decks. Sampson replaced the building's worn-out flooring and won from Congress an appropriation for new buildings. He also after four years of persuasion acquired as an athletic field for midshipmen a triangle of land containing the unsightly gasworks of Annapolis and an area of slum shacks whose lack of sewage facilities had long threatened the health of the station.[24]

In March of 1889, during his final year in Annapolis, Commander Sampson was examined by a promotion board of rear admirals and former superintendents of the Naval Academy and was promoted to captain.

With four daughters just entering society to assist him, Sampson made headway in improving the social life of the Academy. Mrs. Sampson devoted somewhat less time than her daughters to social life, for the reason that during her husband's superintendency at the Naval Academy she bore him two sons, Ralph and Harold. The first child of Sampson's second marriage had died at four months. The second, and more robust boy, named Ralph Earle for a naval officer kinsman of Mrs. Sampson, was born on December 15, 1886, in the southeast room of the superintendent's quarters.

"Dear Auntie," Sampson wrote a member of the family the day following the stork's visit, "I know you will be pleased to hear that we have a fine boy. The big fellow (he weighs 12 lbs.) appeared yesterday morning about 3:30 o'clock. Bess got through in the very best manner and has since been very comfortable. She says if she has plenty of milk for the youngster she will have nothing left to wish for. Of course, we are greatly pleased. I must confide to you, however, that he is monstrously homely. I know Bess would never confess this, but I think that you should, as a near relative, know the true state of the case. You need not mention this when you write. She sends you lots of love and I hope will be able to write herself very soon. Yours affectionately, Robin."[25]

June Week following Ralph's birth was a busy one. The engagement of Margaret Sampson to Roy C. Smith was announced, and the Secretary of the Navy and Mrs. Whitney were guests of the superintendent and his wife. "Secretary and Mrs. Whitney arrived Friday morning," writes Mrs. Sampson, "They were the easiest possible people to entertain; and their being here gave us only pleasure. Friday after the address by President Gilman, the Secretary & Mrs. Whitney & Mrs. Dyer went to dine on the *Dispatch*. Robin & I were too tired to accept the invitation. From 4 to 6 the ladies and gentlemen throughout the Academy grounds were invited to come in and meet the Secretary & Mrs. Whitney. At half past six we had a pleasant supper; and at nine I was dressed and ready to go with Mr. Benham to receive at 'the June Ball.' It was a very handsome affair, nearly 2000 people can testify to that. The bouquet which the Class of '88 gave me was almost entirely of orchids."[26]

After delivering the opening lecture of the fall term at the Naval War College in Newport, Sampson hurried home to attend the wedding of his eldest daughter, in October 1887.

The eleven-months'-old son with whom Sampson now played ball every day as regular routine was growing into a healthy child. Old Sam Brown, a servant, noticing the child's "funny little mouth," made the discovery that he was tongue-tied and his parents at once had the cord cut. "Robin was also tongue tied, when a little fellow," wrote Mrs. Sampson. "He declared that he can remember being taken by his mother to the Dr.; and that he was still in long clothes!! We wish that his memory of recent events were as good." Again like his father, Ralph was fond of "snapping his thumb & forefinger, which in his Papa he admires greatly." He could make the motion all right, but the clicking noise he was forced to make with his mouth.

Commodore Dewey (*left*) at Manila Bay after the Fleet "Hauled off for Breakfast."

The Naval War Board. Sketch by T. V. Chominski. (From W. N. King's *Story of the Spanish-American War*, Peter Fenlon Collier & Son, N. Y., 1898.) *Left to right*: Mahan, Crowninshield, Long and Sicard.

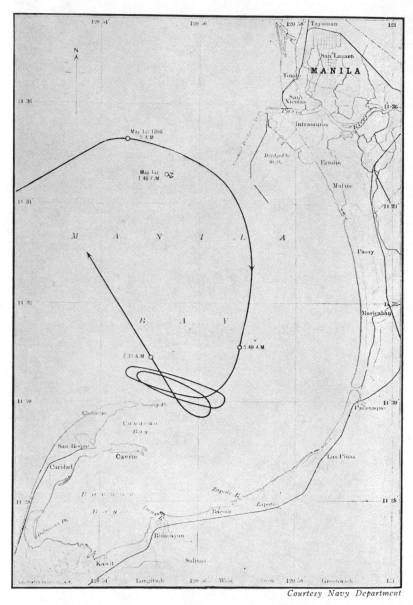

Track of Commodore Dewey's Squadron During the Battle of Manila Bay.

Margaret came home for her first confinement while her husband was at sea, and so fond was Superintendent Sampson of his new grandson that he postponed an inspection trip to Newport "because the little fellow was still so 'under the weather.' "

On November 14, 1889, while the Naval Academy was playing host to members of the Pan-American Congress and of the International Marine Conference then meeting in Washington, the Sampsons' last child, Harold, was born. "Harold's coming took us a little by surprise, as we had not invited him to the reception of Nov. 16. . . . His Papa was fortunately at home that night, and received him with due honor."

On November 23, 1889, on the eve of Sampson's departure for service afloat, the *Baltimore Sun* appraised his superintendency as "one of the best the institution has ever had. . . . Captain Sampson is a tall, straight man of 49, military in appearance and precise in everything he does. His executive skill has been of great service to the Academy." During a total of twelve years at the naval school on the Severn, the scientific spirit of William T. Sampson had become a part of the training of nearly every young officer who was to fight the New Navy in the War with Spain.

Part Three

THE NEW NAVY, 1890-1898

10. DEWEY TO THE ASIATIC

IN THE decades before the war with Spain it was not possible for American naval officers on duty around the globe to ignore the mounting importance of Europe's empire building.

France's conquest of Algeria was completed while Dewey and Sampson were junior officers on the Mediterranean Station in the 1860's. Twenty years later Captain Dewey of the *Pensacola* and Admiral S. R. Franklin over their whist table in Villefranche could discuss France's new venture in Tunis, with devout Mrs. Franklin possibly interjecting a hope that the back-country Berbers might profit spiritually through contact with their Christian conquerors. It happened that when Commander Schley visited Cape Town, Sir Bartle Frere, the colonial governor, was absent attending to the extension of Her Majesty's interests in Natal. In his absence Lady Frere saw to it that the American commander and his officers were entertained with excellent Constancia wines by the wealthy Van Clutes and Van Renans. Commander Schley noted only the attractive side of British imperialism in Cape Colony.

In strategically located Aden, at the mouth of the Red Sea, the ascetic Mahan winced at the squalor and filth of backward peoples. To Mahan it seemed that the British rulers had exercised a benevolent influence over such people. Nor could Mahan regret that China's thriving Treaty Ports had been pried open by force. The star of Cecil Rhodes was ascending as Mahan returned home via Europe. London music halls at this time echoed imperial rivalries in the jingle:

"We don't want to fight,
But by Jingo if we do,
We've got the ships, we've got the men,
We've got the money too."[1]

Henry Morton Stanley, after his trek across Africa in search of the Scottish explorer David Livingstone, stirred the imaginations of merchants and missionaries everywhere in his speech to the Manchester Chamber of Commerce: "There are forty millions of people beyond the gateway of the Congo, and the cotton-spinners of Manchester are waiting to clothe them. Birmingham foundries are glowing with the red metal that will presently be made into ironwork for them and the trinkets that shall adorn those dusky bosoms, and the ministers of Christ are zealous to bring them, the poor benighted heathen, into the Christian fold."[2]

In 1890 at the opening of the Mauve Decade the stage was set for America's own emergence as an empire. America's continental frontier had disappeared and her industrialists had begun their clamor for high tariffs to protect their domestic market. Westward, beyond the Pacific frontier, the sons of American missionaries had entered business and these John-the-Baptists of American empire had for many years been intriguing with the natives of Hawaii and Samoa and urging American naval officers and State Department officials to take steps to secure America's birthright overseas. Mahan's great book, *The Influence of Sea Power upon History*, was published in May 1890. In November the battleship *Maine* was launched. Benjamin F. Tracy, Harrison's Secretary of the Navy, obtained record-smashing appropriations for naval construction. The steel barons at Midvale, Bethlehem and Pittsburgh were building giant presses to forge armor plate for the New Navy. . . .

When Captain George Dewey at the age of fifty-one took the oath of office as chief of the Bureau of Equipment, there were no signs or portents whatever that ten years later he rather than another man would become the living symbol of American expansion overseas. New York papers published his portrait and retold the story of the new bureau chief's liver operation in Malta. "He is said to be a constant sufferer from the effects of the marvellous excision"; commented the *New York Herald*, "but by means of unremitting vigilance in the care of his health, he keeps up and around, does business at the Department about as regularly as anybody, and maintains, rather sedately though it be, a membership in the noted Metropolitan Club of Washington. He keeps a blooded horse on which he rides moderately every pleasant day, almost invariably alone, through the beautiful byways of Rock Creek."[3]

With ill health to handicap him, Dewey was compelled throughout the 1890's to lead a quiet, even pampered, existence. His bachelor's apartment on the third floor of the Hotel Everett, at 1830 H Street, N. W., was only a few blocks from his office. Other tenants in the Everett knew him as a quiet gentleman, affable but "unneighborly," who never came down to the common dining room but always ate breakfast alone in his parlor. Dewey arose every morning at six, scanned the papers, and precisely at eight his colored waiter brought his breakfast. Invariably this meal consisted of fruit, two soft-boiled eggs, orange marmalade and corn muffins. Domestically he was so completely a creature of habit, so prompt in payment of his rent and so opposed to a change in his servants that his chambermaid Rhoda Wilder after her promotion to housekeeper continued to care for Dewey's rooms. Rhoda rated him as her neatest tenant. "He never left a match on the floor, scrap of paper, or any of his clothing scattered about. He even hung up his nightshirt in its proper place, and his clothing for washing was always in the hamper. . . . He was what women would call a very 'easy man on his clothes.' "[4] Though a stickler for having his domestic wants cared for on an inflexible schedule, he was a pleasant and generous master, adored by his servants. Whenever his shirt needed mending, Dewey in violation of traditional New England thrift, gave it to one of the domestics.

Only one of his habits was reminiscent of his former impetuousness when he had scurried up the ratlines as an example to sailors. He would never wait for an elevator. In that great architectural monstrosity, the State, War and Navy Building, Captain Dewey climbed the marble stairs at an easy, regular pace.

After entering Captain Dewey's private office through a door hung with heavy portieres, a visitor would find a large, neat room with white walls, mahogany doors and a two-tone marble mantelpiece. In the center of the room stood an enormous mahogany desk. Scattered over and partially hiding the somewhat rococo Victorian drugget were small Persian rugs probably acquired by Dewey in the Levant. On the mantelpiece were the captain's binoculars, several small pictures of his family, a ship model and odds and ends of bric-a-brac. On the white walls were pictures of ships in neat frames. There was an air of easy comfort about the room. In winter Captain Dewey would hang his tweed coat in the dressing room and wear a woolen smoking jacket over the tweed waistcoat, which he kept buttoned almost up to his wing collar. In summer one might find him wearing a linen suit and the russet-yellow shoes which had caused such a stir when Dewey had first introduced them in Washington. According to Navy Department "scuttlebutt," the first day Dewey had worn them to the office the yellow shoes had become the jest of the officers in the Department. Early in the afternoon one of his feet began to swell, and the pain being acute he retreated to the chief clerk's office to loosen the strings but would not take them off. "I suppose I can't take these things off now," he remarked with a bitter smile, "for those fellows'll think they have driven me to it!"[5]

In his *Autobiography*, twenty years later, Dewey accurately recorded that there had been "nothing showy" about his four years in the Bureau of Equipment. "The detail was not exacting, but vitally engrossing and important."[6] Perhaps to lighten the duty for an officer whose health was uncertain, Secretary Tracy at the beginning of Dewey's tenure shifted the administration of recruiting and apprentice training to another bureau and assigned to Dewey the supervision of the Naval Observatory. To Dewey's desk came reports on the Nautical Almanac, the Commercial Time Service, the construction of the new Naval Observatory and the Eclipse Expedition. With these highly specialized matters he had little to do beyond digesting information for the Secretary's annual report. His prime concern was equipment, which included the outfitting of ships with anchors, chain cables, wire rigging, etc., and the procuring of coal. For surviving relics of the sail-steam Navy he provided fresh suits of sails, and for the new cruisers of the *Baltimore* class he wrestled with the desk work behind the installation of electrical and telephone systems. Compass compensation, a major difficulty on the new steel ships, was solved in part by two young inventors whom Dewey encouraged, Lieutenant S. W. B. Diehl and Ensign John Gibson.

From the diverse technical work of his bureau it is impossible to separate out for appraisal the personal contribution of the bureau chief. On the *Narragansett,* as surveyor of the Gulf of Lower California, Dewey had been schooled in thoroughness and scientific accuracy. He was a swift and canny observer. Abroad on the wooden *Pensacola* he had had many opportunities to observe the latest technological devices on foreign ships. His background for his job was certainly as good as that of the average officer of his age and rank.

As fate willed, however—since in garbled form the story later influenced Assistant Secretary Theodore Roosevelt to send Dewey to the Asiatic Station—Dewey's most important service as chief of the Bureau of Equipment was persuading Congress to make adequate appropriations for coal to run the New Navy. The essence of the story, with inaccuracies in details, is thus presented by Roosevelt in his *Autobiography:* "I had been struck by an incident in [Dewey's] past career. It was at a time when there was threat of trouble with Chile. Dewey was off the Argentine, and was told to get ready to move to the other coast of South America. If the move became necessary, he would have to have coal, and yet if he did not make the move, the coal would not be needed. In such a case a man afraid of responsibility always acts rigidly by the regulations and communicates with the Department at home to get authority for everything he does; and therefore he accomplishes nothing whatever, but is able to satisfy all individuals with red-tape minds by triumphantly pointing out his compliance with the regulations. In a crisis, the man worth his salt is the man who meets the needs of the situation in whatever way is necessary. Dewey purchased the coal and was ready to move at once if need arose. . . . I knew that in the event of war [with Spain] Dewey could be slipped like a wolf-hound from a leash; I was sure that if given half a chance he would strike instantly and with telling effect; and I made up my mind that all I could do to give him that half-chance should be done. . . ."[7]

So many character-revealing anecdotes were related of Dewey at each stage of his career that no one will ever know in what form the coal story was first told to Assistant Secretary Roosevelt, or what flourishes that story owes to the latter's imagination at the time he wrote it down. The facts are that Dewey never commanded a ship "off the Argentine," and that in 1891 when war with Chile over the *Baltimore* incident hung in the balance, Dewey was living quietly in Washington as chief of the Bureau of Equipment. Not niggling facts, however, but the impression the story made on Roosevelt's mind was important to history.

The real story of Dewey's procurement of coal was by no means unimpressive. When Dewey took charge, the bureau had an annual allotment of $625,000 with which to purchase both equipment for the vessels of the Navy and coal for ships and shore stations. Since the upturn in the Navy's fortunes in 1882 all the political energies of the Department had been directed to obtaining appropriations to build ships. The Equipment Bureau, charged with outfitting the new steel Navy, had been compelled to scrimp and salvage and manage to get by with its old lean-years' allotment. Equipment for the modern vessels—electric instead of oil lamps, wire instead of hemp ropes, steam-geared instead of hand-turned capstans—was more expensive than the trappings for wooden ships had been. The new ships, carrying less sail, and those of latest design, none at all, were increasingly dependent upon coal supply. Bureau Chief George Dewey at once declared war on this "most rigid, and in some instances unprofitable parsimony." In his annual reports for 1889 and 1890 Dewey presented to Congress and to the nation a fair and trenchant analysis of the situation that faced his bureau. He demanded, and obtained, a considerable increase in his allotment. Thus it came about that in 1891, when the Chilean difficulty occasioned an extraordinary amount of naval activity on the Pacific coast, Dewey could supply the ships with the necessary coal. On these facts the story which Theodore Roosevelt heard was based.

Dewey was a member of Washington's Metropolitan Club. After Admiral Porter's death in 1891 the club purchased the admiral's fine three-story mansion at 1710 H Street which was a few doors down the street from Dewey's apartment house, and here Dewey took his noon and evening meals. At the club he played a good game of whist or poker and was moderately skilled at billiards and pool. His friends often referred to him as "the man without a liver," "not a good liver but a good half-liver," "Dewey with half a liver which is better than

none at all." But the most flattering bon mot on this soon-hackneyed
subject was the remark of a rear admiral, "I don't know how much
liver Dewey lost, but of what he has left not one atom is white!"[8] At
no little cost to his own health Captain Dewey the widower supervised
the cuisine of the Metropolitan Club, and endeared himself to his fellows.

Both as chief of a naval bureau at a time when naval affairs were
gaining attention and as a prominent citizen in Washington society,
George Dewey was often mentioned in the press. The chief of the
Bureau of Equipment was noted as returning from a month's vacation
in the mountains of New Hampshire "looking brown and hearty."
The chief was "called to Florida on Monday last by a telegram from
his sister announcing the dangerous illness of her husband." On November 19, 1892, the *Army and Navy Journal* reported that Captain
Dewey had "been confined to his room for several days past as a result
of a recent accident while horseback riding. He was thrown from his
horse by reason of the animal stumbling over a stone, and, falling on his
head, became unconscious. He soon recovered from the shock, however, and mounting his horse returned to his quarters at the 'Everett,'
where he is nursing a sprained wrist, which, luckily, is the only damage
done to body or limb."[9]

For Dewey to fall from his horse was a blow to Ben Harris' pride.
Ben was an ancient Negro messenger at the Navy Department who
served as Dewey's stable boy and admired the "mighty fine" corduroy
riding habit with shining boots and spurs which he might one day in-
herit from the captain. Ben delighted in the fact that Dewey sat a
horse not like a sailor at all, but like a cavalry officer.

At the end of his four-year term in the bureau in 1893, Dewey's
naval career reached its low-water mark. For the next two years he
served as president of the Lighthouse Board. Dewey's service as lighthouse inspector while a junior officer during the naval depression of
the 1870's had been nothing out of the ordinary; but now, in his prime
at 56, and during the most interesting naval renaissance in 50 years, to
be shunted out of the Navy into a post *under the Treasury Department*—even into so dignified a berth as that of the president of the
Lighthouse Board—was an anticlimax.

In a visit to Montpelier about this time Captain Dewey confided his
disappointment to his friend Judge Fifield: "Judge, you have had a

successful record as a lawyer; you are known in this State as having accomplished something, and you can be satisfied with what you have done. With me it is somewhat different. I have always worked faithfully in the Navy, and trained myself for what responsibilities might come; but I am approaching rapidly the years of retirement and will soon be out of it all, with nothing to my credit but gradual and honorable promotion. I do not want war, but without it there is little opportunity for a naval man to distinguish himself. There will be no war before I retire from the Navy, and I will simply join the great majority of naval men, and be known in history only by consultation of the records of the Navy Department as 'George Dewey who entered the Navy at a certain date and retired as Rear Admiral at the age limit!' "[10]

As often as his duties permitted Dewey visited his sister Mrs. Mary P. Greeley, a widow living in Montpelier, and his son, George Goodwin Dewey, twenty-one and a student at Princeton. Captain Dewey, for two decades a widower, scarcely knew his son who had been reared by his maternal grandmother and an aunt in Portsmouth.

In 1895 Dewey's fortune as a professional naval officer began to mend with his assignment as president of the Board of Inspection and Survey. "This," as Dewey rightly notes in his *Autobiography*, "was a very important duty," for the Board of Inspection and Survey supervised the final trials of the new "coast defense" battleships. "Ours was the responsibility that the construction from stem to stern was sound and that the builders kept the letter of the specifications."[11] The specifications were most exacting. The United States might have acquired her New Navy many years sooner had she been willing to purchase her ships abroad. Her fleet was delayed, however, by Congressional insistence that home industry be patronized and by the fact that before modern armor plate could be produced there must come entirely new industrial plants and testing laboratories especially designed for this purpose. Most exasperating delays had set back the building program. The *Maine*, though launched in 1890, had to wait three years for her American-built armor to be completed. Dewey as president of the Board of Inspection and Survey witnessed her final trials in Newport Harbor and made a special trip to the Navy Department to urge her acceptance despite a minor flaw—the freezing of her hydraulic gun controls—which had developed during the trial. The *Maine* was our first modern battleship.

Dewey continued with the Inspection Board for another year and thus he "presided," as he expressed it, "at the trials of the *Texas, Maine, Iowa, Indiana,* and *Massachusetts*—all the battleships except the *Oregon* which were to demolish the Spanish squadron at Santiago."[12]

Newspaper comments on Dewey at this time reveal something of his service reputation and character as a naval officer. "He has never had the reputation of being a specially studious officer; indeed his reputation has been rather that of a society man." He "has certainly never been a plodding student, seeking like the little busy bee to improve the shining hour." "It is told of him that when a member of a board on torpedoes he saw so much more in the course of the experiments, and took in so much knowledge by a process of mental absorption, that he was able to make a better report on the subject than others who had been 'boning up on torpedoes.' "[13] Clearly Theodore Roosevelt's impression that Commodore Dewey did not have a red-tape mind was an impression generally held throughout the service.

He was widely known as a Beau Brummell, whose hat was blocked every day and whose trousers always had the proper crease; an all-around good fellow, who loved to listen to and to tell a good story. According to report he had a "due appreciation of his own humor, joining heartily in the laugh his jests excite." He was "exact, not to say finical in matters of form."[14] Once he sent for a young officer who had failed to salute properly when he went aboard ship and gave him a brisk lecture on naval etiquette which he never forgot. Another time Dewey called to account a staff officer who obeyed an order to appear in white trousers by wearing a pair of flannels having a tint of yellow in them. Colorful anecdotes from Dewey's earlier years in the wood-sail Navy were current in Washington when young Theodore Roosevelt was casting about for an officer to command the Asiatic Station, and these stories no doubt entered into the Assistant Secretary's rough and ready conception of Dewey's fitness as a fighting officer. One was the probably apocryphal tale of how Dewey had quelled a mutiny on board the *Dolphin.* A young seaman, according to the story, had refused to obey an officer's order and was reported to Captain Dewey. Dewey went on deck, looked the seaman in the eye a minute and explained that failure to obey an order was mutiny. The sailor maintaining a silent rebellion, Dewey ordered a file of marines to load their rifles. "I will now give five minutes to execute that order," Dewey announced, and, after taking out his watch, began to call off the minutes. The sailor reddened and clenched his fists, but at the count of "four" marched off to obey the order.[15] A retired sea captain, John H. Buckman, who had once sailed with Dewey, related the following: A group of Irish laborers had been sent to Dewey's ship as seamen. Dewey ordered them aloft, but they refused to go, apparently afraid to risk their necks so far from deck. Dewey thought this over a moment and sent out to a store for half a dozen hods. When they were obtained, he ordered the Irishmen to carry bricks to one of the crosspieces and lay them there. Buckman and his comrades were amazed at the alacrity with which the men, hods over their shoulders, climbed aloft.[16]

Immediately after his promotion to commodore on June 17, 1896, Dewey applied for sea duty in the Pacific. The *Army and Navy Journal* on June 20 predicted that he would shortly be given this assignment. Yet months dragged by. In November he wrote impatiently, "No orders to sea for me yet, and probably none will come before Spring unless we have a brush with Spain, which is not likely."[17] His saddle horse no longer pleased him. Dewey gave the animal away. "There is nothing new with me," he wrote his sister Mary on November 30. "I lead a very quiet life, reading a great deal and getting my exercise by walking."[18]

In the spring of 1897, after McKinley's administration had begun, Dewey was still waiting for his command afloat and marking time on the Board of Inspection. In May he noted: "Tomorrow I go to Bridgeport to try another new warship, the 'Nashville,' and soon after to Bath, Maine, to try another."[19]

In July when it became known that there would be a vacancy on the Asiatic Station in December, Dewey at once applied for this duty. So also at the same time did Commodore John Adams Howell. Howell, a member of Dewey's class at the Naval Academy, and distinguished for his invention of the Howell Torpedo which the Navy had accepted, stood one number ahead of Dewey on the Navy list. What worried Dewey was that the officer responsible for the distribution of assignments, Captain A. S. Crowninshield, chief of the Bureau of Navigation, was, as Dewey saw him, "a pronounced bureaucrat, with whose temperament and methods I had little more sympathy than had the majority of officers of the Navy at that time." Crowninshield, an officer of scholarly and scientific bent who moved in the circle of Sampson and Chadwick, was inclined to favor Howell; and, as Dewey bitterly wrote, "He would hardly recommend me to any command; and his advice had great weight with John D. Long, who was then Secretary of the Navy."[20] But happily for Dewey, Theodore Roosevelt was the Assistant Secretary.

By 1899, when Dewey was on his way home from the Philippines, a curious story was making the rounds in naval circles. As this story ran, the day Dewey received his orders to the Asiatic Station, "he went to the Secretary and said, in the velvety voice that with him indicates suppressed passion: 'Mr. Secretary, you listened to a story to my discredit coming from a damned liar and slanderer. I did not like this yesterday, and I don't like it any better today. Good morning, Sir!' " "The officer referred to by Admiral Dewey," amplified the *Army and Navy Journal*, "has the reputation of being a wholesome hater, and others complain of having been made the victim of his disposition to settle old scores."[21]

Here, as in most Dewey anecdotes, a grain of truth is hidden in two bushels of chaff and is not easy to find. The three memoirs left by the principals in the case—Secretary John D. Long, Assistant Secretary Theodore Roosevelt and Commodore Dewey—while perforce agreeing on the fact of Dewey's appointment, bristle with contradictions in minor details.

Each of the principals, we may be sure, desired the approval of posterity. Long, a conscientious politician from Massachusetts, was kept in such a perpetual state of trepidation by the vigorous, red-blooded warmongering of his Assistant Secretary that his reliability as a historian suffers. Roosevelt, the fire-eating imperialist, fearful lest America lose her place in the sun through plutocratic, fatty degeneration of the warlike spirit, was a Procrustean historian and a notorious distorter of fact. Of the three, George Dewey has left perhaps the most trustworthy record of the crucial moment of his selection to command the Asiatic Station. Dewey's narrative reveals the following:[22]

Roosevelt, having investigated the two candidates, declared his belief that Dewey ought to have the Asiatic Squadron. "I want you to go. You are the man who will be equal to the emergency if one arises. Do you know any Senators?"

Dewey, after expressing "a natural disinclination" to use such influence, admitted that Senator Redfield Proctor from Vermont was a friend of his family.

"You could not have a better sponsor." Roosevelt now informed Dewey that "one letter from an influential source in favor of Howell had already been received by the Department." The Assistant Secretary urged Dewey to lose no time in having the Senator speak a word for him.

"I went immediately to see Senator Proctor, who was delighted that I had mentioned the matter to him. That very day he called on President McKinley and received the promise of the appointment before he left the White House.

"When I next met Crowninshield he told me that, although I was to have the appointment—a fact which did not seem to please him any too well—Secretary Long was indignant because I had used political influence to obtain it. I went at once to see Mr. Long, and said to him:

" 'Mr. Secretary, I understand that you are displeased with me for having used influence to secure command of the Asiatic Squadron. I did so because it was the only way of offsetting influence that was being exerted on another officer's behalf.'

" 'You are in error, commodore,' said Mr. Long. 'No influence has been brought to bear on behalf of any one else.'

"Only a few hours later, however, Mr. Long sent me a note in which he said that he had just found that a letter had been received at the Department which he had seen for the first time. It had arrived while he was absent from the office and while Mr. Roosevelt was acting secretary, and had only just been brought to his attention." The *deus ex machina* who held up the Howell recommendation until after Dewey had been selected was undoubtedly the amazing and somewhat preposterous human dynamo in the assistant secretary's office.

Dewey's detachment from duty as president of the Board of Inspection and Survey and his orders to relieve Rear Admiral McNair in the Far East were signed by the Secretary on October 21, 1897. War with Spain was threatening, yet to all appearances not imminent.

"Yes I am to be congratulated," Dewey wrote on November 1, in response to a note from a relative, "as I have received what is *to me* the best gift the President could make. I leave here about the twenty-seventh of this month and sail from San Francisco by steamer of 7th of December. Expect to join my flagship *Olympia* at Yokohama about Christmas. I go out as Commodore, and will not receive my promotion to Rear Admiral until next summer, a new rule to that effect having been recently made."[23] Rightly or wrongly Dewey felt that the new rule, which barred him from hoisting an acting rear admiral's pennant, was spite work on the part of those who had opposed his selection. He was approaching sixty and he was hypersensitive on matters of rank or personal prerogative. He might very well have stormed into Secretary Long's office and vented his anger in a low furry voice, according to the story later printed in the *Army and Navy Journal*. His friends, at any rate, attempted to lessen the "personally unpleasant" "little pin-pricking slight" when they reminded him that Matthew C. Perry, the only one of his predecessors to win fame on the Asiatic Station, had also held the rank of commodore. . . .[24]

On the evening of November 23, a week before his departure for San Francisco, the swank Metropolitan Club gave him a farewell banquet. After the clinking of glasses subsided and cigar smoke was peacefully curling upward, Colonel Archibald Hopkins, clerk of the Court of Claims and a good friend of Dewey's, arose and declaimed a rousing farewell:

> "Fill all your glasses full tonight;
>   The wind is off the shore,
> And, be it feast or be it fight,
>   We pledge the Commodore.
>
> "Through days of storm, through days of calm,
>   On board Pacific seas,
> At anchor off the isles of Palm,
>   Or with the Japanese.
>
> "Ashore, afloat, on deck, below,
>   Or where our bulldogs roar,
> To back a friend or beat a foe,
>   We pledge the Commodore.
>
> "We know our honor'll be unstained,
>   Where'er his pennant flies;
> Our right respected and maintained,
>   Whatever power defies.
>
> "And when he takes the homeward tack,
>   Beneath an Admiral's flag,
> We'll hail the day that brings him back,
>   And have another jag."[25]

11. MENTOR TO IMPERIALISTS

DURING a year of "exile," Captain Mahan as president of a board of naval officers helped to choose the site for a new naval base near Seattle. From this duty he returned East in the summer of 1889, refreshed from his vacation in the open air and glad to get back to his books. In the fall term he lectured at the War College.

Secretary Whitney, lately the nemesis who had interrupted Mahan's work at the War College, had been supplanted in Washington by an aggressive, forward-looking New York lawyer, Benjamin F. Tracy. To Mahan's immense good fortune Tracy was a zealous advocate of naval expansion. One of Tracy's first acts was to incorporate Mahan's ideas about a battleship navy in his first annual report as a means of persuading Congress to appropriate for such a force.

Benjamin F. Tracy was the first politician in high office to adopt Mahan's doctrine as a program of action and thus deserves to stand in the front rank of American expansionists. In 1889 while Henry Cabot Lodge was yet a junior Senator with his program unformed, while Theodore Roosevelt was but a young and uncomfortably active member of the Civil Service Commission, Secretary of the Navy Tracy held the executive post most vital to the achievement of America's place in the sun. He wanted battleships. He wanted overseas bases. He wanted colonial empire. Secretly in 1890 he had Mahan and Captain Folger draw up plans for naval operations in case of war with Spain and at some length discussed with Mahan the "general question of Pacific Coast operations."[1] The spectacular Samoan hurricane, which drove three old-fashioned American warships on the rocks and in one blow all but wiped out our Pacific fleet, was utilized by Secretary Tracy as a tragic demonstration of our naval weakness. The blackness was suitably highlighted with stories of personal courage of our officers and seamen. Taken together, Mahan's ideas, the hurricane and Secretary Tracy's driving energy bore fruit in the epochal appropriation for three of the heaviest battleships, the so-called "seagoing, coast-line" battleships *Indiana, Massachusetts* and *Oregon*.

Through his friend Professor James Russell Soley, lecturer on International Law at the War College, Mahan found a publisher (Little, Brown and Company) for his first series of lectures on the influence of sea power. In January of 1890, Secretary Tracy's new home on Farragut Square burned down. Mrs. Tracy and a daughter were burned to death; Secretary Tracy himself, though overcome by smoke, was rescued. Tracy's subsequent near-breakdown led him to revive the office of Assistant Secretary of the Navy, and Mahan was pleased when this post was given to his colleague Professor Soley.

With two warm friends of the War College at the head of the Navy Department and with his book on sea power, which was about to come off the press—to carry the War College fight to the nation as a whole—Mahan hoped against hope that Congress might appropriate money for a new War College building and thus bring the institution literally out of the poorhouse. The publishing date for *The Influence of Sea Power upon History, 1660-1783* was May 13, 1890.[2]

Civil Service Commissioner Theodore Roosevelt reviewed the book for the *Atlantic Monthly*. "My dear Captain Mahan," exulted Roosevelt in a letter on May 12, "During the last two days I have spent half my time, busy as I am, in reading your book; and that I found it interesting is shown by the fact that having taken it up I have gone straight through and finished it."[3] Roosevelt, now a combative young man of thirty-one, wished that the Navy's enemies in Congress would read it.

Mahan inscribed one of the first copies to his friend Admiral Luce, thanking him for having supplied the original "impulse" for the book, and at once Mahan set himself the task of writing a sequel dealing with sea power during the French Revolution and the Napoleonic era.[4] In the summer Congress appropriated the necessary funds for a new War College building. Mahan, given nominal duty as supervisor of the building's construction, was enabled to spend most of the time in the New York libraries. His time—to the dismay or envy of many an old sea dog—was now completely his own to devote to scholarship, as in 1890 and 1891 no sessions of the college were held. Ground was broken for the new building on September 14, 1891. On the crest of the hill on Coaster's Harbor Island, some hundred yards west of the old poorhouse, the new granite structure materialized. It was 210 feet long and 48 deep, with three stories and a basement. Two of its 100 rooms were lecture halls, 45 by 35 feet, with sky-lighted ceilings 22 feet high.

Mahan's reputation as a naval strategist and imperialist was growing rapidly. The *Army and Navy Journal,* while according only mild praise for Mahan's first sea-power book, quoted Mahan on Caribbean interests and American naval policy: "The motive, if any there be, which will give the United States a Navy, is probably now quickening in the Central American Isthmus. Let us hope it will not come to the birth too late."[5] Impressed by Theodore Roosevelt's glowing review, the *Atlantic Monthly* asked Mahan to write an article on naval policy. Mahan's "The United States Looking Outward," appeared in the December issue. The article was pitched in a strongly imperialistic key: "beyond the broad seas, there are the markets of the world, that can be entered and controlled only by a vigorous contest . . . it is safe to predict, that when the opportunities for gain abroad are understood, the course of American enterprise will cleave a channel by which to reach them." In Haiti, Central America and Hawaii there were "dangerous germs of quarrel, against which it is prudent at least to be prepared." Open a canal at Panama; and the Caribbean, "this now comparatively deserted nook of the ocean, will become, like the Red Sea, a great thoroughfare of shipping, and will attract, as never before in our day, the interest and ambition of maritime nations."[6] Thus was the stuff and marrow of imperialist doctrine flung to a wide audience beyond the elite circle of Tracy, Roosevelt and Lodge.

In the fall of 1891, when the *Baltimore* affair threatened to involve the United States in war with Chile, Mahan was called in as a member of a strategy board with Assistant Secretary Soley and officers of the Bureau of Intelligence. Mahan, who held a high opinion of the German General Staff and hoped that the Navy Department would set up a similar body, was displeased to find that the Secretary wanted merely informal consultation. "I was . . . directed to study the military side of the question, to be ready to prepare plans, or to express opinions, as a result of my reflections; but Mr. Tracy kept matters in his own hands, consulted when he wished to consult, and acted without consultation as he chose. . . . Occasionally, once or twice, I gave brief written expression to my views; but these were simply memoranda, and I do not think they ever went on file."[7] The war scare subsided and in the summer of 1892, the new building made of gleaming Fall River granite having been completed, Mahan was assigned duty as president of the War College.

Seven years after it was founded the college's existence was still being deplored by the Old Guard as an intellectual frill, and Mahan as its guiding genius was still being denounced as an impractical theorist.

"Do you expect a session of the College this year?" an officer stopped Mahan on the steps of a Washington club to inquire. Mahan replied that he hoped so. "Well, are you going to do anything practical?" "What do you mean by practical?" snapped Mahan. "Torpedo boats and launches and that sort of thing." On every hand Mahan received gratuitous advice. "If you want to attract officers to the College," counseled a cynic, "give them something that will help them pass their next examination."[8]

In the summer of 1892 Mahan's first biography, *Admiral Farragut*, appeared; and in December, after a season's use of the material as lectures at the War College, came the second sea-power book, under the ponderous title *The Influence of Sea Power upon the French Revolution and Empire, 1793-1812*. "If the children do not exactly cry for it, they may possibly cry for the mothers whose attention is absorbed by its fascinating pages," playfully observed the *Army and Navy Gazette* of London.[9] Together, the two sea-power books took England by storm. The *Edinburgh Review* hailed Mahan's writing as "a splendid apotheosis of English courage, of English skill and of

English power," a book important "to the statesman, the administrator, the ship owner, the merchant and the tradesman, equally with the naval officer."[10] The *Army and Navy Journal* noted that Mahan's "two books have done much to restore our [United States] naval prestige. . . . If the College had done nothing more than to inspire these admirable studies in naval history it would have fully justified its existence."[11]

Mahan now saw "a fair promise of success in professional writing," in which he found he had become "exceedingly interested."[12] But along with this came the dark prospect of sea duty. If he could avoid sea duty until 1896, he might retire under the forty-year law. President Harrison had lost the November election, however, and Mahan's friends Tracy and Soley left the Navy Department in March 1893.

In April Mahan learned that the chief of the Bureau of Navigation had slated him to command the *Chicago*, the flagship of the European Squadron. The chief was Commodore F. M. Ramsey, for six years an influential and avowed opponent of the War College; and the flag officer under whom Mahan was to serve was Rear Admiral Henry Erben. "Bully" Erben was a jolly seaman, "not a squarer toed" man in the Navy. A Naval Academy graduate, he seemed more like "a midshipman who had been brought up in the steerage in the time of Marryat or even Smollett."[13] He was widely known for his bumptious sense of humor, and he was a two-fisted admiral. As a junior officer on the eve of the Civil War, he had engaged in a hand-to-hand clinch with a pro-Secessionist officer and had rolled over and over down a staircase at the Pensacola Navy Yard without loosening his grip on his opponent. He was famous for making a world-girdling cruise in the old *Pensacola* and for his cleverness as an after-dinner speaker. Erben was, indeed, everything that the reserved Mahan was not. Like Ramsey, Erben considered the War College unnecessary and believed that scribbling books was not part of a naval officer's job.

Mahan in desperation called upon relatives, friends and publishers to use their influence with the Navy Department. Unhappily for Mahan, Hilary A. Herbert, the new Secretary, had been the chairman of the House Naval Committee which, four years before, had been chiefly responsible for killing the college's appropriation.

Theodore Roosevelt jumped into action at Mahan's request. On April 30 he held a "solemn council of war" with Senator Lodge,

Admiral Charles Henry Davis and Admiral Luce. Taking advantage of a temporary absence of the Secretary, Roosevelt approached the "more civilized" Mr. MacAdoo, the Assistant Secretary, and besought the adamant Commodore Ramsey to shift Mahan into some sinecure like the command of the Civil War monitor *Miantonomah*, in which his duties would be nominal. Roosevelt was not encouraged. "I fear all hope for the Naval College *(which is nothing without you)* has gone; our prize idiots have thrown away the chance to give us an absolutely unique position in Naval affairs; but I made a very strong bid to at least give you the *Miantonomah*. The *obstacle is of course Ramsay*, who is bitterly opposing it, or anything else that will help you; he is a blind, narrow, mean, jealous pedant; if I can ever do him a bad turn I most certainly will and I'll see that Lodge does. Lodge will see Herbert about the *Miantonomah* business."[14]

A few days later Mahan's younger brother Frederick, an Army engineer stationed in Washington, relayed hopeful rumors: "My dear Alf,—There was a reporter in here yesterday who told me that he had learned at the Navy Department that your orders for sea would not go into effect for a year yet. . . . I met Dewey this morning and he tells me that there has been a tremendous pressure brought to bear from naval officers themselves to keep you on shore . . ."[15]

The pressure failed in the desired effect. On the afternoon of May 11, 1893, Alfred Mahan, having been granted no reprieve from sea duty, took command of the U. S. S. *Chicago* in North River off Seventieth Street, New York. He did not know whether he should be able to continue his writing and at the same time manage the ship. He wanted to carry his sea-power series through the War of 1812, and he wanted also to do a biography of Lord Nelson. "I am forced daily to realize that I am growing old," he wrote Ashe in discouragement, "and especially that all charm ship life ever had is utterly gone. . . ."[16] Mahan put the *Chicago* into drydock to check the hull. In June Admiral Erben hoisted his flag and the *Chicago* bearing her scarcely compatible admiral and captain set out for Europe.

Mahan, fearing that his late efforts to avoid sea duty boded no good for his relations with Admiral Erben, minded his naval *p*'s and *q*'s by being always on deck when the ship came about or passed another ship. To Ensign John M. Ellicott, who occasionally fell into step with the "tall and spare" captain as he paced the quarter-deck during the "first dog watch" (4:00 to 6:00 P. M.), Mahan seemed "courteous, yet always aloof; uninterested in the interior details of ship keeping and crew drilling, and always intensive and scholarly in his conversation. I could readily understand how he could be looked upon by the average naval officer of that day as a crank."[17] Mahan's unusually frequent collision drills convinced Ellicott that he was obsessed with fear of collision. Admiral Erben, "a very quick-tempered man, even over trifles, and sometimes profanely explosive in his tempers," regarded Mahan as hesitant and indecisive and on several occasions could not refrain from back-seat driving.[18]

One day, in approaching a collier, Mahan put the *Chicago's* helm this way and that several times and each time he veered away the craft ahead yawed about to a collision course.

"Damn it, Mahan!" Erben blurted out, "Show him your nose and then hold your course. He'll get out of your way."[19]

Mahan set the ship on her original course, turned her over to Ellicott with orders to "maintain our present course" and left the bridge.

Another time Mahan was maneuvering the ship in a crowded harbor. Erben on the quarter-deck shouted a "brusque message" for Ellicott to carry to the captain who was forward on the bridge. Before Ensign Ellicott could repeat the message Mahan checked him: "Don't distress yourself by repeating that message, sir. I heard it."[20]

For a while Mahan attempted to write in the evenings. He was 53 and did not wish to get out of the swing of writing and lose his new-found career. To that end he had brought along a considerable library. In fact the bookshelves Mahan had constructed against the normally removable bulkhead between his cabin and Erben's prohibited firing practice with one of the cruiser's five-inch guns—a circumstance that began to look worse and worse to Admiral Erben as time wore on. There was a story that Admiral Erben placed several cages of canaries on his side of this partition to drown the scratching of Mahan's pen.[21] After a time the pen scratched less and less reguarly. "Neither a ship nor a book is patient of a rival," Mahan concluded sorrowfully and gave up attempting to write on shipboard.

Mahan and Erben got along moderately well during their first six months in Europe. The mayor of Queenstown, Ireland, entertained "Erbyne" and "Mahon" with a pleasant trip to Blarney Castle. The First Lord of the Admiralty gave a state dinner in London for Admiral

Erben and Captain Mahan at which many ranking naval officers and government officials were present. There followed an endless stream of invitations, but few of which could be accepted, and many of which included Admiral Erben only out of courtesy. As Lord Rosebery remarked to Mahan, the situation of his admiral was somewhat like that of a chaperone who accompanies a popular debutante. There were *faux pas* made when the admiral was inexcusably ignored, but if one may judge from Erben's version of one such affair, he was capable of straightening things out with tact and humor.[22]

"Captain Mahan at Portsmouth brought to me in my cabin a personal invitation to him from H. R. H. the Duke of York to a banquet on shore a day or two afterward. This invitation was simply a deserved compliment to Captain Mahan's writings, but, of course, it was strictly contrary to naval etiquette, and Captain Mahan was troubled.

"He said, 'Admiral, what shall I do about this?' and I replied, 'Leave it with me, I'll answer it.' And I answered it something in this wise:

" 'Rear Admiral Erben, U.S.N., presents his compliments to H. R. H. the Duke of York, and begs to acknowledge the receipt of an invitation to his flag captain, Captain Mahan. Rear Admiral Erben regrets to state that Captain Mahan is on the sick list.'

"Well, sir, my boat had hardly had time to get ashore with that message when another boat came off from shore with an invitation for me to this banquet, quite in correct form, and I answered something like this:

" 'Rear Admiral Erben, U.S.N., presents his compliments to H. R. H. the Duke of York and accepts with pleasure H. R. H.'s invitation to a dinner on the ——— instant. P.S.—Rear Admiral Erben informs H. R. H. the Duke of York that for this occasion he has taken Captain Mahan off the sick list.' "

Playing second fiddle, however, was scarcely to the admiral's taste. No doubt he was pleased to escape from English seas to spend the winter in the Mediterranean; while Mahan, for all his honors, considered his command of the flagship "an uncompensated bore." To a member of his family Mahan confided, "Erben is as little trouble as possible, I suppose; but as Admiral there is practically nothing to do except visiting on this ridiculous station; so he is a kind of supernumerary Captain, to fret himself by trifles and talk shop."[23]

A trifle which annoyed the admiral was the shabbiness of the Marines' uniforms. Erben wrote Mahan a formal order: "You will please direct Captain W. F. Spicer, U.S.M.C., to make a written report to me as to the shabby appearance of the marine guard of this ship."[24] The fault, as Spicer satisfactorily explained, lay in the poor quality of the government-issued clothing and in the fact that only 27 of the 39 men in the guard had been equipped with the new-style red shoulder knots when they joined the ship; the remainder, as yet, had been unable to replace their old-style yellow epaulettes.

From the correspondence which Erben sent to Washington, it is clear that Erben was aiming his fury at the Navy Department rather than at Mahan. The captain, however, sensitive on other scores and considering that a good share of it was directed at himself personally, retaliated by keeping notes on the admiral's own personal appearance! "On Sunday, February 25, leaving Naples, the Admiral was on deck without a cravat at all—and blouse one button (the 2nd) only buttoned. I make this note, not to attack him but to defend myself if attacked, as, e.g., he criticized much smaller matters of men's uniforms. This is not the first time. A.T.M."[25]

The open break came in January 1894, when Erben reported Mahan to the Navy Department as "an inefficient commander." Mahan requested the Navy Department to hold a court of inquiry to investigate his fitness. In Washington, meanwhile, Roosevelt and Lodge had made headway with Secretary Herbert. The Secretary had been induced to read Mahan's books and together with Roosevelt and Lodge was now actively opposing Mahan's chief enemy, Commodore Ramsey.[26] When Erben's complaint came in, the Secretary pigeonholed it as quietly as possible. The New York Tribune, however, carried the full story on April 6, 1894, under the headline COMMODORE ERBEN AND CAPTAIN MAHAN AT ODDS. "Officers who know both," concluded the Tribune, "say: the two officers are as unlike in nature as it is possible for two men to be. Erben is an old salt who attaches much importance to details of his command. Mahan is an officer of marked ability but he is more of a student than a sailor."

Mahan and Erben did a neat job of concealing their animosity toward each other from the ever-present public in foreign countries, a feat most necessary in the spring of 1894 when the Chicago returned to northern European waters for a further round of naval-diplomatic amenities. As flagship of the squadron and as one of the first ships of the New American Navy, the gleaming white cruiser was everywhere an object of attention. For several weeks while she was anchored off Gravesend, the town in her honor was bedecked with United States flags, and harbor boatmen reaped "small fortunes" from carrying out sightseers to circle around the *Chicago*.

British naval leaders, made uneasy by Germany's new naval building program, sought to extract from Mahan some statement which would serve to popularize their own increased program. Mahan declined to comment specifically on the Admiralty's plans, but he more than satisfied his interviewers with his pronouncements that naval power was now more vital to Britain than ever and that "the future of naval warfare rests upon the battleship."

"Captain Mahan is the greatest living writer on naval history," affirmed the *London Times*. "The entertainment which will be offered to him and his brother officers will be . . . a spontaneous welcome by the nation to the writer who told the story of its naval achievements with philosophic and strategic insight, which while it explains the fate of nations in the past, goes far to determine it in the future."[27]

Banquets tendered by Mahan's London publishers and by naval officers and statesmen were all eclipsed by the dinner at St. James's Hall on May 24, 1894, on the occasion of Queen Victoria's seventy-fifth birthday. The hall of state was decorated with the American and the British colors. The legend BLOOD IS THICKER THAN WATER surmounted the orchestra stand. Ambassador Bayard and Admiral Erben made brief speeches. Mahan then read an address and acknowledged the cheerful assistance in his research which had been given him by his British friends. At the end he proposed the toast that Britain's future be "as beneficent as its past has been glorious."[28]

On June 2 Mahan became the first foreigner to be entertained by the exclusive "Royal Navy Club of 1765 and 1785." Since Erben at the time was obligingly indisposed, Mahan had the field to himself and enjoyed it. "You may imagine," he wrote Mrs. Mahan, "I was somewhat overwhelmed at being greeted by a hundred British admirals and captains. I think it was perhaps the most spontaneous and affecting testimonial I received while in England."[29]

The British press in general dropped all reserve in praising Mahan for his understanding of British character and for his cementing of

Anglo-American friendship. In all London only one paper seasoned its judgment with mild criticism. "Captain Mahan," reported the *Pall Mall Gazette*, "who was the central figure at the banquet, the man at whom everybody talked and about whom everybody, except a few, thought, spoke well, but he does not speak as well as he writes. He knew what he was going to say, and he said it, but he said it in a manner that was prejudicial to enthusiasm."[30]

Not since Admiral Farragut's triumphal tour of Europe after the Civil War had an American received such ovations. The *Boston Advertiser*, noting that some of Mahan's brother officers were inclined to be cynical about the feting of Mahan by the British, observed that "Englishmen recognize now that the American Navy is growing and is now powerful and becoming more powerful every day . . . it would be for the interest of John Bull to simulate a friendly feeling for us, even if he does not feel it."[31] Said the *Army and Navy Journal*, "What a stomach for flattery our good cousin John Bull has. To recognize his merit is to establish your reputation upon the enduring basis of Anglo-Saxon approval."[32] There was, it is true, a group of Englishmen in high position seeking an alliance with America at this time, and Mahan's visits to England gave a real fillip to their agitation in that direction. The big-navy advocates in their celebrations for Mahan were not unmoved by self-interest. Yet the English were by no means alone in their hero worship. The Japanese, too, were quick to sense the importance of Mahan's doctrine and to commence translating Mahan's works. And the German Kaiser, while the Mahan celebrations were at their height in London, sent the following effusively pro-Mahan telegram to a personal friend. "May 26, 1894. To Mr. Poulteney Bigelow, London, Chelsea Embankment 10. Many thanks for kind letter. Am just now not reading but devouring Mahan's book and am trying to learn it by heart. It is a first-class work and classical in all points. It is on board all my ships and constantly quoted by my captains and officers. I shall be glad to see you at the Manoeuvres and at that splendid Marienburg. William I. R."[33] Alfred Thayer Mahan, the mentor of Roosevelt and Lodge, had now become tutor to an enormous British following and to the imperialistic Kaiser of Germany as well. "In his Sea Power books," confessed an admiring British author C. C. Taylor a quarter of a century later, "Mahan gave away to the enemy England's whole system of peace."[34] As Captain W. D. Puleston expressed it in his biography of Mahan, Mahan's writings on sea power "became a campaign handbook for the advocates of a two-power standard for the British fleet. It might have been written to order for the British cabinet, so clearly did it support all their contentions."[35]

"Buy Mahan," the Admiralty advised naval authorities in Cape Town who requested suggestions for their library. Cape Town wired that they had bought a number of copies of Mahan's books. Back cabled the Admiralty, *"Buy more Mahan."*[36]

In mid-June the *Chicago's* shift from Gravesend to Antwerp failed to check the stream of invitations that poured in on Mahan. From Oxford and Cambridge came offers of honorary degrees, which carried Mahan back to England the last week in June.

As Mahan walked down High Street in Oxford toward the Sheldonian Theater, "with cocked hat, red silk gown, and sword, the railroad trousers modestly peeping beneath" he felt that in matters sartorial his life had achieved a climax. Inside the circular auditorium as the candidates were solemnly marching down the aisles, Oxford youths in the gallery, indulging their ancient custom of mingling horseplay with cheers, welcomed Mahan with "Yankee Doodle" and called out irreverent jibes. In his autobiography Mahan tells how at this moment someone aloft shouted, " 'Why don't you have your hair cut?' which I afterwards understood was a delicate allusion to my somewhat unparalleled baldness; but it happened that two behind me in the procession was a very distinguished Russian scientist, like myself a D.C.L. *in ovo*, whose long locks fell over his collar, and I innocently supposed that so pertinent a remark was addressed to him on an occasion when impertinence was lord of the ascendant. Thus the shaft passed me harmless, or fell back blunted from my triple armor of dullness."[37]

One of the subjects on which Mahan and the admiral disagreed was the labor situation. Subversive influences, Mahan believed, were at work at home and in the Navy. "Mahan is a deep thinker—thinks too damned much!"[38] Erben commented to Ensign Ellicott. Mahan's return to Antwerp in July coincided with the arrival of news that Cleveland had called out troops to quell the Chicago Pullman strike.

It was Sunday, July 8. Church was "rigged" on the gun deck in the usual manner, with benches for the crew facing Chaplain Frederick Sherman's reading desk and with chairs for officers arranged in a semicircle behind it. Chaplain Sherman, writes Ellicott, "prefaced his sermon by saying he had intended to preach on another subject, but the news of the crisis at home had decided him to make a short address on law and order. At this Captain Mahan sprang up in alarm and started toward the Chaplain, but was pulled back by the Admiral with an undertone admonition: 'Sit down, Mahan. Let him go ahead.' This, and one or two subsequent impulses of Mahan, were unseen by the Chaplain as they took place behind him and he concluded what proved to be quite a harmless address. As he was going toward the companionway after the service, however, Captain Mahan intercepted him, saying he wished to see him in the cabin. After removing his vestments the Chaplain went to the cabin and found Mahan pacing it in much excitement. A heated colloquy ensued during which the Captain charged the Chaplain with not confining himself to preaching the Gospel. Mahan ordered the Chaplain henceforth to submit his sermons to the Captain on Saturdays for revision."[39] Sherman appealed to Erben. Mahan explained in writing that while the spiritual care of the ship's company is committed to the chaplain's charge, "he, like all other officers, is subject to the orders of the Captain, where the discipline of the ship is, in the Captain's opinion, involved. . . . I consider the use of the ship's pulpit as a platform for utterances on such matters injurious to military discipline."[40] Admiral Erben quietly endorsed on the back of Mahan's paper his opinion that the "commanding officer had the right to stop utterances if discipline is involved."[41] Narrating the incident later, the humorous Erben—after many a solemn tug at his white, spiky side-whiskers—turned the story into a joke. "As Chaplain S. claims this to be a matter between himself and his God," Erben misquoted himself, "I do not feel that I have sufficient power to adjudicate it. I therefore refer it to the Navy Department!"[42]

Early on the morning of July 11 the lookout sounded the collision alarm. Mahan rushed from his morning bath half-clad up on deck. Through the drizzle he saw the English tanker, the S. S. *Azov*, bearing down on the *Chicago* out of control. The *Chicago* at anchor in the river below Antwerp had no chance to dodge as her boilers were lying open for repair. The *Azov* like a drunken man cut into Mahan's ship at the forward sponson and damaged his steam whaleboat.[43] Mahan's well-drilled seamen had a collision mat over the side and instantly plugged the opening as the tanker drifted away. What struck young Ellicott as unusual about the incident was Mahan's complete freedom from embarrassment, though he was clad only in a short smoking jacket and slippers. "He was a man who under any and all circumstances maintained an impressive dignity."[44]

In September, upon the retirement of Admiral Erben, Mahan's chief burden was lifted. His new superior, Admiral William A. Kirkland, was as pro-Mahan as Erben had been anti-Mahan. As an amiable gesture toward Mahan, Kirkland went out of his way in an official letter to the Department to contradict Admiral Erben on the subject of Mahan's fitness as a naval officer, a breach of naval etiquette for which he was rebuked by the Navy Department. The *Chicago* was in Algiers when orders were received in February for her to return to the States. Kirkland transferred his flag to another ship; and on the twenty-first the homeward-bound pennant, 360 feet long, was broken out at the *Chicago's* main truck. Every man of the ship's company sent up a cheer. A dummy, resembling a man, which was cast overboard out of the forerigging, symbolized the pitching of Jonah into the sea to propitiate the gods of the deep and to invoke fair weather for the homeward voyage.[45] Mahan's last sea duty ended in New York on March 23, 1895.

New York society welcomed Mahan with a flurry of invitations. But the Mahans had been too long out of the swing of social life to relish its "frivolities." Mahan himself was dominated by his single interest in professional naval writing, and anyone who sought to lionize him was apt to find him an unwilling and diffident lion. Ellen Mahan, his faithful helper in the long struggle, when the invitations descended upon her, was the possessor of but a single dinner dress![46]

To some extent the circle of Mahan's American readers had widened during his absence in Europe. *The Fortnightly Review* in 1894 noted that Mahan "has found listeners among his own countrymen. They know that neither a mercantile marine alone nor a navy alone can make seapower . . . they mean to be in all senses of the words a great nation."[47] But in 1895 the number of American converts to Mahan's naval principles was not large.

Some of Mahan's most literate and vocal readers were isolationists, who labeled him a "jingo" and dismissed his theories as "patriotism with a gun in its hand." To the general public in the United States Mahan was as yet simply that American naval officer who had been banqueted abroad by queens and emperors. "My books here," Mahan wrote Ashe in November 1896, "don't pay me for the time and trouble."[48] It was in Germany—where Mahan's first sea-power book,

Der Einfluss der Seemacht auf die Geschichte, was appearing serially
in a naval magazine—and in England—where naval imperialism aroused
all the political passion that Bryan's free-silver question did in this
country—that Mahan's ideas had really taken root, and it was from
these countries that most of his royalty money came. Nervous, energetic America found his books long and heavy. His fellow countrymen preferred to take smaller doses of Mahan's strong medicine, not
of book length but of a magazine-article size.

Secretary Herbert now obligingly detailed Mahan as lecturer at the
Naval War College in order to allow him time for his writing, and in
November 1896, after it had become certain that there would be no
war between the United States and Great Britain over the Venezuela
boundary dispute, Mahan requested to be retired from the Navy
under the act authorizing retirement after forty years' service. He
was fifty-six years old. "I shrink from further separation from home,
and have a number of literary projects in view, to follow out which I
need a certainty of non-interference to which I have no claim unless
I retire," he explained to Ashe; "I have just finished and sent to the
publishers a long and elaborate Life of Nelson. . . . I have here . . . an
opening for magazine writing; and I own to a wish to run the remainder of my course as a literary man, taking an active interest in
the State, Church, and social movement about me, leaving the active
pursuit of the sea and its new naval monsters to younger men. . . ."[49]

The Navy Department granted his request and placed him on the
retired list.

In his magazine articles the foremost American imperialist issued a
challenge to his isolationist opponents. "How much poorer would the
world have been had Englishmen heeded the cautious hesitancy that
now bids us reject every advance beyond our shore-lines!"[50] Even if
his plea for the world's welfare were "a cloak for national self-
interest," he felt that we should accept this new role frankly.[51]

The more he considered the arguments of the small-navy isolationists the more Mahan became convinced that the isolationist's position
was fundamentally ignoble. "Ease unbroken, trade uninterrupted,
hardship done away, all roughness removed from life—these are our
modern gods; but can they deliver us, should we succeed in setting
them up for worship?"[52] Mahan, in a somewhat heavy style, glorified
the martial spirit as a safeguard of modern civilization. No longer
ought we to "hug an ideal of isolation," to shirk what Kipling had

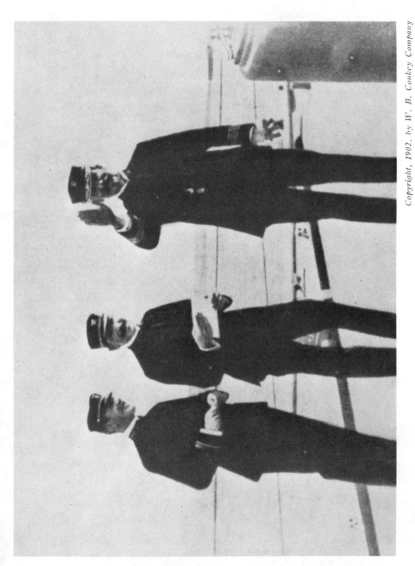

Commodore W. S. Schley, Making an Announcement to His Men.

Rear Admiral Sampson (*left*) with Captain Chadwick and an Aide on Board the *New York*.

named the "white man's burden." "If our own civilization is becoming material only, a thing limited in hope and love to this world. I know not what we have to offer to save ourselves or others."[53] The strategic necessities of the nation, which a later generation of American readers found most interesting in Mahan's writing, was apparently for the author largely incidental to his spiritual message.

Alfred Mahan knew what he had to say and said it. And if to certain audiences the restraint of his style seemed "prejudicial to enthusiasm," there was Mahan's great understudy Theodore Roosevelt to drive the message home in a more popular and emphatic way. Teddy minced no words in his denunciation of the "timid Scholar," hugging shelter in his cloister, and the "timid man of wealth," fearful of unsettling his stock market. Both were "good people with parochial minds," snarled Teddy, "the people who cannot understand that a great country must, whether it will or no, have a foreign policy, and that, after all, there is some nobler ideal for a great nation than being an assemblage of prosperous hucksters!"[54] "A thousand rich bankers cannot leave . . . such a heritage as Farragut left."[55]

Reviewers of the London dailies sat up all night with advance copies of Mahan's two-volume *Life of Nelson*, according to Harold Frederic's cable to the *New York Times*, in order to get their reviews into print the next morning.[56]

Harvard, Yale, Columbia and McGill Universities conferred on Mahan the degree of LL.D. At the Yale ceremony on June 30, 1897, Professor Fisher declared: "By study and experience he qualified himself to write upon naval history with the discernment of an expert. It is not too much to say that his writings make an epoch in this department of literature. . . . It is a pardonable pride that the country may feel in these productions of an American seaman."[57]

On the eve of the epochal war for American empire, Mahan, a retired naval officer, had achieved a reputation as a writer which, as the *Army and Navy Journal* noted, "secures attention for whatever he may write."[58] When in April of 1897 Theodore Roosevelt worked his way into the Navy Department as Assistant Secretary, Captain Mahan had not only a nationwide audience for his writings but a vigorous, forthright executive within the Department who as a long-time friend and pupil was completely sold on Mahan's doctrine and determined, come hell or high water, to put Mahan's program into effect.

12. SCHLEY TO THE FLYING SQUADRON

THE NEW, glistening-white cruiser *Baltimore* was a ship whose mood and temper reflected the pleasing excess of spontaneity and bonhomie in the character of her first skipper. Captain Schley derived a healthy, boyish enjoyment from the mastering of hardships afloat; and when he came ashore he heartily renewed old friendships and on every hand was banqueted and otherwise entertained.

A Washington correspondent of the *New York Herald* thus described a typical instance of Schley's coming ashore: "'Schley!' 'Melville!' The names of the two distinguished naval officers rang out in joyful surprise in a dark corridor of the Navy Building. The two men rushed towards each other, grasped hands, then hugged, and finally danced around in each others' arms. It was the happy meeting of two of our most honored naval heroes—Captain Schley, of the *Baltimore*, and Engineer-in-Chief Melville, of the *Jeannette* Polar Expedition. . . . After reporting at the Navy Department the commander of the *Baltimore* rushed to the Shoreham to greet his wife, whom he had not seen for more than a year."[1] As the world saw him there was about Winfield Scott Schley none of the studied aloofness of the philosophical Mahan nor the shy aloofness of the preoccupied scientist Sampson.

After giving the *Baltimore* her shakedown, Captain Schley proudly took her up the Chesapeake Bay to exhibit this newest craft in the Navy to the people of his native state. In Annapolis Roads he welcomed aboard his ship the superintendent of the Naval Academy, Captain Sampson. The visiting midshipmen, standing around stiffly in awe of the officers' full-dress uniforms, were assured that they might "go where you please on the ship and ask all the questions you wish to."[2]

At the city of Baltimore, the namesake cruiser excited great attention. On May 9, 1890, Captain Schley was accorded a public reception at the City Hall and a parade. In the afternoon Mayor Davidson and Schley's personal friend, General Felix Agnus, publisher of the *Baltimore American*, with other first citizens, returned the captain's visit on board the cruiser. The Citizens' Reception Committee entertained the *Baltimore's* officers at dinner, and the next day the cruiser's bluejackets joined the Maryland 5th Regiment in a second parade. Because the crowd of guests on the eleventh damaged the ship's skylights and removed so many small items of the ship's gear as souvenirs, Captain Schley was compelled henceforth to issue cards of admission for visitors. One of the shrewdest publicity agents for the New Navy, Schley set aside May 12 as "Governor's and Ladies' Day." Salutes welcomed the civil dignitaries, and the captain played a gallant host to 8,000 ladies. Another day while the *Baltimore's* crew went ashore in shifts to regale themselves at Oriole Baseball Park and at Barnum's Circus, the officers enjoyed the races at Pimlico and attended a musical fete. For this "most elaborate" affair the interior of the auditorium of the Academy of Music was converted into a shrubbery and flower garden, with electric lights strung through the trees and along the vines. The illusion of a lawn party was heightened during the evening as dozens of canary birds were liberated from their cages to flit from tree to tree. The Marine Band from Washington and a Baltimore orchestra "discoursed music from concealed positions." The menu was notable "both in substantials and liquids."[3] At banquets the genial captain of the *Baltimore* seldom "got through a whole meal because he talked so much, with his fork waving in the air, that waiters snatched dishes away that he had barely touched." He did, however, save menu cards; perhaps, as a granddaughter later suggested, "to see what he might have eaten!"[4]

Assigned for a short time as flagship to Admiral Bancroft Gherardi's Atlantic Squadron, the *Baltimore* acquitted herself handsomely in the entertainment and the carrying to and fro of distinguished guests. Her captain's ability to ease out an anchor at 7:00 A. M. so noiselessly as not to awaken the admiral, and his affableness as host to President Benjamin Harrison, who was en route to Boston for the twenty-fourth national encampment of the Grand Army of the Republic, won for the *Baltimore* in the summer of 1890 the assignment to carry the remains of the distinguished inventor John Ericsson home to his native Sweden.

The New York ceremony in honor of the *Monitor's* inventor, the biggest event of its kind since the funeral of General Grant, was carefully staged. Following the procession from the cemetery to the Battery, a tug brought the remains out to the *Baltimore's* anchorage off the Statue of Liberty. The funeral tug moved solemnly between a double column of yachts and small boats. All around the harbor American flags and the blue and orange colors of Sweden flew at half mast. Minute guns were fired at the navy yard, while the remains were being hoisted to a catafalque on board the *Baltimore*. Colonel W. C. Church, Ericsson's biographer, committed the remains to the charge of Captain Schley, who responded with an "admirable little speech."[5] Three American rear admirals on the active list, Secretary of the Navy Tracy and retired Rear Admiral John L. Worden, world-famous commander of Ericsson's Civil War *Monitor*, witnessed the ceremony. Finally, as the *Baltimore* sailed down the bay, each ship in the New American "Squadron of Evolution," anchored in a line to the eastward of Ellis Island, flew the Swedish ensign at the fore and fired its tribute of 21 guns.

At Stockholm Schley turned over Ericsson's remains to Admiral Peyron and participated in the final "grandly magnificent" obsequies.[6] King Oscar had a gold medal struck for Captain Schley and invited him to dine with the royal family at Drottningholm. In turn the monarch was entertained at luncheon on board the *Baltimore*. At Kiel Schley enjoyed the hospitality of the port commander, Captain von Diederichs—later the *bête noire* of Dewey at Manila—and of Prince Henry, brother of the Kaiser. In Denmark, too, the *Baltimore's* commander was entertained by King Christian XII. The Danish queen's compliment on the "perfect order and cleanliness" of the ship Captain Schley graciously passed on to his executive officer and "ship keeper," Commander Uriel Sebree.[7]

From northern Europe the ship proceeded to the Mediterranean for several leisurely months before, according to Secretary Tracy's tentative plan, she was to continue her journey through Suez and return home across the Pacific. While normally the idea of an around-the-world cruise would have been most acceptable to Captain Schley, it could hardly have been altogether so at this time. Schley's only daughter Virginia was engaged to be married a few months hence in January of 1891. There is a wistful note in the old seaman's ballad that Schley recalled, as his ship swung at anchor far from home in the landlocked harbor of Port Mahon, Balearic Islands:[8]

> "At Cape de Gatte I lost my hat,
>   And where do you think I found it?
> At Port Mahon under a stone
>   With all the girls around it."

Yet while Captain Schley was trying to console himself by sight-seeing on the Riviera someone back home was interceding in his behalf with Secretary Tracy. Whether this person was the bride-to-be or her mother or one of the New York families who were forever giving a *thé dansant* for the Schleys, or whether it was a combination of intercessors who urged the Secretary to grant "the hero of the Greely Relief Expedition" leave of absence to enable him to be present at the wedding of his daughter is not known. When the cabled authorization reached him at Villefranche on December 19, Schley instantly became too busy telegraphing Paris for the next steamer reservation to wonder how the piece of good luck had come about. Years later in his memoirs he referred to it as an "unsolicited favor." The favor was to lead shortly to Schley's participation in one of the most shocking incidents in the history of the Navy.

After visiting with his family and giving his daughter in marriage to Ralph Montagu Stuart Wortley, a young Englishman engaged in business in Norfolk, Virginia, Captain Schley ran down from Baltimore to Washington to pay his respects to the Secretary and to thank him for granting him his leave. His arrival in Washington coincided with news of the outbreak of a revolution in Chile.

Secretary Tracy had just ordered the *Pensacola* around from the South Atlantic Squadron to Valparaiso, but he needed something more impressive than this wooden Civil War antique to protect United States interests. According to a State Department report just received, the Chilean Congressional Party under Admiral Jorge Montt had seized the country's navy and had set up a rival government at Iquique, in the north, from which it defied the president-dictator Balmaceda at Valparaiso. Since the Chilean Navy in January of 1891 included several ships of latest European build, some naval experts rated it as more powerful than the United States Navy, the keels of whose "coast-defense" battleships had not yet been laid.

At once Valparaiso's promise of excitement appealed more strongly to Schley than the prospect of returning to sight-seeing and banqueting in the Mediterranean. He requested the Secretary to send the *Baltimore* directly to Chile. Should it be desirable for the cruiser to circumnavigate the globe, that could be done later. "When can you start?" asked Tracy. "As soon as the return trip to Europe can be made," said Schley.[9] Tracy assented.

Schley rejoined his ship at Toulon in mid-February and sailed before his new charts arrived. As the cruiser plowed westward across Nelson's famed battleground of Trafalgar, Schley lifted his flat little officer's cap in a votive gesture toward the greatest of naval commanders.

The *Baltimore* cleared the Straits of Magellan on March 29, and after plowing northward through the long swells of the Pacific, reached Valparaiso on the morning of April 7.

Schley reported to Admiral McCann. For the moment the Chilean civil war was quiet. From the beginning of the difficulties Patrick Egan, the American minister, had been willing to gamble that the Chilean President Balmaceda would suppress the Insurgents; and this view, mistaken as it turned out, he had impressed upon Washington. Through their unexpected seizure of the Chilean Navy the Insurgent forces controlled communications along the entire length of Chile's attenuated coast line, and they alone possessed the transport facilities for procuring munitions from abroad. About the time of Schley's arrival at Valparaiso, the Insurgents sent the merchant steamer *Itata* to San Diego for a cargo of arms that had been collected there by one of their agents. When United States officials in California refused to grant the *Itata* a customs clearance, the forbidden arms were secretly run out past the port authorities and transferred to the *Itata* at uninhabited Catalina Island. Washington immediately ordered the *Itata* to be overhauled and seized for violation of American neutrality laws.

Southward from San Diego the cruiser *Charleston* pursued the runaway munitions ship, while the American South Pacific Squadron, augmented by forces from the South Atlantic and by the cruiser *Baltimore*, gathered off the North Chilean, rebel-controlled port of Iquique to arrest her. The presence of so large a force of United States ships off their port induced the Insurgent government at Iquique, against their will, to surrender the *Itata* upon her arrival. She was returned to the United States under American naval escort, to be later freed by an American court after the success of the Insurgents' arms had become certain.

Meanwhile, anti-United States feeling in Chile was whipped up by a second incident. In retaliation for the detention of their munitions ship, the increasingly victorious Insurgents shut off all American cable communication at Iquique. Admiral McCann's reply to this move was to cut the cable on two sides of Iquique and splice it outside of Chile's territorial waters. He thus gave the main American base at Valparaiso an uninterrupted communication with the nearest port in Peru and at the same time by-passed and isolated the port of Iquique.

Since Captain Schley in the *Baltimore* was the officer who supervised the cable-cutting operation and who later informed the Insurgent government of what had been done, much of the ill feeling of the Insurgents came to be directed against the U. S. S. *Baltimore* and her personnel.[10]

Later on Admiral Brown in the *San Francisco,* who had replaced Admiral McCann in the *Pensacola,* found the conquering Insurgents increasingly hostile toward Americans as their armies closed in upon Valparaiso. The movements of the *San Francisco* and the *Baltimore* convinced the Insurgents that the Americans were spying upon their movements in order to assist the Balmacedist Loyalist government which Washington recognized. Insurgent newspapers, their bitterness against the Americans waxing with the success of Insurgent arms, denounced the Americans as "official filibusterers" aiding their enemies, and they continued to hurl these canards long after they had won their decisive victory over Balmaceda on August 21.

Obviously Patrick Egan, the United States minister, had committed that gravest blunder in the diplomatic lexicon, that of cheering for the loser. Equally reprehensible, from the Insurgents' point of view, was Minister Egan's granting of sanctuary inside the American Consulate to discomfited Balmacedists.

During several troubled weeks before the relations of the United States and the new Chilean government became established, Captain Schley kept a bright lookout to forestall any possibility of enemy torpedo action against his ship. The *Baltimore*, swinging at anchor in the middle of the harbor, was once fired at by Insurgents on shore when they opened upon a small Balmacedist craft which lay on a line between the *Baltimore* and the shore battery. Some high shots struck the *Baltimore*, but the fact that his anchorage lay in the line of fire enabled Schley to regard these shots as accidental.

There were a dozen political refugees on board the *Baltimore* at the time, and a guard of bluejackets and marines from the ship was on shore to shield the American Consulate, which was packed with refugees, the release of whom was being loudly demanded by the victorious Insurgents. Little by little the *Baltimore* assumed in Chilean imaginations the lineaments of a scapegoat. After the *Baltimore* had transported a shipload of refugees north to asylum in the neutral Peruvian port of Mollendo, the remainder of the American squadron shoved off, leaving Schley's cruiser alone at Valparaiso to carry on her protective vigil and, as it turned out, to draw upon herself the malice of the Valparaiso mob.

Captain Schley, now senior officer present, made frequent trips ashore in efforts to cultivate better relations with the new authorities. He experienced some difficulty, owing to the widespread Chilean belief that Admiral Brown had taken ex-President Balmaceda north to sanctuary. Actually, as Schley pointed out to the new government, the unhappy Balmaceda had committed suicide within the walls of the Argentine Legation. On September 23, Schley reported to the Navy Department: "Festivities to celebrate anniversary of Chilean independence and peace have passed without political significance. Everything is quiet. Balmaceda committed suicide Sept. 19."[11]

At this point Captain Schley began to sound out Señor Arlegui, the mayor or intendente, about the possibility of granting shore leave to the *Baltimore's* bluejackets who had not been ashore for three months. Schley prided himself on his fluency in Spanish, and in his best Castillian expressed the hope that his own good intentions would be reciprocated. In view of recent events, however, and especially of the still unsettled conditions in the town, Señor Arlegui ought to have advised against the move for the present. Instead, the Chilean official gave Captain Schley bland assurance that there was *no official reason* why the *Baltimore's* crew should not enjoy shore leave.

Accordingly, Captain Schley on the fatal afternoon of October 16, 1891, decided to grant a 24-hour leave to about 120 members of his crew.

At 3:00 P. M. when Captain Schley and Executive Officer Sebree went on shore to see how their men were getting along, they encountered many seamen of the liberty party "strolling about the city, or riding in carriages, apparently enjoying themselves." Schley noted "with much gratification" that they were properly saluting all foreign officers, were "neat in appearance, tidy in dress," and that not one appeared "in the slightest degree under the influence of drink."[12] But this was in the afternoon, before 5:00 P. M., at which hour Captain Schley boarded his gig and returned over the placid water to his ship.

About six o'clock a fight started in a Valparaiso saloon between an American and a Chilean sailor. Details of the wholesale fracas which instantly flared up in widely scattered sections of the city vary with the nationality of the witnesses. The testimony of Schley's distraught seamen, though containing some contradictions and obvious impossibilities, gives a general idea of what happened.[13]

Charles W. Riggin, boatswain's mate, U. S. Navy, was killed by shots fired by a mob.

Testimony of J. W. Talbot, (apprentice seaman, U. S. Navy, who suffered two stab wounds in the back and many bruises): Talbot and Riggin were drinking in the True Blue Saloon with a Chilean sailor. A dispute arose. The Chilean spat in Talbot's face. Talbot knocked him down. Riggin and Talbot, after escaping through a rapidly gathering crowd of Chilean sailors and civilians, jumped on a passing horsecar bound for the downtown section. The mob, crying out against the "Yanks," boarded the car and forced the Americans off the rear platform. Again the two Americans ran, after fighting their way clear.

Testimony of J. M. Johnson, armorer, U. S. Navy: While eating supper in an English boarding house near Calle Arsenal, Johnson heard a commotion in the street and looked down from a second-story window to see his shipmate Riggin, in the hands of the crowd, being stabbed. Riggin was down on the pavement and there were four policemen standing around him. The mob left Riggin to chase Talbot, and Johnson attempted to drag Riggin into a near-by drugstore. He had proceeded only a short distance when police charged him with fixed bayonets. At close quarters they fired on Johnson, the muzzle of one piece being so near that Johnson's face was blackened by the discharge. A second shot was fired from Johnson's right, "the bullet passing over his right breast, through his overshirt, undershirt, and neckerchief, and striking Riggin in the neck. His head fell on Johnson's left arm, as though his neck had been broken."

Coalheaver W. Turnbull, U. S. Navy, received 18 knife and bayonet wounds in the back, two of which penetrated his lungs. He died a few days later.

Testimony of many witnesses implicated the Chilean police in maltreating American sailors. There were serving on the police force at this time several hundred men recently discharged from the victorious Insurgent army. Other witnesses saw both Chilean sailors and police aiding Americans. All told, after the fighting over the city, 36 Americans were arrested, of whom five were sent to the hospital and the rest to various police stations. Several of those arrested were lassoed or nippered with catgut around the wrists, dragged along by the mounted police and beaten with swords when they failed to keep pace.

Schley refrained from bombarding Valparaiso as, immediately after the outbreak, the captain of the American steamer *Keweenaw* urged him to do; but he insisted on a thorough investigation. When the Chilean officials sought to hush the matter up with perfunctory police court hearings behind closed doors, Schley appointed his own board of investigation from the ship's officers to elicit the story as his seamen saw it. In Washington the findings of his board provoked the most warlike stir since the *Virginius* affair. The State Department took over the reins of negotiation, with Schley continuing vigorously to marshal witnesses and unearth facts. To refute the Chilean theory of a drunken brawl, Schley rounded up—among other eyewitnesses—

one Charles Lanctot who swore that Riggin and his companion Talbot had been cold sober when dragged from the streetcar by the mob.

"The attack of 2,000 people upon a few unarmed and defenseless men," wrote Schley to Minister Egan, "(and I say defenseless because, when searched by the police, only six or seven pocketknives were found and returned to me by the intendente after the men's examination), with the death of one on the spot and one subsequently, and the mutilation, by stab wounds in their backs of many others, surely merits to be called a brutal attack."[14]

Charles W. Riggin and William Turnbull, who died later, were buried with full military honors in the foreign cemetery in graves marked by a "handsome marble shaft" paid for by their shipmates. In December the *Baltimore*, having been relieved by the *Yorktown* under Robley D. Evans, sailed for San Francisco, where the Judge Advocate General of the Navy was on hand to conduct a further exhaustive investigation. Schley, meanwhile, was called to Washington to report directly to the Secretary and the President.

As the diplomatic tension mounted there were some who felt that Captain Schley had made too much of a quibble over such details as whether or not his men had been inebriated. "Fighting Bob" Evans, for instance, snorted: "His men were probably drunk on shore, properly drunk; which they did on Chilean rum paid for with good United States money. When in this condition they were more entitled to protection than if they had been sober."[15] Schley's grateful seamen, however, upon his leaving the ship for other duty, presented him with a gold-headed cane, inscribed:[16]

Captain W. S. Schley, U. S. N.
From the Crew of the *Baltimore*,
February 15, 1892.

Schley's eastward trip across the country was a triumphal progression, with crowds yelling their heads off for "Schley" and "the *Baltimore*" wherever his train stopped.

In 1884 Secretary Chandler had utilized the publicity of the Greely Relief Expedition to promote popular interest in the Navy. In 1891 Secretary Tracy, a thoughtful and determined imperialist, in his annual report pointed up the "*Baltimore* outrage" as an obvious indication of our naval needs. "The wooden ships of the Navy have now practically passed out of existence." Safety of our seamen abroad, security of our coastal cities, a share in the commerce of the Pacific—in which our mercantile competitors "are today enlarging their fields of activity with a more aggressive energy than ever before"—all depended, it was urged, upon the continuing development of our New Navy.[17]

For two anxious months Secretary of State Blaine, the "John L. Sullivan of diplomacy," scorched the cables to Valparaiso with threats of war. President Harrison on January 25, 1892, submitted the papers in the case to Congress "for such action as may be deemed appropriate." Red-blooded young Theodore Roosevelt dreamed of leading a cavalry charge against the Chileans. Then, their temporizing having brought Chile to the very brink of war with the United States, the Chileans yielded to the pressure, apologized for the *Baltimore* outrage and agreed to pay an indemnity to the injured American seamen and their families.

After a flurry of dinners in Washington, Captain Schley settled down to work in New York as inspector for the Third Lighthouse District. His new job, involving the purchase of every sort of equipment from shoe lacings to catadioptric lenses, brought him congenially in touch with businessmen, very much as had his earlier job in the Bureau of Equipment. The perfection of electric lighting made the early 1890's an important period for the lighthouse service. Schley supervised the installation of electric buoys for the Chicago Exposition in 1893. This first attempt of the Lighthouse Board to use the high-tension system of alternating currents through its submarine cables was so successful that the system was early adopted for lighting the ship channels into New York Harbor.

Owing to his experience as captain of the cruiser *Baltimore*, Schley was able to make technical suggestions of value in the construction of the newer ships of the Navy. One of Schley's technical reports, dated October 27, 1894, recommended the elimination of wooden ceilings and bulkheads inside warships and the use, wherever possible, of light corrugated steel.

On the social side Schley kept up his fences. Several times in 1893 and 1894 he transported President Cleveland in one of the lighthouse tenders to and from his summer home, Gray Gables. The international yacht race between the *Vigilant* and the *Valkyrie* gave Captain Schley the opportunity on October 5, 1893, to entertain a number of his friends on board the supply ship *America*.

Schley enjoyed shore duty, but he usually kept his "sea dunnage" packed and ready to leave on 24 hours' notice. In October 1895, following a brief tour of duty on the Board of Inspection and Survey, the time came for Schley's "second trick at the wheel as captain." This time he took over from Robley Evans the command of the large cruiser *New York*, the flagship of Admiral F. M. Bunce's Atlantic Squadron.[18] Schley ran the ship safely through a hurricane off Cape Hatteras and helped to work out fleet maneuvers in the drill grounds off Charleston.

On March 6, 1898, after 42 years in the Navy, Schley at the age of fifty-six, was commissioned commodore. Since Schley was accepted by the nation as an officer to cope with such dire emergencies as the relief of Greely and the outrage upon the *Baltimore's* seamen at Valparaiso, it was only natural on the eve of the war with Spain that McKinley's Secretary of the Navy should pick Schley to command a squadron to protect the East Coast. The assignment, as Secretary John D. Long wrote, "was especially desirable, and one to which any one of his seniors might have felt entitled."[19] Schley himself was delighted. And the country generally applauded Schley's appointment as commander in chief of the New Navy's "Flying Squadron."

13. SAMPSON TO THE BLOCKADE

In the building of the New Navy a spirit of rivalry developed between the shipbuilders of the East and West coasts. The Union Iron Works of San Francisco boasted that their California craftsmanship "was equal to the best Cramps," the premier East Coast builders. Irving M. Scott, manager of Union's shipyard, knew how it felt after completing a New Navy ship to have his fellow townsmen unhitch the horses and pull his flower-bedecked carriage around the city. Citizens of San Francisco, quite as noisy as Baltimoreans had been over the new cruiser *Baltimore*, lavished upon their namesake cruiser, the *San Francisco*, a 32-piece silver service worth $7,500, of which each large item was adorned with a California grizzly bear in solid gold.[1]

In midsummer of 1890 Captain William T. Sampson left the superintendency of the Naval Academy to supervise the installation of technical devices on the *San Francisco*.

Sampson brought his entire family west with him, traveling on the *City of Para* to Aspinwall, crossing the isthmus, and then on the *City of Sydney* for the remainder of the 31-day sea voyage to San Francisco.[2] He was greatly pleased with the new cruiser. For the next

174

two months Sampson spent weekdays at the shipyard and evenings and Sundays with his family. Calls upon friends at Mare Island and Vallejo, visits with Ralph and baby Harold to Golden Gate Park, seeing an occasional play with his wife and daughters Catherine, Nannie and Olive filled these pleasant weeks.

The *San Francisco* had a protective steel deck running the length of the ship and sloping down the sides to about four feet below the water line. This light armor plate varied in thickness from one and one-half inches on the flat top to two and one-half inches on the slopes. Three Edison dynamos supplied current for her electric lighting system and her four 25,000-candle-power searchlights. Her main battery of 12 six-inch breech-loading rifles was supplemented by light experimental rapid-fire guns and Gatling guns in her "fighting tops." Unlike the *Baltimore's* engines, the plans for which had been purchased in England, the *San Francisco's* engines were an American product constructed on plans drawn by Commodore George Melville's Bureau of Steam Engineering. All her material was of American manufacture. The *San Francisco* had been designed as a flagship, and the ample mahogany-paneled apartments for her admiral and captain could be thrown into one large room extending across the ship. Owing to a miscalculation for her boiler space, however, because of an overlapping of authority in the naval bureaus, the living quarters for the engineers could be reached only by crawling on hands and knees through a low passageway.

On her trial run in late August the *San Francisco* attained 19.7 knots, "the speed of an express train," and her proud builders were awarded a premium of $100,000 for each knot in excess of her contract speed.[3] Officers of H.M.S. *Warspite*, visiting San Francisco at this time, spoke of the new white American cruiser as "infinitely superior in her fittings and accommodation to her English sisters of the *Galatea* class," but these foreign guests had probably not been shown the engineers' quarters.[4] "Saucier and handsomer than the *Charleston*," wrote an American reporter, who noted also that "a fine spirit is developing among her people."[5]

In February Captain Sampson stood out to maneuver the ship in rough water. When making 75 revolutions per minute in a head sea, she pitched and raced, but set up little vibration. In the trough of the sea she rolled easily, less than 11 degrees. Though a steady ship, and hence a good gun platform, she was a wet ship. Water swept aboard "very freely," drenching points 20 feet high. What was greatly in her favor was that her battery could be fired without straining the frame, although the firing of a broadside cracked the light vertical shields of several guns and carried away a few lugs. These minor defects having been remedied, Rear Admiral George Brown hoisted his broad pennant aboard Captain Sampson's ship on March 31, 1891, and the *San Francisco* sailed south for observation patrol off revolution-torn Chile.

On the South Pacific Station the *San Francisco's* function paralleled that of the *Baltimore*. She posted herself at Callao, Iquique and Valparaiso in such a way as to relay to Washington information on the state of the Chilean war. Her small boats rescued two Chilean seamen who had been hurled overboard by an accidental explosion of a torpedo. She seized the runaway munitions ship *Itata* at the Insurgent-controlled port of Iquique. At Valparaiso she gave sanctuary to political refugees of the defeated Balmacedist party, and several of her crew witnessed the dragging of two dead generals through the streets, "the victors spitting on and kicking the dead."[6] The Valparaiso outrage upon the *Baltimore's* people, and the consequent diplomatic disturbances, brought home two basic ideas to Captain Sampson. Sampson was very much disinclined, ever after, as Robley Evans expressed it, to have "to fight hell with garlic." The United States Navy had to be built up. Also he contracted a deep dislike for the newspaper fraternity, whose extravagant falsehoods about Admiral Brown were being screamed in the Chilean press.

Unlike Captain Schley, who permitted shore leave to his crew at this disordered time, Captain Sampson was inclined to be cautious. It is unlikely that his crew would have requested shore leave; and there can be little doubt that Sampson would have refused it if they had. Sampson held extra target practice during the period of uncertainty following the outrage upon the *Baltimore's* seamen. On February 17, 1893, the Chilean government having acceded to United States demands, the *San Francisco* set sail for Honolulu.

A problem that bothered Sampson, in view of the recent threatening international situation, was the *San Francisco's* limited coal endurance. A full load of coal, according to the original estimate, should have carried the ship 8,333 knots; whereas in actual steaming Sampson found that she would "not exceed 4,412 knots; with the best quality of coal and a clean bottom."[7]

Sampson's voyage to Hawaii was a good-will mission, an important object of which was to consolidate further American control over this essential Pacific coaling base. Mahan and Roosevelt wanted to get Hawaii under the American flag for strategic reasons. Their views found favor with Secretary Tracy and President Harrison; although for the present it was recognized that American public opinion was opposed to annexation.

To Honolulu, to act as hostesses for the flagship *San Francisco*, went Admiral Brown's wife and Captain Sampson's second daughter Catherine. On March 17, Captain Sampson sent the ship's band ashore to help the Royal Hawaiian band provide music for "the grandest ball ever given at the palace."[8] Admiral and Mrs. Brown and Captain and Miss Sampson were among the dancers. Two days later Queen Liliuokalani with fifteen members of her court was officially received aboard the cruiser. On April 8 the queen entertained the *San Francisco's* officers at a state dinner. Twice a month the cruiser held afternoon receptions for Honolulu society. For one of these occasions the seamen had padded out a diver's suit to the shape of a man and had placed an electric light bulb inside the dummy's helmet and felt quite well rewarded for their pains when the guests bowed to this lifelike creation, extending it a hand "of welcome and aloha."[9]

Although Sampson's seamen stood somewhat in awe of their skipper, they knew that on occasion he might relax a rule. On the afternoon of a scheduled boat race against a crew from H.M.S. *Garnet*, the coxswain of the *San Francisco's* boat crew found Captain Sampson seated in his cabin. "Captain," he said earnestly, "do you want us to win this race?"

"Why certainly," replied Sampson.

"Well, Captain, one of my men is under arrest. I have spoken to the First Lieutenant, and he says he can't be released."

"That being the case—the man a prisoner—I don't see what I can do for you."

"But I can't do without him," pleaded the coxswain. "If you don't let that man go, Captain, the Englishmen will beat us!"

Sampson turned suddenly and touched the bell; and as his orderly entered, said: "Tell Lieutenant Moser that I release the prisoner until this race is won." And the race was won.[10]

As a complete surprise came Sampson's detachment, in June, from the command of the *San Francisco* and orders for him to return home immediately and report to the Secretary of the Navy for special duty. The *Army and Navy Journal* detected "considerable curiosity in naval circles to know what the special and important service is that Capt. Wm. T. Sampson is to be assigned to. . . . He will not wait for his own vessel, which will be coming to San Francisco within a month or two, but will return by [passenger] steamer."[11]

On June 7, 1892, Sampson calling all hands to muster, read his detachment orders and turned the command of the ship over to Lieutenant B. F. Tilley.[12] As he left in his gig, the crew of the *San Francisco* swarmed to the rail and gave three cheers for Captain Sampson. A welling up of emotion stopped Sampson's tongue and the coxswain, noting the captain's predicament, cried out, "Oars, boys! And three cheers for the *San Francisco!*" The oars were snapped to attention in the vertical position and the shouts were returned with a will.[13]

When Captain Sampson reached Washington and Secretary Tracy told him that he wanted him to relieve Commander W. M. Folger as chief of the Bureau of Ordnance—a post which to the devotee of gunnery science must have been the most interesting and significant billet in the Navy—Sampson requested first a preliminary assignment as Folger's subordinate in order that he might catch up on the technological advancements that had been made since he had last served in the bureau.

Folger, worn down by patent litigation, adverse newspaper criticism of his policies and by the insistent efforts of a private armor processing company to lure him into their employ, had for several years been suffering from insomnia. His nerves on edge, he wanted to go to Austria to see a specialist. With Sampson on the ground to take over, Commander Folger delayed his resignation for three months, and since Sampson had left his family on the West Coast he took Sampson into his home. Another officer in Sampson's position might have felt a qualm on the score of rank. Folger was four years his junior, but Sampson found his temporary assignment under Commander Folger as inspector of Ordnance at the Washington Navy Yard and the ever-present opportunity to be in intimate association with his predecessor an ideal situation. The arrangement was not so perfect for Folger, who was anxious to shuffle out from under the annoyances of the bureau.

"We talked of little else than ordnance, its history, and present conditions," wrote Folger, noting with disappointment the intense, single-minded interest of his house guest and successor. "He read little but scientific works and periodicals. I do not recall ever seeing him read a novel, and he cared little for historical subjects or general reading. This side of his temperament and taste was often a source of regret to me, as it left us without resource in conversation after discussion of the shop."[14]

The "shop" that so absorbed Sampson's interest was the new gun factory at the Washington Navy Yard which in the fall of 1892 was a center of important activity. The old "mold loft"—a huge structure in which life-size patterns for the hulls of sailing ships had formerly been fabricated—had recently been razed and in its place had been erected a new brick building to house the gun factory. Captain Sampson took over his modest post as Inspector of Ordnance in time to supervise the installation of certain furnaces, overhead cranes and giant lathes that were to turn ungainly ingots of gun steel into trim, sleek, 12-inch guns for the New Navy.

Ever since the *Monitor* fought the *Merrimack* an unremitting contest between armor and ordnance had been waged in the naval laboratories and factories of the world. Guns, down to 1890, enjoyed a margin of supremacy; while belt armor on battleships had been made thicker and thicker with a view to reducing the gun's effectiveness. What gave Sampson's work on 12-inch guns its special significance was the fact that since 1890 American-built armor had undergone so radical an evolution that the best projectiles of the day—12-inch, black powder—were unable to penetrate it.

There being no armor plate factory in the country, the Navy Department in 1887 awarded a liberal contract to the Bethlehem Iron Works on condition that it build an armor fabricating plant. When the *Maine* was launched three years later and was ready to receive her armor, the Bethlehem armor factory was still unfinished. Delays in procuring from abroad certain parts of the $400,000 125-ton forging hammer, delays in experimentation—all reasonable enough excuses— were nevertheless exasperating to Secretary Tracy in 1890 when the first battleship of the New Navy was ready on the stocks to receive its armor. Unwilling to jeopardize the modern Navy by dependence on a single armor firm, the imperialist Tracy called in Bethlehem's competitor, Andrew Carnegie, and after a patriotic exhortation induced him to add an armor plant to his already extensive steel mills at Homestead, Pennsylvania.

With two private armor factories now under construction, Tracy made ballistic tests to determine the best type of armor. The epochal test had occurred at Fort Severn Proving Ground, Annapolis, on June 27, 1890, shortly before Sampson's detachment as superintendent of the Naval Academy. This test had proved that nickel-steel armor developed by the Creusot Company in France when tempered by an American process known as "Harveyizing" produced a new type of face-hardened armor superior to any other armor ever developed. "The substance of the metal," as the *Army and Navy Journal* reported this Annapolis test, "appears to seize upon the projectile and hold it fast, thereby closing the very shot hole that it opens."[15] Tracy immediately built up a stockpile of Canadian nickel to be supplied to the two American armor firms. At Indian Head, Maryland, 30 miles from Washington, he established a new naval proving ground. And he constructed the naval gun factory at the Washington Navy Yard to keep American naval ordnance abreast of the world's best, American-built, armor.

Captain Sampson, relieving Commander Folger as chief of the Bureau of Ordnance in January 1893, leased the fine old Graham mansion at 1729 G Street, around the corner from his office in the State, War and Navy Building. After reconditioning the house, he brought his family to Washington. Mrs. Sampson, who had made a number of close friends in Washington while her husband was on duty at the Naval Observatory and at the Naval Academy, was given, the *Army and Navy Journal* noted, "a warm welcome to the capital."[16]

Even with two firms engaged in the production of face-hardened armor, as Sampson learned, this "best armor in the world" was difficult to produce and costly not only in labor and money but in time. Armor plates for the monitor *Monterey* were so long in coming that that vessel's turret mechanism had to be temporarily covered with timber so as not to delay her acceptance trials. It was May of 1893—three years after the signing of the Carnegie contract—before Sampson was able at the Indian Head Proving Ground to test the first armor from the Carnegie firm, and only half of the armor for the U.S.S. *Maine* had been delivered to the shipyard by October of 1893, three years after the ship had been launched. But by this date armor plate was being produced in moderate quantity by both Bethlehem and Carnegie, and Sampson's testing crews at Indian Head were seldom idle. A substantial advantage of the new American, face-hardened armor was that in addition to increased security for the vitals of a ship it was possible to employ a thinner and lighter armor belt and to devote this saving in space and weight to increasing a vessel's fuel capacity. The *London Engineer*, noting this progress in the fall of 1893, acknowledged that "for a given displacement, America appears to have secured startling advantages compared with European navies."[17]

So impenetrably hard was this armor plate that shipwrights had difficulty boring holes in order to bolt it to the structural frames of the ship. When holes were bored in a plate prior to Harveyizing, they often did not match up with the framing, owing to slight warping of the armor itself during the Harveyizing process. Sampson carried this problem to the General Electric Company and a special torch was designed to soften spots where the builders wished to drill holes.

For several years the armor-maker's art was in a fluid, experimental state. The armorers were obligated by contract to supply the government the "best armor they could make," and the Bureau of Ordnance under Sampson was continually finding ways of improving the quality of armor. Then as soon as a stabilized procedure for quality was determined, Sampson demanded increases in the size of individual plates, since the fewer the number of plates the stronger the entire armoring job would be; and such increases again multiplied the armor manufacturer's difficulties.

In the spring of 1894 charges of fraud in the armor factories were brought before the Navy Department by a Pittsburgh informer. Blowholes had allegedly been plugged and armor plates, following their selection by the ordnance inspector for ballistic tests, had been given additional treatment unknown to the inspector. Captain Sampson headed a board to investigate these serious charges against Carnegie's Homestead plant.

As Sampson testified before a subcommittee of the House in June, the blowholes in the metal were not in themselves grave defects. The serious delinquency was that plates had been "surreptitiously subjected to additional treatment after they had been selected for the ballistic test." The Carnegie Company was fined in consequence, but not because their armor was not good. "In my opinion," testified the chief of the bureau, "every plate would pass the ballistic test . . . every plate was above the requirements." The company had been fined because they furnished *some plates which were not up to their best work.* "The best armor they could make should have been supplied to the Government."[18]

Sampson and the other members of the board found that the workmen implicated in the fraud had received presents and that their promotion and success with the company depended upon the rate at which they turned out their armor.

Because the fraudulent plates did meet the ballistic test, however, President Cleveland remitted to the company a third of the 15 percent fine which his rigid, Scotch-Irish chief of the Bureau of Ordnance had been moved to exact. "Where frauds are perpetrated," wrote Sampson in his annual report for 1894, "they consist usually of substitutions, evasions, secret treatments, and concealments which require rather a knowledge of chicanery and double dealing than metallurgical processes."[19] Following payment of a cash award to the Pittsburgh informant there ensued a great deal of spying and ignorant tattling on all sorts of ordnance contract work; but as a result of the chicanery and suspicion Sampson developed a more alert and critical system of ordnance inspection.

As in earlier days Sampson worked out his scientific tests with meticulous care. On May 16, 1896, he took Secretary Herbert to Indian Head to witness a test firing against a dummy turret made up like those on the battleship *Indiana.* The 15-inch ballistic plate to be fired at was of Harveyized nickel steel manufactured at Bethlehem. Inexpensive cast-iron plates were used to complete the turret. The frame structure weighed 67 tons, the armor 157, and inside there were 180 tons of pig metal to represent guns and gun carriages. The whole weighing 404 tons was mounted on 20 radially placed cylindrical steel rollers, each 10 inches in diameter and 30 inches long. Plumb bobs, cords and the like had been previously put in place for measuring any sliding, rotary or vertical motion of the structure. In addition to testing the target plates the secondary objects of the tests were to determine whether the rollers on which turrets were built would work satisfactorily under heavy shot, to see how the whole structure would withstand the shock and also to ascertain the effect of the impact of a heavy shot upon the "inmates" of the turret.[20]

Just before the first shot was fired a dog was placed inside the improvised turret. Three rounds were fired, a 10-inch with a powder charge of 178 pounds; a 12-inch with 355 pounds; and a 12-inch with 440 pounds. Only the last, a solid 12-inch shot, penetrated the plate before it broke up. Under this final impact the turret revolved around its center to the left through an angle of two degrees. The dog when released from his prison was apparently none the worse for his experience. He had luckily escaped injury from flying fragments of steel which had showered across inside the turret and imbedded themselves in the wooden backing on the opposite side. Sampson and the officers at Indian Head were pleased to find that the turret structure which must support the armor "showed no signs of deformation."[21]

While Sampson was performing these tests at Indian Head, a revolution in Cuba was gaining momentum. By midsummer of 1896 the insurgents had got out of hand, although Spain had built up in the island an army of 135,000 regular troops and 40,000 volunteers—a Spanish soldier to every ten inhabitants, including women and children. Proclaiming Spain "absolutely powerless to make head against the insurgents," the United States press began to talk of the possibility of war. By this time Sampson's bureau had mastered the worst technological riddles about armor. There remained the problems of guns and powder.

The 13-inch guns installed now on three of the Navy's new battleships were not only heavy consumers of powder, but the old-fashioned black powder was itself not satisfactory in those largest guns. European nations had experimented with smokeless powder made from a nitroglycerin base. Professor C. E. Monroe, a Bureau of Ordnance chemist whom Sampson had once brought to the Naval Academy, had developed a smokeless powder from a guncotton base, which Sampson preferred because of its greater stability. But Sampson spent several years in having various formulas tested at the Torpedo Station, and in testing the characteristics of this so-called "smokeless K" when stored at high temperatures such as might develop in the magazines of a ship. The formulas at length perfected, Sampson in 1895 was able to issue "smokeless K" for testing small caliber ammunition in the North Atlantic Squadron.

Guns, gun mounts, turrets, turret-turning devices, ammunition hoists, armor belts, torpedoes—each of these matters challenged the mechanical ingenuity of the Bureau of Ordnance. Each was to some degree experimental. What type of six-inch ammunition hoist, for instance, was most suitable on a modern battleship? No one yet knew. So the Bureau of Ordnance placed a steam hoist on the *Maine*, a hand-power hoist on the *Texas*, a hydraulic on the *Oregon* and a "simple whip" on the *Indiana;* while the six-pounder ammunition for the *Massachusetts* was elevated from the handling room by an electric motor.[22]

So much of the work of Sampson's bureau impinged upon that of other closely related bureaus that much time had to be devoted to interbureau "diplomacy." Which bureau should decide on the type and install the turret-turning mechanism in battleships? The problem concerned Construction and Repair, and Steam Engineering, as well as Ordnance. Sampson, always an advocate of electricity, having persuaded Secretary Herbert to let him install electric turning gear experimentally in half of the turrets of the cruiser *Brooklyn*, in the spring of 1896 wanted electric turning gear adopted also for battleship turrets. Steam "donkey" engines inside the barbette, or armored cylindrical foundation for the turret, raised the temperature inside this narrow powder-handling compartment, and there was danger of steam joints leaking and dampening the powder. Electricity, Sampson believed, would be ideal. The *Army and Navy Journal* reported "quite a controversy" in progress among the three bureaus. "The chiefs of these bureaus appeared before the Secretary and for an hour and a half presented argument in behalf of their respective claims."[23]

Another device which Sampson advocated was the superimposed turret. On the early battleships there were, in addition to two 12 or 13-inch gun turrets, emplacements for a number of eight-inch guns and a considerable assortment of small calibers. When plans were being made for the *Kearsarge* and the *Kentucky*, Ensign Joseph Strauss brought to Sampson his suggestion that two eight-inch guns might be superimposed on each of the major turrets of the new class of battleship. This would give the eight-inchers the full armor protection enjoyed by the main turrets without the additional weight of eight-inch barbettes. The big disadvantage of superimposing the turrets, of course, was that an ammunition hoist should have to be run up through the lower turret. Sampson studied the problem carefully, decided that it was feasible and obtained its adoption by the Navy Department, although there was much sighing and wagging of heads throughout the Navy.

The plans for the *Kearsarge* and the *Kentucky*, however, ran hard aground on a political reef. In the interim since their last armor contract, the two armor firms, in order to break into the European market, had sold an order of armor to Russia at the bargain price of $250 per ton.[24] This fact looked bad to Congress when a short while later Carnegie and Bethlehem submitted identical bids ($552.07 per ton) on the armor for the *Kearsarge* and the *Kentucky*. Senator Smith of New Jersey, sniffing collusion and monopoly, introduced a bill limiting the price of armor to $300. At this figure the companies refused to submit bids. Senator Chandler conducted an investigation of armor prices too technical for the majority of Congressmen to understand and the upshot of Congress' "hot fit of economy" was not only delay in completing the two battleships concerned, but a general postponement in authorizing further new construction. If Sampson at this juncture had not taken strenuous measures to build up a reserve supply of guns, armor-piercing projectiles and gunpowder, the Navy would have been unable a year later to arm and equip its large auxiliary fleet of merchantmen and passenger craft.

During his last year in the bureau, before he resigned from it to take command of the new battleship *Iowa*, Sampson had difficulty over the 13-inch guns. Only 12 of these monsters had been completed at the Washington gun factory; of these four had gone to the *Indiana*, four to the *Oregon*, three to the *Massachusetts* and one to the proving ground at Indian Head. The *Iowa*, which was a larger battleship than any of her predecessors, was given guns of only 12-inch caliber for her main batteries. There may have been technical difficulties which justified the reversion to the smaller caliber; yet there is reason to believe that foreign diplomatic objections to these large guns may have been interposed. Though Sampson habitually never mentioned professional matters at home, there was one remarkable occasion when he departed from this rule. Sampson's eldest son, Commander Ralph E. Sampson, U.S.N. (ret.), who at the time of the incident was eleven years old, writes: "I remember it clearly, as it was the only time I ever saw him provoked. I use the word 'provoked' because if I said he was mad you might think he was excited, and that was impossible for him. It was his last year as Chief of the Bureau of Ordnance just before he took command of the brand new *Iowa*. He came home one evening not at all the man I knew. My mother attempted to find out what the trouble was. His reply was, 'The Dutch have taken Holland,' which was his stock reply to all inquiries over the years. But later in the evening he surprised me with this:

" 'Boy! Always watch the British. They have just objected to the big guns we were going to put on the new battleships. They say they are too big. The White House says we must redesign the ship.' "[25] The stirring events of the next year saved the *Kearsarge* and the *Kentucky* from the caliber limitation that had affected the *Iowa*.

While Sampson was in the bureau his second daughter Catherine, who had been his hostess in Hawaii, was married to Ensign Richard H. Jackson, a survivor and hero of the famous Samoa hurricane disaster of 1889. In 1894 the Sampsons moved from G Street to 1613 New Hampshire Avenue, where they were living on Friday December 21 when the third daughter, Hannah, or Nannie as she was called at home, was presented to society. The Sampson home on the occasion was reported in the press as a "very fascinating rendezvous for their friends after 5 o'clock."[26]

On June 15, 1897, Sampson assumed command of the battleship *Iowa*. This newest "Queen of the Navy" was being eagerly watched by her sailors for any telltale signs of good or bad luck. Her 11,410 tons made her the biggest ship yet commissioned in the New Navy, with a length of 360 feet, beam 72 and draft 24. Would she, like the hoodooed *Texas*, on loading sink so low in the water as to submerge her armor belt? To Sampson's immense relief she proved to have several hundred tons of spare buoyancy beyond the original calculation. And on her trial she developed sufficient speed to award Cramps, her builders, a $200,000 premium. A delegation from the state of Iowa proudly presented her with a 41-piece silver service, with the state seal and motto embossed on each piece. Captain Sampson accepted the gift with a "graceful" speech, which had probably been written for him by his wife who had a pronounced talent in that direction. A writer for the *Midland Monthly* found the belief prevailing among the new battleship's crew that their ship was lucky and would sail "over reefs and sandbars, and ride great storms with little damage to her mighty bulk and complex machinery. . . . Captain Sampson," continued this writer, "is a grave and thoughtful man, the type you would instinctively trust in time of danger, clear-headed and cool, foreseeing emergencies and fully prepared to meet them."[27]

An ordnance expert's paradise, the *Iowa* carried 18 main battery guns; four 12-inch, eight 8-inch, six 4-inch; and 30 smaller guns and quick-firers. In addition she carried seven torpedo tubes. She was a fine and a highly sensitive mechanism, but she had been expensive. Her hull and machinery alone had cost $3,010,000.00. Congress in a fit of "rascally virtue" was trumpeting for lower prices on armor and, to the chagrin of everyone in the Navy, was withholding appropriations for more battleships. Aside from eliminating small mechanical imperfections in the mechanism of new ships, the building up of the New Navy in the summer of 1897 had ground to a stop.

In view of the approaching trouble with Spain—and war was openly talked of now by "jingoes" and the yellow press—this eleventh-hour economy was ill-timed. Feeling the pinch of economy Sampson's gunners on the *Iowa* held target practice only with reduced-caliber guns. They aimed their great 12-inch gun barrels at targets only a few hundred yards distant, but the shots they fired were from Remington small arms clamped inside of the 12-inch bores![28]

Such was the situation of stalemate when that prodigy of American politics, Theodore Roosevelt, became "assistant ruler of Uncle Sam's Navee." Let Secretary Long retire for a quiet week end in the country and the Navy Department was shaken with extraordinary doings. "The liveliest spot in Washington at present is the Navy Department," reported the *New York Sun* on August 23, 1897. "The decks are cleared for action. Acting Secretary Roosevelt, in the absence of Gov. Long, has the whole navy bordering on a war footing. It remains only to sand down the decks and pipe to quarters for action."[29]

Among other innovations, that seem obvious enough today, Theodore Roosevelt called for squadron maneuvers and gunnery practice, despite the expense for ammunition, by the armored ships of the New Navy. On Tuesday September 7, 1897, the Assistant Secretary himself steamed out in the *Dolphin* to the drill ground 30 miles off the Virginia Capes to witness three days of fleet drill. The crack armored cruiser *Brooklyn* was put through her paces and run up and down the firing line. Roosevelt inspected her experimental steam and electric ammunition hoists which Sampson had installed and concerning which interbureau controversy was still raging in Washington. The flagship *New York* repelled an imaginary attack by torpedo boats, making a spectacular display of searchlights and secondary batteries. The next day the great ships got under way early for their first full-dress armored fleet review. Back and forth before the little *Dolphin* the pachyderms of the squadron passed in single column, in double column, in formation *en échelon;* wheels to right and left and other combination movements were made. Two armored cruisers, the *New York*, Rear Admiral Sicard's flagship, and the *Brooklyn;* two second-class battleships, the *Maine* and the *Texas* and three first-rate battleships, the *Massachusetts*, the *Indiana* and the newest and largest of all, the *Iowa*, ran through their evolutions "with splendid precision," cleaving the long swells, their gun crews standing at attention outside their turrets.

The high point of Roosevelt's review of the fleet was the target practice of the *Iowa*. On this occasion, the first since she had been afloat, she was permitted to expend live ammunition and full-sized projectiles against a target. When Captain Sampson received Admiral Sicard's signal that the Assistant Secretary had chosen to watch firing practice on board the *Iowa*, Sampson sent two whaleboats to tow a target into place and cleared the ship for action. Side rails were taken down to give free swing to the guns. Everything liable to damage from concussion was carried to locations of greater safety. Hatch combings were stowed below and in their places heavy steel battle plates were screwed down. Doors were left ajar, window sashes were lowered, breakable articles were removed from insecure shelves. The glass doors of the wardroom cabinet in which the *Iowa's* ceremonial silver service was kept were allowed to swing freely to the ends of pieces of twine.

The Assistant Secretary came on board accompanied by Commander Bronson, Lieutenant Sharp, Mr. Roosevelt's aide and by reporters from the *New York Herald* and the *New York Sun*. "On the occasion of Mr. Roosevelt's visit," reported the *Sun*,[30] "Captain Sampson took position on the bridge with Lieutenant Commander Rodgers, the *Iowa's* executive officer. Captain Sampson is always calm and dignified. He looked the ideal naval commander as he stood on the bridge waiting for the practice to begin. Lieutenant Commander Rodgers, with a speaking trumpet slung over his shoulder, was here, there and everywhere, giving orders that mystified the layman.

"A terrific ringing of a gong was the signal for a scene of activity. Officers took their regular places with alacrity, while the bluejackets and marines scampered to the positions to which they had been assigned. The officers who had charge of the turrets appeared in working clothes, canvas jumpers, old trousers, and caps that had seen better days. Theirs was dirty work. . . . It was close quarters inside the turrets. The day was warm and hardly any air was stirring. . . . Everybody had his station, the little Japanese messboys, not exempted, ran to the powder division.

"On the bridge with Captain Sampson and Lieutenant Commander Rodgers were half a dozen apprentice boys who acted as messengers. . . . A toot from the steam whistle and a bugle blast told the gunners of the battery to commence firing." The ends of the *Iowa's* firing course were marked by two whaleboats, and the target, a five-foot frame covered with strips of canvas, was set adrift about 2,500 yards beyond the firing course.

The *Iowa's* gunners, who had never before fired regular ammunition at a target, were keyed up with excitement, but weather conditions favored them. The sky was clear and hot, with no breeze to disturb the target, which appeared at 2,500 yards "a mere speck slowly wobbling in the gentle roll of the sea."

"Two thousand yards," cried a junior officer with the range finder. "Two thousand yards," repeated the executive officer, and the word was passed along the ship to the officer in charge of one of the eight-inch starboard turrets. A flash of fire, a cloud of smoke and then a thunderous report marked the explosion. The *Iowa's* deck quivered. A column of water shot up in front of the target and a moment later a second column off to the right showed how the shot had ricocheted. Another flash, and the second shot started on its journey. This one sent up a tall column slightly to one side of the target. "Some fell in front, some to the side and one or two went over. . . . The Roosevelt party began to enjoy themselves. They forgot to keep their mouths open and to stand on their toes."[31]

The *Iowa* came about to retrace her course and give the guns on the other side a chance. Officers and men, grimy and sweaty, popped out of the disengaged turrets for a breath of air. On her second run the "12-inch thunderers" shook the battleship, their projectiles leaving the guns with the sound of a heavy wind, deepening in the distance to the "far away rumble of a train of boxcars going over a bridge." Two members of Mr. Roosevelt's party, venturing far out on the bridge to get a better view of an eight-inch turret were caught not 50 feet from the muzzle of a 12-inch gun in the forward turret when it was fired.

The blast lifted them "off their feet straight into the air almost to the top of the bridge railing." They alighted, each wildly clasping the other.

After the 12-inch guns Sampson demonstrated the six-pounder quick-firers. These little barkers, "sharp and unpleasant to the ear," fired 20 shots in 30 seconds. The practice over, the Roosevelt party removed the cotton plugs from their ears and Captain Sampson escorted them on a tour of the ship. Concussions from the heavy guns had smashed a whaleboat, sprung clocks, shattered electric-light globes and glass skylights and knocked several doors off their hinges: petty damages, scarcely noticed by anyone save reporters, so great was the elation over the success of the target practice.

"The trip has been in every way more than satisfactory," the Assistant Secretary told reporters on returning to the *Dolphin.* "The rapidity and precision of the practice with the rapid fire guns and the extraordinary accuracy with which the huge turret guns were fired were equally noteworthy. . . . At last we are beginning to have a navy fit to uphold the interests of our people, a navy which, though too small in size, need fear comparison with no other as regards the quality of its ships and men."[32]

Roosevelt's visit to the fleet apparently convinced him that Sampson was one of the most level-headed and dependable men in the Navy. A month later, when the Assistant Secretary decided to clear up the vexatious personnel problem, he picked Captain Sampson as the senior line officer on this special board. "Novice," "Enfant Terrible," "that blunt old sea-dog, the Assistant Secretary of the Navy"—call him what they might, the shocked Congressmen could scarcely deny Roosevelt's contention that the jealousies of line officers and engineers had too long vexed the Navy. With the New Navy materializing, some settlement of the old feud needed to be made. Sampson and the ten other line and staff officers associated with him decided that the time had now come to amalgamate engineer officers with the line. "Every officer on a modern war vessel in reality has to be an engineer, whether he wants to or not. Everything on such a vessel goes by machinery."[33] "We are not making a revolution; we are merely recognizing and giving shape to an evolution."[34] Reasonable promotion, the board decided, must be provided for by the selection of the best fitted officers and the enforced retirement of others. These problems were not solved

yet; but Sampson and the other members of Roosevelt's Personnel
Board on the eve of the war with Spain worked out the solution
whereby a 50-year-old feud eventually was to be settled.

On January 31, 1898, in the calm before trouble broke with Spain,
Sampson at Dry Tortugas found time to write to his 12-year-old son
Ralph. "My dear Ralph, I wonder if you would not like to change
weathers with me. Here it is warm enough for white clothes and to
sit on the door step after sun down, only we have no door step. I
know you would like the fishing. I have not tried it yet, but I have
had some of the fish others have caught. Among them was a big sea
crawfish. It looks like a lobster except that it has no claws and is covered with pretty spots. It is as large as two or even three lobsters. It
does not turn red when it is boiled. I suppose it is accustomed to a
warm climate and don't [sic!] mind having it boiling hot. Sharks we
have in plenty. We expect to move from here in a couple of days so
that by the time you send me an answer to this, as I hope you will,
we shall be anchored out at sea. I do like to get letters, my boy. I like
to know what you are doing and how you do it, Mamma wrote me
about you having put your little finger out of joint. She told me too
that you did it in a fight. I wonder if you were whipped that time. I
trust you were fighting in a good cause and that the little finger did not
discourage you. It is not a good plan to fight at any time unless you
have a good reason. Good-bye my dear boy. Please give dear Mamma
a good kiss for me. Papa."[35]

After the disaster to the *Maine* in Havana Harbor, Sampson was
ordered to serve as president of the *Maine* Court of Inquiry. The court
was directed to make a thorough investigation of the circumstances
surrounding the loss of the ship. In their report they were asked to
consider whether there had been negligence on the part of any of the
ship's officers or crew and what in their opinion had been the cause
or causes of the explosion.

Sampson convened the court at 10:00 A.M. on February 21, five days
after the disaster. During the first week the court held its sessions on
board the U. S. lighthouse tender *Mangrove*, anchored in Havana
Harbor alongside the wreck itself. In the second week it met in Key
West to question certain survivors hospitalized there, after which it
returned to the scene of the wreck for two final weeks of intensive
investigation.

The *Maine*, with a mean draft of 21.6 feet, had settled to the bottom in water about 32 feet deep. The undamaged afterdeck of the ship was now several feet under water, and much of the totally wrecked forward half of the ship, a mass of shattered and tangled scrap, had been folded back upon the midship section of the ship and stood high out of water.

The almost unanimous testimony of the survivors was that there had been two explosions, first a small one under the portside of the ship like a torpedo or like the report of a 10-inch gun fired close aboard, then within a few seconds an overwhelming, deafening, blinding roar like the explosion of magazines. Might not this initial explosion have been due to internal causes—spontaneous combustion in the coal bunkers, a saboteur's bomb hidden in the coal, inflammable paint supplies or waste materials, a boiler explosion, overheating of the ammunition chambers? Each possibility of laxness in shipkeeping was ruled out by exhaustive and convincing testimony.

Divers were sent down to examine in the muddy blackness the submerged portions of the wreckage. An ensign questioned each diver as he came up, took notes and made sketches of the present positions of the twisted frames, the breaks in the keel plates, etc. Two facts which greatly impressed the court were an indentation inboard of the outside skin of the ship abreast the six-inch shell room, and beneath this indentation a hole in the harbor floor about six feet in depth and 15 in diameter. That the initial explosion did not originate inside the magazines was the apparent meaning of the quantities of unexploded powder cans and shells which littered the submerged wreckage. Much of the ship's powder had been simply spilled out on the bottom of the bay. Two members of the court rowing around the wreckage in a small boat fished up a handful of mud from the bottom.[36] This mud when dried and ignited burned readily and gave off a strong odor of gunpowder. No question was raised as to the stability of the *Maine's* powder. She carried none of the new smokeless powder, but only the stable brown prismatic kind.

At Key West on March 21 the court held its final session on board Sampson's battleship *Iowa*, and signed its history-making report. "At frame 18 the vertical keel is broken in two, and the flat keel bent into an angle similar to the angle formed by the outside bottom plating. This break is now about 6 feet below the surface of the water, and

The *New York* Signaling to Cease Fire after the Surrender of Cervera's Squadron.

Ships on the Blockade, with the *New York* at right.

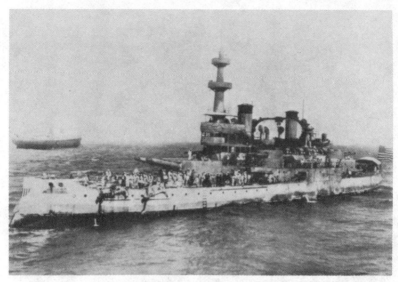

The U. S. S. *Oregon*.

The U. S. S. *Brooklyn*.

about 30 feet above its normal position. In the opinion of the court this effect could have been produced only by the explosion of a mine situated under the bottom of the ship at about frame 18 and somewhat on the port side of the ship. . . . In the opinion of the court the *Maine* was destroyed by the explosion of a submarine mine, which caused the partial explosion of two or more of the forward magazines. . . . The court has been unable to obtain evidence fixing the responsibility for the destruction of the *Maine* upon any person or persons."[37]

During the four weeks while Captain Sampson, Captain Chadwick and the two junior officers of the court were conducting their inquiry, the yellow journals were blatantly trumpeting across the nation that the *Maine* had been deliberately blown up by a treacherous enemy. Lurid stories and highly imaginative sketches of infernal machines purported to demonstrate how the Spaniard had accomplished the *Maine's* destruction.

When the report of Sampson's court was published on March 28, the man in the street was prepared to accept the verdict of an initial external explosion as a verdict against Spain. There were parades with banners demanding retribution against Spain.

The resignation of Rear Admiral Sicard because of chronic malaria led to the appointment of Sampson as commander in chief of the North Atlantic Squadron—the main battle force upon which the heaviest responsibility would fall in case of war. Captain Sampson's pennant was hoisted on board the flagship *New York* at 3:10 P.M. on March 26. On April 21 Sampson was appointed a rear admiral. Next day, upon receipt of orders from McKinley, Sampson disposed his forces for a blockade of northern Cuba. The formal declaration of war followed on April 25.

Part Four

THE BRIEF WAR OF EMPIRE,
APRIL 22-AUGUST 12, 1898

14. DEWEY WINS MANILA BAY

GEORGE DEWEY took over the command of the Asiatic Station from Rear Admiral F. V. McNair on January 3, 1898, hoisting his commodore's pennant on board the cruiser *Olympia* at Nagasaki. The fact that officers in this post normally held the rank of rear admiral did nothing to improve Commodore Dewey's feeling toward Secretary Long, who, he felt, had held him in the lower rank because of his wire pulling to obtain his assignment. Dewey's first gesture was to revive the custom of paying a courtesy call on the Emperor and Empress of Japan which had lately been discontinued.[1] Next he ordered the scattered vessels of his command to concentrate at Hong Kong, an obvious point of departure in case of war with Spain. At Hong Kong, where he received news of the *Maine* disaster, the impetuous Dewey, unwilling to wait for news through ordinary channels, arranged by private subscription among the officers of the squadron to have the admitted facts in the case telegraphed in advance by the editor of the *Army and Navy Journal*.[2]

While official Washington, awaiting the verdict of the *Maine* court, clung to the accident theory, the Assistant Secretary of the Navy from the first interpreted the disaster as an outrage perpetrated by Spain. One Friday afternoon, after the peace-loving Mr. Long had departed for a week end in the country, Roosevelt used his authority as Acting Secretary to alert Dewey with the following historic cablegram: [3]

"Washington, *February 25, 1898*
"Dewey, *Hongkong:*
"Order the squadron, except the *Monocacy*, to Hongkong. Keep full of coal. In the event of declaration of war Spain, your duty will be to see that the Spanish squadron does not leave the Asiatic coast, and then offensive operations in Philippine Islands. Keep *Olympia* until further orders.

"Roosevelt."

Inasmuch as Dewey was 7,000 miles from the nearest American base and since his military preparations in foreign ports would be curtailed by neutrality rules after hostilities had broken out, it was of tremendous importance to him to receive Roosevelt's clear-cut message a month before the *Maine* verdict was published. Dewey put his ships into drydock to have their hulls scraped and painted. Much necessary repair work for machinery was done on shore in Hong Kong. Dewey cabled Consul Oscar F. Williams in Manila a request for information on the Spanish squadron and Manila's harbor defenses. The United States consul in Singapore put Dewey in touch with the Philippine insurgent general, Aguinaldo, whom Dewey agreed to assist. Provisions of all sorts, enough to last the squadron for three months, were transferred to the ships from Chinese sampans.

The British collier *Nanshan* arrived in Hong Kong with 3,000 tons of Welsh coal. On his own initiative Dewey chartered the vessel and, after cabling a request to Washington, purchased this collier and also the supply ship *Zafiro*. [4] He signed on their crews as members of the American merchant marine, and obtained custom house clearances for Guam so as to avoid neutrality restrictions after the outbreak of war. The old paddle-wheeler *Monocacy* he decommissioned and he had her personnel distributed to the combatant ships. The United States revenue cutter *McCulloch* was obtained for use as a dispatch boat.

Commander B. F. Lamberton arrived to relieve Captain Frank Wildes of the cruiser *Boston*. With a prospect of action ahead, Wildes emphatically refused to relinquish his post. Cables sizzled to Washington. Wildes's detachment was canceled and Dewey appointed Lamberton to be his chief of staff. The extra officer might well have taken over Captain Gridley's place as commanding officer of the flagship *Olympia*. Charles Vernon Gridley was an invalid with scarcely two months to live, but the commodore respected his intense desire to stand by his post. Joseph L. Stickney, a journalist who was also an ex-naval officer, had come to the Far East to report on the partitioning of China by European imperialists, but now he came south to Hong Kong instead, traveling on the same steamer as Commander Lamberton. Stickney received Dewey's permission to come aboard the *Olympia*. To give a semblance of legality to Stickney's living on board the naval ship, Dewey with a twinkle appointed him an aide.

During these busy preliminaries the German admiral, Prince Henry, brother of Wilhelm II, whose interest in collecting Far Eastern real estate was notorious, succeeded in infuriating Commodore Dewey. The occasion, as reported to the *New York Times* by Charles N. Post, was a dinner given by Prince Henry to the higher officers of the other fleets in Hong Kong Harbor. At the feast Prince Henry toasted his own country, then England, then all the other powers. Finally, just before the dinner was over he toasted the United States. "When Dewey saw that his country was being slighted, he left the banquet without ceremony. The next day a roundabout apology was sent by Prince Henry. Dewey would receive only a personal or written apology. The Prince then called upon Dewey and explained that in the confusion of the dinner he had thoughtlessly neglected to put the United States in its proper position. When Prince Henry later gave a ball, Dewey did not attend it."[5]

The second week in April Dewey began landing inessential personal belongings of the crews, woodwork and stores that might be useless encumbrance or fire hazard in battle. He was also anxiously awaiting the arrival of the cruiser *Baltimore* with ammunition, and he had urged Consul Williams to come to Hong Kong at once for consultation.

"We are still waiting for the declaration of war to begin our work here," Dewey wrote his sister Mary Greeley on April 18. "I have seven men-of-war all ready for action, and should war be the word I believe we will make short work of Spanish reign in the Philippines.

The insurgents are ready to rise at our first gun, and long before this reaches you we may be masters at Manila and other Philippine cities. But, after all, war is a terrible thing, and I hope some way out of the dilemma may be found without resorting to it. My health continues good, although it is taxed to the uttermost, and my one prayer is that I may be able to hold out until we have finished our work."[6]

The next morning early, bosun's chairs were swung over the rails and the gleaming white sides of Dewey's cruisers and gunboats were dulled by a coat of slate gray. The *Baltimore*, arriving on Friday, April 22, was immediately drydocked to have her bottom scraped and painted.[7] She was out again in 24 hours. While her warpaint was being applied scores of coolie laborers swarmed over her decks from coal junks, water junks, provision junks and sampans, to get her stores on board. The task was completed by Sunday afternoon when Dewey received word from the British governor of Hong Kong that war had been declared between the United States and Spain and that the American Squadron would be given 24 hours in which to leave British jurisdiction. Dewey moved his squadron to Mirs Bay, 30 miles from Hong Kong in Chinese waters, where he would not be hamstrung by neutrality rules. As the American ships left their anchorage at Hong Kong, they passed close by an English army hospital ship whose patients gathered at the port rail and gave them three cheers. The Yankee seamen boisterously returned the compliment.[8]

While waiting for Consul Williams to arrive from Manila, Dewey received Secretary Long's cable of April 24: "War has commenced between the United States and Spain. Proceed at once to Philippine Islands. Commence operations at once, particularly against the Spanish fleet. You must capture vessels or destroy. Use utmost endeavors."[9]

During the few days of waiting in Mirs Bay Dewey's seamen received a final intensive drill at the quick-fire guns and in handling torpedoes. In subcaliber practice they aimed the eight-inch guns of the *Olympia* and the *Baltimore* at points on the brown cliffs of Kowloon Peninsula.[10] Consul Williams, having been delayed by bad weather, reached the fleet on Wednesday, April 27.

Dewey called his captains aboard, to hear Consul Williams' latest information. Coast defense guns were mounted on the Manila water front, at the Cavite base and on Corregidor and Caballo islands in the harbor mouth.[11] According to Williams' informers, the most frequent-

ly used channel entrance, that between Corregidor and Mariveles, had
been extensively mined. A munitions ship, the *Isla de Mindanao,* had
arrived on April 23, the day before Williams had left Manila. Admiral
Montojo's squadron, containing two cruisers and five gunboats, had
recently withdrawn from its base at Cavite inside Manila Bay to a prepared position in Subic Bay, some 30 miles north of Manila Bay.

All anchors were immediately raised and at 2:00 P.M. the flagship
Olympia led the squadron out of Mirs Bay and headed for Manila, 628
miles away. The naval ships steamed in battle order: the *Olympia,* the
Baltimore, the *Raleigh,* the *Petrel,* the *Concord* and the *Boston,* while
in a parallel line a half mile to starboard steamed the fleet train, composed of the *McCulloch,* the *Nanshan* and the *Zafiro.*[12] The entire
squadron perforce moved at the cruising speed of the supply ships.
As they proceeded, the ships, completing the disposal of their woodwork, littered the South China Sea with mess tables, chairs, chests,
planking, turpentine, paint and other waste.[13] Now and then a shout
would go up, "Remember the *Maine!*" As the ships crept southward,
the *Olympia's* band gave a lusty rendition of the march *"El Capitan."*[14]

The squadron sighted Cape Bolinao at 4:00 P.M. on Saturday, April
30. Dewey sent ahead the *Boston,* the *Concord* and the *Baltimore* to
reconnoiter Subic Bay, and when the scouts reported that Montojo
was not there Dewey headed for Manila Bay. The run was made
through the little used Boca Grande passage between the islands of
Corregidor and El Fraile. Corregidor's lighthouse was dark. In the
fleet no lights were shown save a carefully hooded stern lantern on the
taffrail of each ship to enable following vessels to keep in line. While
they were running the gantlet of the forts at the entrance to the bay,
the supply ships were stationed in line behind the naval craft, with
the revenue cutter *McCulloch* bringing up the rear. The night was
sultry, with the moon early in the evening showing occasionally between banks of clouds. At 9:42 P.M. all hands were called to quarters.[15]
The approach was fitfully illuminated by lightning, and at eleven a
light rain fell. "The tension was pretty strong," writes a young officer
on the *Olympia,* "as we did not know what to expect."[16] Not a sound
came from Corregidor until half the fleet had passed beyond the
island's batteries. Then the soot in the *McCulloch's* smokestack took
flame. In a few moments a red rocket streaked upward from the top
of Corregidor and a cannon barked from El Fraile.[17] The *McCulloch*

and the *Boston* returned several shots in the direction of the enemy
flashes. A few shots splattered around the ships, several splashes being
so large as to be mistaken for mines.

When the ships had passed beyond range Dewey reduced speed to
four knots and with red and white lights signaled that all who were
not on watch duty might now relax or sleep at their posts.[18] Throughout the rest of the night Dewey remained on the *Olympia's* bridge,
peering into the darkness and relieving the tension by sipping cold tea.
At 4:00 A.M. hot coffee and hard tack were served to all hands. Dewey
drank his steaming cup along with Captain Gridley, Commander
Lamberton, Lieutenant Calkins and the journalist Joe Stickney. The
hot coffee on top of cold tea did not agree with the commodore, and
there was an embarrassing moment just as dawn was breaking over
Manila when the commodore lost his breakfast.[19]

In the earliest dawn, watchers on the *Olympia* having made out 16
merchant craft at anchor off Manila, but no men-of-war, Dewey left
his supply ships in the middle of the bay and turned his fighters westward toward Cavite. Batteries at Manila fired on the fleet about 5:00
A.M. Their first shots fell short and were not replied to. Off Cavite
seven miles away one could see the smoke pouring up from Montojo's
anchored squadron. At 5:06 A.M. the Spaniards detonated two submarine mines outside of Cavite and some four miles ahead of the
Olympia.[20] The incident gave rise to the American comment that the
Spaniards at Cavite were less perfect in aiming than those who had
sunk the *Maine*. The Spanish, however, had fired their mines not to
sink the *Olympia* but in order to clear a path through which their
own ships might safely sally from their anchorage.

Commodore Dewey took his station on the *Olympia's* bridge, while
Captain Gridley entered the armored conning tower beneath the
bridge and back of the forward turret. As Dewey, in the early morning, moved toward the great battle of his life, his appearance was not
that of the perfectionist in dress which so many newspapers and magazines have depicted. His uniform cap had been lost in the shuffle the
day before when the carpenters had torn out from the commodore's
quarters a bulkhead which interfered with the operation of a secondary gun. He wore instead a casual civilian golfer's cap, which contrasted strangely with his white uniform.

Ever since 9:42 of the night before, the men had been at battle stations. While there were some who had stretched out and slept on deck beside their guns, the nerves of all were now strung up to prebattle tautness. The last detail of ingenuity in preparation had been accomplished. Despite the high temperatures below decks, where full steam had been maintained since leaving Mirs Bay, all hatches were securely battened down. An engineer prostrated by heat during the run past Corregidor had died a few hours before dawn. Doctors, hospital corpsmen and chaplains had distributed emergency bandages and tourniquets throughout the ships and had converted wardrooms into sick bays, with mess tables transformed into operating tables and surgical instruments laid out in readiness.

The batteries along the Manila water front continued their poorly aimed fire at the squadron as it steamed away toward Cavite, where the Spanish fleet was shortly descried. At 5:15 a heavy rifled gun on Sangley Point, Cavite, opened on the challengers. The commodore, personally leading the battle column, withheld his own return fire for a full twenty minutes. His ammunition was not so plentiful that he could throw it away, however satisfying its mere noise might be to the half-naked, tense-muscled gunners in his turrets. Lieutenant C. G. Calkins, the *Olympia's* navigator, kept calling the range as the flagship bore down on the enemy. At about 5,000 yards Dewey turned the column to starboard and straightened out on a course roughly paralleling the anchored Spanish line. Then from the rail of his flying bridge he called down to Captain Gridley in the conning tower below him:

"You may fire when you are ready, Gridley."[21]

The captain nodded to Bugler Charles Mitchell, who in turn blew a blast to transmit the order down the length of the *Olympia's* deck. Lieutenant T. M. Brumby, signal officer, ran up to the foretruck the flag signal "Engage."[22] An eight-inch gun in the *Olympia's* forward battery began the historic duel. Time pieces on the *Olympia* disagreed as to the exact moment when the first American shot was fired. The commodore gave it at 5:41; the keeper of the *Olympia's* log recorded it as 5:35.[23] Instantly, like a series of echoes, came the thunderous challenges of the guns of the other American ships.

At least six Spanish ships could now be distinguished at anchor in a half circle in Bakor Bay just behind Cavite peninsula, the red and yellow flag of Spain at their mastheads. Their puffs of smoke and roars were now added to the smoke and thunder from the batteries on shore. The *Reina Cristina*, Admiral Montojo's flagship, and the *Castilla*, the two largest enemy ships, became Dewey's chief targets.

During the taut and silent approach the *Olympia's* men had stood at their guns with set teeth. Now under the sound of their own guns "salting the enemy in style" they relaxed and worked smoothly.[24]

Five times the commodore charged past the line of enemy targets, with three runs from the eastward and two from the westward. After each turn, shirtless, sweat-dripping gunners of batteries on the disengaged side would come out of their hot turrets for air. Now and then an unconscious fireman would be handed up from the lower decks. Dewey had an advantage of position. The sun, rising behind his squadron, blinded the enemy to the westward. The day turned out to be windless and burning hot. Dr. Charles P. Kindleberger, surgeon on the *Olympia*, having no casualties to care for, watched the spectacle from the six-pounder guns forward of the sick bay. "There was very little for me to do, and as these guns were fired only when the ship was at short range from the shore, my position was an ideal one. Early in the fight I saw what looked like a ten-inch shell coming toward the ship with great velocity. It seemed inevitable that we should be destroyed. The shell struck the water ten feet from the bow and ricochetted clear over the vessel, with a screech that was indescribable. Had it struck five feet higher I should not tell this tale. Other shells fell as near, and the impact sent the water splashing over us."[25] A shell fragment chipped a sliver out of the forecastle deck a few feet below where the commodore was standing. Another snipped in two Lieutenant Brumby's signal halyards.[26] Although the Spanish cruisers had no guns larger than 6.3, the position of the American squadron was well within the range of most of the Spanish guns. The Spaniard was prodigal of ammunition and ineffective in his aim. Dewey and his officers hoped that their own firing was more accurate, but such dense smoke covered the target area that it was difficult to see how effective it was.

Dewey had a man on the bow swinging the lead to avoid grounding, and in his later runs Dewey shifted course nearer to the target line.

Early in the action a yellow-hulled steam launch, which was taken for a torpedo boat, put out from behind Sangley Point and headed toward the *Olympia*. Stickney called Dewey's attention to this boat. "You look after her," Stickney quotes the commodore, "I have no time to bother with torpedo boats. Let me know when you've finished her."[27] The daring craft managed to come within range of the squadron's secondary armament, when it was riddled and sunk. A second such boat was turned back close to shore.

At 7:00 A.M. Admiral Montojo in the flagship *Reina Cristina* made a desperate attempt to break out of his corner and engage Dewey at close range. The *Reina* was hit again and again. In the testimony of Lieutenant Calkins, the *Olympia's* navigator stationed on the bridge beside the commodore, "the Spaniard had only advanced a ship's length or so beyond his line before his progress was arrested by a hail of concentrated fire which produced immediate and visible results. His speed slackened; smoke puffed forward and aft; a white plume of escaping steam showed that his motive power was crippled, and an awkward turn . . . suggested that his steering-gear had met the same fate."[28] As the *Reina* swung about to retreat an eight-inch shell raked her fore and aft. Fires were started throughout the ship and the Spanish admiral's flag was shortly shifted to a small cruiser which disappeared behind Cavite; and a major share of the American fire was now devoted to the large white-sided receiving ship *Castilla*.[29]

After two and a half hours of steady dueling, the smoke was so thick over the targets that it was "almost impossible to distinguish ship or fort except by a gray mass and the sputter of flame."[30]

At 7:35 the commodore received from Captain Gridley a report that there remained only 15 rounds per gun of 5-inch ammunition. This news startled Dewey, whose situation some 7,000 miles from the nearest American base was not enviable. Not knowing what damage he had inflicted upon the enemy, and no doubt fearing that his own fire might have been almost as ineffective as the enemy's, Dewey promptly broke off action and stood out toward the middle of the bay to take stock of his priceless and fast-vanishing ammunition.

When the ships hauled out of action, according to the reporter Stickney, "the gloom on the bridge of the *Olympia* was thicker than a London fog in November."[31] The enemy had proved himself determined and courageous. In two and a half hours of fighting, his fire, however poorly directed, had not appreciably diminished. "Our projectiles seemed to go too high or too low—just as had been the case with those fired by the Spaniards. Several times the commodore had expressed dissatisfaction with the failure of our gunners to hit the enemy. We had begun the firing at too great a distance, but we had gradually worked in further on each of the turns, until we were within about twenty-five hundred yards at the close of the fifth round. At this distance, in a smooth sea, we ought to have made a large percentage of hits; yet so far as we could judge, we had not sensibly crippled the foe. Consequently Commodore Dewey hauled out into the open bay at the end of the fifth round to take stock of ammunition and devise a new plan of attack."[32]

The gunners now popping out of their turrets and untroubled by Dewey's somber responsibilities gave vent to far different feelings. As the cruiser *Baltimore* swung alongside, the *Olympians* cheered her. The *Baltimoreans* returned the cheers with gusto. Stickney, making his way aft, found the gunners confident and eager to get on with the fight. Why, they asked him, was the squadron hauling off? And Stickney's disingenuous reply "that we were merely hauling off for breakfast" caused them to appeal to Lamberton as he came aft a moment later:

"For God's sake, Captain, don't let us stop now. To hell with breakfast!"[33]

In a short time the commodore's mind was relieved when a check on ammunition stores showed that the earlier report had been exaggerated. Instead of the reported 15 rounds, there remained 45 rounds of five-inch ammunition per gun. Even so the situation was none too favorable. Three hundred and fifty rounds had already been expended.[34] Dewey was not at all willing, in the midst of a war, to publish to the world the fact that his ammunition was so low. When Stickney, in his capacity as "aide," suggested that in the news releases the withdrawal from action be attributed merely to the commodore's desire to give his men their breakfast, Dewey assented. In so doing Dewey not only achieved security for vital military information, but also served as an unwitting collaborator in evolving the Dewey Myth, which the newspapers of the United States were shortly to exploit— the heroic image of the Jovelike, confident American commodore who, at the height of battle's fury, coolly and with Olympian calm interrupted the engagement in order to give his men their breakfast!

In response to his signal Dewey's captains came on board the flagship to report damages. Each as he came over the side was asked, "How many killed?" Stickney records their reactions: "Mingled with satisfaction at having lost no man was an evident desire to have it understood that the lack of loss was no proof of an absence of danger."[35]

"Only eight wounded," replied Captain Nehemiah Dyer of the *Baltimore*, "none seriously. But six shells struck us, and two burst inboard without hurting any one."

"Not a dashed one!" jubilated the next captain.

"None killed and none wounded, but I don't know how it happened. I suppose you fellows were all cut up?"

"My ship wasn't hit at all."

When the last of the skippers announced that the *Boston* had suffered no casualties, a cheer broke loose that was echoed as the news spread through the ship.

That this happy condition did not obtain in the Spanish fleet began to be evident to the Americans as the powder smoke cleared away. By 10:30 A.M. there was scarcely anything left of Montojo's forces except three of his smallest gunboats. The *Reina Cristina* was a mass of flames, the *Castilla* had blown up and several other gunboats were sunk in shallow water with their top hampers burning.

At 11:16 Commodore Dewey returned to finish the grim work of the morning. This time, yielding to Captain Dyer's request, Dewey permitted the *Baltimore* to lead the battle line.[36] The remaining enemy gunboats were quickly sunk. The *Baltimore* steamed in close and smothered the shore batteries with her fire. Ensign Montgomery Meigs Taylor, in charge of one of the *Olympia's* batteries, admired the beautiful handling of the *Baltimore* and envied her for her shallower draft. "We drew so much water we could not get very close. My men were mad as pirates, and the profanity was something awful. They begged to be taken closer in, not liking the 4,000 yard business."[37]

At 12:25 P.M. a white flag was run up over Cavite arsenal, and Dewey signaled the *Petrel*, shallowest of his vessels, to go to Sangley Point and seize or burn whatever remained of the enemy's vessels. The *Petrel* applied the torch to partially damaged craft and within a short time returned to the fleet towing a welcome string of small yachts and tugs. The little *Petrel* received the cheers of the fleet. By 12:30 P.M. Dewey noted in his official report: "The squadron ceased firing, the batteries being silenced and the ships sunk, burnt, and deserted. . . . The Spanish lost the following vessels: Sunk—*Reina Cris-*

tina, Castilla, Don Antonio de Ulloa. Burnt—*Don Juan de Austria, Isla de Luzon, Isla de Cuba, General Lezo, Marques del Duero, El Correo, Velasco,* and *Isla de Mindanao* (transport). Captured—*Rapido* and *Hercules* (tugs) and several small launches. I am unable to obtain complete accounts of the enemy's killed and wounded, but believe their loss to have been very heavy. The *Reina Cristina* alone had 150 killed, including the captain, and 90 wounded. . . . I doubt if any commander in chief, under similar circumstances, was ever served by more loyal, efficient, and gallant captains than those of the squadron now under my command. . . ."[38]

Several of Dewey's ships had been hit, but the damages—partly owing to his thorough disposal of woodwork and other inflammable material—were negligible. A broken deck beam on the *Baltimore* and a shot through the mast of the *Boston* were the worst injuries to the ships. The explosion of a box of ready ammunition on the *Baltimore* had slightly wounded two officers and six men. An officer's clothes had been damaged by a shell landing in his locker, and then by being doused with salt water. . . .

"After the muss was over," wrote Ensign Taylor on May 3, "it seemed so absurd that we had knocked those chaps around so much without even skinning our knuckles [that] we looked at each other and laughed. After the surrender . . . the crews lined the rails and cheered themselves hoarse. I was sitting on the 8-inch turret with two or three of the mess, and we yelled ourselves speechless. We cheered each ship, the flag, the American Consul, ourselves, and any old thing that could be used as an excuse. When we stopped the first time one man cried because he could not fire any more. You may imagine how we slept that night after the scrap. We had had no sleep since 8 A.M. the day before and worked under a big strain for twelve hours, from the passage of the forts to the surrender, and when it was all over the men just dropped where they stood and slept. . . . It was great while it lasted, and I never expect to see a grander sight in the rest of my life."[39]

Early in the afternoon Dewey dropped anchor about four miles offshore and gave his attention to Manila, whose water-front batteries since before sunup had never ceased their long-range sniping at his fleet. Dewey sent a message to the Spanish governor threatening to bombard the city unless the Manila batteries stopped firing. This requirement was promptly acceded to. Dewey's further demand that he be allowed the use of Manila's cable to Hong Kong was refused.

Dewey promptly caused the *Zafiro* to drag the harbor and cut this cable.

In severing Manila's only cable communication with the outside world, Dewey was motivated by simple military necessity. And once again, as in his sanctioning of the hauling-off-for-breakfast story, he unconsciously furthered the Dewey Myth by creating an atmosphere in which, as in a hothouse, the myth might flourish. The fragmentary and misleading dispatches which the Spanish authorities had already sent out over their cable before it went dead had been enough to give the outside world a vague sense of the magnitude of the Spanish disaster and an inkling of the overwhelming character of the American success. For more than a week the silencing of the Manila cable kept the world in the dark. The most exciting news in a generation had been no sooner turned on than it was turned off. Manila might as well have been on another planet. The atmosphere of tenseness of doubt, of hope, which this first news from Manila had engendered in the rest of the world, and particularly in America, where the nabobs of yellow journalism were waging their circulation war, was precisely the atmosphere in which myth and legend flourish. Dewey, serenely unaware of the journalistic panic elsewhere in the world, devoted himself first to his immediate and essential military chores: receiving the surrender of Cavite, salvaging as many tugs as possible, receiving the surrender of the forts at the entrance to the bay and demilitarizing them, paroling the Spanish prisoners and looking out for the Spanish wounded in the hospital at the Cavite base.

At length on May 4, with all of Manila Bay in his possession, the leisurely commodore dispatched the *McCulloch* to Hong Kong. From Hong Kong on May 7 his first reports were cabled to Washington. Congress rushed through a vote of thanks "to Commodore George Dewey, United States Navy, commander in chief of the United States naval force on the Asiatic Station, for highly distinguished conduct in conflict with the enemy. . . ."[40] McKinley signed the act on May 10, and Secretary Long dispatched the belated rear admiral's commission to Dewey.

A wave of popular applause swept the nation, affecting high and low, rich and poor, huckster and rhymster.

'They're making Dewey buttons,
  They're making Dewey hats,
And 'Dewey's' imprinted
  On collars and cravats.
They're making Dewey tobies,
  And thus they name cigars;
They're making Dewey cocktails
  To push across the bars . . ."[41]

And while the folks at home wore Dewey buttons and downed Dewey cocktails, their inaccessible idol in the romantic, far-off Philippines, sweltering without collar under a copper sun, fanned himself with a palm-leaf fan and eyed his novel domain from his wicker chair on the *Olympia's* forward deck under white awnings and waited for the next move. He had carried out his orders to the letter, and, as Captain Wildes put it, "with no flukes and misses . . . on ground of the Spaniards' choosing."[42] He had captured or destroyed the enemy fleet. But his orders had not specified what he should do afterward. Return to Hong Kong and be handicapped by neutrality rules? Return to the States? Not a supply base within 7,000 miles was open to him. But Manila Bay was his, and here he stayed. And the mere fact that Dewey stayed in Manila Bay made imperialism popular in America. The reinforcements for Dewey, an army of occupation to take over the city of Manila itself, were neither planned nor organized until *after* Dewey's epoch-making victory—and the commitment of these reinforcements to a campaign in the Philippines constituted the logic which converted the nation to the shining new goal of American Empire.

"Admiral Dewey," beamed Teddy Roosevelt, "has won a victory greater than any since Trafalgar, with the exception of Farragut's. It is one of the great sea fights of all time, and every American is his debtor."[43]

15. MAHAN ON THE WAR BOARD

In the fall of 1897 Mahan's fifteen-year-old son Lyle Evans suffered a heart attack, and after the first of the year Mahan planned to take him abroad to recuperate.[1] Assistant Secretary Theodore Roosevelt, who was keeping in touch with Mahan at this time, tried to persuade Secretary Long after the sinking of the *Maine* to order Mahan back to active duty in the Navy Department so as to have him immediately available for consultation in case of war. Long was unwilling to do so. In consequence Mahan, now a retired officer, went ahead with his plan to take his family to Europe, even though war was fast approaching and Roosevelt was leaning more and more heavily upon his advice.

Through Roosevelt, Mahan tried to influence the Navy Department to adopt what he considered to be a correct strategy in case of war. Mahan wanted the fighting fleet concentrated in the West Indies. The Navy Department, though it did not agree to station the entire fleet in the West Indies, ordered the *Oregon* to proceed from her base at Puget Sound around South America to join the Home Squadron in the West Indies. Mahan was not able, however, because of the popular clamor for ships to defend the various ports on the Atlantic seaboard, to persuade the Navy Department to concentrate the entire fighting fleet at Key West as correct strategy demanded. The fleet thus concentrated, Mahan believed, would be able to blockade Havana and at the same time fall back to protect any threatened area.

"I . . . agree with you with all my heart about local coast defense," Roosevelt wrote Mahan on March 14. "I shall urge and have urged the President and the Secretary to pay absolutely no heed to outcries for protection from Spanish raids."[2] A few days later Roosevelt sent a plan of campaign upon which he wished Mahan's comments. On March 24, 1898, two days before Mahan embarked on the S. S. *Fulda* with his family for Europe, Roosevelt wrote that he was sending all of Mahan's letters down to Captain Sampson at Key West. For the moment young Roosevelt was discouraged. He had "advised the President and the Secretary to treat the sailing of the [Spanish] torpedo flotilla from the Canaries for Porto Rico as an act of hostility. I have repeated the advice today. I do not think it will be regarded." Mahan's European address would be kept, wrote Roosevelt, "and I can assure you we will communicate with you at once in case of need."[3]

Mahan arrived in Rome a few days before the declaration of war, and was mortified to read in the papers the garbled notions about naval strategy which newspaper writers were attributing to him. On April 25, 24 hours after Spain declared war, a messenger from the American Embassy handed him the following cablegram:[4] "Captain Mahan, Hotel d'Italie, Rome. Long Washington twenty-fifth cables proceed to United States immediately and report to Secretary Navy. (Signed) Stevens. (Received in Rome April 25, 1898)"

Leaving his family, Mahan went immediately to the embassy, where Ambassador Draper telegraphed ahead for a reservation on the Cunard liner *Etruria*. The reservation, for reasons of security, was obtained under the assumed name of A. T. Maitland, and the necessary telegrams were sent in the State Department's cipher.[5] To Mahan's chagrin, owing to a leakage of information in Washington, the newspapers in Rome now published more information about Mahan's assignment to the Strategy Board than Mahan himself knew, and at least one New York correspondent attempted to interview him before he left Rome. Thus unofficially assured of the Department's plans for himself, he dispatched through the embassy the following dossier of advice on strategy:[6]

"Captain Mahan offers following suggestions:

"First. If two or three enemy's battleships enter Porto Rico, or elsewhere, they should at once be blocked by a force superior to any combination possible by the enemy at the moment. Second. In such case and in existing conditions it seems probable that Havana could be left to light vessels, swift enough to escape if unfortunately surprised by superior force. Third. It is improbable enemy fleet would seek to enter Havana, adding to the burden of food subsistence, unless meaning to fight, which of course we wish. Fourth. M. does not think any enemy large ship would venture to enter any of our Atlantic ports. Torpedo vessels might, but they can be handled. Fifth. M. heartily approves naval strategy up to date, especially refusing to oppose ships to the Havana forts. He would not favor any dispersal of battleships as he is reported to have done to guard ports against attack. Sixth. M. requests secrecy as to his movements till his return."

After this he removed his closely cropped, too-well-known mustache and Van Dyke beard and returned to New York as the clean-shaven Mr. A. T. Maitland.

A story is told that reporters, who were eluded by Mahan at the pier in New York, seized instead upon Captain Paget, a Royal Navy attaché, and quizzed this obliging person about Mahan. "Why yes," said Paget, "I met him on the boat. A very pleasant man—very. Traveling incog., tho, very much incog. Doesn't want to be interviewed. Said he wouldn't be interviewed on any account. God bless my soul, perhaps I shouldn't have said even so much!"[7]

Mahan's arrival in Washington coincided with the arrival of the first reports from Commodore Dewey via Hong Kong. He found that the capital, as well as the country, was going wild over the wonderful news. A War Department order that officers must discard civilian dress and wear their uniforms brought forth on the streets of Washington "galaxies of stars, eagles, shoulder straps, and red and white or yellow stripes," as well as a "pungent odor of mothballs."[8] Washington and the nation felt inclined to swagger over Dewey's astonishing success. "This war will entirely change our policy," a normally sedate editor proclaimed. "We must become one of the powers, prepared to take our part in the preservation of the balance of power. Matters have most remarkably changed since the days of the Fathers. We are now a nation with interests extending beyond our territorial limits. We have created and are increasing a Navy to subserve those interests. . . ." The first reaction of the *New York Sun* was that while it would be foolish to saddle ourselves with "the mutinous and half-caste population" of the entire Philippine archipelago, we did need Manila "to safeguard our Asiatic interests."[9]

A reporter, inviting Mahan's comment on the Manila victory, found the long-time advocate of acquiring overseas bases disinclined to blow the trumpet when everyone else was at it so vociferously. "The result of this engagement," Mahan remarked, "plainly indicates that a cool-headed commander who gets into the fight first and proceeds to business has the best of the battle from the start."[10] The Washington correspondent of the *Army and Navy Journal,* a long-time supporter of Mahan's ideas, wrote: "The great victory of Commodore Dewey at the Philippine Islands has opened the eyes of those who have heretofore been blind, and they are beginning to see objects, like the man in the parable, 'as trees walking.'. . . Instead of pursuing a penurious and provincial policy in regard to the expansion of our Navy, they are now disposed to make it one of the greatest on the globe. . . ."[11]

At the Navy Department Secretary Long informed Mahan that he wanted him to serve as a member of the Naval War Board. This body, popularly credited with formulating the general strategy of the war, had been set up during Mahan's absence, and included Assistant Secretary Roosevelt, Rear Admiral Montgomery Sicard, Captain Albert S. Barker, Captain Arent S. Crowninshield, chief of the Bureau of Navigation, and Commander Richardson Clover, chief of Naval Intelligence. When Mahan arrived, the War Board as at first constituted was breaking up. Barker and Clover had asked for active duty. Teddy Roosevelt, whose company of cowboy Rough Riders was being recruited in Texas, had resigned only a few days before Mahan reached Washington, and Mahan's arrival solved Roosevelt's last-minute problem of what to do about his Washington house. Roosevelt simply turned over his residence to Mahan for the duration of the war.

From the start, resignations of the original members of the board were not reassuring; nor were the board's purpose and responsibilities entirely clear. As a matter of fact the original purpose of the War Board appears to have been whatever its members had chosen to make it. The *Army and Navy Journal* deduced its main objects to be "uttering warning cries" and prodding the administration into this or that course of action. "Every little while we hear of one or more of them going to the White House and urgently impressing upon the President something which they think he ought to do, which he seems to listen to amiably, and then does not do. Then at other times they turn up before the Secretary and fiercely prod him, the result of which is that he gets his hat and escapes as quickly as possible in the direction of the Executive Mansion, whence he returns confirmed in his belief that further delay is indispensable." The *Journal* writer feared that the board might undertake directly to manage fleets; "in which case," he concluded, "its abolition should promptly follow."[12]

Mahan's first disgruntled reaction to the Naval War Board was that it ought to be disbanded. In the first place the Navy Department had had so little regard for the functions of the board as to provide no proper place for its meetings. To Admiral Luce, Mahan wrote in August: "When I arrived we were under the eaves of the Department Building in a room with one window, which theretofore had been used as a lumber room for books no longer needed for the library. As the Board was supposed to furnish the Dept. with brains for the trivial and secondary purpose of carrying on the operations of the war, the high eligibility of this pasture for broken down books 'turned out to grass' was immediately clear, and the forcing process of a Washington summer under such conditions upon our mental faculties was evident also." Moreover, in Mahan's opinion, Admiral Sicard was not the right person to head the board. "Sicard is a clear headed man for Bureau work, but very second or third rate for what we had to do."[13]

Feeling this way, Mahan, the second day after his arrival, "before any difference with my colleagues has arisen, or could arise," respectfully recommended that the "board of war" be abolished. In place of this "council of war, which the board virtually is, with corporate responsibility," Mahan proposed the appointment of a single officer who would be assisted by experts in various lines but who would be singly and individually responsible for the expert professional opinions which had hitherto been supplied by the board. "I do not forget that the secretary himself exercises such single responsibility. But with the varied and onerous duties resting upon him, it is inevitable that, in such highly technical matters as the conduct of war, he must depend largely upon the technical familiarity with the subject that only seamen, and military seamen, can possess. Professional opinion should come to him, not as the result of a majority vote, but with the far weightier sanction of a single competent man, acting under the high sense of personal responsibility."[14]

Mahan sent in his official recommendation via Admiral Sicard, who forwarded it without comment to the Secretary. Whether Mahan felt that he might himself be selected to fill the unique position it is impossible to say. He certainly regarded himself as especially qualified by his years of study and research in naval strategy and administration. So did others. A few weeks later, when it appeared that the War Board was continuing its existence and that the entire strategic direction of the war was not to be turned over to Mahan, the *New York Sun* thus took the administration to task: "Captain Crowninshield has about as much as one human being can do in attending to the Bureau of Navigation. . . . However great his attainments or those of Admiral Sicard may be in the art [of strategy], it is undeniable that they are eclipsed in the public eye by the capacities ascribed to Capt. Mahan, who now gets the opportunity of his life to demonstrate whether he be the consummate strategist which the English have been insisting for years that he is."[15] As the *Sun* was very much opposed to the War Board as such, it presumably would have favored vesting Mahan with full responsibility.

Secretary Long, however, elected to continue the present setup of the board without change. "The War Board," he explained to his critics, "is not a formal body. It has no set rules and regulations, and is not composed of a certain number of men. Its members are officers in whose judgment and ability the Secretary of the Navy has confidence, and they act merely as advisers. The principal function of the Board is to collect information about the enemy and furnish it to the commanders of American squadrons or single vessels. The Secretary of the Navy is not bound by its advice, and there has never been any intention to have the Board determine what Adml. Sampson, for example, should do in certain cases. The Board has means of securing information not accessible to squadron commanders, and it considers all the data and news it receives and transmits them in compact form to the officer or officers to whom they will be valuable."[16]

After the war, Secretary Long implied that the board had exercised considerable authority. "It was eminently fitted," he wrote in *The New American Navy*, "to coordinate the work of the department and the fleet, and to keep a general surveillance over the larger strategical and technical questions which could not be dealt with by the commanders-in-chief of the several squadrons. . . . To my mind the board possessed high intelligence and excellent judgment, and its service was invaluable in connection with the successful conduct of the war."[17] The fact is that the Secretary rejected Mahan's proposal for a sort of one-man chief of staff for the Navy and kept in his own hands the power of ultimate decision. No doubt he was influenced by a highly vocal body of naval opinion which was averse to the War Board in general and to Captain Mahan in particular. Admiral Belknap, for instance, did not hesitate in the *New York Times* for May 11, 1898, to belittle the board as "a body of men not celebrated as sea fighters, sitting in the comfortable retirement and reposeful comfort of the capital. . . ."[18]

As Mahan had foreseen, the development of cable and telegraph had made it possible to unify and direct operations, at least in the Atlantic and Caribbean, in a way that had never before been possible. That his idea of a one-man chief of staff was essentially sound was to be proved later in World War II when Admiral King was vested with vast powers similar to those which Mahan wished the Secretary to give to some one individual. But in May of 1898 the idea of a naval general staff was too novel and there was too much adverse opinion both inside and outside of the service. Had Roosevelt remained in the Department, Mahan might conceivably have got his chance. From the tone of the article he wrote for the May issue of *Scribner's Magazine* in 1903, it is clear that Mahan's disappointment was acute.

"During the Spanish war," wrote Mahan in retrospect, "an *ex-tempore* Board was constituted to give purely military advice upon the strategic movements of the fleet. It had no powers and, therefore, no responsibility, except for expert advice given; all orders were the Secretary's own. It is open to serious question whether in actual war such a recourse is desirable. Responsibility for advice as well as for action, should then be single, undivided."

As a matter of fact at the time Mahan became a member of the War Board, on May 9, there was little left to be done in the way of strategic planning. In the Pacific one brisk morning's work by Commodore

Dewey had eliminated the Spanish fleet in Asia. In the Atlantic the early strategic dispositions of the fleet, when the whereabouts of Cervera and the Cape Verde fleet were unknown, had already been made. But these dispositions—Sampson's force blockading Havana, Schley's Squadron tied down to the Hampton Roads base and the miscellaneous rag, tag and bobtail of newly purchased and converted craft stationed off New York and New England to allay the popular panic that had been whipped up by the yellow press—these disposi-tions, Mahan felt, only betrayed our naval weakness.[19] They would have to be changed the instant Cervera was located.

On May 10, the day after Mahan joined the War Board, orders were written for the chartered steamer *City of Pekin* to carry troops and supplies to Manila. The *Pekin* was to join the U.S.S. *Charleston* in Honolulu, and together the two were ordered to proceed to Manila. They were directed on their way thither to take possession of the Spanish island of Guam as a safeguard for the supply line to the Philippines.

On May 12 Cervera, who had been at sea for two weeks, was sighted off Fort-de-France, Martinique. The news was at once cabled to Wash-ington by the United States consul in St. Pierre, Martinique, and was shortly afterward verified by the fast lookout cruiser, the U.S.S. *Har-vard*,[20] which was posted off Martinique. For two weeks in cities and towns on the Atlantic coast the fever of apprehension had been mount-ing. With Cervera located in the Caribbean the public's temperature subsided. The War Board now recommended, and Secretary Long approved, that complete realignment of American naval forces which was to smash Cervera's force of armored cruisers as quickly and as completely as Dewey's force had defeated Montojo's unprotected ves-sels. Sampson, who had gone to San Juan in anticipation of Cervera's arrival at that most logical destination, was recalled to Key West. Schley from Hampton Roads was also ordered to Key West. In the passages around either end of Cuba were stationed fast converted liners as lookouts. According to secret intelligence reports Cervera was bringing ammunition stores desperately needed by the Spanish army in Havana. It was expected, therefore, that he would attempt to force his way through the United States Navy's blockade off Havana or off some near-by port, possibly Matanzas or Cienfuegos, which were con-nected with Havana by rail. The fast scout *Harvard* was ordered to

Curaçao to shadow Cervera and report his movements. By all means the enemy was to be prevented from entering Havana.[21] If he should make some other harbor, he must at once be blocked in by a superior force and not allowed to escape without a fight to the finish.

Cervera, after coaling at the Dutch Guiana port of Curaçao, entered Santiago on the southeastern shore of Cuba at 6:00 A. M. on May 19. Owing to faulty transmission of dispatches and to the difficulties of coaling experienced by the Flying Squadron off the south coast of Cuba, a blockade was not established off Santiago until May 29. Cervera thus had ten days in which to finish coaling his fleet and, so the War Board feared, to escape to sea for a possible raid on the American coast. The troops now assembling in Florida could not be embarked for Cuba, nor could the East Coast be safely stripped of fast cruisers, until Cervera's force was securely cornered.

On the large map of the Caribbean which covered a wall of the War Board's office in the State, War and Navy Building, colored pins were fixed to represent the various elements of the American forces as they closed in upon the elusive Spaniard. Each day copies of reports from all naval sources were furnished to the members of the board and the three officers, Sicard, Crowninshield and Mahan, deliberated, made decisions and cast their ideas into the proper form of official orders for Secretary Long's signature. The Secretary, while never committing himself to accept the board's judgment, seems to have done substantially just that.

The War Board, as a new institution made possible by the development of rapid communication, was frankly experimental. Wrong opinions as to its organization and powers were widespread; and from the beginning of Mahan's service on May 9, the board labored under a constant fire of popular criticism. The fact that Dewey had finished his job so promptly with no assistance from Washington was prima-facie evidence to many that Sampson and Schley, if only they were unhampered by the Strategy Board, could finish their work with equal dispatch. "It is generally understood that both Sampson and Schley have little, if any, freedom of action and are held in check by the authorities in Washington," announced Senator Samuel Pasco of Florida; and he concluded, "It was a good thing that Dewey cut the cables. Both Schley and Sampson ought to take a hint in this respect."[22] The *Army and Navy Journal*, seldom critical of the administration, took up the popular cry: "If William T. Sampson and Winfield Scott Schley are not competent to command let them be relieved without further delay and other officers assigned to command their fleets. If they are competent they should be given full liberty of action without interference from War Boards or paper strategists. If the gentlemen who assume direction from Washington are more competent put them in command of the fleets and place the responsibility on them. . . . Does anyone believe that [Dewey] could have accomplished what he has if he had been at the end of a wire running into the Navy Department?"[23]

The *New York Sun* pitched into the Secretary for presuming ever to accept his own judgment against that of the professional experts on the board. If he could reject their advice, of what use was the board? If the board was merely advisory, of what use was the Bureau of Intelligence? "The simplest way out of the difficulty," the *Sun* concluded, "is to abolish the Board and give Capt. Mahan charge of the Bureau of Intelligence, which is not an 'informal body,' and the functions of which are perfectly understood and highly appreciated. No duty could be given him where his known abilities in gathering and weighing the facts of a naval war, and of suggesting the correct inferences to be drawn therefrom—abilities which already command the willing deference of the service—could be more adequately utilized or prove of greater service to the country."[24]

The amiable Secretary, annoyed by the almost daily criticism of the press, undertook to refute in the *New York Herald* the charge that the board's function was "merely to suggest counsel to him wherefrom to make up his mind what to tell Sampson, Schley, & Co." His detractors retorted that the position of the Strategy Board became "funnier" each time the Secretary attempted to defend it. Long's administration of the Navy struck the *New York Sun* as indecisive, and likely to confuse a commander at the front. "Despite official denials," the *London Times* commented on one of Mr. Long's explanations, "the proceedings of the United States Board of Strategy unquestionably indicate diversity and even conflict of councils and the absence of a strong directing hand."[25]

The newspaper fraternity's sniping at Mr. Long on the subject of his Strategy Board was promptly stilled on July 3 when the forces under Sampson and Schley won their sudden and startlingly complete victory over Cervera. In retrospect the *Army and Navy Journal* now discovered that, after all, the War Board had had much to recommend it. "If all boards," said they, "were as discreet and intelligent as the Naval War Board has shown itself to be the objection to boards would disappear. They have left nothing to be criticized in the management of our naval war, and are entitled to the thanks of the country."[26]

As a military man Mahan failed to make a just estimate of the real power which the Naval War Board had exercised. Accustomed to have the letter of his responsibility clearly stated in official order and Navy regulation, he was misled by the superficial mantle of informality with which the Secretary had cloaked the board. Of literal military responsibility it had had little. Yet the board's real power had lain in the Secretary's very real dependence upon their advice. John Davis Long, as Teddy Roosevelt and the news reporters had discovered, was a most unmilitary executive who knew little of, and cared nothing about, the canons of military etiquette. With such a man the letter of the bond was unimportant. On August 21, as the war drew to a close, Secretary Long wrote a letter of honest appreciation to Admiral Sicard, and through him to his associates, Crowninshield and Mahan, in which he virtually gave the Naval War Board credit for the real direction of the war. "But from my personal knowledge and observation," he wrote, "I desire to add . . . that equally marked have been the intelligence, the wise judgment, the comprehensive forethought and the unfailing competency to every contingency which have distinguished *their deliberation and action.* May it not be said that not one error has been made? *Proper control of the Department has been exercised over all movements in the field. . . .*"[27]

While agreeing at the end of the war that Secretary Long had "had the sound sense to see that he was being well served by a number of capable men, in the Board & the Bureaus and to allow them scope," Mahan was nonetheless piqued that Long should have written so flatteringly of the admiral who had been the nominal head of the board. "I have written & talked and stormed for three months before the Board, the Sec'y. & the President," Mahan confided to his close friend Admiral Luce, "and I feel now very much like the teacher who after laborious explanations, receives from one of his boys one of those answers we see in the funny columns of a newspaper. . . ."[28]

16. THE SEARCH FOR CERVERA

WHEN in March the newspapers intensified their crusade to drive out Spain from the Western Hemisphere, the people of the nation with surprising unanimity joined in the war cry:

> "Remember the Maine,
> To hell with Spain!"

Winfield Scott Schley, chairman of the Lighthouse Board, called on Secretary Long to offer the services of all the tugs, tenders, etc., under the control of the Lighthouse service. A few days later the Secretary summoned him to his office, as Schley thought, to arrange for transferring these vessels to the Navy. Instead, Mr. Long notified him of his selection to command the Navy's Flying Squadron.

The new squadron, Mr. Long explained, was to be formed at Hampton Roads. "When shall you be ready to take command?" Schley, who always kept a traveling bag packed and ready, answered, "To-morrow."[1]

Although the details are not on file in the Navy Department, there can be little doubt that Schley's appointment was primarily due to political considerations. The Spanish admiral Pascual Cervera y Topete with his armored cruisers and torpedo vessels, it was popularly feared, would cross the Atlantic in secrecy, appear suddenly off the poorly defended seaboard cities and threaten to bombard them. That New York should have to pay a king's ransom to escape destruction was a theme upon which a sensational press rang all the changes. Secretary Long, an ex-governor of Massachusetts, and Theodore Roosevelt, his aggressive assistant, were both sensitive to this popular opinion, however well or ill founded it might be. Commodore Schley was a choice well calculated to allay this unreasonable fear along the Atlantic seaboard.

In view of the later Sampson-Schley controversy it is worth noting that Schley, standing Number 18 on the active list at this time, was hoisted over at least a dozen admirals and senior commodores. Moreover, the chief of the Bureau of Navigation, whose province it was to detail officers, was by no means friendly to Schley. In the circumstances, the appointment of Schley marked a departure from routine which can scarcely be credited to the very mild-mannered, conservative Governor Long. Very likely it was the forthright, tradition-smashing Assistant Secretary who turned the trick. In addition to all his other duties in preparation for war, Teddy Roosevelt was at this time vigorously serving as head of the Strategy Board, of which the chief of the Bureau of Navigation was a junior member and open to suggestion from the dominant Roosevelt.

Schley ran up his broad pennant on the fast cruiser *Brooklyn* on March 28. For six impatient weeks political necessities penned him in Hampton Roads, subject to the jealous direction of the Roosevelt-controlled Strategy Board. His Flying Squadron became a "fettered" squadron. False alarms of enemy ships off the New England coast caused Washington to detach two of Schley's fast ships (the *Columbia* and the *Minneapolis*) for separate missions.[2] To take the place of these nimble 20-knot cruisers, Schley was given the ponderous, leisurely paced battleships *Massachusetts* and *Texas*—after which his squadron, if and when it should "fly," must do so with clipped wings at about half its original speed.

In theory the mission of the Flying Squadron, as its name implied, was to dash out from its centrally located lair at Hampton Roads and intercept any enemy attacking Boston, New York or Charleston. Yet, owing to the compromise of its original character and the reduction of its squadron speed, the Flying Squadron was no longer suitable for fast countermoves over a virtually limitless expanse of ocean. Actually it was chiefly New England Congressmen and the yellow journalists who indulged in strategic nightmares about Admiral Cervera. As naval men knew, Cervera's ships—with the limited coal capacity of all ships at this time—enjoyed only a restricted operational radius. After their voyage across the Atlantic, the Spanish war vessels could not possibly raid any point on the American coast without first stopping at a port in the West Indies to refuel. Schley's presence at Hampton Roads, needless from a strategic point of view, did act as a sedative for the nation's nerves. "The flying squadron," Theodore Roosevelt later recalled, "was looked upon with hysterical anxiety by the Northeast and its representatives in Congress as a protection against a Spanish attack!" To pacify Congressmen who wanted ships sent "to protect Portland, Maine, Jekyl Island, Narragansett Pier, and other points of like importance," Roosevelt wrote that he "arranged to send them a Civil War monitor with twenty-one New Jersey Naval Militia aboard, which satisfied Portland entirely! It would have been useless against any war vessel more modern than one of Hamilkar's galleys."[3] A number of Civil War relics were recommissioned to stand guard inside of harbors, and an offshore Northern Patrol Squadron of yachts and light steamers was organized under Commodore John A. Howell (of Howell torpedo fame) eventually to relieve Schley of his functions as a pacifier of the public. Schley's slow force, fit only for heavy slugging duty, could then move down the coast nearer to Havana, where the showdown with Cervera was most likely to occur.

Until Cervera's whereabouts should be disclosed, however, each passing week increased the public tension which held Schley in Hampton Roads and at the same time heightened the restlessness of the squadron to get started. Schley used the delay to drill his men. After the report on the *Maine* had reached Washington, Schley was ordered to keep enough fire under his boilers to enable him within an hour to attain a speed of ten knots. Subcaliber firing practice, ammunition-handling drills, and endless coaling of the ships occupied the days; while at nights there were small-boat patrols to guard the battleships against a

The *Oregon* Engaging Shore Batteries at Santiago. (From the Journal of Cadet C. R. Miller.)

The Burning Spanish Ships, *Oquendo* and *Teresa*. (From the Journal of Cadet C. R. Miller.)

The *Oquendo*, Destroyed and Run on the Beach West of Santiago.

sneak torpedo attack. Schley obtained from his captains a mass of data on the fuel consumption of the various ships. Coal supply was a major problem. It was in fact a new problem of the Machine Age for which the Navy, in its eagerness to obtain modern ships, had made scarcely any preparations at all. At Key West, our most advanced base, small ships only could come alongside the single fueling dock; all heavy ships had to be coaled in the bay or in the open roads outside from colliers or lighters. The Navy, moreover, had no colliers of its own, equipped with special side guards so as not to be stove in by overhanging sponsons of battleships like the *Texas;* and furthermore most of the commercial colliers, which the Navy depended on, lacked mechanical coal-hoisting gear and relied upon the warships to furnish coal heavers. These operations would be man-killers in the tropics.

On April 13 Schley, firing a signal gun, recalled all hands from shore leave and ordered the ships to put to sea. This was a novel experience for the Navy wives who had congregated at Old Point Comfort. "The windows at the hotels went up," the chaplain on the *Texas* noted, "and the ladies were seen looking out at us, and in a little while they were all down on the beach."[4] Some crowded in the launches from the ships. Others hired private boats to take them off to bid their husbands a tearful farewell. One canny news reporter, noting the exemplary composure of Mrs. Schley, predicted correctly that the Flying Squadron was not yet leaving for the front. Commodore Schley merely intended to test the main battery guns at the Southern Drill Grounds, 15 miles east of Cape Charles Lighthouse; in formation he plowed around a while through seas rough enough to wash across the gun decks and give his raw recruits a taste of salt. Within a day and a half the squadron was back at anchor off Old Point Comfort.

For 37 days the Flying Squadron was held in readiness to sail *on one hour's notice*. The idling battleships ate steadily into their coal, and the expended fuel had to be replaced daily. Dust and grime from these numerous petty fuelings made it imperative to scrub decks, instruments, hammocks and clothing more frequently than usual. Yet Schley managed to keep everyone in good spirits. For one thing he was lavish with praise. The "well done" signal was often made from the flagship, or if there were greater leisure, such wordy messages were wigwagged as: "The commander in chief appreciates the prompt action of the captain, his officers and crew this morning." Scrupulously Schley relayed to the squadron odd bits of news, like the appointment of a new postmaster general, or the disquieting rumor: "Mexico intends to present Spain with one battleship and 1,500,000 pesetas."[5] Receiving the good news of Manila Bay, he at once cabled to Dewey: "The Flying Squadron says to the Asiatic Squadron, bully boys, congratulations. Schley." And to his own men he signaled: "The Associated Press correspondent has kindly cabled to Commodore Dewey the congratulations of the Flying Squadron for his great victory."[6] The reporter thus singled out was naturally pleased, and Schley's men, who were impatient to get off and follow Dewey's bold example, yelled themselves hoarse.

During the preliminary stage of the war in the Atlantic, before Cervera's fleet disclosed its whereabouts on the American side of the ocean, Acting Rear Admiral Sampson at Key West worked to overcome the disadvantages of an inadequately prepared advanced base and to whip into shape a heterogeneous blockade fleet which might at some unpredictable moment have to encounter a homogeneous and speedy enemy. By all canons of naval strategy, the war must be lost or won in the Caribbean area. Here Spain had fine naval bases at Havana and at San Juan, Puerto Rico, in which to refuel and service Cervera's fleet. Sampson hoped that his blockade might deny Cervera the use of Havana, and in case Cervera should put into San Juan he hoped to surprise him at anchor inside of that openmouthed harbor, in which case Sampson would endeavor to sink the enemy at anchor before he could break off coaling and refitting.

As for Havana, Sampson preferred to adopt the Civil War strategy of Farragut off New Orleans. Immediately after his appointment to command the North Atlantic Station, Sampson submitted a strategic plan to the Department. "My present plan contemplates an attack [upon Havana] the very moment the dogs of war are let loose. My force is now too small for that purpose. . . . The *Indiana* is retubing her boilers but will probably have the work finished this week. The *New York* is hardly suitable for such work, though she would have to do her share if it were to be now. I would commence with one ship if necessary. . . ."[7] Sampson's plan, in which all his capital ship captains concurred—F. E. Chadwick of the *New York*, H. C. Taylor of the *Indiana* and R. D. Evans of the *Iowa*—involved first knocking out the forts at the entrance to the harbor and then paralyzing Havana into surrender by a threat of bombardment. To insure success Sampson asked the Secretary to return to his squadron the *Massachusetts*, which had been assigned to Commodore Schley. "I am convinced that the country has nothing to fear from an attack along our northern coast."[8] Secretary Long, impressed rather by the clamor on the seaboard, vetoed the naval commander's proposal and enjoined him not to risk his ships in fighting shore fortifications until after Cervera's fleet had been disposed of.

Even more important, if Washington were determined to call the moves in this war, was the need to clarify the responsibilities of the two major Atlantic squadrons. Sampson understood his own mission, but on April 8 he requested the Department to clarify the assignment that had been given to Schley. "It is highly important," he urged, "that the scheme of operations against the forces and possessions of Spain should be clearly and cogently laid down and thoroughly understood by all officers in position of command and responsibility. There are now, as I understand the situation, two squadrons ready for offensive operations; the one which I have the honor to command, and the Flying Squadron under the command of Commodore Schley. I request that I may be informed as to the scope of action of the two forces, and especially as to the portion of the line of operations which is to be taken care of by the Flying Squadron."[9] One recalls Mahan's futile attempts to induce the unbusinesslike Secretary Long to assign full responsibility for strategic decisions to one individual. Sampson's plea was also in vain. Time drifted on. War was declared on April 22. Sampson established his blockade off Havana and along 30 to 40 miles of coast on either side of the city, and the question of the "line of operations" which Schley's squadron was to pursue was left for time to decide.

Theoretically in this early stage of the conflict Sampson's job was solely to prepare to meet Cervera. Practically he found little privacy for this somber job, since his every move was scrutinized by the ubiquitous reporters as avidly as were Schley's at Hampton Roads. Rightly shunning publicity, on April 8 he had telegraphed the Secretary, "It is considered best and more just to forbid all press associations being in squadron."[10] His excellent suggestion was turned down in Washington.

At Key West each leading newspaper in the country maintained a staff of six or eight news gatherers under a "war-correspondent-in-chief," and operated at least one fast dispatch boat. The Associated Press reporter, W. A. M. Goode, who was billeted on board the flagship *New York*, had four dispatch vessels at his command. The Associated Press boats, together with those of the *New York Journal*, the *World*, the *Sun*, the *Times*, the *Herald* and the *Tribune*, followed the fleet to Havana, where they frequently hovered like a brood of ducklings around the flagship.[11] The joke circulated that "Admiral Sampson gave orders for the flagship to move northward, and received information that it was impossible, as there were three dispatch boats tied to the anchor-chains. He gave orders to go south, with the result that several others were reported fastened to the rudder and propeller blades."[12]

Shortly after the Havana blockade was established, the *New York*, the largest and speediest of the blockaders, chased and captured a prize vessel that was attempting to run supplies into Havana. The press boats, which raced to keep up and were quickly outdistanced, cheered the *New York*, upon her return. An artist for *Century Magazine* on board a press boat relates: "We steamed alongside the *New York*, shouted our congratulations to Admiral Sampson, who stood upon the bridge, and offered to take to Key West any mail or dispatches he might have. He accepted our offer. Suddenly a blue-shirted, bare-armed creature with flying hair appeared through the superstructure door, and spoke to an orderly, who, raising a megaphone to his lips, shouted: 'Mr. ——— wants to know how long you will wait for him to finish his article for the ———?' And picturesque Mr. ———, stripped for action, was given ten minutes."[13] George Kennan estimated that the newspapers had at least 15 or 20 seagoing yachts and tugs, with perhaps an equal number of steam launches for smooth-water use. Whenever anything of importance occurred in any part of the war theater, these boats were expected to be on the spot and observe it and then to speed the news home by way of the nearest cable station—Kingston, Cap-Haitien, St. Thomas, Port-au-Prince or Key West. A correspondent from the *Chicago Record*, presenting to Admiral Sampson a letter from President McKinley, asked:

"Can you give me any directions or instructions, Admiral, with regard to approaching your fleet in hostile waters? I don't want to be in your way, or to do anything that would imperil my own vessel or inconvenience yours."

"Where do you propose to go?" inquired the admiral.

"Anywhere," replied the correspondent, "or, rather, everywhere that you do."

The admiral smiled dryly and said, "You may approach and hail us in the daytime if you have occasion to do so, but if you come within five miles of the fleet at night there is likely to be trouble."[14]

Although the press boats by their mere presence created many a needless annoyance, they were, in the peculiar circumstances of the Cuban blockade, at times useful. Walter Russell, the *Century* artist, gathered the impression that the press boat was "the Navy's source of luxury." "Alongside the *New York* I saw the *Sommers N. Smith* [a *New York Herald* boat] lowering bags of potatoes, sacks of provisions, boxes of vegetables, bread, etc., into the *New York's* small boat for the wardroom mess. These supplies had been brought from Key West by request."[15] They sent aboard also a live chicken as Gunner Morgan's reward for taking photographs for the press. More than once, owing to the small number of naval dispatch vessels, the newspaper craft performed yeoman service for the Navy in carrying dispatches. But on the whole these vessels were a nuisance. They were responsible for numerous calls to battle quarters. Sometimes they would send back to the States as information what actually was nothing more than rumor, to the discomfiture of the high command. Unwittingly, also, some of these lubbers invested the rankest naval scuttlebutt with the garb of truth, thus implanting in the public consciousness that flotsam of false impressions which spawned the Sampson-Schley controversy.

The first few weeks of the war were a busy time for the flagship, the *New York*, which alone of Sampson's heterogeneous squadron was capable of high speed and heavy fire power. The *New York* was thus invaluable for giving chase to blockade runners. For want of dispatch boats Sampson had to use his fragile torpedo boats or if an unusual burst of speed were immediately required, his own flagship. The *New York Herald*, which made a specialty of covering the admiral, found Sampson at this time a "smiling, tactful, self-poised . . . mild-spoken man" who sat down to breakfast only after he had received the reports of his captains and had gone over the work of the day. "His quickness of thought and rapidity of action are marvellous. . . . A sail is sighted in the distance. Away goes the flagship *New York* to make it give an account of itself. A transport is to be overhauled for new duties and no torpedo boat is at hand. Off flies the *New York* to overhaul it."[16]

Many of the auxiliaries which the Navy Department sent to the blockade at this time proved almost worthless. The revenue cutter *Morrill* carried a good battery, but only enough coal for four days' steaming. Other vessels were entirely dependent on an outside supply of fresh water. At Key West, where there was no fresh water except in rain-water cisterns, the recently ordered distilling apparatus for the naval base was being installed but had not yet commenced to function. On May 1 the unseaworthy tug *Algonquin* with several of Sampson's staff came near foundering while crossing the Gulf Stream. The *Algonquin's* stores had to be sacrificed and her invaluable supply of fresh water pumped out to keep her afloat. Such vessels, Sampson reported, "are a drag on this squadron . . . making demand upon our scanty supply of artisans and limited facilities for work at Key West which are needed for ships of greater value."[17]

Early intelligence reports informed Sampson that Cervera had left the Cape Verde Islands at 10:00 A. M. on April 29. If the Spaniard made anything like his rated squadron speed, he could reach San Juan, Puerto Rico, his nearest West Indian base, about May 8. Sampson decided to go to San Juan to meet Cervera. For this move he requested that his squadron be reinforced by the battleships *Massachusetts* and *Texas*, but Secretary Long declined to detach these from the Flying Squadron on the score that Army movements, the details of which had not yet been settled, made this at present undesirable.

On May 3 Sampson headed east with the best makeshift squadron he could muster: the flagship *New York*, the battleships *Iowa* and *Indiana*, two monitors, the *Amphitrite* and the *Terror*, the torpedo boat *Porter*, two auxiliaries and a collier. The anchorage in San Juan Harbor lay open to attack from the sea, and here Sampson hoped to surprise Cervera at work coaling and refitting. With the heavy guns of his battleships and monitors he planned to cap the entrance to the harbor and destroy the enemy's ships at anchor, while smothering the shore batteries with an overwhelming volume of fire from his secondary quick-fire guns.

Only an urgent need for the services of their great guns could justify Sampson's taking the unseaworthy monitors on this 2,000-mile round trip to San Juan. These craft, like their Civil War prototype, the "cheesebox on a raft" invented by John Ericsson, had so little freeboard that waves rippled across their decks. As they had no adequate space for stowing coal, the monitors had to be towed. Hawsers parted; steering gear became disabled; boilers sprang leaks. At one time the *New York* was forced to tow both the bulky monitor *Terror* and the torpedo boat *Porter*. One day while Goode, the Associated Press correspondent,* was discussing these vexatious difficulties with the admiral in the latter's cabin, a hawser snapped overhead, making "a report like the firing of a 4-inch gun." The flagship quivered as if she had been jerked out of the water.

"I am afraid she's gone," said Sampson.

"Who's gone?" asked Goode.

"The *Terror*," he replied, taking his cap and going on deck. The *Terror's* steering gear had broken down again and her cable had snapped.[18]

Off Cap-Haitien, from a cable station extensively used by Americans on the north coast of the Republic of Haiti, Sampson received a message from the Department: "Do not risk so crippling your vessels against fortifications as to prevent from soon afterward successfully fighting Spanish fleet . . . if they should appear on this side."[19]

Sampson, delayed by the monitors so that he was only halfway to his destination by May 8, in a conference of captains determined in spite of obstacles to push on and deny to Cervera the chance to coal and overhaul in San Juan and escape unmolested.

He arrived off San Juan early on May 12. As dawn broke he saw that none of the Spanish vessels was in the harbor. After a brief attack against the batteries defending the port—in order to develop their positions and strength—Sampson once more took the monitors under tow and retraced his laborious steps to the westward, fearful lest Cervera break the weak blockade and enter Havana.

Sampson misjudged by four days the time required for Cervera to cross the Atlantic. On May 12, during Sampson's bombardment of San Juan, Cervera appeared off Martinique. The Spanish consul, no doubt,

---

* From *With Sampson Through the War,* by W. A. M. Goode, copyright 1899, by Doubleday & Company, Inc., p. 64.

informed him that the port of San Juan was then under attack, for Cervera at once disappeared to the westward in the direction of Curaçao, Dutch Guiana.

This news, flashed promptly to Washington, was sent out at once to Sampson and Schley. Sampson received it on the fourteenth. Leaving the battleships to tug the monitors back to port, Sampson in the *New York* raced ahead toward Key West.

The Flying Squadron, meanwhile, released from its tether in Hampton Roads, was at the same time rushing south through storms and fog in which Schley's one collier, the *Sterling*, became separated from the other ships. Schley's ill-matched ships cruised in a battle line led by the fast cruiser *Brooklyn*, flagship, which had to restrict herself to half speed to keep within sight of the battleships *Texas* and *Massachusetts*. The squadron of heavy ships had only one small escort craft, the armed yacht *Scorpion*, to serve as a screening force against the torpedo craft of Spain.

Off Charleston light, as directed, Schley picked up further orders to proceed on to Key West and report to the commandant of the naval station, Commodore George C. Remey. The lighthouse keeper having also supplied him with a bundle of fresh newspapers, Schley signaled the latest news after the fleet got under way: "Papers say Spanish fleet at or to westward of Curaçao. Cables at Cienfuegos cut under fire. Maynard, Winslow and an Ensign wounded, one or more men killed. Sampson's position not known. Supposed to be at Porto Plata, San Domingo."[20]

Schley arrived off Key West before dawn on May 18, and by day-break the coal lighters, which had been awaiting his arrival, were tugged alongside the ships. Outlying dispatch boats of the *New York Sun* and the Associated Press, having missed the big ships in the night, now discovered them coaling at anchor in the outer roads and raced into the harbor under full steam with much blowing of whistles to announce the Flying Squadron's arrival from Hampton Roads.[21] Welcoming flags were displayed from the halyards of the station ship *Miantonomah*. Eleven-gun salutes were exchanged. Commodore Remey handed Schley the latest order from the Department, which directed him to blockade Havana.

The Havana blockade was precisely what Schley wanted. Cervera, according to naval intelligence, had a cargo of ammunition and other supplies for Havana, and Cervera's orders to deliver these were said to be imperative. Off Havana was the likeliest spot in the West Indies, indeed in the entire world, for the next American naval victory. To have the Department's unequivocal orders defining his mission was, no doubt, a matter of satisfaction to Schley. Schley did not openly raise the question—no one raised the question—yet Schley must have been something less than human had he not already asked himself: "What about Sampson?" Just as Schley had been "jumped" over the heads of commodores and rear admirals, so Sampson had been jumped over the heads of these same people—*and also over Schley!* Sampson, Schley's junior in rank but his superior in present assignment, was now en route to Key West from Puerto Rico. Schley probably hoped to get his blockade at Havana established before Sampson's arrival.

In the late afternoon of May 18, while Commodore Schley was making his way back out of Key West Harbor to the *Brooklyn*, the flagship *New York* of the North Atlantic Squadron, bearing the flag of Acting Rear Admiral William T. Sampson, hove into view. The *Brooklyn* rendered the 13-gun salute due a rear admiral, and the *New York* returned a commodore's 11 guns.

Schley went on board the *New York* to pay his respects and confer on the situation. He found Sampson affable but weary from his operations off San Juan. Schley, Sampson and the latter's fleet captain, French E. Chadwick, conferred in the admiral's office. "We had quite a talk together," Schley later testified, "I told him that I had been ordered to report to . . . [Commodore] Remey, and I imagined necessarily to himself, and that I wanted to assure him at the outset that I should be loyal, absolutely and unreservedly, to the cause that we were both representing. Captain Chadwick . . . said 'Of course, Commodore, anyone who has known your character, would know that it would be impossible [for you] to be otherwise than loyal.' "22

The three examined charts of Cuba and the surrounding waters. Cienfuegos, on the south side of the island, was the only South Cuban port that had rail connections with the capital. Sampson, expressing the belief that Cervera would try to head in at Cienfuegos rather than risk breaking through the Havana blockade, assigned to Schley the mission of blockading Cienfuegos. Schley, whose ships were now busy coaling, was to get off early the next morning. To make doubly certain that Schley's force could outmatch Cervera's, Sampson gave

Schley the battleship *Iowa*, which, under Captain Robley D. Evans, was now en route from Puerto Rico.

Shortly after Schley's return to the *Brooklyn*, the steamer *Algonquin*, sent out by Remey, brought Schley repeat orders from the Department to go to Havana. Schley at 10:40 P. M. signaled to the *New York* by Ardois lights: "Have just received orders to go to Havana immediately. Must have tug to remove lighters at once."[23]

Sampson: "Finish coaling and be ready to carry out plans decided on this afternoon. Namely to proceed to Cienfuegos. *Iowa* following as soon as she gets coal."

Schley: "Did Remey inform you of contents of the dispatch brought me by the *Algonquin* . . . just now, dated 6:40 P. M. today?"

Sampson: "Yes. The order Remey received for you from the Department I understand to be modified by my arrival."

Next morning the Flying Squadron set out into the war zone. In response to a query by Captain Philip of the *Texas*, Sampson had a signal boy wigwag to the Flying Squadron: "You are bound for Cienfuegos, Cuba, to bag the Dons; and may good luck go with you!"[24] The delighted seamen of the Flying Squadron chased one another around the decks, jumping high backs and speculating as to who would get the first crack at the Spaniards.

As his battleships headed south at 8:00 A. M. on May 18, Commodore Schley faced the most exasperating conditions and the most exacting test of his career. He could not fix his eye solely on the horizon and on his gunsights. His attention must necessarily be often, too often, deflected to the state of his coal bunkers and to mechanical breakdowns among his hastily improvised auxiliary craft. For Schley personally, his present lack of adequate facilities was more distressing than it would probably have been to the average officer, since Schley had always generously estimated his material needs. As commander of the Greely Relief Expedition he had insisted on and had obtained about two or three times the amount of supplies actually required for the mission. As chief of the Bureau of Equipment and Recruiting, where his prime preoccupation had been supplies, he had acquired a certain apprehensiveness on the subject. Finally, during the recent anxious weeks at Hampton Roads, when he had *coaled ship every day*, Schley's passion for full bunkers had grown into an obsession. Thus during the forthcoming campaign—during the uncertain, time and fuel-consuming blindman's buff to locate Cervera—Schley was prone to be apprehensive about his fuel supply. He assumed, for instance, that when he sighted the enemy, the enemy with fleeter ships would seek to lure him away from his fueling bases and thus trick him into running out of fuel. Accordingly, when at any given moment he estimated the amount of coal he had on hand for offensive operations, Schley fell into the habit of mentally subtracting from the total the amount necessary to get his squadron back to Key West. In the end this process so influenced his thinking as to lead him into a major error in judgment which, at the most critical moment of the search for Cervera, was to throw Washington into consternation and to force Sampson to recast his entire plan of campaign.

A gross, though unwitting, fault in communications occurred an hour and a half out of Key West when the Flying Squadron exchanged identification numbers at long range with the cruiser *Marblehead*, Commander B. H. McCalla. McCalla, a lone wolf, was one of the most energetic, but also one of the unluckiest, officers in the service. After cutting the telegraph cables out of Cienfuegos, McCalla had succeeded in establishing contact with Cuban rebels in that vicinity. He was now bound for Key West to get coal for himself and ammunition for the rebels, with whom he had arranged a secret mode of signaling. Fearing publicity, as there were press boats everywhere, McCalla had shared this secret with no one else on board the *Marblehead* or her escorts.[25] It would have been of inestimable value to Schley, had McCalla now come on board the *Brooklyn* and informed Commodore Schley of this secret code. McCalla did not, however, know that Schley's destination was Cienfuegos and the *Marblehead* was lying to, some three and one-half miles distant from the *Brooklyn*. Hence the *Marblehead* merely requested permission to proceed in the usual way, while her consort, the small auxiliary *Eagle*, relayed by megaphone that there was no news of Cervera![26]

The Flying Squadron, bucking the stiff current of the Gulf Stream, churned a wide loop around the western lizard's tail of Cuba. As they were now entering the war zone proper, orders were given for the ships to complete their clearing for action, to load their batteries and keep the brightest of lookouts. The chaplain on the *Texas* reported a lively scene of tables, benches and ditty boxes being thrown over the side, as well as an amply stocked refrigerator of the officers' mess sacrificed because it had "stood right between two of our six-inch guns."[27] Two smokes on the horizon off Cape San Antonio brought a call to quarters until the strangers could be identified as American blockaders. Captain Chester of the *Cincinnati* was called on board the *Brooklyn* for consultation. Chester's request to be attached to Schley's squadron flattered the commodore, but Schley explained that he had no power to authorize such a move. He also felt compelled to deny Chester's request for coal from a following collier in order to avoid a trip back to Key West. "I then asked him," Schley testified later, "if he had ever cruised in the West Indies, as I had never been on the south side of Cuba, and if he knew any place that would be favorable for coaling, where fairly smooth water could be expected. He suggested that he had no more information than that given him by the charts, and suggested a place some 30 miles to the eastward on a bank, or to the southward, on another bank, coaling upon which would be problematical and dependent entirely upon the state of weather and the sea."[28] Upon the captain's departure, Schley published nothing of his apprehensions about future coaling but wigwagged to the squadron: "Had long communication with Captain Chester concerning methods on blockade. They turn night into day and sleep by their guns. We must do the same. . . ."[29]

About 5:00 P.M. on Saturday, while still 30 miles off Cienfuegos, Schley heard six or seven guns fired with the cadence of a salute. Others on the bridge at this time who also heard the reports shared the commodore's surmise that there must be "some kind of jubilee going on," very possibly a welcome to Cervera. This impression was heightened the next day when several plumes of smoke were seen rising from the harbor; although, when Schley steamed in close across the entrance, he found the view blocked by a tongue of land; nor could he see any tops of masts above the harbor's girdle of high hills.

The *Iowa*, with her midget torpedo boat *Dupont*, arrived during the afternoon. Evans, the *Iowa's* captain and a critic of Schley at Valparaiso in 1891, because of a shoulder injury was unable to come on board the flagship, but sent his executive officer to report. Schley set up a blockade with ships steaming back and forth across the harbor mouth at a speed which gave them just enough headway for steerage. By the *Dupont*, whose commander was literally worn out from tossing on the heavy seas, Schley received a letter from Sampson enclosing a telegram dated May 19 from Washington: "The report of the Spanish fleet being at Santiago de Cuba might very well be correct, so the Department strongly advises that you [Sampson] send word immediately by the *Iowa* to Schley, to proceed off Santiago. . . ."[30] Sampson's accompanying letter, written early on May 20, was cordial and informal in tone and in it Sampson discounted the Department's information: "Dear Schley: The *Iowa* leaves this morning at 11 o'clock bound for Cienfuegos. The *Marblehead* and the *Eagle* will both be ready to join you. Enclosed is a telegram received at Key West, May 19th, Marked A. After duly considering this telegram I have decided to make no change in the present plans, that is, that you should hold your squadron off Cienfuegos. If the Spanish ships have put in to Santiago, they must come either to Havana or Cienfuegos to deliver munitions of war which they are said to bring for use in Cuba.

"I am therefore of opinion that our best chance of success in capturing their ships will be to hold the two points, Cienfuegos and Havana, with all the force we can muster. . . ."[31]

During the next two days Schley's growing belief that he already had Cervera bottled up in Cienfuegos was confirmed by additional circumstances. Sunday night three lights appeared, evidently signal bonfires, arranged in a straight line on the hills some six or seven miles to the west of Cienfuegos.[32] In attempts to plot the locations of these signals on their charts, Schley and Captain Cook could not make out whether the lights were intended for a fleet outside or inside the harbor. Knowing nothing of Commander McCalla's secret code for communicating with the Cuban rebels, Schley "was satisfied" that he had Cervera trapped. There was this second item: Early Monday morning the British steamer *Adula* from Jamaica approached the blockaders with a request that she be permitted to bring refugees out from Cienfuegos. From the *Adula* Schley's boarding officers obtained a war bulletin from Kingston, Jamaica, "in the nature and shape of a handbill," which said that Cervera had entered Santiago on the nineteenth, Thursday, and left on Friday.[33] There had been ample time for Cervera to reach Cienfuegos by Saturday afternoon when Schley had heard the distant salute guns! Schley granted the *Adula* permission to enter Cienfuegos on condition that she come out again early the next morning and verify for the American squadron the presence or absence of Cervera. The *Adula's* failure thereafter to reappear was another link in the chain of circumstantial evidence which convinced Schley that he had Cervera bottled up in Cienfuegos.

This belief was not shaken by a fresh dispatch from Admiral Sampson which reached Schley via the yacht *Hawk* about 7:30 on May 23, in which Sampson, apparently in the belief that Cervera was in Santiago, instructed Schley carefully to mask his departure from Cienfuegos and to proceed to Santiago. "It is thought the enclosed instructions," wrote Sampson from off Havana on the twenty-first, "will reach you by 2 o'clock A. M., May 23. This would enable you to leave before daylight (regarded very important) so that your direction may not be noticed and be at Santiago A. M., May 24. . . ." If he found that Cervera had left Santiago, Schley was directed, "Follow the Spanish squadron whichever direction they take."[34] Schley, on the scene of action, gave credence not to the "Havana rumor" but to the Jamaica "handbill" from the *Adula* and to the "salute guns" which he himself had heard.

At 1:05 P. M. he felt so certain of his prey that he wigwagged the following message to his squadron: "News from Jamaica reports Spanish fleet arrived Santiago Thursday and left Friday. I think they are in Cienfuegos now as I heard heavy guns firing on Saturday about four o'clock thirty miles S.W. from here. I interpreted this as welcome to the fleet."[35]

Meanwhile coaling operations had already commenced. Upon receipt of Sampson's "Dear Schley" letter, Schley had sent the *Scorpion* eastward to scout Santiago. This had left inshore patrol duty to the torpedo boat *Dupont*, newly arrived with the *Iowa* and out of fuel. Tediously coal was hoisted in buckets through the *Brooklyn's* ventilators and rowed by cutter across choppy water to the *Dupont*.

By the unusual standards of coaling set up in Hampton Roads, Schley's battleships were now seriously short on coal. On the morning of the twenty-third, the collier *Merrimac* appeared. The *Massachusetts*, signaling that she was 450 tons short, requested permission to coal, and the *Texas*, most difficult to coal because of her projecting gun sponsons, made a similar request. Schley, however, gave the favored coaling berth to the *Iowa*, which had left Key West with a short supply. The *Iowa* on this placid day took on board 250 tons. Next day an attempt was made to coal both the *Massachusetts* and the *Texas* by placing the collier between them, but this unconventional procedure had soon to be broken off because of swells whipped up by increasing southeast winds. Captain Jack Philip of the *Texas* was not worried by a few bent plates on his own ship, but rather by the danger of the fragile collier's being stove in between the two heaving battleships. Schley wrote to the Department that henceforth colliers expected to coal ships at sea should be provided with heavy bags, instead of buckets, and with cotton bales or heavy wooden camels six to eight feet broad to serve as fenders.[36] Without such equipment it was impractical to coal in a rough sea.

While coaling conditions were rapidly becoming worse on the morning of May 24, the arrival of the cruiser *Marblehead*, under Commander McCalla, and her light escorts, *Vixen* and *Eagle*, further complicated Schley's supply problem. On the other hand, within a few hours Commander McCalla had answered the question of Cervera's presence in Cienfuegos. While on board the *Brooklyn*, to pay his respects to the commodore and to request leave to put ashore the quantity of dynamite and small arms ammunition he had brought for the Cuban rebels, McCalla inquired whether Schley had recently noticed along the beach three white horses in a row, or at night three lights in a horizontal line. Schley, learning now that these lights had been Cuban and not Spanish signals, sent McCalla at once to communicate with the insurgents and by noon had received intelligence that *Cervera was not inside Cienfuegos!*

The afternoon of the twenty-fourth saw a frenzied battle to coal ship in the face of worsening weather. "Report at once," the *Brooklyn* ordered, "how many days' coal at ten knots you have on board."[37]

Texas: "We have 550 tons aboard. Less than eight days' supply."

Castine (the vessel which towed the collier): "Fifteen days."

Marblehead: "We have five and one-half days' coal steaming at ten knots."

Massachusetts: "Have coal for twelve days at ten knots."

Eagle: "Nine days at ten knots."

Iowa: "Can do ten knots on a hundred tons a day—about nine days."

Worried over the *Texas*, the unit which had most difficulty coaling on the open sea, Schley wrote dispatches for Key West to relay to Washington and for Admiral Sampson off Havana, asking that two properly equipped colliers be sent to him at once. "I have ascertained from the insurgents that the Spanish fleet is not in this port. As it is not practicable to coal the *Texas* from the collier here, where there is so much swell, I shall proceed tomorrow off Santiago de Cuba, being embarrassed, however, by the *Texas'* short coal supply, and her inability to coal in the open sea. I shall not be able to remain off that port, on account of general short coal supply of squadron, so will proceed to the vicinity of [St.] Nicholas Mole [Haiti], where the water is smooth, and I can coal *Texas* and other ships. . . ."[38]

Having no vessel suitable for carrying dispatches, Schley was compelled to detach his sorely needed torpedo boat *Dupont* to carry these important messages. "There is a *Sun* [of London] Press boat here," Schley wrote to Sampson, "which I may utilize to send dispatches to you via Jamaica."[39] Immediately after the *Dupont's* departure, Schley decided to break off further unsatisfactory efforts to coal the *Texas* and to move on at once toward Santiago. It would have been a relief both to Washington and to Admiral Sampson to know of Schley's new decision *to push on immediately* rather than to wait until morning, but Schley had not the means of sending that important message.

He got under way at 6:00 P. M., steaming slowly in two columns, auxiliaries to the right of the battle line, course southeast. "We are bound for Santiago," he signaled to the Flying Squadron. "In case of separation rendezvous off Gonaïves Bay, Haiti, outside marine limit."[40] In the present lumpy sea it was impossible to think of coaling. At ten knots the *Eagle* dipped her bow so far under that the squadron had to be slowed to five knots while a bucket brigade bailed out her forward compartments. When an engine on the collier *Merrimac* broke down, Schley's fleet engineer brought the parts over by rowboat to be repaired on the *Brooklyn*. Sacrificing speed in order to keep his heterogeneous auxiliaries in company with his battleships—he felt that he could hardly dispense with their services as torpedo-boat destroyers, dispatch boats and as fuel reserve—Schley arrived off Santiago about 6:00 P. M. on May 26.

Here he found three converted cruisers: the *St. Paul*, the *Minneapolis* and the *Yale*. The nearest captain, Captain Sigsbee of the *St. Paul*, was summoned on board the flagship. Sigsbee, formerly commanding officer of the U.S.S. *Maine*, brought with him a native Negro pilot, Eduardo Nuñez, who was familiar with Santiago Harbor. Schley met him at the gangway and asked: "Have we got the Dons in here, Sigsbee?"[41] And Sigsbee's answer, as witnessed by Lieutenant Sears, Cadet Marble and Associated Press Correspondent George E. Graham, was "No. They are not here. I have been here for a week, and they could not be here unless I knew it." Graham, a privileged character on the flagship, followed the officers aft on the quarter-deck and heard Schley repeat: "Are you sure they are not in there?" To this Sigsbee is said to have responded: "I have been very close to the harbor entrance two or three times, and Cotton [captain of the cruiser *Harvard*] has been in and cut a cable, and they are not there."[42] Schley, logically enough, got the impression that this opinion was not merely Sigsbee's personal opinion, but the combined views of Sigsbee and of the other officers on the station as well.

Schley, who spoke Spanish fluently, now questioned the Negro pilot. The latter doubted that the Spanish warships could negotiate the narrow and tortuous channel, except in perfectly smooth weather: even then, according to Nuñez, they should have to be worked around the curves by tugs. Nuñez, with 16 or 18 years of experience piloting in these waters, was rather positive that such deep-draft vessels as the *Cristobal Colon* could not take refuge in Santiago.[43]

Again, as in the first days at Cienfuegos, Schley was faced with incomplete and disturbing evidence. But this time he was farther from home; his auxiliaries were developing mechanical difficulties; and every minute his battleships were eating more and more of their precious coal supply. Because her coal had become dangerously low, the *Eagle* in midafternoon was sent to Jamaica. The *Marblehead*, too, was running low. Schley signaled the *Minneapolis* to take the *Marblehead* in tow in the morning. The *Minneapolis* replied, "I am short of coal and machinery in bad condition." Flagship: "Have you enough coal to go to Key West?" *Minneapolis:* "Just enough."[44]

The coal situation, the mechanical situation and the strategic situation, as they appeared to Schley at this moment, were terribly confused. Moreover, Schley's private interpretation of the military situation, as he testified later, was that the telegraphic information from Havana to the effect that Cervera had entered Santiago was very likely "a ruse." "It is precisely what I should have done if I had been militarily managing their situation—to have attracted the squadrons in the direction of either one of these ports and then gone in behind them."[45] Since Sampson's force now lay to the eastward of Havana, it seemed best to Schley to fall back toward Key West via the Yucatan Channel, to the west of Cuba.

To the squadron, Schley at 8:30 P. M. on May 26 flashed the critical orders by Ardois signal lights, "Destination Key West; via south of Cuba and Yucatan Channel as soon as collier is ready. Speed 9 knots."[46]

For Sampson, meanwhile, the critical ten-day period following his dispatch of Schley to the south side of Cuba was one of extreme uncertainty, when events at the front refused to clarify because the enemy could not be located. Preparations back home of the army of invasion demanded that accurate and immediate knowledge of the enemy's whereabouts be obtained. The approach of the hurricane season, when it would be suicidal to throw green, unacclimated troops into the steaming, fever-ridden jungles of Cuba, contributed a fearful urgency to Sampson's problem of locating Cervera.

The first report that Cervera had entered Santiago came 12 hours after Schley's departure from Key West for Cienfuegos. Sampson at first dismissed it as a rumor. Then he received Secretary Long's comment that the Havana report "might very well be correct"; and Sampson's aide, Lieutenant Staunton, calling at the telegraph office in Key West, was whisked aside very secretively by Major Allen, an Army signal officer and told of the circumstances in which the information had been obtained. Allen himself had received the Havana cable at 6:00 P.M. the night before. Only the commander in chief and his staff were to be notified; otherwise the Cuban agent employed in the Havana telegraph office would probably lose his life and further messages become unlikely. The Cuban agent had explained that he would get in touch with Key West each evening at six o'clock, since at that hour the other operatives in his office were out to dinner. Explaining none of the circumstances, Sampson sent word of this rumor to Schley via the *Iowa* and the *Dupont*, without as yet making any change in Schley's assignment off Cienfuegos. When he himself moved on to the Havana blockade, he left his aide in Key West to learn at the earliest moment whether the report from Havana would be confirmed. Promptly at 6:00 P.M. on May 20 the Cuban agent again called and confirmed his earlier report that Cervera had entered Santiago.

At 3:00 A. M. on the twenty-first, Sampson sent Schley a conditional order by the *Marblehead*: "Sir: Spanish squadron probably at Santiago de Cuba—4 ships and 3 torpedo boat destroyers. If you are satisfied that they are not at Cienfuegos, proceed with all dispatch, but cautiously, to Santiago de Cuba, and if the enemy is there blockade him in port. . . ."[47]

In the afternoon of the twenty-first, Sampson rushed to Schley a second dispatch via the *Hawk* which he regarded as a definite order: "It is thought the inclosed instructions will reach you by 2 o'clock A. M., May 23. This will enable you to leave before daylight (regarded very important), so that your direction may not be noticed, and be at Santiago A. M., May 24. It is thought that the Spanish squadron would probably have some repairs to make and coal to take. . . ." Sampson revealed that he himself would move eastward from Havana into the Old Bahama Channel to intercept Cervera should he escape before Schley's arrival and come around the east end of Cuba. "If this word does not reach you before daylight, it is suggested to mask your real direction as much as possible. Follow the Spanish squadron, whichever direction they take." Sampson then telegraphed the Secretary: "Schley has been ordered to Santiago de Cuba."[48]

Sampson stripped the Havana blockade of its strongest ships and proceeded to a location 200 miles east of Havana, where for several days he patrolled the narrow and most frequented passageway around eastern Cuba, hoping that Cervera would appear.

For five days he heard nothing from Schley, owing to difficulties in communication. His anxiety was further increased by orders from Washington to prepare to convoy 30 troop transports from Tampa. Until Cervera had been located and pinned down, however, these orders were impractical.

On the twenty-fourth Mr. Long, in excitement over Schley's failure to move immediately to Santiago, issued two orders which might better have been issued a month earlier. They were:[49] To Sampson: "Till further orders the Flying Squadron is under your orders, and Schley will be so informed." To Schley: "Till further orders the Flying Squadron is under the orders of Sampson, Commander-in-Chief, North Atlantic Station."

Coming at this late date, these orders afforded a vent for Washington's pent-up anxieties, but did not by one iota increase the already complete military authority over Schley which Sampson had exercised since the eighteenth, when the two men joined forces at Key West. To press and public, such orders, in the circumstances, could only mean that something had gone wrong in the relations of Schley and

Sampson; and from this point on, with no conscious encouragement from either of the two principals involved, the people of the country and many in the Navy and in political life commenced to align themselves as pro-Sampson or pro-Schley.

On May 25 the perplexed commander in chief wrote to Commodore Remey: "My dear Commodore: We are still waiting for information about the Spaniards, from Schley. He should have reached Santiago yesterday, and by this time I hoped to hear that he had them blockaded in port. I have proceeded during the past two days, on the theory that the Spanish fleet might have eluded Schley, and started up the north coast to reach Havana, or have gone West on the South side in order to go into Cienfuegos. The delay has been so great that there is the possibility that, if they got away from Schley, they could have gone around Cape San Antonio and reach[ed] Havana. For that reason I have fallen back, and when this reaches you, will be at the Western entrance of Nicholas Passage, and unless I hear from you by the *Vesuvius* tomorrow morning, I shall be quite at a loss to know in what direction it will be necessary for me to move. . . . I have, in my dispatch to the Secretary, informed him that it would be impossible to detach an armor-clad to assist the landing of the Army until this question of the disposition of the Spanish ships has been decided."[50]

Then, on May 25, a procession of dispatch vessels from Haiti and Key West relayed the bewildering early reports of Schley from Cienfuegos. At 1:00 P. M. Sampson sent the *Vesuvius* back to Key West with identical orders to the commanding officers of the fast scouts *Yale, Minneapolis* and *St. Paul:* "Spanish squadron is at Santiago. If Schley has not arrived there, go to Cienfuegos and inform him."[51] At 9:30 P. M. came Schley's report of the twenty-third, saying that he believed he had Cervera bottled up in Cienfuegos! Lieutenant Hood of the *Hawk*, who had carried Schley's dispatch to Key West, had affirmed that "a good number of officers [of the Flying Squadron] do not believe the Spaniards are there [at Cienfuegos] at all, although they can only surmise."[52]

With dismay Sampson wrote to Schley via the *Wasp:* "Sir—1. Every report, and particularly daily confidential reports received at Key West from Havana state Spanish Squadron has been in Santiago de Cuba from the 19th to the 25th instant inclusive, the 25th being the date of the last report received. 2. You will please proceed, with all possible dispatch, to Santiago to blockade that port. If on arrival there, you receive *positive* information of the Spanish ships having left, you will follow them in pursuit. Very respectfully, W. T. Sampson."[53] Sampson also detached from his own meager squadron the cruiser *New Orleans,* under Captain Folger, whom he instructed to direct Commodore Schley "to remain on the blockade off Santiago at all hazards, assuming that the Spanish vessels are in that port." Schley was to obstruct the harbor by sinking a collier across its narrow entrance. "Inform Commodore Schley that the details of this plan are left to his judgment. In the meantime he must exercise the utmost care that none of the vessels already in the port are allowed to escape; and say to the Commodore that I have the utmost confidence in his ability to carry this plan to a successful conclusion and earnestly wish him good luck."[54]

Sampson now returned to Key West to arrange the convoy for the Army and to be near the center of information. He arrived at 2:00 A.M. on the twenty-ninth to find good news. The new battleship *Oregon* had arrived safely at Key West. This first-class ship, the first battleship of the New Navy to be built on the West Coast, had been caught in California when war broke out, nearly 15,000 miles from the Caribbean theater of action. In the face of unpredictable hazards, at one time even threatened with enemy action—when the *Oregon* crossed Cervera's track near the Windward Islands—this fine ship had completed a record voyage around Cape Horn at an average speed of 11.6 knots. Sampson rejoiced in the welcome addition to his blockade squadron. The *Oregon,* moreover, as reported by her skipper Captain Clark, was mechanically fit for active service in spite of her long cruise and would be ready for duty as soon as she got her coal on board.

Earlier plans had been to land the military force near Havana, but at Key West Sampson found a directive from the Department to prepare to convoy 10,000 men to Santiago. As yet no recent word had been received from Schley, but to Sampson's delight the usual 6:00 P. M. telegram from Havana placed Cervera still in Santiago. "This makes it more and more probable," Sampson wrote to Commodore J. C. Watson, his deputy commander off Havana, "that Schley is at that place [Santiago] blockading. Until Schley is heard from I think that it will probably relieve your anxiety on this score to know that I believe those Spaniards are now safe. . . ."[55]

Sampson's optimism concerning the situation off Santiago received a jolt when, two hours past midnight on May 29, he received an agitating telegram from Long: "Schley telegraphs from Santiago de Cuba he goes to Key West with his squadron for coal, though he had 4,000 tons of coal with him in a broken-down collier. How soon after arrival of Schley at Key West could you reach Santiago de Cuba with the *New York* and the *Oregon*, the *Indiana*. . . . Schley has not ascertained whether Spanish division is at Santiago. All information here seems to show that it is there."[56]

By 3:00 A. M. Sampson's reply was on the wire to Washington. He could reach Santiago in three days, but asked permission to leave immediately, hoping to meet Schley's principal force on the way and turn it back to Santiago. While he awaited word from Washington, he hurried his preparations for sailing. The *Oregon* was at the moment en route to Havana to relieve the *Indiana*, which had to come to Key West for coal. Sampson could not wait for the slow *Indiana*. He wrote Watson off Havana a summary of events, since the latter would control everything afloat on the north side of Cuba during Sampson's absence. "We are still coaling, but ready to start as soon as a reply has been received from the Department to my telegram. I am entirely unable to understand why Schley said he must leave his station for the purpose of obtaining coal, when he undoubtedly has his big ships half full of coal and at least four thousand tons in his collier. I also fail to understand why the Department should wish me to remain here until Schley arrives for, in the meantime, the Spanish ships would be unopposed at Santiago for the space of four days. . . . Notwithstanding Schley's statement that he must leave Santiago and come to Key West, it is possible that after receiving my communication sent by Folger [commander of the *New Orleans*], which should reach him this morning, he may change his mind and remain on the blockade."[57]

At noon with an impatience unusual for him, Sampson telegraphed the Department urging an immediate reply to his request. "Failure of Schley to continue blockade must be remedied at once if possible. There can be no doubt of presence of Spanish squadron at Santiago."[58]

Through these difficult hours the commander in chief justified his reputation for being as cool as a block of ice, though Captain Chadwick, his chief of staff and closer to Sampson personally than anyone else on board the *New York*, detected in him the same deep-seated apprehensions which he had seen only once before—during the run to San Juan when the towlines of the monitors had so often snapped. After hours of strain, Chadwick, a ruddy and genial individual, bald and "built on the rotund plan" with every line of his physique "a graceful outward curve," and "to all appearances one of those jolly sea dogs that was as ready to quarter an enemy as to eat a square meal," felt not at all charitably inclined toward Schley.[59] During the afternoon of this critical day when Sampson received Schley's infinitely more hopeful dispatch saying that his collier *Merrimac* had been repaired, that the weather was moderating and he was remaining on the blockade, Sampson telegraphed Schley at once: "Congratulate you on success. Maintain blockade at all hazards. . . ."[60] Captain Chadwick, after all the anxiety that Schley had caused, protested against the admiral's sending Schley congratulations; but Sampson, as Chadwick later testified, "persisted in putting it that way, and I asked him why, and he said, 'Oh, I want to encourage him.' "[61]

Having received in the afternoon the Secretary's telegraphed authorization to act at his discretion, Sampson after sundown on the twenty-ninth departed for Santiago.

Schley's pace, as he retreated toward Key West from Santiago on the night of May 26, was geared to that of the cruiser *Yale*, which was towing the collier. Owing to the inability of the *Merrimac's* crew to attach the towing cable securely, the *Yale* was forced to make frequent stops. In 12 hours the squadron moved only 25 miles. Then it was overtaken by the scout cruiser *Harvard*, bringing an urgent dispatch via Haiti from the Department. This dispatch was in answer to Schley's dispatch of May 24 off Cienfuegos, and it betrayed the Navy Department's mounting concern over the whereabouts of Cervera. It read: "*Harvard*, St. Nicholas Mole, Haiti: Proceed at once and inform Schley, and also the senior officer present off Santiago, as follows: All Department's information indicates Spanish division is still at Santiago. The Department looks to you to ascertain facts, and that the enemy, if therein, does not leave without a decisive action. Cubans familiar with Santiago say that there are landing places 5 or 6 nautical miles west from the mouth of the harbor, and that there insurgents probably will be found, and not the Spanish. From the surrounding heights can see every vessel in port. As soon as ascertained, notify the Department whether enemy is there. Could not squadron and also *Harvard* coal from *Merrimac* leeward of Cape Cruz, Gonaïves Channel, or Mole, Haiti? The Department will send coal immediately to Mole. Report without delay situation at Santiago de Cuba."[62]

The element of doubt in Secretary Long's dispatch weighed heavily with Schley. "The Department looks to you to ascertain facts, and that the enemy, if within . . ." Schley, having already satisfied himself that the Spanish were not there, that the "Havana rumor" had been only a ruse, at once returned the following telegram via Jamaica: "*Merrimac's* engine is disabled, and she is helpless; am obliged to have her towed to Key West. Have been absolutely unable to coal the *Texas, Marblehead, Vixen,* and *Brooklyn* from collier, owing to very rough seas and boisterous weather since leaving Key West. *Brooklyn* is the only one in squadron having more than sufficient coal to reach Key West. Impossible to remain off Santiago in present state of coal account of the squadron. Not possible to coal to leeward of Cape Cruz in summer owing to southwest winds. *Harvard* just reports to me she has only coal enough to reach Jamaica, and she will proceed to Port Royal. Also reports only small vessels could coal at Gonaïves or Mole, Haiti. *Minneapolis* has only enough coal to reach Key West, and same of *Yale,* which will tow *Merrimac.* It is also to be regretted that the department's orders cannot be obeyed, earnestly as we have all striven to that end. I am forced to return to Key West via Yucatan Passage for coal. Can ascertain nothing certain concerning enemy. Was obliged to send *Eagle* to Port Antonio, Jamaica, yesterday, as she had only twenty-seven tons of coal on board. Will leave *St. Paul* here. Will require 9,500 tons of coal at Key West."[63]

During the afternoon Schley ordered the *St. Paul* to remain off Santiago until her coal supply reached the danger point and then to head for Key West. "If Sampson comes here, tell him half of squadron short of coal and collier engine broken down."[64]

The rain squalls of the morning gave way to a steady barometer and fine weather by night. The collier, too, by this time had had her engines repaired and was able to handle herself in coaling operations. The sea being suddenly quieter than it had been for six days, both the *Marblehead* and the *Texas* went alongside her and took on coal.

By 10:45 P.M. of the twenty-seventh, Schley had determined to remain off Santiago, coaling if necessary off Haiti. Working all night and loading coal at the rate of 20 tons an hour, the *Texas* almost filled her bunkers by noon of the twenty-eighth. The chafing of their hulls against one another sprang leaks in both ships, but these were of little consequence. This was the hottest day yet; pitch ran "like water" out of the seams of the deck.[65] On recommendation of the surgeon, who feared exhaustion of the crew in the intense heat, coaling of the *Texas* was halted at 11:00 A.M.

From May 26 to 28, in the so-called "retrograde" movement, when it was under orders to return to Key West, the Flying Squadron, owing to mechanical breakdowns, made very little headway; and its course on the last day, because of coaling, was a zigzag one. Thus at 8:05 A.M. on the twenty-eighth, when Schley announced to his squadron his intention to return to Santiago he was not more than 50 miles to the west of the harbor mouth. The squadron returned to Santiago at a leisurely pace during the night of the twenty-eighth-twenty-ninth.

Early the next morning, as the shadows vanished, the Flying Squadron made out the dim shape of a Spanish warship lying inside the canyonlike mouth of Santiago Harbor. The fact that her smokestacks were located between her military masts clearly identified her as Cervera's speediest armored cruiser, the *Cristobal Colon.* Beyond the *Colon* were visible Cervera's flagship, the *Infanta Maria Teresa,* and several torpedo boats.

Schley's usual good luck, which had deserted him during two arduous weeks of searching for Cervera, had returned. The Spanish admiral, having entered Santiago on the nineteenth, as the Havana operator reported, was by coincidence preparing to leave the harbor just as Schley's ships hove into view.

Schley, after calling a conference of commanding officers, established a blockade and sent off the *St. Paul* to communicate with Admiral Sampson and to dispatch from St. Nicholas Mole the following telegram to the Department: "Off Santiago de Cuba, May 29, 10 A.M. Enemy in port. Recognized *Cristobal Colon, Infanta Maria Teresa,* and two torpedo boats moored inside Morro, behind point. Doubtless the others are here. I have not sufficient coal. Making every effort to get coal in. *Vixen* has blown out a manhole gasket. I have sent boiler makers on board to repair. Collier repaired, machinery being put together. Have about 3,000 tons of coal in collier, but not easy to get aboard here. If there is no engagement in next two or three days, Sampson's squadron could relieve this one to coal at Gonaïves or Port au Prince. Hasten me dispatch vessels for picket work. The *Brooklyn, Iowa, Texas, Massachusetts, Vixen,* and collier compose squadron here. I am sending *St. Paul* to communicate with Sampson."[66]

Several earlier telegrams from the Navy Department, which now arrived by various tugs and dispatch vessels, showed how greatly the game of blindman's buff had strained official nerves in Washington, where military arrangements had been held up pending the definite locating of the enemy squadron.

As a kind of celebration after his long chase, Schley on May 31 shifted his flag to the *Massachusetts* and took the three battleships in for a distant bombardment of the forts at the harbor mouth. Though everyone was hoping that they might "pot" the *Colon*, which still lay in full view in the inner harbor, Schley, obeying the Department's policy, kept a safe distance from the forts. His main object was to induce the latter to open up at extreme range so as to disclose their strength. Captain Evans in his zeal to score a hit on the *Colon* gave the *Iowa's* guns so extreme an elevation as temporarily to disable them. No hits were scored on either side. As the fleet withdrew, the very devout Captain Philip megaphoned to Captain Evans: "I have been trying to get the chaplain to swear for me." To which "Fighting Bob" Evans retorted, "Shoot the chaplain! I have been doing it myself all the afternoon. I have strained one of my twelve-inch guns trying to hit the *Colon*. I think I did hit her once. We should have sunk her though, but we kept too far out."[67]

Sampson, coming around the eastern end of Cuba, met the *St. Paul*, from whose commander, Captain Sigsbee, he learned that Schley's force had returned to Santiago and had actually located two of the principal Spanish warships inside of the harbor. "At the same time," reported Sigsbee—and this alarmed Sampson—"Commodore Schley was blockading, but at a distance of twenty-five miles to the westward of the harbor!"[68] Because the facilities at Key West were overtaxed, Sampson sent Sigsbee to New York for coal. To enable Secretary Long to obtain as clear a picture as possible of the situation off Santiago, Sampson orally directed Sigsbee to report in person to the Navy Department.

At 6:00 A.M. on June 1, Sampson arrived off Santiago and found the enemy still in the harbor and the Flying Squadron in column a few miles outside the entrance. The commander in chief was no doubt relieved to find that Commodore Schley was maintaining a blockade at close range, rather than, as had been reported, from a distance of twenty-five miles!

17. SANTIAGO

THE first night off Santiago, Sampson was compelled to warn certain newspaper boats, which kept moving around the fleet and blinking their lights, that they should have to keep at least five miles outside the fleet or be fired on without warning. Before the cheers for the *Oregon*, "Pride of the Pacific," "Bulldog of the Fleet," had died away, a pro-Schley reporter for the *New York Herald* had already sharpened his pen to write the admiral down. "The appearance of Sampson on the scene," this fellow wrote, "was not relished by the officers of Schley's squadron, who think it bad taste on the Admiral's part to interfere at this juncture. Some think it would be graceful for Sampson to return in front of Havana and leave Schley to deal with the situation. . . ."[1]

The slight shade of difference between pro-Schley and anti-Sampson was rapidly vanishing. Of the fact that Schley had virtually requested the Navy Department to send Sampson to Santiago, the reporter was, of course, unaware.

Schley came on board at 6:30 A.M., and, as the *New York* moved across the entrance to the harbor, pointed out to Sampson what he could about the enemy fortifications. A shot from the *Colon*, still at anchor inside the harbor, splashed in the water about two miles ahead of the *New York*. The imminence of American troop movements now required an early settling with Cervera. But how to do this was the problem. Cervera would never willingly come out in the face of the overwhelming force now concentrated against him. Nor, despite the tall talk of newspaper strategists, was it feasible to repeat Farragut's performance at Mobile or Dewey's at Manila, by steaming boldly into the harbor without regard to its protective mine field. The Spanish mines of 1898 were infinitely more destructive (witness the *Maine* disaster) than the so-called "torpedoes" of 1864 which Farragut had damned; and, whereas the Manila channels had been wide and deep, the channel at Santiago at its narrowest was only a ship's length wide and was so shallow that battleships could enter only during high tide. Should the attempt be made to force a passage, the sinking of a single battleship in the channel might prove disastrous to Sampson's forces. There was also the possibility that Cervera might sneak out on some dark, rainy night and fall upon the United States convoy or perpetrate a much dreaded coastal raid. The one correct course seemed to be to bottle up Cervera. And this Sampson proceeded to do.

While en route from Key West, Sampson had perfected plans for sinking a collier across the narrow entrance to the harbor; and Naval Constructor R. P. Hobson with a special crew had made a string of torpedoes to do the work.

Hobson's torpedoes were transferred to the *Merrimac*, and while special workmen installed them, others stripped the ship of valuable gear. A crew of eleven was picked from the hundreds of seamen who volunteered for what was thought to be a suicide mission. Six torpedoes were lashed against the port side of the ship, about 12 feet below the water line. In the early hours of June 3, between the setting of the moon and the first crack of day, Hobson charged into the entrance. Ensign Joseph Powell with the *New York's* steam launch trailed him as far as the entrance to bring off survivors.

The *Merrimac* was quickly discovered by the enemy and subjected to a galling fire from ships and forts. Captain Robley Evans, whose ship was detailed to move in close and shield the *Merrimac*, described the scene as "hell with the lid off."[2] When day broke, Ensign Powell could see the tops of the *Merrimac's* masts rising above the water, but no sign of the raft with survivors.

In the afternoon Admiral Cervera's aide came out to the fleet under a flag of truce. The Spanish admiral in person had helped to rescue Hobson and his men, and with a touch of old-school gallantry had sent Captain Bustamante to congratulate the American admiral on having such men under his command, and to inform him that they were all safe, though two were slightly wounded, and that all were in need of clothes. While garments were being collected for Hobson and his men, Admiral Sampson entertained Captain Bustamante, whom he knew as the foremost torpedo expert in Spain's Navy. "It was curious," wrote Goode, the Associated Press writer on the *New York*, "to see Captain Bustamante, Cervera's envoy, sitting chatting with Sampson on the quarter-deck of the *New York*. . . . The mission of Bustamante and the spirit that prompted it made us proud of our enemies."[3]

Hobson's attempt evoked wild popular applause in the United States but did not obstruct the entrance to Santiago Bay. As could be seen from outside the harbor the blockship had sunk lengthwise in, rather than athwart, the channel. Cervera must still be penned in by the tedious process of a close blockade.

Having an ample force of auxiliary craft, as well as a landing force of marines, Sampson now seized the placid Bay of Guantánamo, 40 miles east of Santiago, and thither he sent the battleships, one at a time, to be coaled.

Sampson reorganized his force into two divisions and stationed the battleships on an arc six miles from the Morro, with steam up and heading toward the entrance. By placing the division leaders, the *New York* and the *Brooklyn*, on the east and west flanks respectively, he assured advantageous positions to these fast heavy cruisers in case Cervera should manage to slip out. Inside of the semicircle of battleships were light auxiliaries and, yet closer in, torpedo-boat destroyers and yachts. At night the cordon of battleships was drawn in to four miles distance. The Navy Department's prohibition against bombarding forts being no longer applicable, Sampson on June 6 led the first of a series of fleet bombardments of the Santiago forts. This steady and monotonous punishment fell, as the rain itself, almost every day. Lieutenant Commander Seaton Schroeder of the *Massachusetts* wrote that Sampson's methodical bombardments "seemed so one-sided that toward the end the men got to calling them target practices."[4] Indeed, this was the first extensive opportunity that the battleships of the New Navy had had in which to unlimber their great guns, and Sampson, the expert in ordnance, was determined to eliminate all possible difficulties in mechanism and operation before the showdown with Cervera should come. Even the *Vesuvius*, the "dynamite" cruiser, was permitted to test her long pneumatic tubes for hurling guncotton projectiles, although it was impossible to aim these curious guns, save by pointing the ship itself, and the operation had to be conducted in pitch blackness from close range.

Despite careful attention to keeping ships in position they drifted from their appointed stations at night. To overcome this difficulty, Sampson on June 8—for the first time in history—inaugurated a system of battleship searchlight patrols. By turns the battleships took station within two miles of the Morro and sent their blinding beams directly up the channel. It was touchy and difficult business at first to hold the beams steadily on the channel. Often they accidentally illuminated the yacht patrol that plied in the blackness under the enemy cliffs; but with practice the technique of handling the lights was mastered. Sampson's "bottling" of Cervera, as Mahan pointed out, was no ordinary operation such as "the careless shoving of a cork into a half-used bottle—it is rather like the wiring down of champagne by bonds that cannot be broken and through which nothing can ooze."[5] Sampson himself considered the searchlight as "one of the most important elements in making the blockade successful. . . . The entrance was by this means brilliantly lighted, so that the movements of the smallest boat could be seen within."[6] The British naval attaché, Captain Paget, could scarce believe his eyes when he saw the American battleships one after another move up right under the Morro and illuminate the harbor. "What damned impertinence!" was his comment.[7]

If the Army intended to invade Cuba, they should, in Sampson's opinion, make their campaign at once before the hurricane season set in, or else they should delay until dry weather in the fall. The admiral, having been led to expect a military effort against Havana, had planned to return to the north side of the island immediately after blocking the Santiago channel. But two factors caused him to remain off Santiago: the failure of the *Merrimac* effectively to block the channel, and the War Department's sudden shift of its objective from Havana to Santiago itself. Long's telegram of May 31 informed Sampson that the Army was "now embarking" some 25,000 men at Tampa, "to proceed to Santiago as soon as you inform me the whole Spanish fleet in harbor," and the next day General Shafter set June 4 as the date of departure.[8] A naval convoy was ordered. Then the sailing was delayed because of higgledy-piggledy congestion and mismanagement at Port of Tampa.

On June 6, following his initial full-scale bombardment, Sampson pleaded for troops to storm from the rear these forts at the harbor entrance. "If 10,000 men were here, city and fleet would be ours within forty-eight hours. Every consideration demands immediate army movement. If delayed, city will be defended more strongly by guns taken from fleet."[9] But the convoy's sailing was further delayed when by error two groups of American ships meeting off Cuba at night reported each other as enemy cruisers. Sampson quickly checked the logs of the vessels concerned and detected the mistake. To make doubly certain that he had all of Cervera's ships inside of Santiago Bay he sent Lieutenant Victor Blue on a daring reconnaissance which carried him (in full uniform and sword) over mountainous jungle and through enemy lines to a hilltop from which he could actually count and identify the types of ships in the harbor. Blue's report allayed further fear of an enemy raid, and the troop convoy, having deferred its sailing until the rainy season was about to begin, set out for Cuba.

Preparatory to the Army landings, Sampson had already, by landing marines, taken possession of the fine harbor of Guantánamo and he had also opened communication with forces of the Cuban rebels. Cuban General Calixto Garcia in a conference on the flagship furnished a full account of the enemy's military strength and positions and offered to place his insurgent troops under American orders. "He was a large, kindly-faced man," writes Chadwick, "with an extraordinary deep vertical furrow in the forehead made by a pistol bullet in an attempted suicide while captured and in prison. He inspired much confidence in Sampson, who was usually slow to make up his mind to such trust. The general unfortunately suffered much from the motion of the ship, and during most of his stay aboard, which would have been prolonged but for this, was lying stretched upon a sofa in the cabin. Sampson mentioned the possibility of an attack by the Spaniards upon Garcia's force. Lifting himself at once upon his elbow Garcia replied with great impressiveness, 'The Spaniards never attack; they never attack!' "[10]

On June 20 when General Shafter arrived with his 32 transports and

17,000 men, Sampson and his chief of staff Captain Chadwick at once laid before the general their plan of campaign. It involved eliminating enemy batteries at the entrance, sweeping mines from the channel and sending the fleet in after Cervera. Once the Spanish squadron was destroyed, Sampson believed, the entire resistance in Cuba would soon collapse. General Shafter assented to the plan and looked over Sampson's map upon which were marked the Spanish positions at the mouth of the harbor which the admiral wished the Army to assault from the rear while the ships attacked from outside. Later that same afternoon the admiral and the general landed at Aserraderos, west of the harbor and rode muleback to the headqaurters of General Garcia. Here the plans were rehearsed and Cuban advice was sought on where to land the troops and how to co-ordinate the activities of American and Cuban forces.

The Army lacking small boats, it was necessary to strip the fleet of its boats, tugs and lighters to put the troops ashore at a point 15 miles east of Santiago. Landing operations consumed five days and were accompanied by diversionary bombardments along a considerable stretch of coast. Everything had to be done the hard way. The blockaders must not only supply landing vessels, but officers and crews to man them. The *Massachusetts*, for instance, had to detail 70 of her crew of 400 to this unexpected chore at a time when coaling, blockading and bombarding were proceeding more vigorously than ever.[11] Fortunately Sampson had a fine group of naval cadets from Annapolis—Thomas C. Hart was one of these—to rely on for handling picket launches and landing craft. While the troops were being landed Sampson received word from Washington that the Spanish Admiral Camara had set out to menace Dewey in the Far East and that in consequence a new Eastern Squadron was to be formed under Commodore Watson as a counterthreat to the Spanish homeland. Sampson was notified on June 25 that he must part with one of his cruisers and his two best battleships, the *Oregon* and the *Iowa*. Sampson hoped, however, that Cervera might be forced out before Watson's squadron had to leave.

Difficulties of the Army on shore further complicated the naval problem. Green troops outfitted with clothing suited to a campaign in Alaska were rushed during the sickly, rainy season into tropical jungle. Many threw away their gear, some even their rations, as they slogged

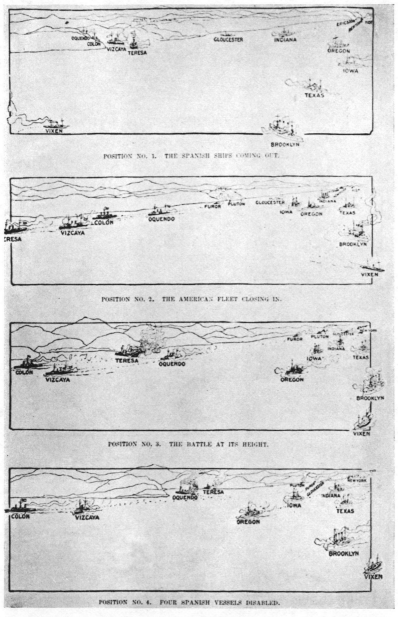

POSITION NO. 1. THE SPANISH SHIPS COMING OUT.

POSITION NO. 2. THE AMERICAN FLEET CLOSING IN.

POSITION NO. 3. THE BATTLE AT ITS HEIGHT.

POSITION NO. 4. FOUR SPANISH VESSELS DISABLED.

Pictorial Map of the Battle of Santiago, Drawn by Howard F. Sprague. First Four Positions. (*See next page.*)

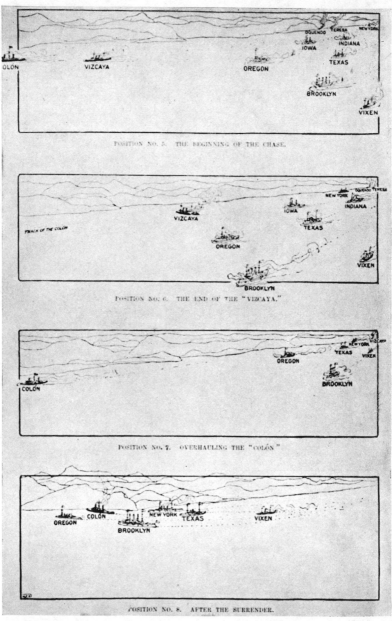

POSITION NO. 5. THE BEGINNING OF THE CHASE.

POSITION NO. 6. THE END OF THE "VIZCAYA."

POSITION NO. 7. OVERHAULING THE "COLÓN"

POSITION NO. 8. AFTER THE SURRENDER.

Pictorial Map of the Battle of Santiago, Drawn by Howard F. Sprague. Last Four Positions.

inland. After the troops had been put on shore it became a major operation to land supplies rapidly enough to feed and equip them, and this gratuitous task also fell to the Navy's small boats. To a suggestion that after landing the troops, these craft be returned to their ships, the quartermaster of the expeditionary force threw up his hands. "Take these boats away," he announced emphatically, "and the Army falls back!"[12] Even more fatal to Sampson's plan of operations, the mule trails which ran inland from the landing beach, the preliminary tracings through the jungle along which the Army was now busily clearing trees and building roads, led not to the harbor forts which Sampson wanted the Army to attack, *but toward the city of Santiago itself some four miles inland from the coast!*

General Shafter, himself weighing some 300 pounds, was no nimble leader in this steaming climate, and there were too many younger men, like the romantically bellicose Teddy Roosevelt and his Rough Riders, to whom Admiral Sampson's plan of campaign had not been divulged. The Navy bombarded the Morro, the Socapa and the Punta Gorda batteries, expecting momentarily a signal to delay their operations in favor of an Army assault force in the rear of these enemy positions. No such attack materialized. Instead, Shafter was five or six miles inland striking at San Juan Hill and El Caney, on the outskirts of the militarily insignificant city.

On July 2 Sampson's aide telephoned to General Shafter that Admiral Sampson had silenced the forts, but could not get at the mine field until "after the forts are taken possession of by your troops."[13]

Shafter, ill in his tent at the front and appalled by his own unexpectedly heavy losses, replied sharply: "It is impossible for me to say when I can take batteries at entrance to harbor. If they are as difficult to take as those which we have been pitted against it will be some time and a great loss of life. I am at a loss to see why the Navy cannot work under a destructive fire as well as the Army. My loss yesterday was over 500 men. By all means keep up fire on everything in sight of you until demolished. I expect, however, with time and sufficient men to capture the forts along the bay."

And an hour later he telegraphed: "Terrible fight yesterday, but my line is now strongly intrenched about three-fourths mile from town. I urge that you make effort immediately to force the entrance to avoid future losses among my men, which are already very heavy. You can now operate with less loss of life than I can. Please telephone answer."

Sampson sent a calm note explaining once more his tactical problem: "Our trouble from the first has been that the channel to the harbor is well strewn with observation mines, which would certainly result in the sinking of one or more of our ships if we attempted to enter the harbor, and by the sinking of a ship the object of the attempt to enter the harbor would be defeated by preventing further progress on our part. It was my hope that an attack, on your part, of these shore batteries from the rear would leave us at liberty to drag the channel for torpedoes. . . ."[14]

The next day was Sunday, July 3. Off the entrance to Santiago, searchlights were turned off shortly before dawn and the solemn semi-circle of battleships resumed daytime stations about five miles off the Morro. Church pennants fluttered from the flagstaffs. Sampson signaled his fleet to disregard the movements of the commander in chief and turned the *New York* eastward toward the coastal hamlet of Siboney, from whence Sampson planned to ride muleback to the front to confer with Shafter. Goode has left a thumbnail glimpse of the admiral at this moment, standing "on the quarter-deck of the *New York* as that vessel neared the brown hills of Siboney, wearing his leggings, and all ready for the long, hot ride that lay before him. He was not in very good health, and was well-nigh worn-out with the tremendous strain of the past month. . . . The physical and mental strain . . . had confined him once or twice to his bed, much against his will. . . ."[15] Beside Sampson stood Naval Cadet Needham Jones, also in leggings. A few days ago the cadet had obtained permission to accompany the admiral the next time he went ashore to see his wounded brother who was a captain in the Army. Sampson had remembered the youth's request.

Suddenly a man yelled from the signal bridge: "Smoke in harbor! The fleet's coming out!"[16]

Sampson lowered his glass and remarked quietly to Lieutenant Staunton, his assistant chief of staff. "Yes. They're coming out. Hoist 250." The signal, "Close in towards harbor entrance and attack vessels"— though too far away to be read by the already alerted blockaders— was quickly run up.[17] "Mr. Jones—" the admiral turned to the naval cadet—"I'm afraid you won't see your brother today."[18]

Had Cervera turned eastward in his attempted flight through the American line, Sampson would have been ideally situated to head him off. But the Spanish admiral turned westward, thus presenting to Commodore Schley and the *Brooklyn* at the western extremity of the line the fairest opportunity for distinction in battle.

Cervera's black-hulled flagship the *Infanta Maria Teresa*, shooting her way out of the canyonlike gulch of the harbor, appeared to Sampson, seven miles to the eastward, as little more than a dark cloud low on the water which was rifted every few seconds by gun flashes. With intervals of six to eight minutes between them, three other Spanish cruisers darted out: the *Vizcaya*, the *Cristobal Colon* and the *Oquendo*. Each in turn followed in the track of the leader to the westward. Last of all came the little torpedo boats *Furor* and *Pluton*, braving like the larger ships the concentrated fire of the American battleships, which were just now commencing to straighten out on westerly courses; although from Sampson's quarter-deck, seven miles directly astern of the Spanish, the pursuing American ships were lost to view in a panorama of smoke. Suddenly Schley's 400-foot *Brooklyn* with her high freeboard and three tall funnels appeared out of the white cloud, apparently heading south. There were gasps of dismay on the flagship, *New York*. "The *Brooklyn's* hurt!" Sampson more than once exclaimed: "What can be the matter?"[19] The crippling of this swift cruiser—officially rated as the fastest ship at Santiago—at the beginning of the pursuit would give Cervera an excellent chance to escape with some of his vessels. But the *Brooklyn* presently straightened out on a westward course and the watchers on the flagship sent up a cheer. Gunners on the *New York* who had stripped off their Sunday attire and were congregated on deck preparatory to getting into action, called down the ventilators to the firemen, "For God's sake get those engines going! Make us move! Burn any old damn thing! Get us there! Get us there!"[20] Quickly fires were spread under the spare boilers, and at 10:10 the fourth boiler was connected.

The most direct line toward the fleeing enemy carried the *New York* close under the Morro, whose shells splashed around her. "Shall we answer them?" Captain Chadwick asked. "No, let us get on—on after the fleet! Not one must get away!"[21] Sampson spoke without taking his binoculars from the smoky turmoil ahead.

At 10:30 one of the larger Spanish vessels burst into flame and ran for the beach, "black smoke laying over her upper works, from aft." "At this time," Admiral Sampson's writer, Chief Yeoman Fred J. Buenzle records, "a shell from the western battery burst over our quarter."[22]

Well past the entrance to the harbor the *New York* now came upon the fierce struggle between the *Gloucester* and the Spanish torpedo boats. The financier J. P. Morgan's yacht *Corsair*, mounting three-inch quick-fire guns and rechristened the *Gloucester*, was being skillfully handled by Lieutenant Commander Richard Wainwright, a *Maine* survivor. One of the torpedo boats, *Pluton*, ran on the rocks and vanished in a geyser of steam, the other circled and headed menacingly toward the *New York*, which pumped four four-inch shells into the craft and left the *Gloucester* to pick up survivors.

At 10:50 across a point of land was seen the military mast of the flagship *Infanta Maria Teresa*, which for a moment across the treetops seemed to be moving out to sea, but this illusion was instantly dispelled when the *New York* came around the point. Cervera's stricken flagship on fire had been headed in to the beach and her seamen were stripping off their clothes and abandoning her.

"10:55 A.M." wrote Chief Yeoman Buenzle. "Threw life preservers to a Spaniard in the water. Now abreast of the two burning ships, the *Maria Teresa* and the *Almirante Oquendo*."[23] A few minutes later another cry arose from the water: "Amerigo! Amerigo! Auxilio! Auxilio!" There being no life preserver handy, Captain Chadwick's coxswain tossed overboard the ship's pulpit, which a few hours earlier had been set up for church services.[24]

At 11:15 the *Vizcaya* turned toward the beach at Aserraderos, struck her colors and exploded, hurling burning debris as high as the Cuban hills. The *New York* having overtaken the *Iowa*, Sampson hailed her to ask how many men she had lost. Her captain, Robley Evans, stood on the stern, and behind him—the *Vizcaya* having been disposed of—were his gunners, crowded on turrets, superstructure and decks, dirty, grimy and most of them naked to the waist. As these men of the *Iowa* saw Sampson, their one-time captain, now admiral, they gave him cheer after cheer. Evans had to wave them down before he could megaphone his report: "Not a man hurt aboard this ship."[25]

Sampson left the *Iowa* to rescue the shipwrecked Spaniards and pushed on after the one remaining fugitive, the *Colon*. This vessel, uninjured in the early stages of the action, had by noon outdistanced her pursuers. She was at this time approximately four miles ahead of the nearest American ships, the *Brooklyn* and the *Oregon*, and about eight miles ahead of the *New York*. There was thus a chance that she might make good her escape. There was a chance, too, that the swift *New York*, which during the past two and a half hours had cut in two extra boilers and had driven her speed upward to 16 knots, might at the eleventh hour get in on the kill. . . .

Meanwhile, more favored by circumstances than the commander in chief, Commodore Schley had been conforming at every point to the journalistic ideal of a hero in action—and that with the utmost sincerity and lack of artfulness.

The *Brooklyn*, flagship of the Second Division of the fleet, was ideally situated at the western end of the line of blockade ships. After his usual morning turn around the deck, the commodore had just seated himself under the awnings on the fantail for a chat with Captain Cook and reporter Graham when Navigator Hodgson shouted by megaphone:

"After bridge, there! Report to the Commodore and the Captain that the enemy's ships are coming out!"[26]

Reaching across Graham, Schley grabbed his binoculars off a hatch cover and sprang forward through the superstructure. Bells for battle stations were sounding throughout the ship as he elbowed through crowds of seamen who were stripping off Sunday shirts as they ran to their stations. The commodore noticed quickly that the *New York* could not be seen from the *Brooklyn*. To Schley's right lay the *Texas*, and beyond her in order the *Iowa*, the *Oregon* and the *Indiana*.

To be near Captain Cook, whose battle station was inside the armored conning tower forward, and at the same time to allow himself a maximum view of the battle, Schley had constructed a wooden platform or gallery about three feet high and extending around the outside of the conning tower. As Schley reached his platform, the *Iowa* got off the first shot, a sharp high-pitched, six-pounder.

The *Brooklyn*, heading toward the left of the entrance to Santiago, began slowly to get under way. The signal "Close up" was raised. "Commodore, they are coming right at us," the navigator called down from the upper bridge. "Well, go right for them," Schley directed.[27]

The vessel was brought around and headed toward the leading enemy. Two of Cervera's ships were now visible, the flagship *Teresa* and the *Vizcaya*. Their black hulls with golden figureheads and their bright yellow superstructures contrasted sharply with the dull gray of the American warships. The Spanish decks, moreover, were gay with colored awnings, and from their halyards fluttered silk flags embroidered in gold with the coat of arms of Spain.

Sampson's plan had been for his gray ships to close in upon the enemy and sink him in the entrance to the harbor or drive him on shore there. The enemy, however, emerging under full steam and enjoying the initial advantage of high momentum, was able to frustrate this move on the part of the blockaders, who, although they had some steam in their boilers, were lying to and motionless when the enemy appeared.

As the distance narrowed between the *Brooklyn* and the *Infanta Maria Teresa*, other enemy ships became visible through the smoke: the *Vizcaya*, the *Colon* and the *Oquendo*. The Spanish, as they cleared the shelf to the west of the harbor mouth, in succession turned west at full speed. To the American ships, from their positions six miles off the entrance, the enemy vessels seemed to spread out fan-wise.

Anticipating that the frail enemy torpedo craft would be sheltering behind their big ships, awaiting a chance to attack the American line, Schley detailed quick-fire gunners to keep a bright lookout for such craft. For ten minutes or more the *Brooklyn* wove a sinuous course toward the *Teresa;* then, when the two came within a mile of each other, the *Teresa* sheered to port as if to ram the *Brooklyn*.

"Hard aport, Cook," Schley called into the conning tower, and Captain Cook answered that the helm was already over hard aport. As the *Brooklyn* veered in a loop to starboard, she was so close to the on-rushing enemy line that Schley could see men on board their second ship, the *Vizcaya*, running from turret to superstructure, and without his glasses he could distinctly see "the daylight between their legs as they ran."[28] It was essential to get the *Brooklyn* turned immediately to prevent the enemy's escape. During the turn Lieutenant Hodgson warned, "Commodore, if you go to starboard you will run into the *Texas*."

"Damn the *Texas*. She must look out for herself!" answered Schley.[29] The commodore's idea was to get around fast. Had the fleet-footed *Brooklyn* been shaken off at the outset of the pursuit, the chances of the slower-paced battleships working up sufficient speed to catch the enemy were slight indeed. Between the speeding *Brooklyn* and the other American ships, there was at this moment an immense pall of smoke, which for a time obscured the *Texas*, the nearest ship. When suddenly through a rift in the smoke the men on the *Texas* sighted the high-sided *Brooklyn* coming toward them, they experienced a moment of near-panic and threw the *Texas'* engines in reverse.

Although witnesses disagreed as to her margin of safety, the *Brooklyn* got turned around safely and quickly, and she held her proper place at the head of the American line, which now straightened out on a westerly course parallel to the enemy.

At this juncture the *Brooklyn* was within point-blank range of the first three enemy ships, and the battleships supporting her were obscured by a wall of black smoke.

"We must stay with this crowd," remarked Schley to Captain Cook. Enemy projectiles fell all around the *Brooklyn*, raising "jets of water ahead and astern and over and short," and the roar they made was that of express trains. For a long while the enemy showed no sign of injury, and the thought passed through Schley's mind "that after all of our precautions and waiting these fellows would get away."[30]

Then, as though in answer to prayer, a white line, like a heavy surf, became visible through the smoke that trailed the *Brooklyn*. In a few minutes the bow of the *Oregon* appeared, racing ahead, perhaps 400 or 500 yards away on the *Brooklyn's* starboard quarter. Men on the *Brooklyn* cheered. Schley wigwagged, "God bless the *Oregon!*"[31] To the *Brooklyn's* eight-inch guns were added thunderous salvos of 13-inch from the *Oregon*, as well as continuous sprays of metal from the quick-fire guns. "I never saw such a fire and never realized what rapid gun fire really meant before," Schley testified later, "because both ships were at that time a sheet of flame.[32]

About ten o'clock the *Teresa* started to lag astern and soon Schley saw smoke rolling out of her ports, then from her hatches. Columns of smoke rose almost straight in the air as the vessel lost speed and curved toward the beach about six miles west of the Morro.

"We have got one. Keep the boys below informed of all the movements"; Schley said to Captain Cook. "They can't see and they want to know these things."[33] Every few minutes messages were sent down the voice tubes and the cheers of the men inside the ship reverberated up the ventilator shafts.

Twenty minutes later the burning *Oquendo* ran aground also, leaving only the *Vizcaya* and the *Colon*. While the *Vizcaya* engaged actively in the unequal duel with the *Oregon* and the *Brooklyn*, the *Colon*, Cervera's speediest vessel, working her way inshore where she was screened by the *Vizcaya*, dropped out of action and bent all her energy toward escaping.

During the 30-minute duel with the *Vizcaya*, the *Brooklyn* received several injuries. Her signal halyards were shot away, and a speed cone crashed on deck not far from Schley and bounded overboard. Yeoman George Ellis, an expert in the use of the stadimeter, whose business was to keep Schley informed of the range, was standing on the deck a few feet below the commodore when a shot took off his head above the mouth. Schley was spattered with bits of the man's brain. A few minutes later he took his eyes off the battle long enough to stop Ensign McCauley and Dr. De Valin from heaving the body over the side. He directed them instead to cover it with a blanket until it could be given decent burial.

At 11:00 A.M. the *Vizcaya*, after surviving thirty minutes of concentrated pounding, received a mortal wound. She turned, and for a moment seemed as if about to charge the *Brooklyn* or the *Oregon*, when simultaneously one of her own bow torpedoes exploded inside of its tube and a heavy American shell raked her deck fore and aft. As she nosed toward the land, some 15 miles from the Morro, Schley told the signal officer to direct Captain Philip of the *Texas* to save the stricken vessel's crew. The signal officer reported that the *Texas* was too far astern to receive the message. "Well, Philip is always sensible," Schley reflected; "he needs no instructions about such things."[34]

By the time the *Vizcaya* had lowered her colors and run on the beach, the *Colon*, which had followed the contour of the coast, had got well out of range. Schley signaled to the *Oregon* to cease firing, and to Captain Cook he suggested that he get the men out of the turrets for fresh air and a bite to eat.

Schley himself at this time went inside the battle tower and sang down the voice tubes "that we had got all hands of them except one and that I thought they could be relied upon to catch that other vessel." Throughout the ship the pleased commodore heard merriment and rejoicing, and he returned to the bridge satisfied that his "bully boys" were doing their best. Impatient to crowd on more speed, Schley detected "a jingle to the rails and a vibration," and sent the carpenter to examine the hull of the ship to see why her motions were so sluggish.[35] The carpenter reported that an after compartment had filled with water, and that the damage could not be repaired while under way. Schley dropped the idea and the *Brooklyn* pushed on despite her vibration.

The *Colon*, approximately six miles distant from the *Brooklyn* when the *Vizcaya* was driven ashore, held her lead and was outside of range for an hour and a half.

After 12:30, however, the *Brooklyn* signaled to the *Oregon* to fire one of her 13-inch shells. The message, as wigwagged, was "Try one of your railroad trains."[36] Since the *Oregon* was about half a mile to landward of the *Brooklyn* and approximately in the wake of the *Colon*, it was possible during the next half hour for the two American warships to fire alternately and to spot the splashes for each other. A few minutes after 1:00 P.M. a 13-inch projectile from the *Oregon* dropped beyond the *Colon*, and the Spaniard read his doom. At 1:15 the *Colon* struck her colors, fired a gun to leeward and nosed into the bank at Tarquino River, some 50 miles west of the Morro.

Schley gave the order to cease fire and sent Captain Cook in the ship's boat to receive the surrender of the *Colon*.

At 1:30 Schley signaled the *Oregon:* "Congratulations on the grand victory. Thanks for splendid assistance."[37]

"Thank you," responded the *Oregon*, "more than words can express."

At 1:45, as the flagship *New York* came within signal range, the *Brooklyn* wigwagged to her: "We have gained a great victory. Details will be communicated."

Five minutes later, the flagship acknowledged receipt of the message and signaled back, "Report your casualties."

Brooklyn to flagship: "Killed one. Wounded two."

Sampson could scarcely believe that Yeoman Ellis was the sole fatality in the entire American fleet. Against this, as later verified, the enemy had lost 260 dead. The Spanish ships with a great deal of woodwork in their superstructures had burned like torches.

Sampson made provision for the rescue and care of prisoners and

ADMIRALS OF AMERICAN EMPIRE

tried unsuccessfully to keep the *Colon* afloat—she had been scuttled after her surrender. The report that another Spanish cruiser had appeared off Santiago caused Sampson to send the *Brooklyn* and the *Oregon* out at once to investigate. The stranger proved to be an Austrian man-of-war.

Exhausted, but with good reason to be pleased with a fleet that could "win a war in an afternoon," Sampson dispatched the following message to Washington:[38] "The fleet under my command offers the nation as a Fourth of July present the whole of Cervera's fleet. It attempted to escape at 9:30 this morning. At two the last ship, the *Cristobal Colon*, had run ashore seventy-five miles west of Santiago and hauled down her colors. The *Infanta Maria Teresa, Oquendo,* and the *Vizcaya* were forced ashore, burned and blown up within 20 miles of Santiago. The *Furor* and *Pluton* were destroyed within 4 miles of that port. W. T. Sampson."

Part Five

FULFILLMENT

18. IMPERIALISM'S DARLING

THE twofold task assigned to Dewey had been "to see that the Spanish squadron does not leave the Asiatic coast, and then offensive operations in the Philippine Islands."[1] As to the first part, Montojo's fleet now rested on the mud bottom of the bay off Cavite. The second, "offensive operations in the Philippine Islands," might mean anything or nothing. The chances are that the firebrand imperialist Theodore Roosevelt, who had written Dewey's orders and who had been instrumental in placing Dewey in command in the East, had also reached with his naval commander a preliminary oral understanding on the importance of acquiring overseas naval bases. And there is every reason to suppose that Dewey, though he loathed writing and was not outspoken as was Mahan, was yet a natural advocate of such acquisitions.

Dewey's first move was to clear the Spaniards out of Cavite and get that Spanish naval base into operation as an American naval base. He paroled and sent his naval prisoners to Manila, where, although their numbers were added to the 10,000 Spanish soldiers already in

Manila, Dewey felt he had nothing to fear. The city lay under his guns and he could force a surrender or blow the town to bits whenever he chose. From the very beginning Dewey seems to have assumed . that the United States would take Manila. "I control bay completely and can take city at any time, but I have not sufficient men to hold," he reported on May 4.[2] A week later, in response to Secretary Long's inquiry, Dewey reckoned that the city could be captured by 5,000 well-equipped troops, who would be aided by a native rebel force estimated at 30,000.[3]

Dewey's game was to watch and wait, and perhaps to let the fruit of war fall of its own ripeness into his country's lap. But other nations also seemed to be tempted by this exotic fruit: other nations who had definitely committed themselves to a policy of overseas expansion, and who were busy rivals in the partitioning of China into so-called spheres of influence. Within ten days after Dewey's victory, six foreign men-of-war had dropped in at Manila to observe—two British, one French, one Japanese and two German.[4] It was doubtful whether the British economic stake in Manila, which was by far the largest foreign holding, was sufficient to justify the presence of two British cruisers; and certainly Manila's single German firm was a wholly inadequate warrant for the presence of two German cruisers.

Dewey's victory in the unknown East touched off a storm of popular applause which two months of unromantic searching for Cervera and weary blockading in waters nearer home tended not to diminish but rather to heighten. Congress accorded Dewey a vote of thanks. McKinley sent him a rear admiral's commission. Secretary Long (the Manila cable was cut anyway) tendered him carte blanche to "exercise discretion most fully in all matters, and be governed according to circumstance which you know and we can not know. . . ."[5] Thousands of letters and presents were forwarded to Dewey, which the whimsical admiral to the amusement of reporters filed in waste baskets on top of and on the floor around his desk.[6] Patriotic societies sent him such luxuries as clam juice, lemons, beef extract and jellies; while the Navy dispatched ammunition stores and white uniforms for the marines. A preliminary expeditionary force of 1,200 troops was embarked for the Philippines. And in the meantime Dewey brought the professional Philippine insurrectionary leader, Emilio Aguinaldo, to Cavite, gave him some old Mauser rifles and ammunition captured from the Spaniards and set him to organizing native resistance around the city so as to cut off any source of supply by land, just as Dewey's blockade was eliminating water-borne supplies.

For three months Dewey waited for troops and reinforcements. Seated in a comfortable wicker chair on the deck of the Olympia, shielded by "weather breaker" awnings from the rays of a tropical sun and puffing a cigar or patting his shaggy chow dog Bob, the admiral could generate the impression of having not a care in the world—yet in a twinkling his temper might flare up and recall the young officer who had been too free in his use of the speaking trumpet. The lubberly mismanagement of a Philippine gig once moved him to dress down a lieutenant. Another day one of several insurgent officers on board the flagship, to receive regulations concerning small boats in the harbor, made the mistake of mumbling a disrespectful remark; whereupon, the story goes, Dewey's face went white and in a furry voice rising to high pitch he ordered the man tossed overboard.[7]

While the Spanish themselves presented no serious problem, there were numerous other difficulties to annoy a sensitive and punctilious admiral. For one thing Dewey had no sooner given encouragement to Aguinaldo by supplying him rifles and ammunition, than he was warned by Washington that he was not to enter into any sort of political alliance with the insurgents. Dewey's explanation to the Secretary that his relations with Aguinaldo were "of a personal nature" and that he was bound by no formal agreement, precipitated that coolness toward the insurgents which eventually led to a two-year campaign of pacification and subjugation of the insurrectionists by American arms.[8]

Less serious in its consequences, but more exasperating to Dewey at the time, was his trouble with the Germans who increased the number of their ships in Manila Bay until they had five there. Two were heavily armored battleships whose ten and 12-inch guns could easily have smashed Dewey's unarmored cruisers which had no guns greater than eight-inch. The German ships had a disquieting habit of entering the bay at odd hours of the night and anchoring as they pleased with no regard for the authority of the blockading admiral, although warships of other nations requested permission to anchor.[9] Thoughtlessly they took soundings of the bay and sent their small boats prowling at night, a time when Dewey's men were on the alert against torpedo attack. Report was current in Manila that an alliance would be made between Spain and Germany, and Dewey heard that the morale of the beleaguered Spanish garrison had improved since the arrival of the Germans. Vice-Admiral Otto von Diederichs, to Germans a national hero because of his recent seizure of China's port of Kiaochow, arrived in Manila Bay on June 12 on board S. M. cruiser *Kaiserin Augusta*. Rear Admiral Dewey, being junior in rank, paid the first call on Vice-Admiral von Diederichs. For several weeks thereafter Dewey's situation grew worse. From Gibraltar came word that the Spanish Admiral Camara's battleships were on their way to relieve blockaded Manila. Every American battleship at this time was tied down by Cervera off Santiago. Only the slow monitors *Monterey* and *Monadnock* had set out to cross the broad Pacific as naval reinforcements for Dewey, and General Merritt's transports with 4,000 troops had had to sail from San Francisco without a convoy. When on July 7 Aguinaldo complained that one of von Diederichs' cruisers was protecting the Spanish garrison on an island in Subic Bay, Dewey sent the *Raleigh* and the *Concord* to Subic to capture the Spanish, and the same day he sent his aide, Lieutenant Thomas M. Brumby, with a list of infractions of the blockade to protest to Admiral von Diederichs. A few days later an officer from von Diederichs, Flag Lieutenant Hintze, presented himself on board the *Olympia* with an oral explanation of Dewey's complaints against the Germans and also a countergrievance that the United States revenue cutter *McCulloch* had improperly stopped and boarded the German cruiser *Irene* off Corregidor.

Dewey burst into a fury, crying out, as Hintze reported it immediately after the occurrence, "Why, I shall stop each vessel whatever may be her colors! And if she does not stop I shall fire at her! And that means war, do you know, Sir? And I tell you if Germany wants war, all right, we are ready. With the English I have not the slightest difficulty, they always communicate with me, etc."[10]

The German, quite unprepared for so heated an outburst, backed out of the admiral's presence and in a subdued tone remarked to Lieutenant Brumby, "Your Admiral seems to be much in earnest."

"Yes," replied Brumby, "and you can be certain that he means every word he says."[11]

Sir Edward Chichester of the British cruiser *Immortalité*, a stout old sailor shaped like a typical English squire, heard Dewey's complaints and assured him that the Germans, new to the seagoing profession, were in this instance chiefly guilty of "bad sea manners."[12] The incident passed, with Dewey making no mention of it at all in any of his official writings; although for many months afterward rumors about it pricked the curiosity of press and public in the United States. The incident seems to have cleared the atmosphere a bit, since a few days later Dewey accepted the offer of a departing German ship to carry a bundle of his dispatches to Singapore. Dewey, however, never lost his feeling of prejudice against these possible rivals for the prize of Manila. And like Mahan, Dewey contracted a decided liking for the British. Captain Chichester, the explorer Sir George Younghusband, who visited Dewey on the *Olympia*, Governor Black of Hong Kong and British friends who had given him a send-off in Hong Kong as he left for Manila had engendered in him sympathies that were firmly and lastingly pro-British.

Through the British consul at Manila, Dewey had early opened negotiations with the Spanish Captain General of the Philippines, looking toward a peaceful surrender. But Dewey's move was frustrated: (1) by Dewey's own obvious inability to protect the surrendered Spanish garrison from violence on the part of the insurgents, and (2) by Madrid's recalling the Captain General. With the arrival of Major General Wesley Merritt, Dewey reopened his negotiations, this time through the Belgian consul, M. Edouard André, the Britisher having been taken ill. Spanish General Jaudenes made it plain to André that he wished to surrender but could do so only after Spanish "honor" had been satisfied by an exchange of shots.[13]

A ticklish three-cornered situation now developed, with the insurgent leader Aguinaldo attempting to appear as an ally of the Americans, the Americans awkwardly fending off rebel aid and brandishing without actually using their overwhelming force; and, caught between Americans and Filipinos, the unlucky Spanish Dons, wanting both "honor" and surrender to the Americans with as little bloodshed as possible.

Aguinaldo, having proclaimed himself dictator, fatuously demanded that the Americans officially request his permission before landing their troops on Philippine soil. He was stalled off, and as General Merritt's army moved around the coast and entrenched themselves outside Manila, their chief problem was to avoid officially undesirable cooperation with the Filipinos.

Preliminary to their attack on the city, Admiral Dewey and General Merritt notified the Spanish authorities of their intention to bombard the town, in order that women and children might be removed to a position of safety. As the only such positions were on the refugee ships in the bay, which had already been loaded some days ago, and as the city was surrounded by insurrectionary forces, General Jaudenes pointed out that to move women and children was impossible. Dewey and Merritt then called on him in the interest of humanity to surrender. Jaudenes requested time for the demand to be submitted to Madrid. The American answer was No.

The assault on Manila now proceeded, on August 13, ironically enough, one day after the preliminary articles of the peace had been signed in Washington. According to the arrangement made through the Belgian consul, Dewey would not fire into the town unless Manila's coastal guns opened on the fleet. After the action commenced, Dewey was by flag signal to demand surrender, and the Spanish commander was to hang out a white flag on a particular building inside the town. Early in the morning Dewey's heavy ships took position off Manila's water-front batteries, while several lighter craft moved inshore to afford artillery support for the advancing army. "The operation had been planned with care to avoid loss of life on both sides, and there is evidence that only a formal resistance was expected from the Spaniards," wrote a correspondent for the *London Times*.[14]

The morning was thick and hazy with frequent squalls of rain. With their battle flags hung from every truck and gaff, the American ships fired very deliberately so as not to land a shot in the town. A dozen carefully placed shots were required to get range of the enemy batteries, which, as had been previously agreed, maintained silence throughout the entire affair. A downpour of rain ceased at 10:30, and the *Olympia* signaled, "The enemy's camp is breaking up." At 10:50 she ordered, "Cease firing." Meanwhile the danger of a real fight developed when a mix-up occurred and American troops advancing in two columns against an outlying fort were met by a fusillade which killed 11 and wounded 39. At 11:00 Dewey hoisted his prearranged signal demanding surrender.

Across the town a white flag was broken out on the appointed building.

Lieutenant Brumby, after going ashore with two apprentice boys, made his way through the crowds of Spaniards. At the flagpole in front of the cathedral he hauled down the red and yellow colors of Spain and hoisted the Stars and Stripes, just as an Army band leading a body of troops up another street started to play "The Star-Spangled Banner."

For months after the "reduction" of Manila, the feeling between the American Army of Occupation and the followers of Aguinaldo was one of suspended hostility. Despite General Merritt's clumsy precautions, the insurgents entered certain quarters of Manila along with the victorious American troops and stayed there until General Merritt resigned the awkward task and went home. His more tactful successor, General Otis, succeeded in peaceably moving the insurgent forces out into the countryside, with the understanding that they might re-enter the city whenever they wished as long as they came unarmed. While the United States held the city of Manila only, Aguinaldo held all the back country. He retained his weapons on the ground that he might need them against the Spaniard in case the United States should decide to withdraw from the Philippines. When the treaty with Spain was concluded in December, and President McKinley announced the American intention of holding all of the Philippines, the Aguinaldists prepared for open rebellion against the Americans.

Meanwhile for several months Admiral Dewey hoped that the gathering storm might somehow be averted. On the basis of his early contacts with Aguinaldo he felt that he understood the native Filipino. From Aguinaldo he had received a handsomely carved baton, a cigar case and a cordial letter of congratulation upon his May Day victory.[15]

Two days after Manila fell, the admiral went ashore to find American troops instead of Spanish policing the city and peaceful business being resumed. Once more he enjoyed the little amenities for which, during months aboard ship, he had hungered. From a vendor of antiques he purchased a snuffbox made from mulberry wood "planted by Shakespeare in his garden at Stratford."[16] To the mother of Captain Gridley he wrote what for Dewey was a long letter of condolence over the loss of her son, who had been Dewey's "friend and . . . gallant assistant." A Miss Thompson, an American newspaper woman in Manila, tells that during the occupation she complained to the admiral that "the officers' wives would not notice me because I was a breadwinner." Thus appealed to, Dewey called upon and dined with her, enabling her to boast that then she "was the first lady in the land."

When asked about the incident later, after his plans for matrimony had become known, Dewey is said to have shown annoyance, "Why that wasn't anything. Every American woman is the first lady of the land."[17] To Admiral Montojo the American admiral sent a message that, peace or war, he would have great pleasure in clasping by the hand one who had fought so gallantly. Aboard ship at this time the admiral relaxed. "He was given to banter and what is called leg pulling," writes Frederick Palmer. "Between the laughter in his dark eyes and their flash of indignation there was a wide middle ground of whimsicality that left you in doubt where seriousness began and ended."[18] In the officers' mess, mention having been made of the sentimental naming of the converted cruisers *Yale* and *Harvard*, Dewey was asked to give a collegiate christening to some of the sunken Spanish ships when they were raised. "Certainly," replied the admiral, "I will call one the Massachusetts Institute of Technology and another the Vermont Normal College for Women."[19]

One of his first messages over Manila's newly spliced cable was a request that the Secretary not order him home. "Should regret very much to leave here while matters remain in present critical condition." According to Frederick Palmer, who was with Dewey in Manila and who later served the admiral as ghost writer of his autobiography, Dewey was not prepared to see his country undertake to hold the entire Philippine archipelago.[20] He foresaw "ructions" in Congress and thought that an American empire could maintain no such consistent and long-range colonial policy as European empires did. "If we want colonies . . . why not take Mexico or Central America? That seems to be much more sensible and businesslike."[21] Dewey probably favored keeping only Manila as a naval station that would safeguard our Asiatic commerce. As a correspondent for the *New York Sun* expressed it, "Manila should be made the Hong Kong of America in the Far East!"[22] The Filipinos might conceivably have been willing at this time to surrender Manila and its superb bay in exchange for independence elsewhere throughout the archipelago.

As the months passed Aguinaldo tightened his lines around Manila; while General Otis, his force increased, prepared to extend American hegemony over the archipelago. As the atmosphere became more tense, Dewey on January 7, 1899, cabled a suggestion that a "civilian commission" composed of men skilled in diplomacy and statecraft should be sent out to the islands to make a study of the situation and adjust differences. To his friend and sponsor Senator Proctor he wrote at the same time that the present situation was one to be handled by the civilian, rather than by Navy or Army. "These people [the Filipinos] are afraid of us, navy and army, but would listen to you while they would not to us. They should be treated kindly, exactly as you would treat children, for they are little else, and should be coerced only after gentler means of bringing them to reason have failed."[23] The President appointed a Philippine Commission, mixed civilian and military, and therefore scarcely the thing that Dewey had recommended. It was composed of Jacob Gould Schurman, president of Cornell; Professor Dean C. Worcester of the University of Michigan, author of a book on the Philippines; and Charles Denby, a former minister to China. To this group of civilian experts were added the names of Admiral Dewey himself and of General Otis. The civilian members of the Philippine Commission, however, did not arrive in Manila until after full-scale warfare had broken out.

Trouble began the night of February 5, when two or three insurgents who attempted to pass through the American line were fired on by pickets. Immediately fighting became general all along the line. The insurgents held a series of blockhouses and entrenchments extending from the bay north of the city for about seven or eight miles around to the bay south of it and standing several miles from the outskirts of Manila. Early the next morning the Americans inside the city assaulted along the whole arc of insurgent positions. Dewey stationed vessels to bombard the enemy on either flank of the city. Rebel-infested villages surrounding Manila were burned, and a small boat captured from the Spanish was sent up the Pasig River to clean the rebels out of rice fields along its banks. According to American estimates, Aguinaldo had 20,000 troops in the battle, and the Americans 13,000. In this opening shock of the bloody struggle against Aguinaldo and the hazards of the Philippine jungle, the American army lost four officers and 53 men killed, eight officers and 207 men wounded. Dewey had only two men wounded on board the monitor *Monadnock*.

Henceforth Dewey's task was to support the Army by blockading all areas through which military supplies could reach the rebels and to ascend each creek and bayou where gunboat artillery could be of use. Small craft taken from the Spanish and from the rebels themselves were repaired at Dewey's navy yard at Cavite and rushed into all sorts of service among the myriad islands of the archipelago.

The Manila climate favored a lush growth of Dewey anecdote. Rear Admiral Ammen Farenholt of the Medical Corps tells how the nondescript assortment of riverboats under General Otis managed to fray Dewey's nerves. Occasionally these boats would come out of the Pasig River for a turn about the bay. "Now the waters of the bay were the Admiral's particular bailiwick and each time they were reported beyond the lighthouse Dewey would become nearly apoplectic with wrath and would order them back. Finally he sent a direct order to General Otis to the effect that if he ever caught them outside of the river again he would sink them. They never reappeared in those forbidden waters." Farenholt also reminisces on the "Society of the Dog." "Admiral Dewey had on board the *Olympia* as his pet a badly spoiled dog. . . . The afterguard sweepers detested the animal. The dog was smart enough to know that his sole protector was the Admiral and ran back to him as if he had been maltreated whenever anyone touched or made a pass in his general direction. Several men were punished . . . and a quartermaster disrated. Partly in a spirit of waggishness . . . before the fall of the city the men formed a very secret organization called the 'Society of the Dog.' To be an ordinary member a man had to have kicked the brute, but to become a member, first class, he had to have kicked him when the Admiral was on deck and could possibly have seen him do it. . . . There were very few of these. The organization lasted as long as the dog did, for one morning he turned up missing. That day a first-class member was hurriedly promoted to the office of 'Chief Superior Dog' and the society prudently disbanded."[24]

With the opening of the war against the Filipino rebels, George Dewey's fame at home achieved new pinnacles. The story of his tilt with von Diederichs received a rich embroidering by naval officer speakers at banquets. Preachers sought to influence the young by upholding the Hero of Manila as a paragon who never swore or touched hard liquor. A politically minded New York City divine on March 5, 1899, after proposing Dewey for President of the United States, depicted him as "a Gibraltar against which the waves of corruption, bribery, injustice, stolen wealth and political infamy would beat only to break at his feet powerless as the wind-whipped foam."[25] Dewey's native Vermont was ransacked for anecdotes of the famous man's youth. That these be plausible was not at all requisite to insure publication and general circulation. In Manila the admiral declined to pose for a new picture and turned down tempting offers from magazines. "Why, a thousand words would make four pages of typing," he objected. "You would turn me into a chatterer." Nor would he consent to don his golf cap and walk up and down in front of one of the new moving picture cameras to simulate his actions during the naval battle. "How do I know how I walked up and down the bridge during the action? It wouldn't be real. It wouldn't be honest. No, no antics at all."[26]

In spite of Dewey's lack of co-operation with press agents, the Washington authorities proceeded to revive for him the rank of Admiral of the Navy, which only two officers, Farragut and Porter, had held before him. It was recalled that Dewey's first reward, given him in May of 1898, had raised him but two numbers on the Navy list and brought him his rear admiral's commission only four months sooner than he might have obtained it by seniority, "had he remained quietly ashore during the war."[27] On March 2, 1898, Congress authorized the President to appoint Dewey an "admiral of the navy, who shall not be placed upon the retired list except by his own application," and whose office should cease to exist after his death.[28] Dewey's services in testing the New Navy, declared Secretary Long, "stamp him as being of larger mould than great captains usually are or need to be cast in."[29]

Dewey, as his writer friend Palmer knew him in Manila, was simple and straightforward, punctilious but not at all infatuated with "fuss and feathers." The great honor, of course, delighted him, just as the hundreds of small gifts and letters from the "little people" moved him. "The home-folks in Vermont will agree that Doctor Dewey's son has done quite well."[30] The new honor, moreover, gave him an economic independence which he had never before enjoyed. His annual pay of $14,000, together with what he might collect as prize money for the Spanish fleet he had sunk, enabled him to propose marriage to his long-time friend, Mrs. Mildred McLean Hazen. It seems probable that he proposed by letter before beginning his triumphal voyage home. At any rate by the time he had reached Trieste in July he had received Mrs. Hazen's affirmative reply, and the joyful bridegroom-to-be confided the information to Palmer while the *Olympia* was at Trieste.[31]

In May 1899, a year after his victory, Dewey turned the prow of the

Olympia homeward. To have proceeded via San Francisco, as the railroad companies begged him to do, would have entailed listening to too many speeches across the continent. He chose rather to return via Singapore, Suez and New York, as this would get him to Washington with the minimum of to-do. In a leisurely cruise that took over six months, he combined rest and relaxation with the entertainments which were everywhere showered upon him. Only one reporter, Frederick Palmer, was allowed to accompany the admiral on the *Olympia*, and that, in his capacity as a personal friend, and only upon the understanding that he should not be permitted to write.[32]

At Trieste, where the admiral revealed to Palmer his engagement to Mrs. Hazen, he encountered his first trouble with the press. In Manila he had enjoyed a working agreement with reporters and had always spoken as freely as he pleased. In Trieste, with Manila rules no longer applicable, he fell into conversation with an engaging traveler who failed to mention that he was also a reporter. Dewey was led to make some unguarded remarks about the Germans, and to his astonishment read the next day in the papers of an "interview" in which the "master diplomatist of Manila Bay" predicted that Kaiser Wilhelm I was going to make trouble in the world. Palmer suggested that since Dewey had not spoken for publication he might simply deny the statement. "But I said it," replied Dewey. "Yes, damn it. I said it. It's true. I can't deny what I know I said. I can't lie."[33]

Because Dewey was known to be fond of music, the Italian composer Mascagni, of *Cavalleria Rusticana* fame, dedicated one of his songs to him.[34] At Naples, in mellow mood, the admiral was attracted by an eleven-year-old girl member of a troupe of musicians who serenaded the *Olympia*. The child slipped past the sentry and kissed the admiral's hand. Dewey patted her on the head and, graciously concealing his distaste for the odor of garlic, invited the accompanying musicians to come on board to perform during the supper hour.[35]

In Gibraltar Dewey raised a purse for a gunner who had been injured in a powder explosion on H.M.S. *Devastation,* and himself delivered it to the sufferer. Four hundred shipmates of the unfortunate Gunner Peppiatt lined the rails and cheered themselves hoarse as the *Olympia*, symbol of a new and friendly sea power, steamed away.[36]

Meanwhile in America plans were maturing for vast celebrations in New York, Washington, Vermont and elsewhere. A National Dewey

Committee headed by Secretary of the Treasury Vanderlip collected funds to purchase a home for the admiral. Theodore Roosevelt, the newly elected governor of New York State, obtained from the legislature an appropriation of $75,000 to bring the National Guard troops of the state to the place of celebration.[37] The governor of Vermont laid plans for a three-day entertainment in Montpelier. In New York City the architectural climax of a $150,000 ovation was a 70-foot lath-and-plaster triumphal arch embellished with a frieze of the Battle of Manila Bay and numerous symbolic statues, the whole being the work of 30 architects and sculptors. All over the country projects for Dewey celebrations were organized. "All a man has to do is to talk mysteriously about a mythical letter he has got from Dewey and about equally mythical 'leading men' who are behind his scheme, to get plenty of names on a subscription paper for a dinner in honor of the Admiral," lamented the *New York Tribune;* "Dewey is not to be welcomed by the three tailors of Tooley Street. It would be a big feather in the cap, no doubt, if Messrs. Miggs and Snooks and Spifkins were to be permitted to pose as the organizers of the city's greeting to the Nation's hero. . . ."[38] And the *New York Times,* itself a leader in the House-for-Dewey Movement, took note of the "pathetically uncouth proposals that have been made to do him honor, including a dinner 'at $100 a cover,' such as might be bestowed upon a plain millionaire by another plain millionaire."[39]

Penalties which the darling of the new American empire would have to endure in the future were accurately foretold by the *Chicago Tribune:* "In addition to all the dogs and cats that are named 'Dewey,' he will find innumerable 'George Dewey' babies cutting their teeth on Dewey teething rings and amusing themselves by shaking rattles surmounted by the well known Dewey physiognomy in rubber. He will see young men on the street wearing Dewey neckties, into which are stuck Dewey scarf pins, and displaying cuffs ornamented with Dewey cuff buttons. He will see canes with a reproduction of his own head as a handle. If he should go into the barber shop to be shaved, he is apt to find his own features looking at him from the side of the shaving mug, and when he washes his hands at a hotel he is likely to pick up a bar of Dewey toilet soap. In the lunch rooms he may find Dewey paper napkins, and the tops of some of the butter dishes consist simply of Dewey's head, which is used as a handle. In the toy stores are offered for sale a number of novelties which would call a blush to the cheek of the modest Admiral. . . ."[40]

The outspoken admiral had not learned his lesson in Trieste. In New York he was as pleased as a child to see the electric-light WELCOME DEWEY sign blazing across Brooklyn Bridge in letters 36 feet tall. He was pleased to have the entire Atlantic Fleet dressed in parade, pleased to be personally welcomed by the President, the Secretary, Governor Roosevelt, the Vermont Deweys—"They didn't wait for me in Vermont, bless them!"—pleased with the gigantic parade and with the regal splendor of the Dewey Triumphal Arch. There had, indeed, been nothing in American history to compare with this celebration. Dewey talked. And the newspaper folk took down verbatim what he said. Palmer found the chagrined hero in his suite at the Waldorf-Astoria "in a mixture of rage and humiliation, with the newspaper of his interview spread before him on his table. . . . 'They printed it all. You didn't do that in Manila. Look at it—all this stuff from me. But I said it! God almighty!' "[41]

He recovered himself quickly and was whisked to Washington where again the dignitaries of the nation took him in tow.

At the station he was greeted briefly by Mrs. Hazen, with her mother, Mrs. Washington McLean, and her sister, Mrs. Ludlow. Mrs. McLean had vacated her mansion to put it at Dewey's disposal, and nothing would suffice but that Dewey must occupy it during his stay in Washington for the ceremonies.[42] On a platform off the east portico of the Capitol Dewey received an ovation from the people, and Secretary Long presented to him the golden sword voted by Congress. By his sinking of a hostile fleet, said Long, Dewey had ". . . demonstrated the supremacy of American sea power and transferred to the United States an imperial cluster of the islands of the Pacific." In presenting him this sword, added Long, the nation recognized "not only the rich fruits which . . . you have poured into her lap, but also her own responsibility to discharge the great trust which is thus put upon her and fulfill the destiny of her own growth and of the empire that is now her charge. . . ."[43]

This was the supreme moment of George Dewey in the uncomfortable role of hero.

Next month the admiral, ill at ease under the spotlights, eluded the public and took a quiet morning drive with Mildred Hazen out U

Street. In the rectory of St. Paul's Catholic Church—the bride being a Catholic—and with no witnesses save the bride's mother and sister and the admiral's aide Lieutenant Caldwell, the two said their marriage vows. Nor did the admiral consult the public when he deeded to his bride the house at 1747 Rhode Island Avenue which had been purchased for him by popular subscription.

Dewey now discovered that hero worship of the ecstatic kind is short-lived. As Mark Sullivan writes, "it was as if the American public had elected itself to be Admiral Dewey's bride; and as if the admiral had committed bigamy; or, at best, it was as if he had procured a divorce, abruptly and without just cause."[44]

The hero's position was further shaken in April of 1900 when Dewey announced his candidacy for the Presidency. When this subject had been broached in Manila, Dewey had turned it down flatly. However, a steady stream of "fan mail" since his return home, and above all, his marriage to a socially prominent and ambitious wife gradually wore down his first resolve. Invitations from all over the country, which Dewey as a widower might have declined, he now accepted. Everywhere he went, crowds shouted, "Dewey for President" as a sort of special greeting. At Savannah he was vociferously assured that the Spanish War had at last healed the breach between the North and South. In St. Louis, Mayor Ziegenhein himself shouted to the masses, "Give three cheers for the Admiral! Call him Uncle George!"[45] In April 1900, after many months of refusing even to consider the idea, Dewey, who knew absolutely nothing about politics, who in his sixty-two years had never even voted, broke down and gave a Washington reporter for the *New York World* an exclusive interview: "If the American people want me for this high office, I shall be only too willing to serve them. . . . Since studying this subject I am convinced that the office of the President is not such a difficult one to fill, his duties being mainly to execute the laws of Congress. Should I be chosen for this exalted position I would execute the laws of Congress as faithfully as I have always executed the orders of my superiors. . . ."[46]

Had the election occurred before Dewey's return from Manila, or had the sixty-two-year-old admiral himself been mercifully afflicted with what William Jennings Bryan called "military lockjaw," he might have been elected. But six months had passed, and, as the *Review of Reviews* put it in May 1900, "people are thinking more of business and less of glory. They . . . are not in a mood for electing a hero regardless of his politics."

To the end of his life, the admiral remained on active duty as a member of the Navy's General Board. As president of the Schley Court of Inquiry, his name figured prominently in the news for a time. For a brief period in 1902-1903, about the time of the difficulty with Germany over the Venezuela Debts matter, Dewey was afloat in command of the fleet maneuvers in the Caribbean area. On occasion he continued to speak out of turn on matters involving foreign relations, particularly with Germany. On March 30, 1903, for example, President Theodore Roosevelt before leaving town for a speaking tour felt moved to caution the admiral in the following note:[47] "To Admiral George Dewey: Good-by and good luck to you while I am gone! Now, my dear Admiral, do let me beg of you to remember how great your reputation is—how widely whatever you say goes over the whole world. I know that you did not expect the interview you had to be printed, but do let me entreat you to say nothing which can be taken hold of by those anxious to foment trouble between ourselves and any foreign power or who delight in giving the impression that as a nation we are walking about with a chip on our shoulder. We are too big a people to be able to be careless in what we say."

He keenly enjoyed the social life of the wealthy set into which he had married. His honored position, his friendship with Theodore Roosevelt and his genuine affection for his wife made his declining years comfortable and pleasant. Dewey relished Washington's social whirl, perhaps because of its analogy to sea fighting in its endless jockeying for position. At the White House on New Year's Day, 1900, Mrs. Dewey, with many blandishments, induced Secretary Long to escort her ahead of her turn through the receiving line. "Tempers were ruffled . . ." wrote the Washington correspondent of the *New York Sun*, "in consequence of the question of precedence existing between the wives of Admiral Dewey and General Miles. The matter was finally settled—in as great a degree as these social controversies ever can be settled—by the decision that, inasmuch as the War Department was established prior to the Navy Department, the General commanding the Army was entitled to precedence over the Admiral of the Navy at official functions. When the men are entertained as individuals, however, Admiral Dewey, being of superior rank, takes precedence."[48]

As he advanced in age he became increasingly complacent. He enjoyed his rank. He even became less shy of reporters, who, on occasion, were invited out to his country home, Beauvoir. "I should like the American people to know Mrs. Dewey better," he would explain.[49]

He died on January 16, 1917, at the ripe age of 79. Chaplain Frazier, a shipmate on the *Olympia*, read the funeral service and the Battalion of Midshipmen from Annapolis provided an honor guard for the burial in Arlington. "I do not wish them to come," the dying man had whispered to Mildred, "because they are under orders. I wish them to come as friends."[50]

19. THE SAMPSON-SCHLEY CONTROVERSY

THE victory over Cervera, since it followed two days of bloody and discouraging fighting at San Juan Hill and El Caney, burst for a moment like sunlight through low-hanging clouds. The spectacular victory, with battleships as protagonists, was as swift and complete as Dewey's had been. Yet in the case of Santiago there was an ominous difference. The principal leaders, Sampson and Schley, beheld with chagrin a mad tussle of press and public to pick "the Dewey" of the Santiago Campaign.

On July 4 the *New York Times* headlined "Sampson's Fourth of July Victory," and at Palmyra, Sampson's home town, a salute of 100 guns was fired. Reporters descended upon Glen Ridge, New Jersey, to interview Mrs. Sampson and the admiral's exultant young sons Ralph and Harold. The *New York World* conveyed to Sampson cablegrams from his wife, "Accept congratulations. All well and very happy. Elizabeth." And from his sister Hannah: "Dear Brother: We congratulate you on your recent victory. We always knew you would do the right thing at the right time. Your devoted sister. H. C. Sampson."[1]

Then Sampson's publicity went sour. During the 12-day interval before his battle report could be completed a phenomenon occurred which defies precise explanation. Reporters hinted at dissension between the two leaders. Editors noticed that in his first brief announcement, "The fleet under my command offers the nation a Fourth of July present," Sampson *had not mentioned Schley*. The *Baltimore American* under Schley's close friend General Felix Agnus proclaimed on July 6 that "Schley is the real hero," and that Sampson had not had "the grace even to mention Schley's name. . . . He was in command. He began the destruction of the Spanish Fleet. . . . He did the work. Now give him the honors."[2] On July 5 Representative Berry of Kentucky, apparently anxious to be the first to propose it, moved that Congress tender to Commodore Schley a vote of thanks. Said Berry: "Schley is the real hero of the incident. Sampson commands the fleet in those water, but it was Commodore Schley in command when Cervera and his fleet made the plucky attempt at escape and it was under Schley that every one of that Spanish fleet met its destruction. . . ."[3]

An unbiased observer at Santiago might indeed have detected a coolness between the top commanders without understanding the causes back of it.

By an irony of circumstance, denied a position in the front of the fray, and with all his energies bent on watching his other ships perform, the commander in chief no doubt did have a most intent, single-minded expression, but the reporter was probably guilty of maudlin exaggeration who expressed the belief that Sampson would have committed suicide had Cervera's fleet escaped. And after the end of the race, when the *New York* caught up with the *Oregon*, the *Brooklyn* and the *Colon*, and when Schley signaled, "We have gained a great victory. Details will be communicated," it was natural, perhaps, for some disappointed souls on board the flagship to misread the intent of this signal as a "boast" on the part of the more fortunate Commodore Schley. On board the *Brooklyn*, which had been hilariously swapping congratulations with the *Oregon*, it had seemed only right and natural, when the flagship came up, to hail to her some sort of message. And the *New York's* response, "Report your casualties," sounded cold and curt to battle-excited junior officers and newsmen unaware that the "Report your casualties" had been a stock signal kept bent on the signal halyards for directing at each ship in the squadron as it had been overhauled.[4]

At this moment, indeed, the taut and serious commander in chief ("Covenanter afloat" was the name his Chief of Staff found for him to express his unbending Presbyterian will) might appropriately have relaxed his rule against "back-slapping" and, with perhaps a touch of Schley's enthusiasm, have returned a graceful word of congratulation. But the commander in chief's situation at the moment was one which he could not divorce from the background of Schley's as yet unexplained conduct during the search for Cervera. Schley's "retrograde" movement off Santiago, following his announced intention of returning to Key West to coal, was a matter so serious that Sampson in his various conferences with him since the first of June had never once mentioned this subject to Schley. He felt naturally reluctant to come to grips with a senior officer in a matter about which he himself felt so strongly and about which such captains as Chadwick and Evans were furious with rage; he had every reason to expect the Navy Department to handle the case; and he was in the midst of an arduous military campaign. His decision was unfortunate, perhaps, but understandable. The fact that the Schley Court of Inquiry, which was convened eventually at Admiral Schley's request, consumed 40 days in its investigation and ran to about 2,000 pages of print without satisfactorily settling the issue, is proof enough that the issue was not one to be hastily judged on the eve of battle. The circumstance did, however, color Sampson's thinking and influence his reports.

"With regard to [rewarding] Commodore Schley," Sampson surrendered the initiative to the Department in his letter of July 10, "I much prefer that the Department should decide his case. I am unwilling to fully express my own opinion. His conduct when he first assumed command on the South coast of Cuba I assume to be as well known to the Department as to myself. Had the Commodore left his station off Santiago de Cuba at that time he probably would have been court-martialed, so plain was his duty. Were I alone in this opinion I would certainly doubt my judgment, but so far as I know this opinion is confirmed by that of other commanding officers here acquainted with the circumstances. This reprehensible conduct I can not separate

Sampson's Fleet Steams into New York Harbor on Its Return from
Cuba. (From the Journal of Cadet C. R. Miller.)

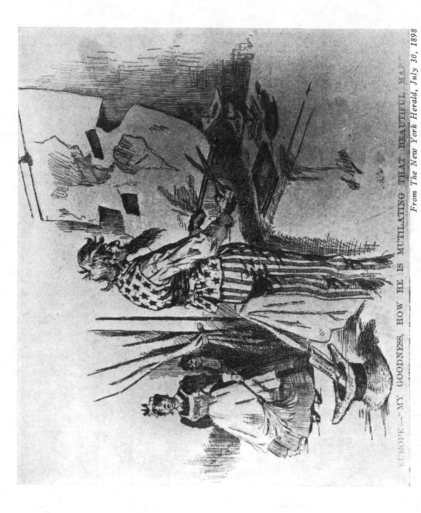

EUROPE.—"MY GOODNESS, HOW HE IS MUTILATING THAT BEAUTIFUL MAP!"

From The New York Herald, July 30, 1898

"My Goodness, How He Is Mutilating That Beautiful Map!"

from his subsequent conduct, and for this reason I ask you to do him ample justice on this occasion."[5] From this moment on, Admiral Sampson, as far as is known, had no further word to say, orally or in writing, on the hotly debated issue of Schley's management of his search for Cervera.

Toward Schley personally, Sampson's manner continued to be scrupulously courteous, as did Schley's toward himself. When the first batch of newspapers arrived lauding Schley and minimizing Sampson's share in the victory, the commodore hastened to the flagship to permit the admiral to read a disclaimer he had written to the Secretary:[6] "Feel some mortification that the newspaper accounts of July 6th have attributed victory on July 3rd almost entirely to me. Victory was secured by the force under command Commander-in-Chief, North Atlantic Station, and to him the honor is due. The end of line held by the *Brooklyn* and *Vixen* was heavily assailed, and had the honor, with the *Oregon*, of being in the battle from the beginning to the end. And I do not doubt for a moment full and proper credit will be given to all persons and all ships in the official report of the combat. W. S. Schley."

Meanwhile, the city of Santiago not immediately capitulating, General Shafter had again importuned Sampson to run into the harbor and compel the city to surrender. Sampson again refused to risk his ships because of the mine field, and in so doing incurred the ill will of many of the 89 reporters whom General Shafter had brought down as passengers on his headquarters boat. Shafter now asked the Secretary of War to exert pressure on Sampson, appealing on July fifth as follows: "Navy should go into Santiago Harbor at any cost. If they do, I believe they will take the city and all the troops that are there. If they do not, the country should be prepared for heavy losses among our troops. . . ."[7] Shafter's strictures on Sampson, given freely to the press, were seized by pro-Schley papers as the basis for bare-faced propaganda. Schley, it was alleged, with no truth whatever, had all along wanted to dash heroically past the Santiago batteries into the harbor. Schley, as well as Sampson and the Navy Department itself, was equally at the mercy of newsmen, not a few of whom had mastered the art of "irradiating" the grist for their mill with "peculiar and intuitive" information of their own.

Secretary of War Alger, as incapable as Shafter of understanding the naval point of view, again on July 13 pressed the Navy in a conference of the War Board and Cabinet and thoroughly aroused the ire of Mahan. "There was a pretty scrimmage between Captain Mahan and Secretary Alger," Long recorded in his journal. "We have furnished him [the Secretary of War] transports to carry his men, on account of his own neglect in making provision for transportation. We have landed them; have helped him in every way we can; and have destroyed the Spanish fleet. Now he is constantly grumbling because we don't run the risk of blowing up our ships by going over the mines at the entrance of Santiago Harbor and capturing the city, which he ought to capture himself, having some 20,000 troops against perhaps 5000 or 6000. Of course the Navy ought to help all it can, and it is under orders to do so. But Mahan, at last, lost his patience and sailed into Alger; told him he didn't propose to sit by and hear the Navy attacked. It rather pleased the President, who, I think was glad of the rebuke. The matter was at last settled by an order to the Commanding Officer of the Army in Santiago, and today I think something will be done one way or the other—that is, either a surrender made on our terms or an assault begun."[8]

Santiago did surrender the next day. Sampson and Schley participated together in the ceremonies that were held in the town; but the press continued to play up the false story in which Commodore Schley was reported to have declared that ships could enter the harbor "notwithstanding the mines." Schley voluntarily paid a call on Sampson to deny this preposterous story and to assure Sampson that he had always entirely agreed with him on this question. At Sampson's request Long investigated the matter, and received assurance from an official of the Associated Press that the falsehood had emanated not from accredited writers on the battleships but from a" gentleman who was temporarily on one of our dispatch boats" and had not been subject to censorship![9] The fat being in the fire, the Associated Press made little or no effort to douse the flames.

Mahan on August 5 entered the lists as Sampson's champion with a letter to the *New York Sun*. That Sampson had not been at the head of the fighting line mattered not at all, Mahan pontificated for those who had ears to hear. "With the wise and stringent methods laid down by the Admiral, it would not in the least have mattered, as things happened, with such ships and such Captains, had the Commander-in-Chief and the second in command, either or both, been seventy miles away.

... Few things in the observation of the writer have been more painful than the attempt of a portion of the press and of the public to rob Sampson of his just and painfully won dues."[10]

The signing of the peace protocol on August 12 brought an end to the war with Spain, but only intensified the peculiar battle between two sections of the press which, with no aid from either of the principals involved, had come to be called the "Sampson-Schley controversy." Secretary Long's proposal that Sampson be advanced eight numbers and Commodore Schley six, a move which would promote both men to rear admiral, but place Sampson one number ahead of Schley, opened a bitter battle in Congress which raged intermittently for two years and eventually resulted in the failure of Congress to approve the promotion of either Sampson or Schley. Secretary Long, hauled over the coals by "Schleyites" as a persecutor of their hero, publicly lamented the widespread and senseless scourging of Sampson: "I can think of nothing more cruel than a deprecation of the merit of the faithful, devoted, patriotic Commander-in-Chief, physically frail, worn with sleepless vigilance, weighed with measureless responsibilities and details, letting no duty go undone; for weeks with ceaseless precaution blockading the Spanish Squadron; at last, by the unerring fulfillment of his plans, crushing it under the fleet which executed his commands; yet now compelled in dignified silence to be assailed as vindictively as if he were an enemy to his country."[11]

The *Springfield Republican*, commenting on August 9 upon Schley's public denial "that he had ever said it was possible to enter Santiago Harbor in spite of the mines," laid a finger on an important cause of the Sampson-Schley controversy. "It arose largely from the determination of the slap-dash writers to get a brilliant hero out of the Santiago battle at any cost. Sampson's careful, thorough and comprehensive leadership would not do at all. The hero must be a dashing and devil-may-care officer, 'standing on the bridge,' and fearlessly heading the line of battle against the enemy fleet. It was a great disappointment to the company of newspaper strategists that the battle took place as it did, and even the glory of it all, which they would heap upon Commodore Schley, was a good deal dimmed by the fact that it was a running foe who was assailed and overcome. It was then reported that Schley would have led the fleet into the harbor before Cervera came out could he have had his way. This confirmed his title to the heroship of the whole affair, and placed Sampson in the light of a halting, shrinking, feeble commander, whose fleet had finally achieved victory in spite of him by a stroke of luck and the gallantry of the officers under him." This writer concluded with the platitude that the modern warship "is too intricate and expensive a piece of mechanism to be permitted to pass into the hands of heroes of the slap-dash newspaper variety."[12]

Another pro-Sampson paper noted that Schley might well pray, "Lord, save me from my friends. . . . Admiral Sampson," according to this organ, "is not what is called 'a good fellow;' the kind that everybody slaps on the shoulder. He never plays to the gallery, never gives whiskey to reporters, never hugs a dirty-faced brakeman on the train because he is from his own state. The various methods by which celebrities have, as the papers say, 'set the crowd wild,' do not apply to him. He forever offended the reporters of the yellow journals, by refusing to be 'written up.' He would not receive the representatives of the Daily Screecher and the Weekly Mud-Dredger; it did not flatter his vanity to have his pictures in the Sunday papers, along with the Mellins Food triplets, and Woodbury's soap."[13]

The war over, the fleet was ordered to New York for a review. Off Fort Wadsworth two mines were exploded as a greeting to the victorious ships. The mayor of New York City boarded the flagship New York to extend a welcome to the admiral. Mrs. Sampson, with three daughters, two sons and two grandchildren came out from Hoboken on the tugboat Mutual. Sampson went down to the foot of the flagship's ladder to greet them; although, the New York Times reported, "He thought it not proper to take the family on board."[14] Some well-wishers felt that the "Covenanter afloat" should have been more demonstrative. In the midst of a pandemonium of cheers, guns, whistles, bands and fireworks, Jerry Blake, a one-legged veteran of Farragut's fleet, came alongside the flagship on an excursion boat and shouted above the din, "For God's sake, Admiral, do something. Make a noise! Give us a salute! We are your friends! There is no Spanish blood here."[15] Sampson had the colors dipped.

The line of warships proceeded up the Hudson to fire 21-gun salutes abreast of Grant's Tomb and then retired to the navy yard where Sampson called all the captains on board the New York to be welcomed by Secretary Long.

After a few days at his home in Glen Ridge, New Jersey, Sampson returned to Havana as a member of the Cuban Commission charged with the evacuation of the Spanish troops from Cuba and the preservation of government property and records.

In Havana Sampson fell ill of overwork and malaria. Secretary Long sent Mrs. Sampson down to care for him. He returned North at the end of the year in time to attend the marriage of his youngest daughter Olive to Henry Harrison Scott. Hannah Sampson, who acted as maid of honor for Olive, was herself a short while later married to Ensign Wat Tyler Cluverius, a native of New Orleans and a survivor of the *Maine* tragedy.

For another year Sampson retained command of the North Atlantic Station. During this time he kept the fleet at its peak of wartime efficiency. Working in close co-operation with the War College, Sampson brought his fleet often into Narragansett Bay to permit its officers to attend lectures at the college, and in several brief cruises in northern waters he worked out fleet problems that had been designed by the War College. Although Sampson's health was beginning to fail, this was a happy year for him. Whenever the fleet stopped at the Brooklyn Navy Yard, Sampson was able to spend a few days at his home in near-by Glen Ridge, New Jersey. His sons Ralph and Harold, and sometimes other children from Glen Ridge, were taken on board the flagship to play with Pitch, the goat which the sailors had acquired as a mascot.

At a banquet in the Hamilton Hotel in Bermuda which was tendered to Admiral Sampson by Admiral Sir John Fisher, R.N., who as the foremost English exponent of gunnery was Sampson's counterpart in the British Navy, Sampson succinctly and gracefully returned a compliment to a great sister sea power. It was on Washington's Birthday. "At the banquet I gave in his honor, I proposed his health, and that of the United States," relates Fisher. "He said never a word. Presently one of his officers went up and whispered something in his ear. I sent the wine around, and the Admiral then got up, and made the best speech I ever heard. All he said was: 'It was a d—d fine old hen that hatched the American eagle!' "[16]

At home also, in New York, Glen Ridge, Boston and Palmyra, he was given banquets and receptions. Harvard conferred upon him the Doctor of Laws; President Eliot in so doing, hailed him as "an officer foresighted, forearmed, ready at every point, the American expert in high command." He was everywhere honored by such men as Ex-Secretary Benjamin F. Tracy, who had helped him to obtain the best armor and guns for the New Navy; Governor Theodore Roosevelt of New York, who as Assistant Secretary had aided Sampson in obtaining powder and shell for target practice; Captain Mahan, whose writings had placed the New Navy in the forefront of public attention; and a loyal host of captains who had served under him—Robley Evans, French Chadwick, Henry Taylor and Richard Wainwright, to mention only the most ardent of Sampson's admirers.[17]

The good of the service was always a burning passion with Sampson. The victory, he was ever ready to point out, "was not won by chance . . . to secure victory it is absolutely necessary to prepare for it." Unlike Mahan, Sampson expressed no opinions as to the desirability or undesirability of colonial possessions. That, he evidently thought, was the field of the politician or statesman. As a naval man he looked solely at the new strategic picture. He warned in a speech to Bostonians that "the increased territory which we have added to our country, will probably produce an increase in our chances for war by at least 100 per cent, and that we need to increase the Navy to that extent."[18]

In a cogent article on the United States Navy in the *Independent* for June 8, 1899, Sampson surveyed our new world situation. "Whether or not we desire to have it so, the war has made a great change in our position among the nations. They have gained a new estimate of us, and have put us in the front rank of the powers whose voices decide questions of world politics. At the same time we have greatly extended our coast line and undertaken the government of large and distant territories. We have become an Asiatic power, and cannot evade the responsibilities of such a position. We have great interests in the Pacific Ocean, and must be prepared to cope with any who are disposed to deny us our rights there." The "Covenanter afloat" was not blind to the inadequacies of the forces we had beaten. "If our easy victories over the fleets of a weak naval power fill our people with the belief that we have now a Navy that is large enough for all our needs, then those victories will have done us harm instead of good. . . . We have still much to learn about modern warships. They are as yet in the experimental stage." He urged that we heed the healthy, intelligent criticism of foreigners and that we not fall behind in our naval building. "We must be prepared to strike hard blows at a distance from the United States. . . ."[19]

Late in 1899 Sampson was detached from command of the North Atlantic Station and ordered to Boston as commandant of the navy yard there. The *New York* was lying at Hampton Roads when he left her for the last time. "When he came on deck to go," writes Chadwick, "there were very few officers visible, though there were all the other adjuncts of the regular ceremonial. But when he went over the side, and found the barge manned by the principal officers of the flagship instead of by the barge's crew of bluejackets, and boats from other ships of the squadron present also manned by the officers as a guard of honor, he was deeply moved."[20]

His health failing to improve he was unable to serve his full tour of duty in Boston. He lingered for a year and a half, dying gradually from softening of the tissues of the brain. A few months before his death, while the Schley Court of Inquiry was under way, Sampson requested permission to testify. Had he been mentally and physically able to do so, the whole problem might have been more satisfactorily clarified from the point of view both of Schley and himself. That, however, must remain forever a might-have-been.

On May 6, 1902, Admiral Sampson died in Washington. The funeral from the Church of the Covenant, at 18th and N Streets, was attended by President Roosevelt, the Cabinet, the Supreme Court, many members of Congress and a host of the highest-ranking officers in the Army and Navy. The Battalion of Naval Cadets from Annapolis, wearing plain black uniforms with side arms and rifles, marched with slow step behind the Naval Academy Band in scarlet and gold. A large body of bluejackets from the North Atlantic Squadron at Hampton Roads and a battery of field artillery from Fort Myer completed the impressive funeral cortege which escorted the admiral's remains to Arlington.

Of the four chief naval figures in the war for American empire Schley was by far the most sensitive and responsive to the feelings of other people. In the best sense of the word he was sentimental. Without being "thin-skinned," he was highly responsive to the joys or sorrows of other men, as well as susceptible to their praise or blame of himself. His reactions toward men were generous, spontaneous and enthusiastic. About midnight after the battle, learning that Cervera was a prisoner on the *Iowa*, Schley went on board that ship to pay him a visit. The bedraggled Spaniard, wearing a borrowed suit and feeling greatly depressed by the loss of his men and ships, burst into tears when Schley spoke to him in Castillian Spanish, assuring him of the high regard in which he was held and offering to help him in any way that he could.[21] A few days after the battle a delegation of seamen came up to the quarter-deck where the commodore was reading. "Sir," said their spokesman, "the crew would like to make you a present." Schley was on his feet in an instant, his glasses in his hand and his paper on the deck. "Well, my men."

"We found this compass on the Spanish Admiral's ship, and we thought as how we would like to give it to you to remember how you whipped them."

"I am much obliged to you," said the commodore, "but the great credit of that victory belongs to you boys—the men behind the guns. Without you, no laurels would come to our country. Thank you."

There were three hearty cheers from the men, and then Gunner's Mate Donnelly touched his cap and blurted out: "We hope, Sir, as how you'll steer a straighter course than the other fellow who owned it." The thoughtfulness of the crew, the *New York Times* reported, brought a glistening tear of joy to the commodore's eye.[22]

As the *Brooklyn* entered New York Harbor with the rest of the victorious fleet, bearing her "honorable scars of battle," a small boat with a brass band on board raced up alongside the ship and as a compliment to her commodore played "Maryland, My Maryland." "There was no doubt," noted the *New York Journal*, "about the heart in Winfield Scott Schley's welcome home."[23] "Passing up the harbor," Schley later wrote, "wharves were seen crowded with people, windows and housetops on each side of the river were filled with enthusiastic men and women gathered together to witness the pageant of a lifetime, and to do homage to officers and men who had represented them in their war for humanity. Reaching Riverside Drive, the hillsides from the water to their tops were packed with enthusiastic people, women and children being clad in raiment of every variety of summer colors, which gave to the slopes the appearance of having been padded with flowers."[24]

From a notice tossed on board by a press boat Schley first learned that the Department had raised him to rear admiral for "eminent and conspicuous conduct in battle."[25]

The *Brooklyn's* new paint did not conceal the shot holes in her tall funnels and, as she passed up the river, crowds yelled, "Schley! Schley! Schley!" "Judging by the sound alone," reported the *New York Journal*, "the cheers for Schley were longer and greater than for anyone in the fleet."[26]

Schley spent several days in bed at the home of his daughter Mrs. Wortley in Westport, Connecticut, recovering from the excitement.

Schley knew that his maneuvers off Cienfuegos and Santiago, prior to Sampson's arrival on June 1 had greatly excited the Navy Department at the time, for Mr. Long's increasingly more agitated messages of that period had continued to arrive on board the *Brooklyn* for ten days after June 1. Nevertheless, since the battle had been brilliantly won and since he had received his promotion, he had reason to feel that his conduct during the strenuous period of the search for Cervera was not being held against him. Such, at least, he might infer from the celebration in New York, when arm in arm with Admiral Sampson he had been welcomed bv Secretary Long and other members of the Cabinet.

In Washington he was given a conqueror's welcome. A hundred policemen mounted on bicycles escorted his carriage through cheering throngs to the Navy Department. Assistant Secretary Allen in the absence of Mr. Long at once carried him to the Executive Mansion, where the President welcomed him and appointed him a member of the Puerto Rican Commission, paralleling Sampson's appointment to the Cuban Commission; the wording of Schley's commission noted the President's "special trust and confidence in the integrity and ability of Rear Admiral Winfield Scott Schley, U.S.N."[27]

When he returned to New York he was recognized everywhere in the streets and welcomed by the public. In the office of his son, W. S. Schley, Jr., M.D., a crowd of well-wishers gathered to be introduced. The admiral and Mrs. Schley stopped in a shop to buy gold lace and were welcomed by an impromptu gathering of people, "though no one," observed the *Times*, with Hobson's fate in mind, "made so bold as to kiss him."[28] On August 29, when he returned on board the *Brooklyn* for two days before embarking on a transport for Puerto Rico, his "bullies" turned somersaults. They presented him with the *Brooklyn's* "much riddled and tattered" battle flag, amid cheers which Schley felt "beat promotion all to pieces." "Everybody seemed so sincere, so whole hearted."[29] When the blue flag with its two white stars was broken to the breeze, Captain Cook saluted it with 13 guns. Then the men tossed their caps in the air and embraced one another, while officers and petty officers filed into the admiral's cabin to shake hands and congratulate him. During the two days he spent on board, thousands of people from all parts of the country visited the ship to examine her battle scars and express admiration for her officers and crew.[30]

At San Juan, Puerto Rico, in addition to salutes, Rear Admiral Schley was greeted by cheers and a tiger. Someone in the crowd— and this was a year before Dewey's great *faux pas* in politics—even shouted, "Hurrah for the next President."[31] The work of the commission being to evacuate the Spanish troops with as little friction as possible, Schley's knowledge of the Spanish language proved useful. At noon on October 18 when the American colors rose over the city of San Juan, signifying the transfer of sovereignty, the ceremony also marked Schley's share in obtaining for the United States not only an economically valuable overseas colony but a repair and supply station of the greatest strategical value for the Navy.

He returned home expecting soon to obtain command of the European Squadron, a billet of dignity and prestige second only to that of the North Atlantic Station. He found instead that the European Squadron, which had been discontinued during the war, had not yet been reorganized. He learned, too, that the unhappy Sampson-Schley controversy was raging with more heat than ever. Schley's adherents in Congress, unwilling to promote Sampson above Schley, were holding up promotions for all who had taken part in the Santiago Campaign. Also, he found that in the Department's publication of naval records of the war a number of documents necessary to understanding his own actions prior to June 1 had been omitted. An investigation revealed that these papers from the flag office on the *Brooklyn*, which should have been sent to the Navy Department for inclusion in the Secretary's annual report, had been boxed and by mistake sent with Schley's personal effects to Puerto Rico.[32] Before this material was finally placed in the Department, the Senate Naval Affairs Committee in a secret investigation unearthed material which looked so damaging to Schley that the injunction of secrecy was removed and Schley was allowed to defend himself. This he did to the entire satisfaction of the Senate, which body now proceeded to draft a new bill restoring Schley to his original position ahead of Sampson.

Schley's adherents, many of whom were politically aligned against the administration, hailed this as a victory for Schley. Schley himself, having at this time only nominal duty on various boards, busied himself for nearly a year with traveling about the country as the guest of various cities and state legislatures, attending banquets, accepting swords and loving cups and greatly enjoying the praise of his fellow citizens. He had an honest affection for people and they reciprocated that feeling in colorful and spontaneous displays. At North Platte, Nebraska, for instance, where his train stopped for an hour and he was welcomed by a crowd of 10,000, Buffalo Bill, the hero of the Wild West show, lent all his tallyhos and other spectacular trappings to the citizens and everybody had a grand time.[33] No less enthusiastic was the audience at Georgetown University when he received the degree of Doctor of Laws. "As the Admiral stepped to the center of the platform men and women rose en masse and pandemonium reigned. Waving of handkerchiefs, shouts, clapping of hands, and the stamping of feet marked the occasion." Undergraduates cried, "What's the matter with Schley? He's all right!"[34] On July 3, 1899, 250 men of the *Brooklyn's* crew, celebrating the first anniversary of Santiago as "Schley Day," paraded with a brass band in a Long Island park carrying a huge banner with Schley's picture; while their mascot "Billy" pranced in a silver collar and uniform of blue satin and yellow plush.[35]

In November 1899, shortly after the Dewey celebration, Schley was appointed commander in chief of the South Atlantic Station. If by this move the Navy Department sought to silence the pro-Schley agitation by "banishing" Schley to a foreign station, the Department was doomed to disappointment. Ardent Schleyites like publisher Agnus of the *Baltimore American* charged the Department with "persecuting" Schley, and, since the next presidential campaign was approaching, this new hue and cry was not allowed to diminish even though to most people the Sampson-Schley controversy had become tiresome. To quench recurrent flare-ups of the controversy Secretary Long issued a circular prohibiting naval officers from mentioning the case in public; and Captain French E. Chadwick, for subsequently allowing himself to be interviewed on this topic by a reporter, was given a reprimand.[36]

Schley himself was thoroughly wearied of the business and was often reported to have expressed a wish that the matter be allowed to die. At the end of his tour of duty in the South Atlantic, however, he found a new situation at home which forced the whole issue out into the open for a final showdown.

In June of 1901 Schley began to receive in the mail from all over the country clippings from a new book on the Spanish War which he read with dismay and anger. Sample passages quoted in the *Army and Navy Journal* read as follows: "In his report about the coal supply of the vessels under his command Schley exhibited either a timidity amounting to absolute cowardice or a prevarication of facts that were intrinsically falsehoods." "Schley, on May 28, 1898 . . . turned in caitiff flight from the danger spot towards which duty, honor and the whole American people were earnestly urging him. . . ." " 'Let the *Texas* take care of herself,' was the heartless reply, and the shameful spectacle of an American warship . . . deliberately turning tail and running away was presented." "Schley was perfectly willing to avoid blanketing the fire of the American warships, even at the risk of a disastrous collision with the *Texas,* so long as he could escape getting too close to danger. . . . Schley's contribution to naval strategy, as too plainly shown by his conduct throughout the campaign, was, 'Avoid your enemy as long as possible, and if he makes for you, run.' " The offending book was Volume III of *A History of the United States Navy* by E. S. Maclay, the first two volumes of which had been in use for several years as a textbook at the Naval Academy.[37] Confronted with this "perversion of facts, misconstruction of intention," and "intemperate abuse and defamation" of himself, and with the prospect that these ideas might be taught at the Naval Academy to naval officers of the future, Admiral Schley felt that he had but one alternative: to request a court of inquiry. "I have refrained heretofore from all comment upon the innuendoes of enemies, muttered or murmured in secret, and therefore with safety to themselves," he wrote the Secretary. He stated that he now thought the time had come "to take such action as may bring this matter under discussion under the clearer and calmer review of my brothers in arms. . . ."[38]

Secretary Long ordered an inquiry into Commodore Schley's conduct and at the same time investigated the Maclay case. The author, a clerk in the Brooklyn Navy Yard who had derived his prejudices from anti-Schley sources, was dismissed from his job. Congress prohibited the use of his history book at the Naval Academy, and the publishers hurriedly recalled all copies of the book that they could lay hands on and reissued it in a new edition, from which the aspersions upon Admiral Schley's character had been removed.

At noon on September 12, 1901, the most famous and perhaps the most unsatisfactory court of inquiry in American history was opened at the Washington Navy Yard. Its sessions, open to the public, were held in the spacious "Gunner's Workshop." Admiral George Dewey presided. The inquiry lasted for forty days, and scores of naval witnesses of all ranks testified, as well as a few civilian reporters, pilots, cartographers, etc. Reporters from all over the country covered the "trial" and a *Washington Post* cartoonist with a chip on his shoulder against the Navy Department sketched a whole book of cartoons for his paper. From start to finish the case drew large crowds, many of them society women who came early to get seats and brought their lunch.

Unhappily for all concerned, the scope of the inquiry was so hedged in as to admit only such testimony as concerned Schley personally. Anything relating to Sampson was rigorously excluded by the court on the ground that "Admiral Sampson's conduct was in no way under review." Schley's lawyers repeatedly sought to invalidate this ruling by getting the court involved in legal inconsistencies, but the ruling was held to. As Schley pointed out later in his autobiography, *Forty-Five Years under the Flag,* "It was impossible not to . . . [involve Sampson in some way] at every point of the inquiry, owing to the closeness of the official connection of the two officers."[39] What frustrated a complete investigation, although it was given no publicity, was the declining health of Admiral Sampson himself, who was suffering from the mental ailment which would in a few months prove fatal.

On the basis of testimony that was largely incomplete the court decided that Schley's campaign prior to June 1, 1898, was characterized "by vacillation, dilatoriness, and lack of enterprise"; although in the battle of July third he was adjudged to have been "self-possessed," and to have "encouraged, in his own person, his subordinate officers and men to fight courageously."[40] A curious minority report signed by Dewey not only nullified the adverse findings of the majority, but departed from all the rulings in the case to conclude that on July 3

Schley had been "in absolute command, and is entitled to the credit due to such commanding officer for the glorious victory which resulted in the total destruction of the Spanish ships."[41] Dewey's extraordinary judgment, the impulsive, warm-hearted gesture of a lifelong friend, partially assuaged Schley's disappointment. Another friend, Lieutenant General Nelson A. Miles, by publicly announcing his agreement with Admiral Dewey, voluntarily incurred a reprimand from the Secretary of War. Schley's subsequent appeal to President Theodore Roosevelt for relief from the verdict of the court was without avail.

October 9, 1901, on reaching the statutory age of sixty-two Schley was placed on the retired list. His ebullient spirits undimmed by his difficulties, he continued to accept invitations throughout the country. In 1904 he published his memoirs, *Forty-Five Years under the Flag*, which give a remarkably detached and fair appraisal of his long career in the Navy with Farragut in the gulf, vindicating American rights in Korea, teaching at the Naval Academy, the Lighthouse service, the Greely Relief Expedition, chief of a Bureau in Washington, the *Baltimore* Affair at Valparaiso and his part in the War for American Empire.

Vigorous to the last, he fell dead of apoplexy on October 2, 1911, on a street in New York City. The Battalion of Midshipmen from Annapolis marched behind his caisson on the way to Arlington, and a file of bluejackets, whose lot he had helped to improve, fired a last salvo over his grave.

20. THE TRIUMPH OF MAHAN

As a champion of American overseas expansion, Mahan made his bow in January of 1893. He had as yet won no great fame at home; although his first sea-power book had made him a name abroad and he was about to embark with Admiral Erben on the *Chicago* to receive from Great Britain, as the foremost interpreter of the growth of her navy and her empire, a phenomenal homage of banquets and honorary degrees. Hawaii was the first great overseas possession which Mahan sought to induce his fellow Americans to acquire.

While movements to annex Hawaii had been cropping up for half a century, only to be nipped by the frost of our time-sanctified policy of isolation, the Hawaiian Islands had continued inevitably and steadily to be drawn into the American orbit. Americans in Hawaii—missionaries, whalers, traders, sugar growers—a persistent and nagging progeny, never allowed the frowns of the United States Senate to discourage their efforts toward closer bonds with their homeland. In the reciprocal trade treaty of 1887 there was inserted a clause which gave the United States the exclusive right to use Pearl Harbor as a naval station, and in mid-January of 1893, when Queen Liliuokalani sought to promulgate a reactionary constitution, her obstreperous American subjects in Honolulu arose in revolt. With the aid of the United States minister and 150 armed seamen from the U.S.S. *Boston* in the harbor at the time, they deposed the queen and declared Hawaii to be a protectorate under the United States flag.[1]

Mahan's first effort to sway public opinion in favor of annexing Hawaii, a letter published in the *New York Times* on January 31, 1893, pointed out that it was a matter of concern to the entire civilized world whether Hawaii eventually came under Western or Oriental influence; and, he concluded, "our own country with its Pacific coast, is naturally indicated as the proper guardian. . . ." His suggestion attracting the attention of Walter H. Page, editor of the *Forum*, Mahan was promptly engaged to contribute an article on "Hawaii and Our Future Sea Power" to the March issue of that magazine.

The question of Hawaii, Mahan conceded in this first full-fledged argument, was "pregnant of great consequences in one direction or in the other," and the issue could not be dodged. We had filled out our natural frontiers by territorial expansion across the continent so that "today maturity sees us upon the Pacific. . . . Have we no right or no call to progress farther in any direction? Are there for us beyond the sea horizon none of those essential interests, or those evident dangers, which impose a policy and confer rights?" Hawaii, 2,100 miles west of San Francisco and the only possible island coaling base within operational range of our Pacific Coast, would be a menace in the hands of a maritime enemy. In addition to the negative advantage of preventing enemies from acquiring Hawaii, there were positive advantages that impelled the United States to annex the islands. With the opening of an Isthmian canal in the not-too-distant future, Hawaii would become a great natural focus for routes of trade as well as a vital point in our own strategic defense system. Hawaii's nearness to our shores—and proximity had been "always admitted as a reasonable ground for national self-assertion"—demanded that we annex while we could "righteously" do so. "Let us not shrink from pitting a broad self-interest against the narrow self-interest to which some would restrict us."[2]

Thus far in a political sense Mahan's argument had at least one practical advantage: It was directed against a single opponent—the traditional isolationist. Here, perhaps, as a publicist advocating a cause, he should have rested. But he was a novice at the game of shaping and giving direction to public opinion. In his enthusiasm for other pet subjects he went farther and, rather unnecessarily, added hosts of enemies to the cause he was advocating. By upholding Britain's maritime empire as an example to be imitated, by calling for a navy adequate "to secure outlying dependencies," and by viewing Hawaii not as a final goal "but a first-fruit and token" of a new direction in America's foreign policy, Mahan stirred up and arrayed against himself "small navy" enthusiasts, anti-Britishers and anti-imperialists of every shape and hue. Mahan's startling idea of an America departing from her cherished isolation and carrying her flag out beyond her natural frontiers to cover peoples of dissimilar race, culture and religion—peoples, moreover, who could scarcely ever be assimilated and enfranchised as United States citizens—was more than most Americans of that day could endure. Before the machinery of Harrison's administration could handle the question, Cleveland had returned to office. The American-sponsored revolt in Hawaii was declared by the new administration to have been a mistake. Old Glory was hauled down in Honolulu and the reins of government were with an air of gallantry restored to Queen Liliuokalani.

Four years later, coincident with another tremor of feeling against the "yellow peril," the issue of annexing Hawaii again came to the fore. Mahan, fifty-eight years old at this time, retired and living in New York, was riding the crest of fame as biographer of Nelson and author of magazine articles on sea power. Although his writings kept him busy, he was always ready to give thought, and possibly direction, to the policies of his friend, the ebullient young Assistant Secretary of the Navy. With Theodore Roosevelt, as with Mahan, the annexation of Hawaii amounted to a passion. Mahan feared that war with Japan would develop if the issue of Hawaii were not settled before Japan's program of naval construction had been completed. "That there is danger of trouble with her towards Hawaii, I think beyond doubt," Mahan wrote Roosevelt on May 1, 1896; "if this administration is not able to get those islands under our wing, Mr. Cleveland's name will be immortalized a century hence by one thing only, that he refused them when he could have had them. . . . Of course Japan is a small and a poor state, as compared to ourselves; but the question is are we going to allow her to dominate the future of those important islands, because of our lethargy. I do not know your chief [Secretary John D. Long], but only that at his age and having lived his life in what a clever Boston woman styled to me the 'backwaters' of Boston society, he regards the annexation of the islands, if offered, as an insoluble political problem. To this, in my mind, the only reply is: Do nothing unrighteous; but as regards the problem, take the islands first and solve afterwards. . . ."[3]

"As regards Hawaii," replied Roosevelt, "I take your views absolutely, as indeed I do on foreign policy generally. If I had my way we would annex those islands tomorrow. . . . I earnestly hope we can make the President look at things our way. . . . But to no one excepting Lodge do I talk like this. . . . As regards Hawaii, I am delighted to tell you that Secretary Long shares our views. . . . I have just been preparing some memoranda for him to use at the Cabinet meeting tomorrow. . . ."[4]

Mahan out of consideration destroyed Roosevelt's letter, not knowing that Roosevelt himself had kept a copy, and tactfully assured the ambitious young politician that he himself desired to play only the passive role of thinker or backstage prompter, "to suggest thoughts or give information. . . . I have known myself too long," confided Mahan, "not to know that I am the man of thought, not of action. Such an one may beneficially throw out ideas, the practical effect of which can rest only, and be duly shaped only, by practical men."[5]

Mahan's present suggestion was that Roosevelt have the new battleship *Oregon* visit Honolulu to further the cause of annexation. If the move were made, Mahan cautioned, "it is necessary that instructions be perfectly clear on views of the government. All other conscientious scruples in a military mind disappear before the fundamental duty of obedience; but government must speak clearly, without ifs and buts."[6]

"I have shown that very remarkable letter to the Secretary," reported Roosevelt on June 9 to his mentor. "Yesterday I urged immediate action by the President as regards Hawaii. Entirely between ourselves, I believe he will act very shortly. If we take Hawaii now, we shall avoid trouble with Japan, but I get very despondent at times over the blindness of our people, especially the best educated classes. In strict confidence I want to tell you that Secretary Long is lukewarm about building up our Navy, at any rate as regards battleships.

Indeed, he is against adding to our battleships. . . . I feel that you ought to write to him—not immediately but . . . at some length, explaining to him the vital need of continuity in our naval policy. Make a plea that [it] is a measure of peace and not war. I cannot but think your words would carry weight with him."[7]

McKinley's negotiators a week later signed a new annexation treaty, but objections from Japanese empire builders and American isolationists frustrated immediate ratification. As an issue, however, it was not allowed to grow cold. The approach of the war with Spain, plus the high moral fervor of the anti-imperialists, kept the topic alive in popular discussion.

Many Americans sincerely resented the idea of annexing Hawaii or any other overseas colonies. Had not colonial projects brought endless wars and quarrels to the European powers? America ought not to descend from her "pedestal of wise and pacific detachment" or depart from the teachings of the founders of the Republic.[8] The "seductions of imperialism" were denounced as "drawing the United States toward the abyss where all the great democracies of the world have found their end."[9] The deposed Queen Liliuokalani, "dethroned through force and fraud," came to reside in Washington as a living reproach to the republic.[10]

Apparently to offset the moral objections to annexation, Mahan published "A Twentieth Century Outlook" in *Harper's Magazine* in May of 1897. "Bound and swathed in the traditions of our own eighteenth century . . . we, under the specious plea of peace and plenty . . . hug an ideal of isolation. . . ." As inheritors of the culture of Western Europe, we Americans should "look abroad" and "busy ourselves with our duties to the world at large in our generation." Too long have we "stood apart from the general movement of our race." As Mahan saw it, the Western world must either aggressively carry its civilization to the backward regions, "converting them to our ideal," or "go down finally under a flood of outside invasion. . . . Issues of vital moment are involved. A present generation is trustee for its successors, and may be faithless to its charge quite as truly by inaction as by action."[11] And in a lecture before the Lowell Institute at about this time Mahan warned, "The decision not to bring under the authority of one's government some external position, when occasion offers, may by future generations be bewailed in tears of blood."[12]

Not all of Mahan's argument was on the apocalyptic level. "If a plea for the world's welfare seem suspiciously like a cloak for national self-interest, let the latter be accepted frankly as the adequate motive which it assuredly is." Mahan's early article in *Harper's*, reprinted in book form in 1897, was quoted in the *Army and Navy Gazette* of London in January of 1898. "Let us not shrink from pitting a broad self-interest against the narrow self-interest to which some would restrict us. The demands of our three great seaboards, the Atlantic, the Gulf and the Pacific, each for itself, and all for the strength that comes from drawing closer the ties between them, call for the extension through the Isthmian Canal of the broad sea-paths. Let us start with the fundamental truth, warranted by history, that the control of the seas, and especially along the great lines drawn by national interest or national commerce, is the chief among the merely material elements in the power and prosperity of nations. It is so because the sea is the world's great medium of circulation. . . . It should be an inviolable resolution of our national policy that no foreign State should henceforth acquire a coaling position within 3,000 miles of San Francisco, a distance which includes the Hawaiian and Galapagos Islands and the coast of Central America. For fuel is the life of modern naval war; it is the food of the ship; without it the modern monsters of the deep die of inanition. Around it, therefore, cluster some of the most important considerations of naval strategy. In the Caribbean and in the Atlantic we are confronted with many a foreign coal depot bidding us stand to arms . . . but let us not acquiesce in an addition to our dangers, a further division of our strength, by being forestalled in the North Pacific."[13]

Much of what Mahan wrote and said about annexation found its way into the *Congressional Record*, both in its original form and in the paraphrases of senators.[14] In February of 1898 a lively discussion followed an exchange of letters between Mahan and Senator James H. Kyle of South Dakota. Senator Kyle submitted four questions to the authority on sea power: (1) Would the possession of Hawaii strengthen our military position? (2) Would it necessitate a larger Navy? (3) Would it be practicable for a foreigner to invade our Pacific coast without first occupying Hawaii as a base? (4) Would it be a desirable coaling base for the United States? Mahan's carefully phrased answers to these questions constituted a strong plea for annexation and were given wide publicity in the press of the country.[15]

Logic alone, however, was unequal to the task of prying the American people away from the rock of traditional isolation. Mahan's words, cogent enough, and recognized as the words of "the most distinguished writer and authority of our time on the history of sea power," made their appeal to the intellect. What was needed was an emotional pull of the first magnitude. And that was what Commodore Dewey supplied in his spectacular battle of Manila Bay.

Dewey's victory struck the scales from the eyes of politicians at both ends of Pennsylvania Avenue. "Between April 30 and May 1 the weather vane which shows the public breath swung clean around," commented a writer in the London Chronicle. "The practical American read the news, asked himself, 'Well, why not?' and hung another flag out of his window."[16] In the corridors of Congress a few days after Dewey's victory a reporter for the Army and Navy Journal heard "continual talk . . . as to the imperative need of coaling stations for our vessels in every part of the globe. It seems to be tacitly agreed that we must take front rank as a maritime power. . . . The annexation of Hawaii has been given a big impetus by the 'logic of events' within the last week, and it looks now only a question of days before Uncle Sam will be in possession of the Sandwich [Hawaiian] Islands. . . . I have talked with a large number of statesmen, Navy people and New York business men temporarily in the city, and one and all say that the United States has turned a sharp corner in its policy and that hereafter it is bound to play an important part in the progress of the globe. . . ."[17]

In July of 1898 the opposition senators enjoyed a final fling against annexation. "Not conquest, but an act of piracy," declared Senator Pettigrew of South Dakota. "If it [our flag] goes up there [in Hawaii] again, it goes up in infamy and shame, and we join the ranks of the robber nations of the world."[18] But the senator was in a minority. Even Senator George F. Hoar of Massachusetts, a bitter opponent of imperialism who conceived the war with Spain to be a "just and holy" war for the sole purpose of liberating Cuba, conceded that Hawaii should be annexed by the United States to prevent its falling a prey to Japanese immigration.

The joint resolution to annex Hawaii was passed on July 6, 1898, and next day at 7:00 P.M., when McKinley's signature was affixed, became law. For Alfred Mahan, one of the most devoted and influential workers in the crusade for American empire, the victory was very real. It was, perhaps, the greatest victory of his life, since by cutting the ground from under the isolationist opposition it prepared the way for the more extensive annexations that were to follow the war with Spain.

Englishmen very naturally understood the significance of the event. "The apocalyptic vision of a new heaven and a new earth is still unfulfilled," wrote Henry Norman in the London Chronicle in July of 1898, "but there is a new America. The second American revolution has occurred, and its consequences may be as great as those of the first. The old America, the America obedient to the traditions of the founders of the Republic, is passing away, and a new America—an America standing armed, alert and exigent in the arena of the world struggle— is taking its place."[19]

From his magazine articles which were collected and published in 1897 under the title The Interest of America in Sea Power, Present and Future it is clear that the foreign territories which most appealed to Mahan were those that would enhance our naval security. In addition to Hawaii he wanted bases in the Caribbean. In the latter area the most useful locations were those that might afford protection to the Windward Passage approach to an Isthmian canal. This passage, around the eastern end of Cuba, was obviously marked to become the most practicable route for American East Coast shipping proceeding to the canal. At the request of the Senate Committee on Naval Affairs, the Naval War Board drew up a memorandum, in a style unmistakably Mahan's, which clarified this strategic need. The memorandum cited Santiago or Guantánamo on the south coast of Cuba as the base site most desirable for the purpose.

A prime difficulty for the expansionists was the Teller Amendment to the Declaration of War. In this fateful self-denying clause, Congress, swept off its feet by a prewar gale of sympathy for downtrodden Cuba, had in advance of hostilities renounced any intention of annexing Cuba. Some way around this embarrassing self-imposed restriction would have to be found if a Windward Passage naval station were to be obtained. Fortunately, in the opinion of the "large policy" advocates, Congress had said nothing at all about Puerto Rico, the Ladrones in the western Pacific and the Philippines. Before the war was over, Guam, an excellent base in the Ladrones group about halfway between Honolulu and Manila, had been seized as a military measure to secure Dewey's line of supply, and Puerto Rico, not mentioned in the Teller

Amendment bond, came very quickly to be popularly regarded as a fair prize of war. From Tampa, Florida, on the eve of embarkation with his Texas cowboys, Teddy Roosevelt enjoined his friend Senator Lodge to prevent "any talk of peace until we get Porto Rico and the Philippines," and Lodge by mid-June assured him that the whole annexation policy was gaining ground rapidly "under the irresistible pressure of events."[20]

Mahan in Washington, living in Roosevelt's house during the latter's absence in Cuba, saw much of Lodge during the months of the war. One evening after dinner at the Lodges', the captain and the senator spent two hours going over the problem of the Philippines with Secretary of State Day.[21] Whether Mahan wanted Manila only, the Island of Luzon only, or the whole of the Philippines is not clear. In reporting this after-dinner conversation to Roosevelt, the senator did not mention this point, nor did Mahan in his writings specifically clarify it. Like the rest of the country, even the great naval philosopher was somewhat undecided. An indication of his thinking, however, is given in the following note written on July 27 to Lodge: "Public opinion I assume will insist that Spain quit America forever. But feeling as to the Philippines is much more doubtful. I myself, though rather an expansionist, have not fully adjusted myself to the idea of taking them, from our own standpoint of advantage. It does seem to me, however, that the heavy force, army and navy, we have put in Luzon, has encouraged the revolutionists to an extent for which we are responsible. Can we ignore the responsibility and give them back to Spain? I think not. Spain cannot observe a pledge to govern justly, because she neither knows what good government is, nor could she produce it if she knew. As to an agreement with the other Powers, I hope no entangling alliances for us. But we have done nothing in the other islands of the group. Might it not be a wise compromise to take only the Ladrones and Luzon; yielding to the 'honor' and exigencies of Spain the Carolines and the rest of the Philippines."[22]

While it is not possible to measure with precision Mahan's influence upon the drafting and the ratifying of the treaty of peace with Spain, it is nevertheless clear that his impact upon both was considerable. His prestige as the foremost American expert on sea power added weight to his words, and his ideas were eagerly sought by administration leaders, peace commissioners and Congressmen alike. Magazines and newspapers printed and reprinted what he had to say. Other writers and speakers acquired a "Mahanite" manner when dealing with problems growing out of the war.

Originally the struggle against Spain had been undertaken to put an end to unrest and bloodshed and to give a stable government to Cuba. As time went on, their war aims began gradually in the minds of the American people to undergo a sea change. By slow degrees the inexorable logic of events brought the nation around to the point of view of Mahan. Had Dewey sailed back to Hong Kong after his naval victory, his duty would have been regarded as thoroughly accomplished both by ourselves and by the rest of the world. But he stayed, and military reinforcements were sent him. As the size of these reinforcements grew, thrifty Americans began to question the wisdom of such expense. "To spend the millions of dollars we have spent on a purely sterile demonstration," editorialized the *Army and Navy Journal*, ". . . would be a national absurdity deserving the derision of the world. . . ."[23] Certain mutations quite naturally occurred in our war aims. The simple, unmixed humanitarian solicitude for Cuba became alloyed with considerations of overseas expansion, naval bases, power politics, trade routes, the prestige of a "Hong Kong" for America in the Far East. "Every consideration of national pride—national interest and of presenting ourselves to the world as something more than mere tyros in enlarged politics, demand that we hold the islands . . . the Philippines should be American only."[24]

McKinley, who confessed that on May 1 he could not have located the Philippines within 2,000 miles, in October instructed the Peace Commissioners in Paris to demand the cession of the entire Philippine archipelago. "The march of events," he cabled, "rules and overrules human action. . . ." To a group of fellow Methodists the President confessed:[25] "The truth is that I didn't want the Philippines and when they came to us as a gift from the gods, I did not know what to do about them. . . . I sought counsel from all sides—Democrats as well as Republicans—but got little help. I thought first we would take only Manila; then Luzon; then the other islands, perhaps, also. I walked the floor of the White House night after night until midnight; and I am not ashamed to tell you, gentlemen, that I went down on my knees and prayed Almighty God for light and guidance more than one night.

"And one night late it came to me this way—I don't know how it was, but it came: (1) that we could not give them back to Spain—that would be cowardly and dishonorable; (2) that we could not turn them over to France or Germany—our commercial rivals in the Orient —that would be bad business and discreditable; (3) that we could not leave them to themselves—they were unfit for self-government—and they would soon have anarchy and misrule over there worse than Spain's was; and (4) that there was nothing left for us to do but to take them all, and to educate the Filipinos, and uplift and civilize and Christianize them, and by God's grace do the very best we could by them, as our fellow-men for whom Christ also died. And then I went to bed, and went to sleep and slept soundly. . . ."

For weeks Senator Lodge as "whip" for the Republicans in the Senate battled to get the treaty ratified.[26] Finally, William Jennings Bryan, arch foe of imperialism, swung his Democratic following behind the treaty. Ratify the treaty now and unload the Philippines later was his curious scheme! At the last minute a petition to amend the treaty so as not to take the Philippines was sent to Washington, bearing such names as Charles Francis Adams, Andrew Carnegie, Grover Cleveland, Samuel Gompers, Charles W. Eliot, Carl Schurz, Henry van Dyke and Theodore S. Woolsey.[27] On Saturday, February 4, the poll in the Senate was 58 for and 32 against ratification, two votes short of the necessary two-thirds majority.[28] Then, over the week end, shots rang out on the other side of the world as Aguinaldo's forces struck for the first time against the tense and ready ring of United States troops around Manila. On Monday six senators who had been present on Saturday were absent, and three changed their minds. The treaty was now at last ratified, by a vote of 57 to 27. Governor Theodore Roosevelt of New York announced to the press, "I am as glad as a man can be."[29] And Alfred Mahan, also pleased at the results which the war and his own long struggle to inform the public had helped to bring about, sent a note to Senator Lodge "congratulating him upon his able efforts."[30]

One of the first evidences of the new role which the United States had assumed in world affairs was her sending delegates to the First International Peace Conference at the Hague in 1899. The Czar of Russia, alarmed by the mounting costs of armament, initiated the move to disarm; and the Queen of the Netherlands, from May 18 to July 29 acted as hostess to one of the most colorful "gatherings of the nations" since the Congress of Vienna.[31] Since 20 of the 26 participating nations were European, while only two were American (the United States and Mexico) and four Asiatic, this conference was so predominantly European that sections of the press in the United States cried farewell to our tradition of noninterference in Europe's affairs and gloomily predicted the doom of the Monroe Doctrine whenever Europe should decide to intervene in Western Hemisphere problems.

Captain Mahan was picked by Secretary of State John Hay as America's naval representative on a delegation that included Andrew D. White, ambassador to Germany; Stanford Newell, minister to the Netherlands; Seth Low, president of Columbia University; Captain William Crozier, U. S. Army; and G. F. W. Holls, secretary. Why the foremost advocate of naval expansion in America should have been selected as a delegate to a disarmament conference or why Mahan should have accepted the post have never been revealed; although it might conceivably have been because Britain had placed her famed Admiral Sir John Fisher, also a naval expansionist, among her delegates.

The Hague Conference stirred the imagination of idealists throughout the world and the 96 delegates to the conference were surrounded by a colorful array of "millennium-seekers," inspired by hope that somehow with the turn of the century humanity itself might turn over a new leaf and abolish war. One journalist noted that "Young Turks, Old Armenians, emancipated and enthusiastic women, ancient revolutionists of the 'forties, buzzed about The Hague like bees."[32]

Mahan found the conference "interesting in a way" but ten weeks of it "rather too much." From the start he was convinced that Russia had had not the slightest intention of reducing her armaments, or curtailing her building program. "*Neither does she intend to change her forward policy,*" Mahan reported to his friend Ashe; "nor do I think any other state differs from her." The First Lord of the British Admiralty told Mahan that he had offered to stop construction on two battleships, provided Russia did the same, but that Russia had ignored his proposal. Mahan concluded that Russia's real reason for calling the conference had been "the shock of our late war, resulting in the rapprochement of the U. S. and Great Britain and our sudden appearance in Asia, as the result of a successful war. . . . In peace," Mahan wrote,

"Russia's advance moves over the inert Asiatics like a steam-roller; but the prospect of America and England, side by side, demanding that China be left open for trade, means either a change in her policy, or war. Hence she wishes peace by pledge."[33]

On two occasions Mahan spoke out strongly in the conference. Once he rose to point out the logical inconsistency of prohibiting the use of poison gas while permitting the use of submarine torpedoes. The "sharp controversy" on this point between Mahan and the Russian delegates afforded reporters a welcome change from monotony. "A shell charged with asphyxiating gas need not necessarily destroy human life any more than chloroform," contended Mahan, "but might only place men *hors de combat* for a time; whereas a submarine boat, stealthily approaching under cover of darkness, might send a thousand sleeping men to a watery grave. Why forbid retail asphyxiation by air and permit wholesale asphyxiation by water?" A Russian delegate replied that men might be rescued at sea, and Mahan recalled that in the accidental sinking of H.M.S. *Victoria* many hundreds of men had been drowned, "so sudden was the catastrophe and so short the available time to pick up the men," although at the time "an immense fleet was close together and doing its utmost to save life."[34] Ambassador White, who felt unequal to arguing technical issues with Mahan ("What can a layman do when he has against him the foremost contemporary military and naval experts?") told Captain Mahan afterward, "in a bantering way . . . that while I could not favor any of the arguments that had been made in favor of asphyxiating bombs, there was one that somewhat appealed to me—namely, that the dread of them might . . . bring home to warlike stay-at-home orators and writers the realities of war."[35] Ambassador White, striving to maintain a united front among the members of the United States delegation and finding it almost impossible because Mahan "had very little, if any, sympathy with the main purposes of the Conference," conceded that Mahan's views were an excellent tonic to forestall sentimentality. "When he speaks the millennium fades and this stern, severe, actual world appears."[36]

The second time that Mahan, in White's phrase, "threw in a bomb," affords a sidelight on Mahan's intricate and devious habit of thought.[37]

It having become certain that the conference could accomplish nothing in the way of disarmament, a spontaneous movement developed to further the cause of arbitration as a peaceful means of settling

international disputes. A special committee had worked into the form
of a convention a plan for submitting disputes to a permanent court.
As Mahan read it, one clause in the convention confronted signatory
powers with an obligation to intervene with "good offices" in *every*
controversy that might arise between any of the signatory powers.
Mahan objected that this procedure would not only involve the United
States in Europe's domestic difficulties but would also involve Europe
in matters relating to our Monroe Doctrine. His opposition led the
American delegates to sign the convention only after the conference
had accepted a reservation that "nothing contained in this Convention
shall be so construed as to require the United States of America to
depart from its traditional policy of not intruding upon, interfering
with, or entangling itself in the political questions or policy or internal
administration of any foreign State; nor shall anything contained in the
said Convention be construed to imply a relinquishment by the United
States of America of its traditional attitude toward purely American
questions."[38] Mahan's objection to arbitration, as he stated to Ashe on
September 23, 1899, was "that arbitration should always be a nation's
first thought, but that it should never pledge itself, by treaty or otherwise, to arbitrate before it knows what the subject of dispute is. Needless to say, I have no sympathy with those who hold that war is never
imperative."[39] This he amplified in an article, "The Peace Conference
and the Moral Aspect of War," in the October 1899 issue of the *North
American Review*. "Power, force is a faculty of national life, one of
the talents committed by God. Like every other endowment of a complex organization, it must be held under control of the enlightened intellect and of the upright heart; but no more than any other can it be
carelessly or lightly abjured, without incurring the responsibility of
one who buries in the earth that which was intrusted to him to use.
And this obligation to maintain right, by force if need be, while common to all States, rests peculiarly upon the greater in proportion to
their means. Much is required of those to whom much is given." For
nations as for men, as Mahan saw it, conscience was important. There
are times when war is the "moral" course to pursue. The "undiscrim-
inating advocacy of Arbitration," in Mahan's opinion, "may lead men
to tamper with equity, to compromise with unrighteousness, soothing
their conscience with the belief that war is so entirely wrong that
beside it no other tolerated evil is wrong."[40]

After the conference had broken up, Mahan left The Hague on July

31 and arrived home in New York on August 19. Here he was way-laid by reporters. The meager story of his experiences abroad, which was the best the reporter for the *Tribune* could obtain from Mahan himself, was that he had visited various places in Europe and that con-siderable progress had been made at the conference! Mrs. Mahan, as always tactful and capable, interposed when the reporters pressed for further details. "Gentlemen," said she, "I think you might let me talk to the Captain a little while now. I have not seen him for five or six months, and——" The reporters bowed themselves away and Mahan was seen to cast a look of genuine gratitude upon his rescuer.[41]

Mahan, "the sailor student," was to the last modest and retiring. Never could he understand or sympathize with the desire of the news-reading public for information about himself as a public man. The mere idea of talking about himself "makes him tongue tied," wrote one reporter. "He cannot conceive of himself as an object of interest." Yet such was the case. To Charles de Kay, who was writing a series of articles on "Authors at Home" for the magazine *Critic*, Mahan, tem-porarily overcoming his "nervous horror" of the reporter, granted an interview which must have consisted chiefly of a look at the colonial front of the building and a very hasty glance at the hallway and little else inside of 160 West 86th Street. There was, de Kay reports, "noth-ing of the bluff old seadog about the man, and nothing of the seadog's haunt about his house." Order and a sort of Dutch cleanliness reigned. The dwelling suggested the college professor, literary man or artist, but not at all "a famous graduate of the Naval Academy." "The White Squadron is reflected in the color of the façade and the white wainscot-ing of hall and library. One of the most pleasant impressions aboard a man-of-war is that of feeling that everything from rigging to engine room must have been hosed down, scrubbed, scraped and painted just so many times a week. That is the impression one gets from Capt. Mahan's home." As a writer, Mahan was depicted as "a methodical worker who leaves as little as possible to chance. . . . To him a new book is like a naval battle; by far the greater part of it consists of com-plete preparation." As to subject matter, "He writes not only from the sailor's point of view, but from that of . . . the Anglo-American. . . . When nations are reaching out to seize on what is left of the globe un-appropriated, they are glad of arguments that offer a justification for their action. . . ."[42]

Mahan found old age to be "a quiet enough evening tide," with plenty of congenial work, even though it had not quite "the abundance of interest it once had." Thanks to emergency legislation passed in 1898, authorizing the employment of retired officers in peacetime, Mahan was assured of active duty as lecturer at the Naval War College until the expiration of the law in 1912. Throughout this period he gave his lectures and continued steadily with his writing. His last major historical study, *The War of 1812*, was about a period of history not so congenial to him as the eras covered in his earlier studies of British sea power. "It is a very old story, often told, and not a brilliant episode, nor one of which, as a whole, the United States can feel proud."[43] Yet in some respects this work marked an advance over his earlier studies. Elected president of the American Historical Association in 1902, he became progressively more thorough in his research, relying less upon secondary materials and delving more into original sources. Always patient and industrious, he came in later life to consider work itself as more valuable than its product. He undertook to write for *Harper's Magazine* a series of autobiographical articles based upon his own career.

This project, begun as a potboiler, soon awakened his interest, and he produced in *From Sail to Steam* one of the most readable and informative memoirs in American naval literature. His interest in religion deepened as he grew older; he put aside revision of his *Naval Strategy* until after he had completed *The Harvest Within*, which he described as "thoughts on religious subjects . . . which I have imagined fit for modern 'difficulties.' "[44]

The Harvest Within, since it to some extent expresses Mahan's spiritual goals, explains much about the character of its rigidly introspective author. "The poor are not only those who have little money. They are also the poor in native good dispositions, whose hearts know their own bitterness; who fain would in temper, in love, joy, peace, long-suffering, gentleness, meekness, self-control, give to Christ abundantly, if only they could; who from the poverty of a weak or an arid or a perverse nature, can give only the rare cup of cold water, wring the few mites of kindly impulse, realize here and there something of love, not in bare act, which is cheap, but in that steady burning purpose which is life and light."[45] In this stern self-searcher we may identify the cadet who for his rigid adherence to ideals had been put into Coventry by his classmates, and we may see the mature naval officer with a mission, whose dogged persistence enabled the Naval War College to survive exasperating and determined opposition both from Congress and from the service itself.

One might expect the philosopher of naval empire and the former mentor of Theodore Roosevelt to become a power behind the throne during Roosevelt's terms as President. Mahan and Roosevelt continued to correspond with each other. Although their letters were fewer than when Roosevelt was Assistant Secretary, the President had long since adopted Mahan's principles as his own policies. The most important of these were the building up of the battleship fleet, the concentrating of that fleet rather than dividing it between two oceans, the importance of the Isthmian Canal and the fortifying of the canal. Roosevelt on occasion appointed Mahan to membership on various naval boards, and Mahan's magazine articles gave staunch support to Roosevelt in upholding the "Open Door" in China and in sending the United States fleet around the world.

Once, the aging mentor, on the basis of an inaccurate news story that Roosevelt intended to split the fleet by sending four battleships to the West Coast, protested "with dismay," and incurred a royal rebuke.[46] Wrote the momentarily offended Roosevelt: "Don't you know me well enough to believe that I am quite incapable of such utter folly as dividing our fighting fleet? I have no more thought of sending four battleships to the Pacific while there is the least possible friction with Japan than I have of going thither in a rowboat myself. On the contrary, if there should come the most remote danger of war I should at once withdraw every fighting craft from the Pacific until our whole Navy could be gathered and sent there in a body."[47] Mahan was by no means blind to Roosevelt's faults. Concerned over the extraordinary rapidity with which the mercurial President shifted his naval secretaries, Mahan wrote Luce in January of 1908: "The President, confident in his knowledge of naval matters and of his profound interest in the service, has made the grave mistake, since Moody, of filling the Secretary's chair with figureheads, expecting to run the machine himself. Necessary result, hastey [sic!] and mistaken decisions [;] for the Navy is now so big a thing as to demand the sole attention of a first class man for a full official term. No man can run it and the Presidency together."[48]

On December 30, 1906, Mahan was elevated to the rank of rear admiral on the retired list. It was a singular recognition—coming ten years after his retirement from active duty—although he had in spite of retirement continued on active duty as lecturer at the Naval War College.

Following a serious operation in the fall of 1907, Admiral Mahan was a restless but housebound invalid for six months. To Luce he wrote, "I have had a dead beat, head wind, and lee tide. I think a few more tacks will fetch, but don't expect full restoration until spring gives good weather."[49] Under a slower regimen, with a great deal of lying on a couch reading novels and with slowing down in his walking and bicycling, his health improved. He spent much time sunning himself on the beach and surf bathing near his new summer home, Slumberside, at Quogue, Long Island.

In the fall of 1908 he delivered the main address at the unveiling of the memorial window to Admiral William T. Sampson in the magnificent new chapel of the United States Naval Academy. At the close of the ceremony he had the pleasure of meeting Midshipman George Bamford Ashe, the son of his former roommate Samuel A'Court Ashe. The son's resemblance to the elder Ashe carried Admiral Mahan back half a century in time and brought back a rush of happy memories of his lifelong friend. The experience probably recalled those strangely irreverent days when he had himself sat in an older, less pretentious Naval Academy Chapel and had made fun of Chaplain George Jones's rhetoric.

After 1908 Mahan reduced his work load to summer lectures only, and this lasted until June 6, 1912, upon which date the law authorizing retention of retired officers on active status expired. Five days later, on June 11, he celebrated with Ellen Evans Mahan the fortieth anniversary of their marriage.

In the fall of 1914, after several months of correspondence with Dr. J. F. Jameson of the Carnegie Institution, Admiral Mahan at age seventy-four agreed to leave his home in New York and come to Washington as Research Assistant in the Institution. It had been hard to refuse an invitation from Dr. Jameson, whom Mahan had known since 1902 when Mahan became president of the American Historical Association. Mahan was to control his own working hours and to do research looking toward a history of the United States stressing her expansion; but chiefly, Dr. Jameson had made clear, it was Mahan's presence which

UNCLE SAM: "I'll just frame this."—From the *Evening Post* (Denver).

From the Denver Evening Post, May 26, 1898

"I'll Just Frame This."

the Pacific, almost with the importance   and from 25 to 130 miles wide. With its a:

OUR COMING EMPIRE.

	Area. Square Miles.	Population.
Hawaii	7,029	90,000
Philippines	150,000	17,000
Ladrones	450	10,000
Navassa	8	500
Samoa	1,701	34,000
Alaska	570,000	31,795
Cuba	43,319	1,500,000
Porto Rico	3,530	900,000
Carolines	580	40,000
Howland and Baker Islands	1	Uninhabited.
Marquis of Weeks Island	3	50
TOTALS, FOREIGN TERRITORY	777,221	2,623,345
TOTALS, UNITED STATES	3,025,600	75,000,000
THE AMERICAN EMPIRE	3,802,821	77,623,345

Courtesy Commander R. E. Sampson

Our Coming Empire.

Courtesy Rear Admiral W. T. Cluverius

"Well, Who'll Be Next?"

BE IT PEACE OR WAR, UNCLE SAM WILL BE WELL REPRESENTED AT THE HAGUE.—From the *Journal* (Minneapolis).

Reprinted in The American Monthly Review of Reviews, May, 1899

Be It Peace or War, Uncle Sam Will Be Well Represented at the Hague. (A. T. Mahan, second from left.)

was desired as an inspiration to the younger members of the staff. Jameson wished in informal meetings to discuss with Mahan "the nature and uses of the sources of naval history, the genesis of each of your larger historical books, and your present thoughts respecting them, the naval conduct of the Civil War, the Strategy of the War of 1898, the modern development of naval warfare, your thoughts and criticisms upon the various modern historians, and the like."[50] Such a feast of the intellect between congenial spirits all working toward a common goal—precisely the sort of ideal atmosphere that Mahan in his rosiest dreams had projected for the War College—was not to be declined.

Dr. Jameson found a suitable house for the Mahans and their four servants, on Hillyer Place, convenient to a trolley line.[51] Mrs. Mahan, as usual, went ahead to prepare the house, and the admiral followed her on November 1. He rejoiced in his new home; and at the Carnegie Institution, as Dr. Jameson has written, "He charmed us all by his kindness and by the courtesy he showed even to the youngest of the young women in the office."[52]

But Alfred Mahan was ill. On November 22 he attended his last church service and joined in the singing. The excitement of his new project, together with the energy he expended to keep abreast of events in World War I had brought on heart attacks. He entered the naval hospital on the twenty-eighth, and on December 1, 1914, he died. His remains were taken to his home at Quogue, Long Island, where he was buried, according to his request, with no military display, but only the simplest religious ceremony.

ACKNOWLEDGMENTS, NOTES
AND INDEX

ACKNOWLEDGMENTS

To DESCENDANTS and relatives of Admiral Sampson and Admiral Schley the author is indebted for the loan of family papers, scrapbooks and pictures. Commander Ralph E. Sampson, U. S. Navy (Ret.), lent a trunkful of papers, including several of his father's family letters and his mother's diary and scrapbooks. These are cited in the footnotes as "R. E. Sampson Collection." Rear Admiral Wat Tyler Cluverius made available two scrapbooks of news clippings of 1898. Mrs. E. R. Sawtelle lent a fine collection of the journals, pressed-letter books and letters of her grandfather, Admiral Schley; these papers, which she has presented to the Naval Academy Library and the Naval Academy museum, are referred to in the footnotes as "Sawtelle Collection."

The staffs of the Naval Academy Library, the Library of Congress, the Naval Records and Library, the New York Public Library and the National Archives have rendered cheerful assistance. Especially is the author grateful to Mr. Louis Bolander, Librarian of the Naval Academy; Captain John B. Heffernan, Director of Naval History; Lieutenant Commander M. V. Brewington, U.S.N.R., of Naval Records and Library; Commodore Dudley W. Knox, U. S. Navy (Ret.), formerly of Naval Records and Library; Mr. Robert W. Hill, Keeper of Manuscripts, the New York Public Library; Mr. P. M. Hamer, Director of Reference Service, The National Archives; and to Dr. St. George L. Sioussat of the Division of Manuscripts, Library of Congress. Captain H. A. Baldridge, Curator of the Naval Academy Museum, made available a number of photographs.

The following libraries have supplied microfilm or transcripts of materials in their possession: The New York Public Library, The New York Historical Society, Harvard College Library, Duke University Library, the Henry E. Huntington Library and Art Gallery, and the King's Daughters' Free Public Library of Palmyra, N. Y.

For critical assistance in matters of style and organization the author acknowledges a special debt to Mr. Victor F. White of Taos, New Mexico, and to Mr. David Laurance Chambers of The Bobbs-Merrill Company, Indianapolis.

Among the many individuals who aided in the search for materials the following must be mentioned: Mrs. John Hartsook, Annapolis, Md.; Mr. Jeter A. Isely, Princeton, N. J.; Mrs. Richard Wainwright, Annapolis, Md.; Mrs. S. T. Ziegler, Palmyra, N. Y.; Captain W. D. Puleston, U. S. Navy (Ret.), Washington, D. C.; Captain G. H. Wood, U. S. Navy, Bethesda, Md.; Judge E. S. Delaplaine, Frederick, Md.; and Mr. John C. Long of Bethlehem Steel Company, Bethlehem, Pa.

For their kind permission to use on the page following the title page the quotation from Admiral Barker's *Everyday Life in the Navy*, the author is indebted to Bruce Humphries, Inc. of Boston.

In each phase of the book's preparation my wife, Marie McElreath West, skillfully tempered criticism with encouragement and rendered most essential help.

NOTES

1. FOUR NAVAL CADETS

[1] For Dewey's early life, see *Autobiography of George Dewey*, Charles Scribner's Sons, New York, 1913; Murat Halstead, *The Life and Achievements of Admiral Dewey*, Our Possessions Publishing Co., Chicago, 1899, copyrighted by H. L. Barber; Adelbert M. Dewey, *The Life and Letters of Admiral Dewey*, The Woolfall Company, New York, 1899; Laurin Hall Healy and Luis Kutner, *The Admiral*, Ziff-Davis Publishing Company, New York, 1944; Joseph L. Stickney, *Life and Glorious Deeds of Admiral Dewey*, Monarch Book Company, Chicago, 1899.

[2] For the Naval Academy before the Civil War, see Park Benjamin, *The United States Naval Academy*, G. P. Putnam's Sons, New York, 1900, Chapter XIV.

[3] Records, Superintendent's Office, U. S. Naval Academy.

[4] Letter from S. H. Chauvenet to Julian P. Boyd, January 17, 1936, Library, U. S. Naval Academy.

[5] Dewey, *Autobiography*, p. 18.

[6] For Mahan's early life, see Captain W. D. Puleston, U.S.N., *Mahan: The Life and Work of Captain Alfred Thayer Mahan*, Yale University Press, New Haven, 1939; Captain A. T. Mahan, *From Sail to Steam, Recollections of Naval Life*, Harper & Brothers Publishers, New York, 1907.

[7] R. P. Chiles (Ed.), *Letters of Alfred Thayer Mahan to Samuel A'Court Ashe* (1858-59), Duke University Library Bulletin Number 4, Durham, N. C., July, 1931.

[8] Puleston, *Mahan*, p. 23.

[9] Chiles, *Letters of Mahan*, p. 51.

[10] Winfield Scott Schley, Rear Admiral, U.S.N., *Forty-Five Years under the Flag*, D. Appleton and Company, New York, 1904, p. 1.

[11] *Ibid.*, p. 4.

[12] *Ibid.*

[13] Chiles, *Letters of Mahan*, pp. 47-48.

[14] Schley, *Forty-Five Years*, pp. 6 and 8.

[15] *Ibid.*, p. 9.

[16] Chiles, *Letters of Mahan*, p. 79.

[17] S. P. Butler, "Sampson As A Boy," *The Mail and Express Illustrated Saturday Magazine*, New York, May 28, 1898, p. 5.

[18] A. T. Mahan, "Rear Admiral William T. Sampson," *Fortnightly Review*, July 1902 (Copyright by the S. S. McClure Co., 1902), p. 232.

[19] *Ibid.*

[20] *Ibid.*

[21] Charles E. Clark, *My Fifty Years in the Navy*, Little, Brown and Company, Boston, 1917, pp. 24-25.

[22] Benjamin, *Naval Academy*, p. 228.

2. DEWEY IN ACTION

[1] A. M. Dewey, *Life of Dewey*, p. 159.
[2] Dewey, *Autobiography*, p. 35.
[3] *Ibid.*, p. 46.
[4] *Ibid.*, p. 51.
[5] *Ibid.*, p. 55.
[6] *Ibid.*, p. 61.
[7] *Ibid.*, p. 65.
[8] *Ibid.*, p. 69.
[9] *Official Records ... Navies*, Series I, Vol. 18, p. 206.
[10] Dewey, *Autobiography*, p. 82.
[11] *Official Records ... Navies*, Series I, Vol. 19, p. 680.
[12] *Dewey, Autobiography*, pp. 92-93.
[13] *Ibid.*, p. 96.
[14] *Ibid.*, pp. 99, 100.
[15] *Ibid.*, p. 103.
[16] *Official Records ... Navies*, Series I, Vol. 19, p. 681.
[17] Dewey, *Autobiography*, p. 110.
[18] *Official Records ... Navies*, Series I, Vol. 20, p. 334.
[19] *Ibid.*, p. 339.
[20] Dewey, *Autobiography*, p. 120.
[21] *Ibid.*, p. 123.
[22] *Ibid.*, p. 126.
[23] *Ibid.*, p. 132.
[24] *Official Records ... Navies*, Series I, Vol. 11, p. 294.

3. THE INFLUENCE OF WAR ON MAHAN

[1] Mahan, *From Sail to Steam*, p. 112.
[2] *Ibid.*, pp. 114-115.
[3] *Ibid.*, pp. 133, 121-122.
[4] *Official Records ... Navies*, Series I, Vol. 1, pp. 87-88.
[5] *Naval Letters of Captain Percival Drayton*, 1861-1865, New York Public Library, New York, 1906, p. 6.
[6] Mahan, *From Sail to Steam*, p. 164.
[7] *Ibid.*
[8] Mahan to Ashe, Jan. 17 and March 6, 1870. Flowers Collection; and Puleston, *Mahan*, p, 35.
[9] Mahan, *From Sail to Steam*, pp. 174-175, 188.
[10] *Ibid.*, p. 192.

4. SCHLEY TRIES "THIS NELSON BUSINESS"

[1] Schley, *Forty-Five Years*, p. 12.
[2] *Ibid.*, p. 17.
[3] *Ibid.*, pp. 21-22.
[4] *Official Records ... Navies*, Series I, Vol. 5, p. 629.

5 Chiles, *Letters of Mahan*, p. 88.
6 *Official Records . . . Navies*, Series I, Vol. 17, p. 16.
7 *Ibid.*
8 *Ibid.*, p. 61.
9 Schley, *Forty-Five Years*, p. 35.
10 *Official Records . . . Navies*, Series I, Vol. 19, p. 390.
11 Schley, *Forty-Five Years*, p. 40.
12 *Official Records . . . Navies*, Series I, Vol. 20, p. 794.
13 Schley, *Forty-Five Years*, pp. 45-46.
14 C. S. Clark, "Some American Admirals and a Few Other Sailors," *United Service Magazine*, Vol. 17, p. 597.

5. SAMPSON AFLOAT AND ASHORE

1 The record of Sampson's first assignments is detailed in a letter to the author from Captain Dudley W. Knox, of Naval Records and Library, dated April 12, 1944.
2 Schley, *Forty-Five Years*, p. 27.
3 A file of articles from local newspapers about Sampson's early life is in the Palmyra King's Daughters' Free Public Library, Palmyra, N. Y. News scrapbooks in the R. E. Sampson Collection have also been used.
4 Mahan, *From Sail to Steam*, p. 186.
5 Benjamin, *Naval Academy*, pp. 247-248.
6 *U. S. Naval Academy Register* for 1862-63 and 1863-64.
7 *Official Records . . . Navies*, Series I, Vol. 16, p. 177.
8 *Ibid.*, p. 176.
9 A. T. Mahan, "Rear Admiral William T. Sampson," *Fortnightly Review*, July 1902, p. 236.

6. GENTLEMAN GEORGE DEWEY

1 Healy and Kutner, *The Admiral*, p. 88.
2 W. M. Clemens, *Life of Admiral George Dewey*, Street & Smith, New York, 1899, p. 65.
3 Alexander Dennett to commandant, Kittery Navy Yard, April 11, 1864, George Dewey Collection, New York Public Library.
4 *Army and Navy Journal*, Vol. 37, p. 90.
5 Log of *Kearsarge*, 1865-66, National Archives.
6 Quoted in Clemens, *Life of Dewey*, p. 62.
7 Arthur Strawn, "The Rise and Fall of a Hero," *American Mercury*, November 1928, p. 347.
8 Clemens, *Life of Dewey*, p. 63.
9 *Ibid.*, p. 66.
10 Richard S. West, Jr., *The Second Admiral, A Life of David Dixon Porter, 1813-1891*, Coward-McCann, 1937, Chapter 29.
11 Dewey, *Autobiography*, p. 142.
12 *Army and Navy Journal*, Vol. 6, p. 65.
13 *Ibid.*, Vol. 10, p. 366.
14 *Ibid.*, Vol. 22, p. 1015.

[15] *Ibid.*, p. 317.

[16] *Ibid.*, Vol. 9, p. 557.

[17] Dewey, *Autobiography,* p. 146.

[18] *Ibid.*, p. 145.

[19] Dewey's rescue of Brook is told by Lieutenant F. Winslow, U.S.N. (Ret.), in *New York Tribune,* June 16, 1899. See also Dewey, *Autobiography,* pp. 146-149.

[20] A. B. Johnson, *The Modern Light-House Service,* G. P. O., Washington, D. C., 1889, pp. 108-118.

[21] *New York Tribune,* September 20, 1899.

[22] Dewey, *Autobiography,* p. 151.

[23] Clark, "Some American Admirals and a Few Other Sailors," p. 595.

[24] Dewey, *Autobiography,* p. 155.

[25] A. M. Dewey, *Life of Dewey,* pp. 187-188.

[26] "Journal of Rear Admiral S. R. Franklin," New York Public Library, entry for November 3, 1885.

[27] *Ibid.*, January 9, 1886.

[28] Quoted from *Saturday Evening Post* in *Army and Navy Journal,* Vol. 39, p. 71.

[29] Dewey, *Autobiography,* p. 158 and 159.

7. MAHAN TURNS NAVAL PHILOSOPHER

[1] Mahan to Ashe, February 1, 1903, Flowers Collection.

[2] *Army and Navy Journal,* Vol. 4, p. 63.

[3] Mahan to Ashe, n. d., *circa.* 1867, Flowers Collection.

[4] Mahan, *From Sail to Steam,* p. 211.

[5] *Ibid.*, pp. 220-221.

[6] *Army and Navy Journal,* Vol. 5, p. 489.

[7] Mahan to Ashe, August 12, 1868 and October 10, 1868. Flowers Collection.

[8] *Ibid.*, September 21, [1869].

[9] *Ibid.*

[10] *Ibid.*, January 17, 1870.

[11] *Ibid.*

[12] *Ibid.*, July 6, 1870.

[13] *Ibid.*

[14] *Ibid.*, April 25, 1871.

[15] *Ibid.*

[16] Quoted in Puleston, *Mahan,* p. 50.

[17] *Army and Navy Journal,* Vol. 9, p. 109.

[18] Mahan to Ashe, March 28, 1876. Flowers Collection.

[19] *Ibid.*, September 30, 1870.

[20] A. T. Mahan, "The Practical in Christianity," an address delivered in the Church of the Holy Trinity, Middletown, Conn., Wednesday, March 22, 1899. Printed at the end of *The Harvest Within.*

[21] A. T. Mahan, *The Harvest Within: Thoughts on the Life of the Christian.* Little, Brown and Company, Boston, 1909, p. 208.

[22] Puleston, *Mahan,* p. 53.

[23] Mahan to Ashe, May 21, 1875. Flowers Collection.

[24] *Ibid.*, Dec. 27, 1875.

[25] *Ibid.*
[26] *Ibid.*, January 27, 1876.
[27] *Ibid.*, March 27, 1876.
[28] *Ibid.*, October 21, 1877.
[29] *Ibid.*, December 2, 1877.
[30] *Ibid.*, May 9, 1879.
[31] *Ibid.*, March 12, 1880.
[32] *Ibid.*, December 21, 1882.
[33] *Ibid.*, July 6, 1883.
[34] *Ibid.*, August 14, 1883.
[35] *Ibid.*, July 26, 1884.
[36] Mahan, *From Sail to Steam*, p. 197.
[37] Mahan to Ashe, July 26, 1884. Flowers Collection.
[38] Log of *Wachusett*, 1883-85, National Archives.
[39] From *Yarns of a Kentucky Admiral*, pp. 30-31, by Hugh Rodman, copyright 1928. Used by special permission of the publishers, The Bobbs-Merrill Company.
[40] Mahan to Ashe, March 11, 1885, Flowers Collection.
[41] Mahan, *From Sail to Steam*, p. 274.
[42] *Army and Navy Journal*, Vol. 22, p. 168.
[43] Mahan, *From Sail to Steam*, p. 277.
[44] A. T. Mahan, "Naval Education," U. S. Naval Institute *Proceedings,* 1879, p. 375.
[45] *Ibid.*, p. 351.
[46] *Ibid.*, p. 349.
[47] From address by Captain A. T. Mahan, President of U. S. Naval War College, August 6, 1888, U. S. Naval Institute *Proceedings*, Vol. XIV, No. 4, whole number 47, 1888, p. 628.
[48] *Army and Navy Journal*, Vol. 22, p. 444.
[49] Mahan, *From Sail to Steam*, p. 275.
[50] Puleston, *Mahan*, p. 83.
[51] Mahan, *From Sail to Steam*, p. 297.
[52] Mahan to Ashe, August 10, 1888, Flowers Collection.

8. SCHLEY'S TOWERING FAME

[1] *Army and Navy Journal*, Vol. 22, p. 39.
[2] *New York Tribune,* December 18, 1898.
[3] *Army and Navy Journal*, Vol. 8, p. 506.
[4] *Ibid.*, p. 72.
[5] Schley, *Forty-Five Years*, Chapter IX, "Opening Communications with Korea, 1871."
[6] *Army and Navy Journal*, Vol. 8, p. 782.
[7] Accounts of the Korean Expedition may be found in Seaton Schroeder, *A Half Century of Naval Service,* D. Appleton and Company, New York, 1922, pp. 29-59; *Army and Navy Journal*, Vol. 9, pp. 37-38; *Harper's Weekly*, August 1894.
[8] Schley, *Forty-Five Years*, p. 92.
[9] *Ibid.*, p. 93.
[10] *Army and Navy Journal*, Vol. 9, p. 783.
[11] Schley, *Forty-Five Years*, p. 110.

[12] *Ibid.*, p. 112.
[13] *Ibid.*, p. 114.
[14] Schley to Nichols, December 22, 1878. *Essex* Miscellaneous Letters. Sawtelle Collection.
[15] Schley, *Forty-Five Years*, p. 129.
[16] *Ibid.*, p. 112.
[17] *Ibid.*, p. 135.
[18] *Ibid.*, p. 145.
[19] L. B. Richardson, *William E. Chandler, Republican,* Dodd, Meade & Company, New York, 1940, p. 329.
[20] *Report of Winfield S. Schley, Commander U. S. Navy, Commanding Greely Relief Expedition of 1884,* G. P. O., Washington, D. C., 1887.
[21] *Army and Navy Journal,* Vol. 21, p. 778.
[22] Schley, *Forty-Five Years*, p. 154. Also useful for Greely Relief Expedition is the extensive news-clipping scrapbook in the Sawtelle Collection.
[23] Log of *Thetis* for June 22, 1884. National Archives.
[24] A. W. Greely, *Three Years of Arctic Service*, Scribner's, New York, 1886, Vol. 2, p. 331.
[25] *Army and Navy Journal,* Vol. 22, p. 49.
[26] Schley, *Forty-Five Years*, pp. 178-179.
[27] *Army and Navy Journal,* Vol. 22, p. 9.
[28] *New York Tribune,* August 16, 1884.
[29] Clark, "Some American Admirals and a Few Other Sailors," p. 597.
[30] *Ibid.*

9. SAMPSON WHETS NEW WEAPONS

[1] C. F. Goodrich, *Rope Yarns From The Old Navy*, Naval History Society, New York, 1931, p. 23.
[2] *Annual Report, Secretary of the Navy*, 1878, p. 62.
[3] "European Squadron, Charles S. Boggs," p. 68. National Archives.
[4] *Annual Report, Secretary of the Navy*, 1877, p. 63.
[5] *Ibid.*
[6] *Army and Navy Journal,* Vol. 12, p. 298.
[7] *Annual Report, Secretary of the Navy*, 1877, pp. 56-58.
[8] *World's Work,* November, 1901, p. 1421.
[9] R. A. Millikan, "Biographical Memoir of Albert Abraham Michelson, 1852-1931," National Academy of Sciences, Washington, 1938, pp. 121-147.
[10] A. A. Michelson, "Experimental Determination of the Velocity of Light," *Proceedings* of American Academy for the Advancement of Science, 1879, pp. 124-160.
[11] Quoted in Millikan, "Biographical Memoir of Michelson."
[12] *Army and Navy Journal,* Vol. 15, p. 739.
[13] Letter to author from Mrs. Sarah T. Ziegler, April 21, 1944.
[14] Diary of Mrs. W. T. Sampson. R. E. Sampson Collection.
[15] G. A. Weber, *The Naval Observatory: Its History, Activities, and Organization,* Johns Hopkins Press, Baltimore, 1926, p. 39.
[16] Diary of Mrs. W. T. Sampson. R. E. Sampson Collection.
[17] Weber, *The Naval Observatory*, p. 34.

[18] *Army and Navy Journal,* Vol. 22, p. 201.
[19] *Ibid.,* Vol. 21, p. 1013.
[20] *Ibid.,* Vol. 13, p. 321.
[21] *Ibid.,* Vol. 23, p. 321.
[22] *Ibid.,* p. 1037.
[23] R. S. West, Jr., "The Superintendents of the Naval Academy," U. S. Naval Institute *Proceedings,* July 1945, pp. 804-805.
[24] Annual Reports, Superintendent, U. S. Naval Academy, 1886-1889.
[25] R. E. Sampson Collection.
[26] Diary of Mrs. W. T. Sampson, R. E. Sampson Collection.

10. DEWEY TO THE ASIATIC

[1] Quoted in P. T. Moon, *Imperialism and World Politics,* The Macmillan Company, New York, 1933, p. 38.
[2] Quoted in Moon, p. 66.
[3] Quoted in *Army and Navy Journal,* Vol. 28, p. 762.
[4] Murat Halstead, *Life and Achievements of Admiral Dewey,* pp. 160-161.
[5] *Army and Navy Journal,* Vol. 37, p. 127.
[6] Dewey, *Autobiography,* p. 164.
[7] Theodore Roosevelt, *Autobiography,* Scribner's, New York, 1929, pp. 210-213.
[8] M. A. Hamm, *Dewey the Defender,* F. Tennyson Neely Co., New York, 1899, p. 110.
[9] *Army and Navy Journal,* Vol. 30, pp. 52, 312 and 204.
[10] J. Barrett, *Admiral George Dewey, A Sketch of the Man,* Harper & Bros., New York, 1899, pp. 13-14.
[11] Dewey, *Autobiography,* p. 165.
[12] *Ibid.,* pp. 165-166.
[13] *Army and Navy Journal,* Vol. 36, p. 705.
[14] *Ibid.*
[15] J. L. Stickney, *War in the Philippines and Life and Glorious Deeds of Admiral Dewey,* Monarch Book Company, Chicago, 1899, p. 156.
[16] *Army and Navy Journal,* Vol. 36, p. 267.
[17] Halstead, *Achievements of Dewey,* p. 396.
[18] A. M. Dewey, *The Life of Dewey,* p. 410.
[19] Halstead, *Achievements of Dewey,* p. 395.
[20] Dewey, *Autobiography,* p. 167.
[21] *Army and Navy Journal,* Vol. 37, p. 124.
[22] Dewey, *Autobiography,* pp. 168-169.
[23] A. M. Dewey, *Life of Dewey,* p. 411.
[24] Dewey, *Autobiography,* p. 173.
[25] Stickney, *War in the Philippines,* pp. 158-159.

11. MENTOR TO IMPERIALISTS

[1] Mahan to Luce, September 3, 1901. Unless otherwise stated, all of Mahan's letters to Luce are from the Naval Historical Foundation.
[2] A. T. Mahan, *The Influence of Sea Power upon History, 1660-1783,* Little, Brown and Company, Boston, 1890. Cited hereafter as Mahan, *Influence of Sea Power.*

[3] Roosevelt to Mahan, May 12, 1890. Mahan Papers, Library of Congress.

[4] Mahan to Luce, May 7, 1890.

[5] Mahan, *Influence of Sea Power*, p. 88. Quoted in *Army and Navy Journal*, Vol. 27, p. 742.

[6] Article reprinted in A. T. Mahan, *The Interest of America in Sea Power, Present and Future*, Little, Brown and Company, Boston, 1897. Quotations are from pages 4, 8 and 12.

[7] Mahan to Luce, September 3, 1901.

[8] A. T. Mahan, "The Practical Character of the Naval War College," delivered at the opening of the annual session, September 6, 1892. U. S. Naval Institute *Proceedings*, Vol. XIX, No. 2, 1893, Whole No. 66, p. 157.

[9] Quoted in *Army and Navy Journal*, Vol. 32, p. 157.

[10] Quoted in *Army and Navy Journal*, Vol. 30, p. 633.

[11] *Army and Navy Journal*, Vol. 30, p. 532.

[12] Mahan to Ashe, November 24, 1893. Flowers Collection.

[13] Obituary editorial in *New York Sun*, quoted in *Army and Navy Journal*, October 30, 1909, p. 232.

[14] Roosevelt to Mahan, May 1, 1893. Mahan Papers, Library of Congress. The portion of the quotation, "who is bitterly . . . that Lodge does," has been stricken out lightly in the original.

[15] C. C. Taylor, *The Life of Admiral Mahan: Naval Philosopher*, George H. Doran Company, New York, and John Murray, London, 1920, p. 60.

[16] Mahan to Ashe, November 24, 1893. Flowers Collection.

[17] Captain J. M. Ellicott, "Three Navy Cranks and What They Turned," U. S. Naval Institute *Proceedings*, October, 1924, p. 1623.

[18] Captain J. M. Ellicott, "With Erben and Mahan on the *Chicago*," U. S. Naval Institute *Proceedings*, September, 1941, p. 1236.

[19] *Ibid.*

[20] *Ibid.*

[21] Puleston, *Mahan*, p. 151.

[22] *Army and Navy Journal*, October 30, 1909, p. 229.

[23] Puleston, *Mahan*, pp. 141-142.

[24] Erben's out-going correspondence for November 15, 19 and 24, 1893. National Archives.

[25] Puleston, *Mahan*, p. 151.

[26] *Ibid.*, p. 149.

[27] *New York Tribune*, May 11, 1894.

[28] *Ibid.*, May 25, 1894.

[29] Taylor, *Mahan*, p. 65.

[30] Quoted in *Army and Navy Journal*, Vol. 31, p. 742.

[31] *New York Tribune*, June 10, 1894.

[32] *Army and Navy Journal*, Vol. 31, p. 731.

[33] Taylor, *Mahan*, p. 130, gives photograph of telegram.

[34] *Ibid.*, p. 131.

[35] Puleston, *Mahan*, p. 107.

[36] Taylor, *Mahan*, p. 128.

[37] Mahan, *From Sail to Steam*, p. 316.

[38] Ellicott, "With Erben and Mahan on the *Chicago*," p. 1240.

[39] Ellicott, "Three Navy Cranks and What They Turned," p. 1625.

[40] Mahan's endorsement, July 9, 1894, Letter Book *Chicago*, National Archives.

[41] Erben's endorsement, July 11, 1894, Letter Book, *Chicago,* National Archives.

[42] Ellicott, "Three Navy Cranks and What They Turned," p. 1625.

[43] Log of *Chicago,* July 11, 1894, National Archives.

[44] Ellicott, "With Erben and Mahan on the *Chicago,"* p. 1240.

[45] *Army and Navy Journal,* Vol. 32, p. 503.

[46] Puleston, *Mahan,* p. 167.

[47] Quoted in *Army and Navy Journal,* Vol. 31, p. 824.

[48] Mahan to Ashe, November 7, 1896, Flowers Collection.

[49] *Ibid.*

[50] A. T. Mahan, "Hawaii and Our Future Sea Power," *Forum,* March, 1893, reprinted in *The Interest of America in Sea Power, Present and Future,* p. 50.

[51] *Ibid.,* p. 51.

[52] A. T. Mahan, "Possibilities of An Anglo-American Reunion," *North American Review,* November 1894, reprinted in *The Interest of America in Sea Power, Present and Future,* p. 121.

[53] A. T. Mahan, "A Twentieth-Century Outlook," *Harper's New Monthly Magazine,* September 1897, reprinted in *The Interest of America in Sea Power, Present and Future,* pp. 225 and 246.

[54] *Army and Navy Journal,* Vol. 35, p. 463.

[55] Quoted in H. F. Pringle, *Theodore Roosevelt, A Biography,* Harcourt, Brace and Company, New York, 1931, p. 173.

[56] Taylor, *Mahan,* p. 84.

[57] *Army and Navy Journal,* Vol. 34, p. 816.

[58] *Ibid.,* Vol. 35, p. 54.

12. SCHLEY TO THE FLYING SQUADRON

[1] *Army and Navy Journal,* Vol. 29, p. 408.

[2] *Ibid.,* Vol. 27, p. 721.

[3] *Ibid.*

[4] Letter to author from Mrs. E. R. Sawtelle, May 3, 1944.

[5] *Army and Navy Journal,* Vol. 28, p. 8.

[6] *Ibid.,* p. 107.

[7] Schley, *Forty-Five Years,* p. 203.

[8] *Ibid.,* p. 205.

[9] *Ibid.,* p. 210.

[10] *Ibid.,* p. 215.

[11] *Army and Navy Journal,* Vol. 29, p. 74.

[12] Schley, *Forty-Five Years,* pp. 222-223.

[13] *Foreign Relations,* 1891, pp. 206-207.

[14] *Ibid.,* p. 215.

[15] Robley D. Evans, *A Sailor's Log, Recollections of Forty Years of Naval Life,* D. Appleton-Century Company, New York, 1901, pp. 259-260.

[16] Schley, *Forty-Five Years,* p. 236.

[17] *Annual Report, Secretary of the Navy,* 1891, p. 30.

[18] *Army and Navy Journal,* Vol. 30, p. 814.

[19] "History and Rear Admiral Schley," *Independent,* July 25, 1901.

13. SAMPSON TO THE BLOCKADE

[1] *New York Tribune,* August 28, 1890.

[2] Diary of Mrs. W. T. Sampson, R. E. Sampson Collection.

[3] *New York Tribune,* September 1, 1890.

[4] *Army and Navy Journal,* Vol. 28, p. 274.

[5] *Ibid.,* p. 409.

[6] *Ibid.,* Vol. 29, p. 308.

[7] *Annual Report, Secretary of the Navy,* 1891, p. 35.

[8] *Army and Navy Journal,* Vol. 29, p. 590.

[9] *Ibid.,* p. 660.

[10] New York, *The Mail and Express,* May 18, 1898.

[11] *Army and Navy Journal,* Vol. 29, p. 684.

[12] Log of *San Francisco,* National Archives.

[13] Rochester, N. Y., *Post Express.* Clipping, without date, supplied by Mrs. Sarah T. Ziegler, Palmyra King's Daughters' Free Public Library.

[14] Quoted in C. S. Alden and R. Earle, *Makers of Naval Tradition,* Ginn and Company, New York, 1925, p. 279.

[15] *Army and Navy Journal,* Vol. 28, p. 240.

[16] *Ibid.,* Vol. 30, p. 440.

[17] *Ibid.,* Vol. 31, p. 125.

[18] *Ibid.,* Vol. 31, p. 734.

[19] *Annual Report, Secretary of the Navy,* 1894, p. 248.

[20] *Army and Navy Journal,* Vol. 33, p. 681.

[21] *Annual Report, Secretary of the Navy,* 1896, p. 351.

[22] *Annual Report, Secretary of the Navy,* 1895, p. 220.

[23] *Army and Navy Journal,* Vol. 33, p. 413.

[24] *Prices of Armor for Vessels of the Navy,* H. R. Report No. 1453, 54th Congress, 2d Session.

[25] Letter to author from R. E. Sampson, November 26, 1944.

[26] *Army and Navy Journal,* Vol. 32, p. 275.

[27] *Ibid.,* Vol. 34, p. 927.

[28] *New York Sun,* September 24, 1897.

[29] Scrapbooks, Theodore Roosevelt Collection. Harvard University.

[30] *New York Sun,* September 24, 1897.

[31] *Ibid.*

[32] *Army and Navy Journal,* Vol. 35, p. 19.

[33] *New York Tribune,* December 31, 1897.

[34] *Engineering,* January 28, 1898. Scrapbooks, Theodore Roosevelt Collection. Harvard University.

[35] W. T. Sampson to R. E. Sampson. R. E. Sampson Collection.

[36] Charles Sigsbee, *The "Maine," An Account of Her Destruction in Havana Harbor,* D. Appleton-Century Company, New York, 1899, p. 131.

[37] Finding of *Maine* Court of Inquiry. *Appendix to the Report of the Chief of the Bureau of Navigation,* 1898, p. 17.

14. DEWEY WINS MANILA BAY

[1] Dewey, *Autobiography,* p. 176.

[2] J. L. Stickney, "With Dewey at Manila," *Harper's New Monthly Magazine,* February 1899, p. 482.

[3] L. S. Mayo (Ed.), *America of Yesterday, as Reflected in the Journal of John Davis Long,* Little, Brown and Company and the Atlantic Monthly Press, Bos-

ton, 1923, pp. 169-170; Theodore Roosevelt, *Autobiography,* Charles Scribner's Sons, New York, 1929, p. 213; *Appendix to the Report of the Chief of the Bureau of Navigation,* 1898, p. 65 (cited hereafter as *Appendix,* 1898).

4 *Appendix,* 1898, p. 66.

5 *New York Times,* June 2, 1898.

6 Quoted from *Springfield Republican* in *Army and Navy Journal,* Vol. 35, p. 796.

7 F. E. Chadwick, *The Relations of the United States and Spain: The Spanish-American War,* Charles Scribner's Sons, New York, 1911, Vol. 1, p. 156.

8 C. P. Kindelberger, "The Battle of Manila Bay," *Century Magazine,* August 1898, p. 620.

9 *Appendix,* 1898, p. 67.

10 Stickney, "With Dewey at Manila," p. 482.

11 Chadwick, *Spanish-American War,* Vol. 1, p. 157.

12 *Appendix,* 1898, p. 70.

13 *New York Times,* June 19, 1898.

14 G. A. Loud, "The Battle of Manila Bay," *Century Magazine,* August 1898, p. 612.

15 Log of *Olympia,* National Archives.

16 *Army and Navy Journal,* Vol. 35, p. 918.

17 *New York Times,* June 19, 1898.

18 *Leslie's Official History of the Spanish-American War,* Copyright, 1899, General Marcus J. Wright, War Records Office, Washington, D. C., p. 199.

19 Strawn, "The Rise and Fall of a Hero," p. 351.

20 Log of *Olympia,* National Archives.

21 Dewey, *Autobiography,* p. 214.

22 H. L. Williams, *Taking Manila,* Hurst and Company, New York, 1899, p. 71.

23 *Appendix,* 1898, p. 70; *Olympia's* log, May 1, 1898.

24 *Army and Navy Journal,* Vol. 35, p. 918.

25 Kindelberger, "The Battle of Manila Bay," p. 622.

26 Log of *Olympia,* National Archives.

27 Stickney, *War in the Philippines,* p. 53.

28 Chadwick, *Spanish-American War,* Vol. 1, p. 179.

29 *Appendix,* 1898, p. 92.

30 T. J. Vivian (Ed.), *With Dewey at Manila,* R. F. Fenno & Company, New York, 1898, p. 60.

31 Quoted in Chadwick, *Spanish-American War,* Vol. 1, p. 181.

32 *Ibid.,* pp. 181-182.

33 *Ibid.,* p. 182; Stickney, "With Dewey at Manila," p. 477.

34 Lieutenant C. G. Calkins, quoted in Chadwick, *Spanish-American War,* Vol. 1, p. 182.

35 Stickney, "With Dewey at Manila," p. 480.

36 *Appendix,* 1898, p. 70.

37 *Army and Navy Journal,* Vol. 35, p. 918.

38 *Appendix,* 1898, pp. 70-71.

39 *Army and Navy Journal,* Vol. 35, p. 918.

40 *Appendix,* 1898, p. 98.

41 Clemens, *Life of Dewey,* p. 135.

42 *Army and Navy Journal,* Vol. 35, p. 882.

43 Quoted in Clemens, *op. cit.,* p. 128.

15. MAHAN ON THE WAR BOARD

[1] Puleston, *Mahan,* p. 186.

[2] Letters, Book 4, pp. 574 and 604. Theodore Roosevelt Collection, Library of Congress.

[3] Letters, Book 3, p. 549. Roosevelt Collection, Library of Congress.

[4] Taylor, *Mahan,* p. 88.

[5] *New York Times,* May 8, 1898.

[6] Taylor, *Mahan,* pp. 88-89.

[7] *Literary Digest,* December 12, 1914, p. 1193.

[8] *Army and Navy Journal,* Vol. 35, p. 723

[9] *Ibid.*

[10] *Ibid.,* p. 714.

[11] *Ibid.*

[12] *Ibid.,* p. 703.

[13] Mahan to Luce, August 31, 1898. Naval Historical Foundation.

[14] G. W. Allen (Ed.), *Papers of John Davis Long, 1897-1904,* Massachusetts Historical Society, 1939, pp. 119-120.

[15] Quoted in *Army and Navy Journal,* Vol. 35, p. 771.

[16] *Ibid.*

[17] J. D. Long, *The New American Navy,* The Outlook Company, New York. 1903, 2 vols., Vol. 1, pp. 162-163.

[18] *New York Times,* May 11, 1898.

[19] *Army and Navy Journal,* Vol. 36, p. 647.

[20] *Appendix,* 1896, pp. 384-385.

[21] *Ibid.,* pp. 386-389.

[22] *Army and Navy Journal,* Vol. 35, p. 725.

[23] *Ibid.,* p. 746.

[24] *Ibid.,* p. 771.

[25] *Ibid.,* p. 786.

[26] *Ibid.,* p. 1079.

[27] *Ibid.*

[28] Mahan to Luce, August 31, 1898, Naval Historical Foundation.

16. THE SEARCH FOR CERVERA

[1] Schley, *Forty-Five Years,* p. 257.

[2] *Appendix,* 1898, p. 26.

[3] Roosevelt to Mahan, June 27, 1911, Mahan Papers, Library of Congress.

[4] H. W. Jones, *A Chaplain's Experience Ashore and Afloat, The Texas Under Fire,* A. G. Sherwood & Co., New York, 1901, pp. 157-158.

[5] Signal log of *Brooklyn,* Sawtelle Collection.

[6] *Ibid.,* May 2, 1898.

[7] "00 North Atlantic Station," No. 13, March 30, 1898, National Archives.

[8] *Ibid.,* No. 12, March 30, 1898. National Archives.

[9] *Ibid.,* p. 9.

[10] Journal of North Atlantic Squadron, Rear Admiral W. T. Sampson, Official Records from April 21 to May 14, 1898, inclusive, National Archives

[11] George Kennan, "George Kennan's Story of the War: Introductory Letter from Key West," *Outlook*, May 21, 1898, p. 169.

[12] Walter Russell, "Incidents of the Cuban Blockade," *Century Magazine*, August 1898, p. 657.

[13] Walter Russell, "An Artist with Admiral Sampson's Fleet," *Century Magazine*, August 1898, p. 575.

[14] "George Kennan's Story of the War: IV. How War News Is Collected," *Outlook*, June 11, 1898, p. 371.

[15] Russell, "Incidents of the Cuban Blockade," p. 657.

[16] *New York Herald*, April 26, 1898.

[17] "00 North Atlantic Station," No. 63.

[18] From: *With Sampson Through the War* by W. A. M. Goode, copyright 1890, by Doubleday & Company, Inc., p. 64.

[19] *Appendix*, 1898, p. 459.

[20] Signal log of *Brooklyn*, May 16, 1898, Sawtelle Collection.

[21] "George Kennan's Story of the War. III. On the Edge of the War." *Outlook*, June 4, 1898, p. 273.

[22] *Record of a Court of Inquiry in the Case of Rear-Admiral Winfield S. Schley, U. S. Navy*, G. P. O., Washington, D. C., Vol. 2, p. 1344.

[23] Signal log of *Brooklyn*, Sawtelle Collection.

[24] Jones, *A Chaplain's Experience*, p. 169.

[25] Schley Court of Inquiry, Vol. 1, p. 285.

[26] *Ibid.*, Vol. 2, p. 1345.

[27] Jones, *A Chaplain's Experience*, p. 170.

[28] Schley Court of Inquiry, Vol. 2, p. 1346.

[29] Signal log of *Brooklyn*, Sawtelle Collection.

[30] *Appendix*, 1898, p. 393.

[31] "No. 2. Squadron, April 23-July 18, 1898." North Atlantic Squadron, Rear Admiral W. T. Sampson, p. 91, National Archives.

[32] Schley Court of Inquiry, Vol. 1, p. 477.

[33] *Ibid.*, Vol. 1, p. 1193.

[34] Chadwick, *Spanish-American War*, Vol. 1, p. 274.

[35] Signal log of *Brooklyn*, Sawtelle Collection.

[36] *Appendix*, 1898, p. 404.

[37] Signal log of *Brooklyn*, Sawtelle Collection.

[38] Schley Court of Inquiry, Vol. 1, p. 997.

[39] *Ibid.*

[40] Signal log of *Brooklyn*, Sawtelle Collection.

[41] Schley, *Forty-Five Years*, p. 276.

[42] Schley Court of Inquiry, Vol. 1, pp. 1094, 1123 and 1224.

[43] *Ibid.*, Vol. 2, p. 1357.

[44] Signal log of *Brooklyn*, Sawtelle Collection.

[45] Schley Court of Inquiry, Vol. 2, p. 1357.

[46] Signal log of *Brooklyn*, Sawtelle Collection.

[47] *Appendix*, 1898, p. 466.

[48] *Ibid.*, pp. 394 and 466.

[49] *Ibid.*, p. 394.

[50] "No. 2. Squadron, April 23-July 18, 1898," p. 116.

[51] *Appendix*, 1898, p. 473.

[52] *Ibid.,* p. 474.

[53] *Ibid.,* p. 475.

[54] "No. 2. Squadron, April 23-July 18, 1898," p. 124.

[55] *Ibid.,* p. 129.

[56] *Appendix,* 1898, p. 477.

[57] "No. 2. Squadron, April 23-July 18, 1898," pp. 133-134.

[58] *Appendix,* 1898, p. 478.

[59] Scrapbook, R. E. Sampson Collection.

[60] *Appendix,* 1898, p. 478.

[61] Schley Court of Inquiry, Vol. 1, p. 842.

[62] *Appendix,* 1898, p. 395.

[63] Chadwick, *Spanish-American War,* Vol. 1, pp. 306-307. There was latitude for variation in translation of telegraphed cipher. This version varies slightly from that in *Appendix,* 1898, p. 397.

[64] Signal log of *Brooklyn,* Sawtelle Collection.

[65] Jones, *A Chaplain's Experience,* p. 176.

[66] *Appendix,* 1898, p. 400.

[67] Jones, *A Chaplain's Experience,* p. 177.

[68] "00 North Atlantic Station," p. 33.

17. SANTIAGO

[1] Scrapbook, Rear Admiral W. T. Cluverius.

[2] *Army and Navy Journal,* Vol. 36, p. 685.

[3] Goode, *With Sampson through the War,* pp. 152-153.

[4] Schroeder, *A Half Century of Naval Service,* p. 221.

[5] A. T. Mahan, *Lessons of the War With Spain and Other Articles,* Little, Brown and Company, Boston, 1899, p. 33.

[6] *Army and Navy Journal,* Vol. 36, p. 283.

[7] *Ibid.,* p. 200.

[8] *Appendix,* 1898, p. 480.

[9] *Ibid.,* p. 485.

[10] Chadwick, *Spanish-American War,* Vol. 1, pp. 387-388.

[11] Schroeder, *A Half Century of Naval Service,* p. 223.

[12] *Ibid.*

[13] *Appendix,* 1898, p. 608.

[14] *Ibid.*

[15] Goode, *With Sampson through the War,* p. 194.

[16] *Ibid.,* p. 196.

[17] *Appendix,* 1898, p. 507.

[18] Goode, *With Sampson through the War,* p. 196.

[19] Chadwick, *Spanish-American War,* Vol. 2, p. 136.

[20] Goode, *With Sampson through the War,* p. 199.

[21] *Ibid.*

[22] Buenzle's account is inserted in the *New York's* log on July 3, 1898. National Archives.

[23] *Ibid.*

[24] Chadwick, *Spanish-American War,* Vol. 2, p. 148.

[25] *Ibid.,* p. 150.

[26] G. E. Graham, *Schley and Santiago*, W. B. Conkey Company, Chicago, 1902, p. 288.

[27] Schley Court of Inquiry, Vol. 2, p. 1387.

[28] *Ibid.*, p. 1388.

[29] *Ibid.*, Vol. 1, p. 641.

[30] *Ibid.*, Vol. 2, p. 1389.

[31] *Ibid.*, Vol. 1, p. 1034.

[32] *Ibid.*, Vol. 2, p. 1389.

[33] *Ibid.*

[34] *Ibid.*, p. 1390.

[35] *Ibid.*, p. 1391.

[36] *Ibid.*, Vol. 1, p. 1034.

[37] Signal log of *Brooklyn*, Sawtelle Collection.

[38] *Appendix*, 1898, p. 505.

18. IMPERIALISM'S DARLING

[1] *Appendix*, 1898, p. 65.

[2] *Ibid.*, p. 68.

[3] *Ibid.*, p. 98.

[4] Dewey, *Autobiography*, p. 254.

[5] *Appendix*, 1898, p. 101.

[6] Healy and Kutner, *The Admiral*, p. 209.

[7] *Ibid.*, p. 228.

[8] *Appendix*, 1898, pp. 101 and 103.

[9] T. A. Bailey, "Dewey and the Germans at Manila Bay," *American Historical Review*, October 1939, gives a thorough survey of Dewey's relations with von Diederichs.

[10] *Ibid.*, p. 67.

[11] Healy and Kutner, *The Admiral*, pp. 209-210.

[12] Sir George J. Younghusband, *The Philippines and Round About*, The Macmillan Company, New York, 1899, Chapter 9.

[13] *Appendix*, 1898, p. 120ff.

[14] Quoted in *Army and Navy Journal*, Vol. 35, p. 1053.

[15] Younghusband, *The Philippines*, p. 103.

[16] *Army and Navy Journal*, Vol. 36, p. 108.

[17] *Ibid.*, Vol. 37, p. 87.

[18] From *With My Own Eyes*, p. 114, by Frederick Palmer. Copyright 1932. Used by special permission of The Bobbs-Merrill Company.

[19] *Army and Navy Journal*, Vol. 36, p. 539.

[20] Bailey, "Dewey and the Germans at Manila Bay," footnote 37, p. 69.

[21] Palmer, *With My Own Eyes*, p. 110.

[22] *Army and Navy Journal*, Vol. 35, p. 732.

[23] Dewey, *Autobiography*, p. 285.

[24] Rear Admiral A. Farenholt, M. C., U. S. Navy (Ret.). "George Dewey: Admiral of the Fleet," Manuscript in U. S. Naval Academy Library.

[25] *Army and Navy Journal*, Vol. 36, p. 646.

[26] Palmer, *With My Own Eyes*, p. 112.

[27] *Army and Navy Journal*, Vol. 36, p. 480.

[28] Dewey, *Autobiography*, p. 286.
[29] *New York Tribune*, October 6, 1898.
[30] Palmer, *With My Own Eyes*, p. 121.
[31] *Ibid.*, pp. 123-124; for Mrs. Dewey's version of the proposal, see Healy and Kutner, *The Admiral*, pp. 258-259.
[32] Palmer, *With My Own Eyes*, p. 120.
[33] *Ibid.*, p. 123.
[34] *New York Tribune*, July 24, 1899.
[35] *McClure's*, October 1899, p. 495.
[36] *Army and Navy Journal*, Vol. 37, p. 152.
[37] *Ibid.*, Vol. 36, p. 931.
[38] *New York Tribune*, May 12, 1899.
[39] Quoted in *New York Tribune*, May 14, 1899.
[40] Quoted in *New York Tribune*, September 28, 1899.
[41] Palmer, *With My Own Eyes*, p. 125.
[42] Healy and Kutner, *The Admiral*, p. 253.
[43] *Ibid.*, p. 255.
[44] Mark Sullivan, *Our Times, The United States, 1900-1925, Vol. 1, The Turn of the Century*, Charles Scribner's Sons, New York, 1926, p. 332.
[45] Strawn, "The Rise and Fall of a Hero," p. 353.
[46] *New York World*, April 4, 1900.
[47] J. B. Bishop, *Theodore Roosevelt and His Time*, Charles Scribner's Sons, New York, 1920, Vol. 1, p. 239.
[48] *Army and Navy Journal*, Vol. 39, p. 501.
[49] *Woman's Home Companion*, May 1904.
[50] Josephus Daniels, *The Navy and the Nation*, George H. Doran Company, New York, 1919, p. 26. By permission of Josephus Daniels.

19. THE SAMPSON-SCHLEY CONTROVERSY

[1] Scrapbook and album, R. E. Sampson Collection.
[2] *Baltimore American*, July 6, 1898.
[3] *New York Times*, July 6, 1898.
[4] Signal log of *Brooklyn*, Sawtelle Collection.
[5] *Sampson-Schley Official Communications to the United States Senate*, G. P. O. Washington, D. C., 1899, p. 136.
[6] "No. 2 Ciphers Received, Dec. 17, 1897-May 5, 1899," National Archives.
[7] Chadwick, *Spanish-American War*, Vol. 2, p. 200.
[8] Mayo, *America of Yesterday . . . Journal of John Davis Long*, p. 203.
[9] *Army and Navy Journal*, Vol. 35, p. 1026.
[10] *Ibid.*
[11] *Ibid.*, p. 1064.
[12] Scrapbook and album, R. E. Sampson Collection.
[13] "Letter to editor," signed Veritas, R. E. Sampson Collection.
[14] *New York Times*, August 21, 1898.
[15] *New York Journal*, August 21, 1898.
[16] Lord John Fisher, Admiral of the Fleet, *Memories and Records*, George H. Doran Company, New York, Hodder & Stoughton, Ltd., London, 1920, 2 vols., Vol 1, p. 222.
[17] Scrapbook, R. E. Sampson Collection.

[18] *Army and Navy Journal,* Vol. 36, p. 633.

[19] Quoted in *Army and Navy Journal,* Vol. 36, p. 980.

[20] Captain French E. Chadwick, U.S.N., "Sampson the Man," *New York Evening Post,* May 7, 1902.

[21] Schley, *Forty-Five Years,* p. 315.

[22] *New York Times,* July 24, 1898.

[23] *New York Journal,* August 21, 1898.

[24] Schley, *Forty-Five Years,* pp. 341-342.

[25] *New York Times,* August 21, 1898.

[26] *New York Journal,* August 21, 1898.

[27] Schley, *Forty-Five Years,* p. 345.

[28] *New York Times,* August 30, 1898.

[29] *Ibid.*

[30] Schley, *Forty-Five Years,* p. 346.

[31] *New York Times,* September 7, 1898.

[32] Schley Court of Inquiry, Vol. 1, pp. 584-585.

[33] *Army and Navy Journal,* Vol. 36. p. 947.

[34] *Ibid.,* p. 1018.

[35] *Ibid.,* p. 1075.

[36] *Ibid.,* Vol. 38, p. 1164.

[37] *Ibid.,* p. 1116. These excerpts are in order from pages 296, 298, 364, and 365 Vol. 3 of E. S. Maclay, *A History of the United States Navy from 1775 to 1901,* D. Appleton and Company, New York, 1901.

[38] *Army and Navy Journal,* Vol. 38, p. 1166.

[39] Schley, *Forty-Five Years,* p. 415.

[40] Schley Court of Inquiry, Vol. 2, p. 1830.

[41] *Ibid.*

20. THE TRIUMPH OF MAHAN

[1] T. A. Bailey, *A Diplomatic History of the American People,* F. S. Crofts & Co., New York, 1940, p. 470.

[2] *Forum,* March 1893. Reprinted in A. T. Mahan, *The Interest of America in Sea Power, Present and Future,* Little, Brown and Company, Boston, 1897, pp. 31-55.

[3] Mahan to Roosevelt, May 1, 1897. Theodore Roosevelt Collection, Library of Congress.

[4] Roosevelt to Mahan, May 3, 1897. Roosevelt Collection, Library of Congress.

[5] Mahan to Roosevelt, May 6, 1897. Roosevelt Collection, Library of Congress.

[6] *Ibid.*

[7] Roosevelt to Mahan, June 9, 1897. Roosevelt Collection, Library of Congress.

[8] *Forum,* December 1897, p. 25.

[9] *Review of Reviews,* 1897, Vol. 19, p. 336.

[10] *New York Sun,* January 14, 1898.

[11] A. T. Mahan, "A Twentieth Century Outlook," *Harper's New Monthly Magazine,* September 1897. Reprinted in *The Interest of America in Sea Power,* 1897.

[12] Mahan to Roosevelt, May 6, 1897. Theodore Roosevelt Collection, Library of Congress.

[13] *Army and Navy Journal,* Vol. 35, p. 408.

[14] From *Mahan on Sea Power,* by William E. Livezey, copyrighted 1947 by University of Oklahoma Press. By permission. Ch. VIII, "Hawaii."

[15] *New York Journal,* February 10, 1898.

[16] Quoted in *New York Sun,* July 3, 1898.

[17] *Army and Navy Journal,* Vol. 35, p. 714.

[18] *New York Sun,* July 3-7, 1898.

[19] Quoted in *Army and Navy Journal,* Vol. 35, p. 928.

[20] *Selections from the Correspondence of Theodore Roosevelt and Henry Cabot Lodge, 1884-1918,* Scribner's, New York, 1925, Vol. 1, pp. 309 and 311.

[21] *Ibid.,* p. 313.

[22] Mahan to Lodge, July 27, 1898, Lodge Papers, quoted in Livezey, *Mahan on Sea Power,* pp. 182-183.

[23] *Army and Navy Journal,* Vol. 35, p. 1011.

[24] *Ibid.*

[25] *New York Christian Advocate,* January 22, 1903. Quoted in T. A. Bailey, *A Diplomatic History of the American People,* F. S. Crofts & Co., New York, 1940, p. 520.

[26] *New York Times,* February 7, 1899.

[27] *New York World,* February 6, 1899.

[28] *Ibid.,* February 7, 1899.

[29] *Ibid.*

[30] Livezey, *Mahan on Sea Power,* p. 185.

[31] Seth Low, "The International Conference of Peace," *North American Review,* November 1899, Vol. 169, p. 626.

[32] R. M. Johnston, "In the Clutch of the Harpy Powers," *North American Review,* Vol. 169, p. 453.

[33] Mahan to Ashe, September 23, 1899. Flowers Collection.

[34] *London Times,* quoted in *Army and Navy Journal,* Vol. 36, p. 1048.

[35] A. D. White, *Autobiography of Andrew D. White,* D. Appleton-Century Company, New York, 1905, 2 vols., Vol. 2, p. 319.

[36] *Ibid.,* p. 347.

[37] *Ibid.,* p. 338.

[38] Low, "The International Conference of Peace," pp. 636-637.

[39] Mahan to Ashe, September 23, 1899, Flowers Collection.

[40] A. T. Mahan, "The Peace Conference and the Moral Aspect of War," *North American Review,* October 1899, Vol. 169, p. 444.

[41] *New York Tribune,* August 20, 1899.

[42] Charles de Kay, "Authors at Home: Captain A. T. Mahan in New York," *Critic,* May 28, 1898.

[43] Mahan to Ashe, February 1, 1903. Flowers Collection.

[44] Mahan to Luce, November 18, 1907, Naval Historical Foundation.

[45] Mahan, *Harvest Within,* p. 208.

[46] Mahan to Roosevelt, January 10, 1907, Roosevelt Papers. Quoted in Livezey, *Mahan on Sea Power,* p. 233.

[47] Roosevelt to Mahan, January 12, 1907, Roosevelt Papers. Quoted in Livezey, *Mahan on Sea Power,* p. 233.

[48] Mahan to Luce, January 27, 1908, Naval Historical Foundation.

[49] *Ibid.*

[50] Puleston, *Mahan,* pp. 339-340.

[51] *Ibid.,* p. 352.

[52] *Ibid.,* p. 353.

INDEX

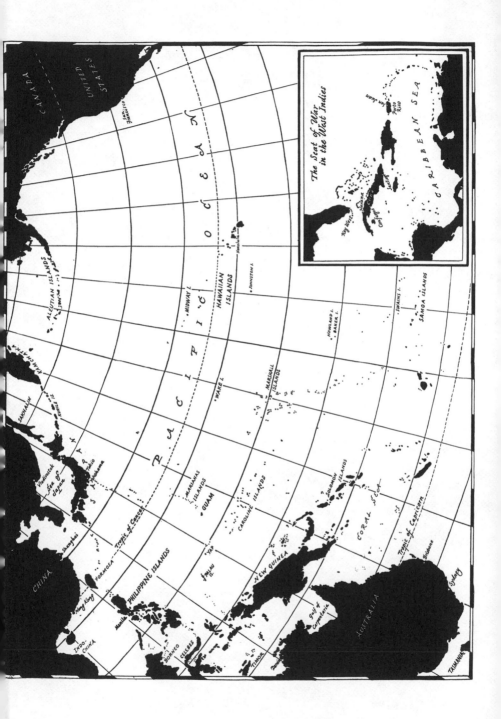

The Seat of War in the West Indies